Stigma, State Expressions and the Law

This book demonstrates the difficulties the law is likely to encounter in regulating the expressive activities of the state, particularly with regard to the stigmatization of vulnerable groups and minorities.

Freedom of speech is indispensable to a democratic society, enabling it to operate with a healthy level of debate and discussion. Historically, legal scholars have under-appreciated the power of stigmatization, instead focusing on anti-discrimination law, and the implicit assumption that the state is permitted to communicate freely with little fear of legal consequences. Whilst integral to a democratic society, the freedom of a state to express itself can however also be corrosive, allowing influential figures and organizations the possibility to stigmatize vulnerable groups within society. The book takes this idea and, uniquely weaving legal analysis with extant psychological and sociological research, shows that current legal approaches to stigmatization are limited. Starting with a deep insight into what constitutes state expressions and how they can become stigmatizing, the book then goes on to look into the capacity the law currently has to limit these expressions and asks even if it could, should it?

This fascinating study of an increasingly topical subject will be of interest to any legal scholar working in the field of freedom of expression and discrimination law.

Paul Quinn is Professor at the Vrije Universiteit Brussel (Brussels Free University).

Stigma, State Expressions and the Law

Implications of Freedom of Speech

Paul Quinn

Routledge
Taylor & Francis Group
LONDON AND NEW YORK

First published 2019
by Routledge
2 Park Square, Milton Park, Abingdon, Oxon OX14 4RN

and by Routledge
605 Third Avenue, New York, NY 10017

First issued in paperback 2021

Routledge is an imprint of the Taylor & Francis Group, an informa business

Publisher's Note
The publisher has gone to great lengths to ensure the quality of this reprint but points out that some imperfections in the original copies may be apparent.

British Library Cataloguing in Publication Data
A catalogue record for this book is available from the British Library

Library of Congress Cataloging-in-Publication Data
Names: Quinn, Paul, 1981- author.
Title: Stigma, state expressions and the law: implications of freedom of speech / Paul Quinn.
Description: Abingdon, Oxon ; New York, NY : Routledge, 201. | Based on author's thesis (doctoral - Vrije Universiteit Brussel, 2015) issued under the title: The importance of stigmatising statements of the state and the problems they pose for the law.
Identifiers: LCCN 2019003039 (print) | LCCN 2019005076 (ebook) | ISBN 9781315136110 (ebk) | ISBN 9781138087705 (hbk)
Subjects: LCSH: Discrimination–Law and legislation. | Discrimination in language. | Freedom of expression. | Stigma (Social psychology)
Classification: LCC K3242 (ebook) | LCC K3242 .Q56 2019 (print) | DDC 342.08/53–dc23
LC record available at https://lccn.loc.gov/2019003039

ISBN 13: 978-1-03-224112-8 (pbk)
ISBN 13: 978-1-138-08770-5 (hbk)

DOI: 10.4324/9781315136110

Typeset in Galliard
by Taylor & Francis Books

For Padraic, Evelyn, Sigrid, Aidan and Maya
Your support and love is my strength.

Contents

Introduction

1 A picture says more than a thousand words, but a presidential tweet says much more still

The journalistic world waits a special moment every day. With a little luck at that moment the pressing of a 'send button' on a phone or computer screen and the posting of a short (and often incoherent) text fragment has the ability to create an intense global polemic. The moment in question is usually between 6 and 8 am East Standard Time in the US. At that moment President Donald Trump will have already arisen from his bed, perhaps have eaten something and will have turned his eye to the various sources of media that interest him. As we have learned in the past few years, the most powerful person in the world has a remarkably thin skin. When he feels he has been maligned he has the propensity to launch a visceral attack on his target of the moment. His preferred weapon is Twitter. The target can range from politicians, to sports individuals, to major multinational businesses to nation states.

To some, the media obsession with Donald Trump's tweets has become tiresome. Are they nothing but a distraction from his situation of *de facto* political impotence given the difficulty he has in getting legislation through Congress? Are they nothing more than a dog-whistle-like attempt to whip up a wave of populism similar to the one on which he rode to power in the 2016 elections? Whilst such thoughts may be at the very least partially true they are not the whole story. This is because of the status of the man behind the message. This man is not merely someone wealthy or a television celebrity (though he is both of those things). More importantly, he is the head of the most powerful state on Earth. He has various forms of power that are arguably matched by few, if any, people on earth. Such power could be thought of in military terms, given that not only does he have direct executive control of a powerful conventional military force but also an arsenal of thousands of nuclear warheads. When he threatens to wage war against another state,[1] would it not be foolish to simply dismiss such expressions? Equally, when President Trump threatens major companies if they don't move factories back to the US, the immediate effect on their share prices clearly demonstrates that his tweets are capable of having a powerful effect given the potential power the president has (at least in theory) to effect regulatory change.

1 https://twitter.com/realdonaldtrump/status/895970429734711298?lang=en

As this book will demonstrate, however, even when Trump's tweets are not intended to be veiled threats of military force or a change in regulatory posture, they are capable of producing important effects (many of which are negative). Even when his tweets are of a purely symbolic nature (i.e. implying physical consequences or regulatory changes) they arguably have an importance that should not be underestimated. This is because the President is often seen as the embodiment of the state, as representing the collective moral authority that is vested in it (and legitimized through the democratic process). Therefore, when he or she speaks their words may be perceived as having moral authority by a large proportion of society. On certain occasions Trump has, for example, criticized sports stars protesting for African American equality as being Un-American.[2]

The condemnation of a particular individual or group in society by the President for 'un-American' behaviour can therefore be perceived (correctly or incorrectly) as a powerful signal of disapproval of the state, and by extension, of certain individuals or groups in society (in this case activist members of the African American community). In short, such comments have an enormous ability to stigmatize. Comments that seemingly label certain immigrant groups as a threat to America may increase the likelihood that such groups suffer not only discrimination but even violence.[3] Some of the targets of the President's criticism have even illustratively become the victims of attempted bomb attacks. In addition to these physical consequences, such expressive activity can also bring about negative psychological consequences whereby the members of such groups question their place in society. These negative psychological effects can often have serious consequences for vulnerable groups in society. As the reader of this book will quickly become aware it is the author's contention that such forms of expression should be taken seriously and, given his background as a legal scholar, merit consideration from a legal perspective (something that is largely missing at present). Given this background it is logical (in the author's eyes at least) to ask what legal approaches may be available to individuals who feel that they have been harmed by such 'stigmatizing state expressions' (SSEs).

With regards to the tweets or other communications of President Trump the legal position is relatively clear. According to the US Supreme Court's doctrine of 'government speech' he, as head of the US executive, has the right to express himself in whatever way he wishes. He is entitled (with very few exceptions) to use the resources of the state to communicate in a manner that he sees fit about anything he chooses.[4] Accordingly, there is relatively little individuals or groups that feel themselves to be negatively affected by such comments can do before a court of law.[5] President Trump's tweets are but one form of state expression. Whilst

2 https://twitter.com/realdonaldtrump/status/911655987857281024?lang=en
3 https://twitter.com/realdonaldtrump/status/673993417429524480
4 N Murphy, "Context, Not Content: Medium-Based Press Clause Restrictions on Government Speech in the Internet Age", *University of Denver Sports & Entertainment Law Journal* 7 (2009).
5 C Taylor, "Hate Speech and Government Speech", *Journal of Constitutional Law* 12, no. 4 (2010).

they illustrate very clearly many of the negative effects that the expressive activities of the state, even in the absence of any other tangible measures, are capable of producing they are by no means alone in this ability. The concept of state expression can encompass an enormous range of activities that may vary in terms of form, substantive content (i.e. message or meaning) and also the context in which they are used. This can vary from crisis communication used in a natural disaster, to public health information, to information bulletins produced by the police after a crime to the erection of statues in a local park. Some may take the form of conventional paper based communication (e.g. leaflets and posters) whilst others might make central use of social media platforms. The legal situation surrounding such various forms of communication may not be as straightforward as the President's tweets however. Different legal regimes (depending on the jurisdiction in question) may or may not be capable of impacting upon state expressions depending upon the particular context. More often than not there will be no specific legal doctrine or approach that has been formulated to deal with matters of state expression. Furthermore, as this book will discuss, a number of important legal approaches that one might imagine would be capable of impacting upon such measures (e.g. administrative law, anti-discrimination law or laws related to hate speech) may in reality not be able to do so. This has the effect of rendering the use of SSEs largely constraint free (at least from the perspective legal challenge).

In this book the author will attempt to illustrate his main thesis – that there are few options for individuals that have been harmed by SSEs to seek redress. In particular, it may be difficult or impossible to seek a remedy in a court of law. Importantly, this is not because of the lack of engagement of any one single legal approach that one might expect to be responsible for the regulation of state expressions (indeed this cannot be the case because in most jurisdictions no such single approach exists). Rather, it is because of the non-engagement of a range of different legal approaches (illustrative examples of which are discussed below in section 3).

It is the author's contention that stigmatization as a phenomenon provides a brilliant 'lens' through which to examine the law's natural limits in terms of its ability to engage such forms of expression and where necessary provide redress. The concept of stigmatization recognizes that even expressive activity (i.e. in the absence any other form of binding measure or physical imposition) is capable of having an important psychological effect on an individual, effects that can in turn lead to very real negative consequences for those concerned, both on the individual and societal level. This book aims to demonstrate how the phenomenon of stigmatization and its associated negative effects highlight the impotence of various legal systems to limit the harm that is produced by stigmatizing state expression. An exploration of these themes is important given that legal scholars have arguably thus far given limited consideration to issues of stigmatization, especially in comparison to related but different concepts such as discrimination.[6] As this book attempts to demonstrate, the resultant ability of the state to stigmatize through its expressive activities without fear of legal repercussion is, given the harm that stigmatization can produce, arguably incongruous with the requirement of liberal democratic states to treat all individuals with respect.

6 I Solanke, *Discrimination as Stigma* (Oxford: Hart, 2017).

2 Key issues that will be raised in this book

The main aim of this book is to demonstrate that '*the law has difficulties in regulating stigmatizing state expressions in a way that one might expect given the negative consequences they can produce*'. Demonstrating this will demand a multidisciplinary approach It involves research concerning areas as diverse as psychology, sociology, social policy, ethics and philosophy and various legal disciplines. In particular, it requires:

i An analysis of what exactly state expression is and how it differs from other activities (or tools of the state);
ii An analysis of how such expression can be stigmatizing;
iii An understanding of what stigmatization is and what harm it can do both to individuals and society at large;
iv Given the nature of such harm, the adoption of a normative position on when the state's use of stigmatizing expressions is acceptable (or not);
v The analysis of various legal approaches to discern whether they are capable of ensuring that the normative position is complied with.

Each of the chapters in this book will deal with one or more of these approaches in the manner outlined below.

Chapter 1 – What are state expressions and how can they be stigmatizing?

The state is capable of expressing itself in an enormous number of ways. Whilst the physical or legal acts of the state may be capable of having expressive content, the state can also engage in purely expressive forms of activity. As Chapter 1 discusses, such forms of activity can be thought of as having expressive meaning but not capable of imposing any binding legal or corporeal effects on individuals.

Given that there is limited discussion in European legal literature concerning the issue of state expression (as a general legal concept) it is necessary to turn to the area of social policy in order to find useful conceptualizations that help to explain what such expressions are, and why they are used by states.[7] In doing so the author will (in Chapter 2) make use of the concept of 'nodality' as described by Hood and Margretts.[8] This concept allows one to compare the use of information (*inter alia* in forms of communication) to other

7 Even in the US where the concept of 'government speech' has been developed by the Supreme Court, the focus has been on separating state expression from private expression and not on defining 'expression' itself. See A Olree, "Identifying Government Speech", *Connecticut Law Review* 42, no. 2 (2009). As the author states on page 368 "Classifying the speech as either government speech or private speech becomes a crucial question—often *the* crucial question—in deciding these speech cases".

8 C Hood and H Margretts, *The Tools of Government in the Digital Age* (New York: Palgrave Macmillan, 2006). See Chapter 2.

'tools' available to the state. Communication or expressive activity is a tool that allows the state and various public bodies to respond to a particular situation in an extraordinarily flexible manner. Compared with other potential tools, the use of 'communication' or 'expressive activities' costs little and requires little or nothing in terms of a legal framework to deploy. Most importantly the use of communication or expression does not usually entail legally binding or corporeal impositions on individuals. This is because individuals are in theory simply able to ignore such impositions if they so wish. It is arguably this factor that is central to the flexibility of communication as a tool. In contrast, other 'tools' which may involve binding impositions on individuals can only be used where the law so describes and in a manner that is compatible with legal norms.

Despite the apparent non-binding nature of purely communicational activities they are nonetheless capable of producing a range of harmful effects. Perhaps the most important is stigmatization, which can in turn increase the chances of other negative effects occurring. Most types of stigmatizing expression can be placed into one of three different categories. The first occurs where the state often has to partake in some form of communication that has an important functional purpose but which may result in certain groups feeling stigmatized ('functional stigmatization'). Imagine a public health message, for example, concerning a condition that was found predominantly in a certain community.[9] The second may occur where the state condemns certain forms of anti-social or harmful behaviour, e.g. drink driving or passive smoking ('fair criticism'). Whilst being unpleasant for those concerned, the ability to express such condemnation may have important benefits for both individuals and society as a whole. A third category concerns the participation of the state and individuals connected to it in processes that are closely linked to the democratic nature of the state, e.g. policy announcements or political debate (statements made for political purposes).[10] Often individuals involved in such activities will occupy a duel or hybrid role whereby they are simultaneously expected to represent the state and exhibit a certain level of neutrality whilst at the same time representing partisan political interests. Unlike 'fair criticism', it may often be objectively difficult to discern any tangible benefit arising from the type of stigmatization that can occur from such expression. Despite this, freedom of expression in such contexts is often seen as an indispensable part of a democratic society.

9 For a discussion on the merits and problems of using stigmatizing messages in healthcare communication see R Bayer, "Stigma and the Ethics of Public Health: Not Can We but Should We," *Social Science & Medicine* 67 (2008); S Burris, "Stigma, Ethics and Policy: A Commentary on Bayer's 'Stigma and the Ethics of Public Health: Not Can We but Should We'". P. Quinn, "Crisis Communication in Public Health Emergencies: The Limits of 'Legal Control' and the Risks for Harmful Outcomes in a Digital Age", *Life Sciences, Society and Policy* 14, no. 1 (2018).

10 D Gelders and I Oyvind, "Government Communication About Potential Policies: Public Relations, Propaganda or Both?", *Public Relations Review* 36 (2010).

Chapter 2 – Defining stigma and its potential harm?

A common theme of legal discourse relating to stigmatization (be it academic writings or in court judgments) is that the phenomenon is often handled in a superficial manner.[11] This has led to both an 'under appreciation' of how the phenomena can manifest itself and also the effects it can produce.[12] These include those related to issues such as 'internalization', 'harm to self-esteem' and 'coping effects'. Such effects can bring about both negative consequences for the individuals concerned and society as a whole.[13] A clear understanding of these effects is needed in order to: (i) understand why stigmatization can so easily be produced by the expressions of the state; (ii) to adopt a normative approach (see description of Chapter 3 below) concerning the permissibility of the use of stigmatizing expression by the state.

This chapter undertakes a general review of the main facets of stigmatization as a phenomenon. This involves presenting the main themes found within the literature on the issue. It is mainly descriptive in nature. It has two main sources of information. The first draws on an extensive body of theoretical and empirically based literature in the field of psychology concerning stigmatization. The focus here is on the effect of stigma at the individual level. In doing this, Chapter 2 draws on the large field of empirically based psychological research available on the manifestation and effects of stigmatization on the individual.[14] The second draws on sociological perspectives of stigmatization and, in particular, the negative effects that stigmatization can have on vulnerable groups in society. Such works are useful in linking stigmatization to other key concepts that may be recognized in the law (e.g. discrimination, stereotyping, marginalization, etc.).[15] The aim of this chapter is to describe stigmatization as a phenomenon and to highlight its various properties.[16] In doing so the author wishes to demonstrate that expressive acts of the state that merely stigmatize cannot be thought of as without consequence simply because they do not impose any 'binding legal or corporeal effects'.

11 P Quinn and P De Hert, "Self Respect—a 'Rawlsian Primary Good' Unprotected by the European Convention on Human Rights and Its Lack of a Coherent Approach to Stigmatization?", *The International Journal of Discrimination and the Law* 14 (2014). On page 31 the authors discuss how the ECtHR has referred to stigmatization in an extremely limited manner, often using what appears to be an intuitive understanding of the phenomenon.

12 Solanke, *Discrimination as Stigma.*

13 B Link and J Phelan, "Conceptualizing Stigma", *Annual Review of Sociology* 27 (2001). Quinn and De Hert, "Self Respect—a 'Rawlsian Primary Good' Unprotected by the European Convention on Human Rights and Its Lack of a Coherent Approach to Stigmatization?"

14 For a discussion on the complementarity of these two approaches see G Scambler, "Health-Related Stigma", *Sociology of Health & Illness* 31, no. 3 (2009). p444

15 See, for example, B Link and J Phelan, "Stigma and Its Public Health Implications", *The Lancet* 367 (2006).

16 For a concise overview of the literature on stigmatization see J Dovidio, B Major, and J Crocker, "Stigma: Introduction and Overview", in *The Social Psychology of Stigma*, ed. T Heatherton et al. (New York: Guilford Press, 2000).

Chapter 3 – Developing a normative approach towards the use of stigmatizing expressions

Stigmatization can be produced by many types of expressive activity by the state. Simply preventing all forms of stigmatization is neither feasible nor desirable. Imagine, for instance, the example of 'fair criticism' (discussed above in Chapter 2). Were states not able to engage in such criticism, it might mean that they were unable to prevent various forms of anti-social/harmful behaviour. Furthermore, some minor forms of stigmatization may be an unavoidable by-product of essential communications concerning areas of critical importance for both the state and the individuals that may be affected (i.e. 'functional stigmatization'). Common examples of this include areas such as public health and security.[17] Whilst communication in areas such as this can produce negative effects for those involved, the consequences of a failure to communicate important information would often arguably be worse. In addition, many democratic processes in which individuals connected to the state (e.g. members of the executive such as presidents, prime ministers, etc.) take part may involve acts of expression that are stigmatizing to particular groups in society (of which President Trump's constant tweeting on political issues is a prime example). Whilst such activities may on occasion be stigmatizing for particular minorities it is difficult if not impossible to imagine how a democratic society would be able to operate without a certain amount of room for freedom of expression for such individuals.[18]

Given these needs, it is arguably necessary when discussing the appropriateness of the use of stigmatizing expressions of the state, to develop a normative stance on their use. In doing so Chapter 3 looks at the phenomenon of state expression from an ethical and philosophical perspective (as opposed to the psychological or sociological perspectives used in Chapter 2) and attempts to make a normative argument concerning the use of stigmatizing expressions by the state. In particular this chapter discusses the potential effect of stigmatization on the concept of 'self-respect', a concept that is central to a number of legal theories concerning the just organization of society including that of Rawls[19], Sen[20] and Nussbaum.[21] A particular emphasis is placed on Rawls' concept of 'justice as fairness' given the importance it attributes to the attitude of the state and the effect such attitudes can have on individuals Given the familiarity of scholars both in Europe and the US with Rawls' ideas, this allows the concept of stigmatization (which is primarily psychological in nature) to be discussed in the context of ethical ideas that purport

17 Numerous examples of this are discussed in Chapter 2 section 2.

18 American scholars such as Post often take a more puritan view on the protection of freedom of speech, even where this means preserving the right to use hate speech. The term 'marketplace of ideas' has been used to describe the need for freedom to convey thoughts and ideas, even where they are repugnant or offensive to others. See, for example, R Post, "Racist Speech, Democracy, and the First Amendment", *Faculty Scholarship Series* 208 (1991). p275

19 J Rawls, *A Theory of Justice* (Cambridge, MA: Harvard Press, 1971).

20 A Sen, *Inequality Reexamined* (Cambridge, MA; Harvard University Press, 1995).

21 M Nussbaum, "Capabilities as Fundamental Entitlements: Sen and Social Justice", *Feminist Economics* 9, nos 2–3 (2003).

to give normative guidance to the arrangements used to regulate society. The aim in attempting to mix these spheres of thinking is to promote a normative debate on the permissible use of stigmatizing expressions by the state in a just society. This allows an argument to be made for the potential existence of legal controls on the use of such expressions by the state in certain contexts. Furthermore, the presence of a normative position will allow existing legal frameworks to be tested against its requirements for the regulation of stigmatizing expressions, something that is important in allowing the main contention of this thesis to be demonstrated.

Given that some forms of stigmatization may occur in expressions or messages that may be considered indispensable (discussed in Chapter 1), it is necessary to discern which are acceptable and which are not. Chapter 3 accordingly develops a set of principles that can be used to analyse various legal approaches (presented in Chapters 4–7) in order to discern their effectiveness in protecting individuals from unjustified stigmatization by the state. These principles are referred to throughout the later chapters of the book. These principles which are elaborated in Chapter 3 are:

- i There are no instances where states need to intentionally damage an individual's self-respect.
- ii The state should only take action that may harm self-esteem (i.e. stigmatize) where doing so would be needed to secure the fundamental liberties or equality of opportunity of others.
- iii There is a duty upon states not to harm individual or group self-esteem through the release of incorrect information.
- iv The state should not criticize individuals for their ideas or lifestyle choices unless they threaten the fundamental rights or the equality of opportunity of others.
- v Stigmatizing statements made during the political process should be clearly identified as neither emanating from, or representing the opinion of the state itself.

It is the author's broad contention it may often be difficult to find legal approaches that can contribute (in part or at all) to ensuring that this normative position is met. The author will attempt to demonstrate this by discussing the potential application of a range of important legal approaches in Chapters 4–7.

Chapter 4 – Stigmatizing expression as hate speech

Chapter 4 begins by looking at what role hate speech laws can play in meeting the normative position described above. Given the existence of numerous criminal law approaches to hate speech in various states, such laws present an obvious candidate in terms of the control of stigmatizing expression.[22] Such laws may, for example,

22 Quinn and De Hert, "Self Respect—a 'Rawlsian Primary Good' Unprotected by the European Convention on Human Rights and Its Lack of a Coherent Approach to Stigmatization?" The authors state on page 43, for example, "First there are a number of important criminal law provisions that apply to both private individuals speaking in

be relevant where public figures target particular groups with stigmatizing criticism or insults. Given that stigmatization as a concept is often not itself described in legal provisions, it is necessary to determine when hate speech approaches are likely to make an impact upon such forms of expression. Many forms of SSE are mildly (and often unintentionally) stigmatizing. Such forms of SSE are often unlikely to qualify as hate speech. The considerable variation in hate speech provisions from state to state also means the ability of hate speech law in a particular jurisdiction to impact upon stigmatizing expression in general may differ. Depending on the jurisdiction in question, offences may apply to remarks made against individuals and groups or even both. Laws may, for example, vary widely in terms of the categories that are protected with some states offering protection to a narrow range of defined categories, e.g. ethnicity, sexuality, etc., whilst others may offer protection to undefined groups or minorities. In addition to the type of categories of individual that may be protected, laws differ in terms of the intensity of the remarks that may be forbidden.[23] Some may, for example, prohibit 'incitement to hatred' whilst others may relate to 'incitement to discrimination'. In some countries such as Germany provisions may be very broad concerning remarks that have the ability to harm the dignity of individuals and groups. Given such variability, and the spectrum of the possible stigmatizing intensity of state expressions, hate speech laws may have some role to play in regulating extreme forms of SSE but are unlikely to engage the vast majority of which are of a more mildly stigmatizing nature. It is also necessary to consider the effects that provisions relating to the immunity of public officials, i.e. the 'human component' (including state employees and individuals with a political function), will have on the application of criminal law provisions where they exist. This will often further limit the applicability of hate speech laws to stigmatizing expressions made by public figures.

Chapter 5 –The importance of the lack of binding effects produced by SSEs

A characterizing feature of the purely expressive activities of the state is that they do not impose binding consequence on those who are subjected to them. This

their capacity as private persons and also to public officials. Examples of such laws include incitement laws which prevent individuals inciting acts that would lead to violence, laws against racist expression, laws against the promotion of religious hatred, laws against vocalizing public support for terrorism and even in some countries laws against denying historical events such as the Armenian genocide or the Holocaust".

23 In France, for example, according to Articles 21 and 22 de la loi du 29 juillet 1881 defamatory remarks are forbidden against an 'ethnic group', a 'nation', a 'race' or a 'recognized religion', a group of persons because of their 'sex', their 'sexual orientation' or a 'handicap'. In Belgium however a larger range of groups is described within Article 453 *bis* of the criminal code, i.e, 'racial origin', 'skin colour', 'family ascendance', 'national or ethnic origin', 'present nationality', 'gender', 'sexual orientation', 'civil state', 'birth', 'age', 'fortune', 'religious or philosophical convictions', 'health status (present or future)', 'disability', 'language membership of a union', 'physical characteristics', 'genetic characteristics' or 'social origin'.

makes their use simpler in both ethical and legal terms. In terms of the latter this is because a number of key legal approaches, which are often useful to individuals in seeking redress for harm produced by the state, may not be applicable to such forms of purely expressive activity. Chapter 5 describes two illustrative examples of this: administrative law and anti-discrimination law.

Administrative law has an important contribution to make in terms of the regulation of acts by public officials, in particular to ensure that the officials responsible for such acts have legal authority and that they are made in compliance with important procedural (or even sometimes substantive) norms.[24] Given, however, that administrative acts are often defined in terms of the ability to create rights or obligations for particular individuals, there is uncertainty as to whether administrative law approaches will apply to acts that are purely expressive in nature.[25] The result of this is that a key legal mechanism that is usually available for the regulation of public bodies and officials may not be applicable to SSEs.

Concerning *anti-discrimination* law, one might expect, given that stigmatization and discrimination are often described as problems occurring in a similar context that it would be a natural first port of call for those who perceived themselves to have been negatively affected by various state expressions.[26] Both phenomena are experienced by vulnerable groups in a relatively weak position in terms of power relations. Both are also linked to the creation of negative stereotypes concerning particular groups in society. Numerous anti-discrimination approaches exist at the national, European and international levels. Two main problems, however, become quickly apparent when looking at such approaches from the perspective of SSEs,[27] First, certain general anti-discrimination approaches (including those that are most general and thus far reaching, e.g. the ECtHR's approach under Article 14 of the ECHR) are focused on the concept of 'treatment'. It is this concept that distinguishes expressive acts which are merely stigmatizing (such as expressions) from acts of 'treatment' which are able to have binding effects on individuals. In the context of anti-discrimination approaches, a requirement of 'treatment' usually equates to the imposition of binding legal changes, something that is not present in many SSEs. A second problem is that whilst there are some anti-discrimination approaches that seemingly recognizes types of discrimination not contingent upon the existence of treatment (e.g. 'harassment' or instruction to 'discriminate') they are often only intended to apply to

24 C Harlow, "Global Administrative Law: The Quest for Principles and Values", *The European Journal of International Law* 17, no. 1 (2006). p193
25 This issue is discussed in greater detail in Chapter 5 section 4.
26 Link and Phelan, "Conceptualizing Stigma"; Quinn and De Hert, "Self Respect—a'"Rawlsian Primary Good' Unprotected by the European Convention on Human Rights and Its Lack of a Coherent Approach to Stigmatization?"; L Sayce, "Stigma, Discrimination and Social Exclusion: What's in a Word?", *Journal of Mental Health* 7, no. 4 (1998); ibid.
27 P Quinn, "The Problem of Stigmatizing Expressions – the Limits of Anti-Discrimination Approaches", *International Journal of Discrimination and the Law* 17, no. 1 (2017).

a narrow range of contextual settings. This, for example, appears to be the case with the European Union's (EU's) 'equality directives' that only apply to certain narrowly defined categories of discrimination (e.g. related to race or ethnicity)[28] or may only apply in a narrow context (e.g. within employment contexts).[29] The result of such limitations is that whilst some specialist discrimination approaches may apply to acts that are of a solely expressive nature, they are only likely to do so in certain restrictive circumstances.[30] As the author points out in Chapter 6, this means the vast majority of stigmatizing expressions created by the state are unlikely to be engaged by anti-discrimination approaches. The likely non-application of approaches such as administrative and anti-discrimination law is important because it arguably means that two important candidate tools that one might assume would be useful in providing for the author's normative position (particularly because they would allow an analysis of necessity and proportionality) will not be available.

Chapter 6 – Stigmatizing state expressions – a threat to privacy?

Stigmatizing expressions of the state may on certain occasions contain information that may be sensitive in terms personal privacy. Given this, it is useful as to enquire what role legal approaches related to various concepts of privacy can play in regulating the use of stigmatizing state expressions.

Chapter 6 looks at how various types of legal approaches linked to ideas of privacy may or may not be able to engage various state expressions. In terms of concepts linked to informational notions of privacy, one can look at the various approaches that exist to ensure the protection of personal data. This chapter focuses on the EU's General Data Protection Regulation which foresees a strong role for consent and lays down a series of important principles that must be followed (guaranteed through a series of mandatory administrative practices). Other sources of law relating to the use of personal data in Europe include the European Court of Human Rights (ECtHR) case law under Article 8. The duty the court has found to protect individual reputation from unfounded attack means that states must have in place laws designed to prevent libel or defamation. As powerful as such privacy tools are however, they are limited to instances where data is used that can be inked to specific individuals. This may be relevant in certain limited

28 Council Directive 2000/43/EC of 29 June 2000 implementing the principle of equal treatment between persons irrespective of racial or ethnic origin.

29 Council Directive 2000/78/EC of 27 November 2000 establishing a general framework for equal treatment in employment and occupation.

30 In the US, for example, the interpretation of the Equal Protection Clause has thus far been restricted to a narrow range of protected categories whereas Article 14 of the ECHR contains the term 'or other status'. This term has been reasoned to allow the protection Article 14 offers protection for groups that are undefined. For a discussion of the former approach see K Yoshino, "The New Equal Protection", *Harvard Law Review* 124 (2011). For a discussion of the importance of 'other status' in the latter see R O'Connell, "Cinderella Comes to the Ball: Art 14 and the Right to Non-Discrimination in the ECHR", *Legal Studies* 29, no. 2 (2009). p221

circumstances where stigmatizing information concerning specific individuals is made public. It is not however likely to apply where statements or expressions are made about broad groups of individuals. Such types of statement do not need to refer to specific individuals to be stigmatizing. This represents an important demarcation in terms of SSEs. This is because the majority of SSEs do not refer to specific individuals and as a consequence will often not be engaged by legal approaches related to themes of informational privacy.

As Chapters 1 and 2 discuss, however, expressions can be stigmatizing even where they do not refer to specific individuals. It is therefore also worthwhile to consider legal measures linked to wider notions of privacy, i.e. not relating to the use information that is linked to specific individuals. This includes, for example, privacy approaches that are inspired by a broader vision of privacy, including the need to allow individuals to determine how they will lead their lives. Such visions may see a role for the law in preventing individuals from being the subject of undue 'pressure' or 'steering' from outside forces to follow one way of living or another. In illustrating the role such approaches may be able to play the author opts to use the illustrative approach of the ECtHR under Articles 8 and 10 of the European Convention of Human Rights. Whilst these articles have been used to push an extremely wide and expansive notion of privacy, there are a number of problems that may limit their potential applicability to stigmatizing expressions of the state.

The first is that the court has not found (with the exception of hate speech) purely expressive acts that are stigmatizing to be capable of engaging a convention right. Thus far engaging acts have always involved the use of personal information or some form of legal or physical imposition. Second, the court has only invoked the existence of a positive duty to prevent stigmatizing remarks where they are sufficiently severe to amount to hate speech. As Chapter 4 discusses, however, hate speech has a high threshold seemingly excluding many forms of stigmatizing expressions which may be more subtle in nature. Third, the court has indicated that the existence of Article 10 means that it will not be able to prohibit remarks that do not amount to hate speech (even if stigmatizing). As the court has indicated, living in a pluralist society means that remarks that are simply shocking, disturbing or offending cannot simply be prohibited. This effectively limits the role that privacy approaches can play in regulating SSEs, especially where they do not refer to specific individuals. As with other legal approaches described in this book this once again means it is not realistic to expect privacy approaches to provide for the normative position described in Chapter 3.

Chapter 7 – Carte blanche to stigmatize or a pragmatic reality in a liberal democracy?

Given the difficulties Chapters 4–6 illustrate in finding legal approaches that allow the author's normative approach to be met one might ask whether such a state of affairs is intentional or merely the by-product of the ways many legal approaches are formulated? This is a question that often does not have a clear answer in most legal systems. In Europe, for example, there are few legal provisions found in constitutions, statutes or human rights instruments that appear to grant the state a high degree of freedom in terms of liberty of expression. Rather it appears that such a situation seems to exist as a result of cumulative non-engagement of a range of important legal approaches (as has been illustrated thus far in this book). One prominent exception to this can however be found in the American concept of 'state speech' – a doctrine developed by the US Supreme Court which grants the executive (of which the President is the ultimate head) the right to express itself almost without restriction on any matter of its choosing. Unlike most European legal systems, the US Supreme Court has thus effectively ruled that the state enjoys a right to freedom of expression under the US Constitution. The far ranging effects of such a doctrine are illustrated on a daily basis for all to see with the incendiary tweets of President Trump and the lack of any possibility to take legal action in response to them.

The fact that there are few hard law approaches available that are capable of impacting upon the expressive activity of the state does not, however, mean that other mechanisms of control do not exist. Whilst this book is primarily concerned with the existence (or not) of binding law mechanisms it is necessary give some consideration to alternative forms of control that may exist upon SSEs. These include control over day-to-day state activities by the executive, intervention by legislatures and the creation and implementation of various forms of soft law pertaining to the conduct of public bodies and public servants. Each of these can provide some form of restraint on the expressive activities of the state. These forms of constraint may have several advantageous properties which hard forms of law do not. This includes the fact that they are relatively inexpensive, fast and flexible, often not requiring the existence or creation of legislation. Soft forms of law can be both more flexible and more precise (applying to very specific contexts) and adaptable to changing situations. Not requiring the same lengthy legislative processes as hard law they can be re-drafted quickly in response to new problems that are perceived, including with regard to discrimination and stigmatization.

Despite these advantages such methods of control also suffer from important disadvantages in comparison to hard forms of law. Perhaps the most important is that they can often not be activated externally and independently by private individuals, e. g. through an independent court. Individuals (without the help of binding law) can do little to compel executives or legislatures to take action. Where soft forms of law are available, they may not provide any mechanisms that can be activated externally by private individuals but may rather depend on individuals who work within the executive for activation. Even where a mechanism (such as a complaints body) can be activated, complaints will usually not be heard in a truly independent court. Weaker, non-independent tribunals may be open to majoritarian forms of control. Given that the prejudices and misconception that lie behind many stigmas are often found in majoritarian attitudes to minorities and vulnerable groups, such forms of control may also be influenced by them. The result is that the individuals involved in creating and operating them (and who are ultimately answerable to masters that derive their power and authority from majoritarian political approval) are arguably less likely to be able or willing to recognize or respond to stigmatizing expressions where they occur.

3 Some comments on the scope of this book

As the reader will already be aware this book involves concepts that are extremely far reaching and which go to the very heart of demographic life. Terms such as 'expression' or 'the state' have no clearly agreed and universally accepted definition. The paragraphs below will attempt to outline the scope of this book and elaborate on certain key terms which the author uses throughout.

A Expressions/expressive acts

Producing a concise and catch-all definition of 'state expressions/expressive acts' is difficult if not impossible. Providing illustrations of expressions is not difficult but defining them in an exhaustive manner is. An enormous range of state acts are capable of having expressive content. When the state enacts a law, opens a school in a new area or provides financial assistance to certain groups, the state, in addition to the corporeal and tangible acts it undertakes, will often be seen as expressing an attitude on something or other. Indeed, such expressive meaning is often implicit in the action undertaken.[31] When the state increases maternity leave, for instance, it shows that it is sensitive to issues of gender equality. When it enacts a law banning violent hate crimes against certain minorities it will likely also be seen as expressing a positive attitude to such groups.[32] This book is not however concerned with such types of activity where expressive content can be deduced from an act that has 'corporeal content'. It is rather concerned with activity that has only expressive content. As Chapter 1 discusses (drawing heavily on Hood and Margretts' concept of 'nodality')[33] one potential way of separating 'expressive acts' of the state from other acts is to define them as those activities that whilst having expressive content are not capable of impacting upon individuals in any ' legal or corporeal sense'. When a minister, for example, speaks about her opinions on a particular subject she may well be expressing herself on a particular issue but she is not imposing any real legal or corporeal changes on a particular individual or group of individuals. Individuals are, in theory (and ignoring for a moment all the psychological effects this book is concerned with), able to simply ignore the opinions that have been expressed and act as they wish. The same is arguably true when a public health service advises individuals to stop

31 For more on the importance of the expressive content of legislation (in the US context) see E Anderson and R Pildes, "Expressive Theories of Law: A General Restatement", *University of Pennsylvania Law Review* 148, no. 5 (2000); D Hellman, "The Expressive Dimension of Equal Protection", *Minnesota Law Review* 85, no. 1 (2000–2001); A Strudler, "The Power of Expressive Theories of Law", *Maryland Law Review* 60 (2001).

32 L Ray and D Smith, "Racist Offenders and the Politics of 'Hate Crime'", *Law and Critique* 12, no. 3 (2001). p213 "Advocates of hate crime statutes take the position that alongside the additional hurt done by these crimes the laws are justified by their expressive function. That is, they publicly denounce acts motivated by hate and (in Durkheimian fashion) affirm a set of collective commitments to harmony and equality."

33 Hood and Margretts, *The Tools of Government in the Digital Age*. See Chapter 2.

smoking, continue breastfeeding or have safe sex. Unlike the types of acts that are discussed above, purely expressive activities do not affect the legal rights of an individual, i.e. they do not create binding legal rights or duties upon individuals. As examples in this book will show again and again, this situation makes it difficult for various legal approaches to gain traction. This may be because of the absence of an 'administrative act' (with administrative law), or because of the absence of 'treatment' (with anti-discrimination approaches).[34] It is precisely such an aspect which gives 'expressive acts' of the state their peculiar legal character. Referrals to 'expressive acts' in this book can thus be understood to concern *actions of the state that have an expressive character but which do not create any direct corporeal impact, impose rights or duties upon individuals or alter their legal rights in any way.*

B The state

Another important term found within the title of this work that will likely invoke many questions in the mind of the reader is that of 'the state'. This is a concept that raises obvious problems in terms of definition. When individuals speak of the state, they may often have different things in mind. Some, for example, may be speaking about the governing structure of the state and the political machinery that controls it, i.e. 'the executive'. This is understandable given that this is the most prominent aspect of the state, one that is omnipresent in the media and societal discussion.[35] Viewing the state in terms of its legal character however allows a much wider conception to be developed. It involves considering not just the most prominent aspects of the executive but all of the bodies and 'emanations' that lie under its control.[36] This extends our view of the state to include not only obvious entities such as the police but also potentially other aspects such as schools, local government and public utilities (not to mention entities under the control of the other two arms of the state, i.e. the judiciary and the legislature).

A useful source of reference for this concept can be found in the case law of the US Supreme Court concerning its doctrine of 'government speech' (discussed in

34 These two aspects are discussed in greater depth in turn in Chapters 5.

35 For an interesting discussion of how our concept of the state has evolved over time see Y Barzel, *A Theory of the State: Economic Rights, Legal Rights and the Scope of the State* (Cambridge: Cambridge University Press, 2002). See in particular Chapter 1.

36 'Emanations' is a concept developed by the European Court of Justice in the case *Foster, A. and others v. British Gas PLC*, Case C-188/89, [1990] para 20. An emanation of the state is described as a "body, whatever its legal form, which has been made responsible, pursuant to a measure adopted by the state, for providing a public service under the control of the state and has for that purpose special powers beyond that which result from the normal rules applicable in relations between individuals. The government, local authorities, health authorities and the police are emanations of the state. An employer carrying out a public service which is in the control of the state (such as managing a prison or governing a school) may also be classed" as an emanation of the state.

further detail in Chapter 7). Its cases on this aspect have involved diverse forms of expression from billboard advertisements[37] to statues in parks.[38] Interestingly it has not actually defined what expression is, looking at each expression on a case-by-case basis. In such cases the main area of contention has often rather been the issue of whether the expression in question was indeed speech of the state or of a private individual.[39] In doing so the main test which the court has set has been the existence of some form of executive control over the speech in question. This usually entails the ability of the executive to control the types of expression conducted or prevent them from occurring. In this manner, the ability of individuals in the executive to fire individuals, withdraw funding or any other legal methods of control will be of high evidential value.[40] Such a loose concept of control allows a very wide range of possible expressive activity to be understood as being connected with the state.

The author will employ a similar definition of 'the state' in this work though he would broaden it to include the entities and individuals connected to such bodies that fall under control of one of the three branches of the state, i.e. the executive, the legislature or the judiciary. Given the size of the executive branch (and the entities under its control) most cases of state expression will fall under the first category. Whilst most of the examples used in this work represent speech that would fall under the control of the executive branch, one should also be aware of the potential importance of the other two branches of the state. This includes, for example, the expressive activity of parliamentarians (activity that may often be protected from prosecution under hate speech laws by provisions granting immunity).[41] In addition, though not covered explicitly in this book, similar arguments could also be applied to stigmatizing expressions made by the judiciary.

C The 'human component'

In addition to considering the potential range of entities (e.g. bodies and organizations) that could fall within the concept of the state, it is also important to recognize that in most cases, the state (i.e. an abstract concept) cannot make expressions alone. In reality there is always human input behind the expressions of the state, though in some instances it may be difficult, if not impossible, to determine who the exact individuals were, or assign legal responsibility to them.[42]

37 *Johanns v. Livestock Marketing* 544 U.S. 550 (2005).
38 *Pleasant Grove City v. Summum* 129 S. Ct. 1125 (2009).
39 See Olree, "Identifying Government Speech". As the author states on page 368, "Classifying the speech as either government speech or private speech becomes a crucial question—often *the* crucial question—in deciding these speech cases".
40 H Norton and D Keats Citron, "Government Speech 2.0", *Denver University Law Review* 87 (2010).
41 Several examples of stigmatizing expressions by parliamentarians are discussed in Chapter 2 part 2 and Chapter 4 (concerning criminal law).
42 A good example of this may be a monument that may have been erected in a public park many years ago. The US. Supreme Court heard a case in a similar context to this in the case of *Pleasant Grove City v. Summum* 129 S. Ct. 1125 (2009).

Such individuals are referred to as 'the human component' throughout this book. It is the connection of such individuals to the state and their ability to speak on behalf of it (or be perceived as speaking on behalf of it) that makes their expressions interesting from the point of view of this book and, depending on the content and context potentially stigmatizing. It is for this reason necessary to consider not only the expressions of the state as an 'abstract entity' but also the expressions of those individuals that are linked to it. Such individuals are important because when they express themselves their views may be perceived as representing 'the state' in general. Imagine, for instance, overtly racist expressions made by police officers or teachers. One could argue that in instances where the state failed to take action (e.g. disciplinary sanctions), individual citizens would likely conclude that the ideas behind such expressions were also held by the state. From a legal point of view the existence of this 'human component' is interesting because such individuals may be susceptible to certain forms of legal challenge even when the state itself is not susceptible (e.g. with criminal law in the case of hate speech).[43] A recognition of the 'human component' as a group that also has rights is important as in some instances the rights of these individuals may prevent the state from taking action to restrain their expression (even where it may be stigmatizing to certain groups in society).[44]

Bibliography

Anderson, E, and R Pildes. "Expressive Theories of Law: A General Restatement." *University of Pennsylvania Law Review* 148, no. 5 (2000): 1503–1575.

Barzel, Y. *A Theory of the State: Economic Rights, Legal Rights and the Scope of the State.* Cambridge: Cambridge University Press, 2002.

Bayer, R. "Stigma and the Ethics of Public Health: Not Can We but Should We." *Social Science & Medicine* 67 (2008): 463–472.

Burris, S. "Stigma, Ethics and Policy: A Commentary on Bayer's 'Stigma and the Ethics of Public Health: Not Can We but Should We'." *Social Science & Medicine* 67 (2008): 473–475.

Dovidio, J, B Major and J Crocker. "Stigma: Introduction and Overview". In *The Social Psychology of Stigma*, edited by T Heatherton, R Kleck, M Hebl and J Hull. New York: Guilford Press, 2000.

Gelders, D, and I Oyvind. "Government Communication About Potential Policies: Public Relations, Propaganda or Both?" *Public Relations Review* 36 (2010): 59–62.

Harlow, C. "Global Administrative Law: The Quest for Principles and Values." *The European Journal of International Law* 17, no. 1 (2006): 187–214.

Hellman, D. "The Expressive Dimension of Equal Protection." *Minnesota Law Review* 85, no. 1 (2000–2001): 1–70.

Hood, C, and H Margretts. *The Tools of Government in the Digital Age.* New York: Palgrave Macmillan, 2006.

43 The difference between the susceptibility of the state to criminal prosecution and those who work for it is discussed in Chapter 4 sections 7–8.

44 This concept is discussed further in Chapter 7 section 10 with regards to the rights of state employees under Article 10 ECHR (a right to freedom of expression).

Link, B, and J Phelan. "Conceptualizing Stigma." *Annual Review of Sociology* 27 (2001): 363–385.

Link, B, and J Phelan. "Stigma and Its Public Health Implications." *The Lancet* 367 (2006): 528–529.

Murphy, N. "Context, Not Content: Medium-Based Press Clause Restrictions on Government Speech in the Internet Age." *University of Denver Sports & Entertainment Law Journal* 7 (2009): 26–61.

Norton, H, and D Keats Citron. "Government Speech 2.0." *Denver University Law Review* 87 (2010): 899.

Nussbaum, M. "Capabilities as Fundamental Entitlements: Sen and Social Justice." *Feminist Economics* 9, nos 2–3 (2003): 33–59.

O'Connell, R. "Cinderella Comes to the Ball: Art 14 and the Right to Non-Discrimination in the ECHR." *Legal Studies* 29, no. 2 (2009): 211–229.

Olree, A. "Identifying Government Speech." *Connecticut Law Review* 42, no. 2 (2009): 365–433.

Post, R. "Racist Speech, Democracy, and the First Amendment." *Faculty Scholarship Series* 208 (1991).

Quinn, P. "The Problem of Stigmatizing Expressions – the Limits of Anti-Discrimination Approaches." *International Journal of Discrimination and the Law* 17, no. 1 (2017): 23–50.

Quinn, P. "Crisis Communication in Public Health Emergencies: The Limits of 'Legal Control' and the Risks for Harmful Outcomes in a Digital Age." *Life Sciences, Society and Policy* 14, no. 1 (2018): 4.

Quinn, P, and P De Hert. "Self Respect—a 'Rawlsian Primary Good' Unprotected by the European Convention on Human Rights and Its Lack of a Coherent Approach to Stigmatization?" *The International Journal of Discrimination and the Law* 14 (2014): 19–53.

Rawls, J. *A Theory of Justice*. Cambridge, MA: Harvard Press, 1971.

Ray, L, and D Smith. "Racist Offenders and the Politics of 'Hate Crime'." *Law and Critique* 12, no. 3 (2001): 203–221.

Sayce, L. "Stigma, Discrimination and Social Exclusion: What's in a Word?" *Journal of Mental Health* 7, no. 4 (1998): 331–343.

Scambler, G. "Health-Related Stigma." *Sociology of Health & Illness* 31, no. 3 (2009): 441–455.

Sen, A. *Inequality Reexamined*. Cambridge, MA: Harvard University Press, 1995.

Solanke, I. *Discrimination as Stigma*. Oxford: Hart, 2017.

Strudler, A. "The Power of Expressive Theories of Law." *Maryland Law Review* 60 (2001): 492–505.

Taylor, C. "Hate Speech and Government Speech." *Journal of Constitutional Law* 12, no. 4 (2010): 1115–1189.

Yoshino, K. "The New Equal Protection." *Harvard Law Review* 124 (2011): 747–803.

1 What are state expressions and how can they be stigmatizing?

1 Introduction

> How do you want a French worker who works with his wife, who earn together about 15,000 FF and who sees next to his council house, a piled-up family with a father, three or four spouses and twenty children earning 50,000 FF via benefits naturally without working … If you add to that the noise and the smell, well the French worker, he goes crazy. And it is not racist to say this. We no longer have the means of honoring the family regrouping [policy], and we need to finally start the essential debate in this country, as to whether it is moral and normal that foreigners should profit to the same extent as French people, from a national solidarity to which they don't participate, as they pay no income taxes.
>
> Jacques Chiraq, Mayor of Paris 1980[1]

In all societies, one can easily find examples of statements made by the state, or those in its employment that are capable of stigmatizing groups of individuals. Common examples include statements made by politicians that occupy government posts (including not least the US President), the actions of civil servants such as the police or through organized press releases and information campaigns by government agencies tasked with a particular function, e.g. public health. Given this wide variety, one might ask, what do such activities have in common, and perhaps even if it is possible to categorize them as the same type of activity.[2] In order to answer these questions it is necessary to look at how states use expressive activity and what their effect is on individuals and groups in a society.

Accordingly, this chapter will look at both of these issues. The first part will consist of a discussion of what state expressions actually are and how they can be categorized in relation to other functions of the state. In doing so the author will make use of the concept of 'nodality' as described by Hood and Margretts.[3] Their

1 http://en.wikipedia.org/wiki/Le_bruit_et_l'odeur

2 D Gelders and I Oyvind, "Government Communication About Potential Policies: Public Relations, Propaganda or Both?", *Public Relations Review* 36 (2010).It is often difficult, for example, to separate propaganda and informational activities of the state, with some activities performing both functions.

3 C Hood and H Margretts, *The Tools of Government in the Digital Age*, ed. Palgrave Macmillon (2006). See chapter 2.

approach views the activity of the state primarily in 'policy' and not in 'legal' terms. Such an approach allows the expressive activity to be envisaged in a way which the law and legal scholarship often do not.[4] This part will attempt to demonstrate how and why the state uses expressions and why they can often be stigmatizing. The concept of nodality is useful in explaining why the state (and the individuals working for it) may often use expressions with the expectation that they will not be subject to restraint (including legal restraints) given the common assumption that they do not impose binding legal or corporeal changes on individuals.

The second part of this chapter will provide a range of examples of stigmatizing state expressions (SSEs). As this chapter will show, there is a wealth of examples available that go far beyond the Presidential tweets referred to at the beginning of this book. Most of these can be placed into one of three different categories. The first occurs where the state often has to partake in some form of communication that has an important functional purpose but which may result in certain groups feeling stigmatized ('functional stigmatization'). Imagine a public health message for example concerning a condition that was found predominantly in a certain community.[5] The second may occur where the state condemns certain forms of anti-social or harmful behaviour, e.g. drink driving or passive smoking ('fair criticism'). A third category concerns the participation of the state and individuals connected to it in processes that are closely linked to the democratic nature of the state, e.g. policy announcements or political debate (statements made for political purposes).[6] Often individuals involved in such activities will occupy a duel or hybrid role whereby they are simultaneously expected to represent the state and exhibit a certain level of neutrality whilst at the same time representing partisan political interests

Part 1: Expression as a function of the state – comparison to other functions

In addition, to the many corporeal functions of the state (e.g. providing services such as healthcare, social and physical security and various types of infrastructure), the state is able to act in other instances by making various public statements or releasing information. In doing so the state is often utilizing information to bring about a certain end. On many occasions such pronouncements fulfil an important

4 Chapter 7 points out that most states do not have specific legal approaches designed to deal with state expression. The US forms an exception to this trend given its doctrine of 'government speech'.

5 For a discussion on the merits and problems of using stigmatizing messages in healthcare communication see R Bayer, "Stigma and the Ethics of Public Health: Not Can We but Should We," *Social Science & Medicine* 67 (2008); S Burris, "Stigma, Ethics and Policy: A Commentary on Bayer's 'Stigma and the Ethics of Public Health: Not Can We but Should We'."

6 Gelders and Oyvind, "Government Communication About Potential Policies: Public Relations, Propaganda or Both?"

function – providing citizens with information that they may need in order to protect themselves or their interests.[7] On other occasions such pronouncements reflect a normal aspect of democratic life whereby public officials make their views known on issues that are of interest to the public at that moment.[8] The varying aim, context and scope of such activities raises the question as to whether it is possible to group such activities together as being similar. One might wonder whether this is like 'comparing apples and pears' or do they have much in common from both the point of view of the state that uses them and the law that is intended to regulate them?

This section will attempt to answer such questions by attempting to assess what aspects such acts have in common and how they can be categorized. The author will make use of ideas concerning government capabilities and 'tools' put forward by individuals such as Hood and Margretts.[9] Such an approach attempts to classify government 'tools' in terms of their ability to achieve certain of the state's policy objectives. 'Statements' and 'expressions' seen from such a perspective form one type of 'tool' that is available for use by the state in conjunction with others in order to achieve its aims. This chapter will not focus on how such acts are recognized by the law (this will be done in subsequent chapters), but rather the uses that are made of such acts and why they are particularly useful in certain contexts. The aim will be to identify why, from a state's perspective, it is often desirable to use such tools and also how, on occasion, their use can bring about the stigmatization of various kinds of individuals in society.

1 Public statements as a mode of operation for states – the art of governance

Defining what public expressions are, or how they may be categorized is not simple. Several questions immediately come to mind. What, for example, differentiates a government act that is an expression from one that is not? What is the correct way to describe such a category of acts? Can all forms of expression, including, for example, speech and printed messages, be classified as the same, or do they represent entirely different categories of activity? Does the practical use of 'statements' correspond with their actual recognition in legal terms?

One can, in attempting to answer the first of the above questions, start by analysing the functions that the state carries out in order to attempt to make a distinction between statements or expressions and other types of competences. This is no easy task as the modern state can be seen to carry out an enormous range of functions or operations and it is indeed beyond the scope of this (or any

7 P. Quinn, "Crisis Communication in Public Health Emergencies: The Limits of 'Legal Control' and the Risks for Harmful Outcomes in a Digital Age", *Life Sci Soc Policy* 14, no. 1 (2018).

8 Gelders and Oyvind, "Government Communication About Potential Policies: Public Relations, Propaganda or Both?"

9 Hood and Margretts, *The Tools of Government in the Digital Age.*

other) work to describe them all.[10] Imagine, for example, all the various interactions the average individual has with the state in a year, from medical intervention, to receiving a tax rebate, to sending his or her children to school, etc. A more realistic option than going through all the possible activities of the state is to attempt to categorize activities into more generalized groups which are capable of corresponding to the actual activities the state engages in. Hood and Margetts[11] perceived the state as ultimately a structure that engages in numerous forms of social control.[12] In attempting to exert such social control, states have four basic categories of actions available. These are, according to Hood and Margretts, capable of encapsulating the numerous and varied functions of government that we as citizens are familiar with. They describe these as 'nodality', 'authority', 'treasure' and 'organization'. These functions are utilized by the state to achieve its primary purpose – the exercise of social control. All state activity can be broken down into one of these categories that can be used in different guises in different contexts.

The first, 'nodality', would encompass the types of government 'statement' or 'expression' that this book is interested in. This category effectively involves the use of information by the state to achieve particular aims. The term 'nodality' refers to the ability of the state, through its various structures, to assemble, sort and distribute information. This involves the collection and dissemination of information to and from sources external to the state itself. Actions that fall under the categorization of nodality could, for example, include the distribution of information to the population on a mass basis, e.g. a public health campaign, or on a more restrictive basis, e.g. through letters or targeted emails.[13]

'Authority', refers to the unique authority of the state in condoning or condemning various actions by individuals or groups in society. Such actions are capable of ranging from hard laws to declarations by the state indicating that it 'frowns' upon certain activities and sees them as 'un-citizenly'.[14]

'Treasure' involves the use of economic resources as an incentive for individuals to act in a certain way. Individuals may be induced, for example, to register their

10 Not only are such interactions large in number, but their very nature is changing given the increasing prevalence of e-government. Compare the way interaction is described as a meeting of individuals or a "dyad – two people" in C Goodsell, *The Public Encounter: Where State and Citizen Meet* (Bloomington, IN: Indiana University Press, 1981). and a world of e-government where much interaction is less personalized and there is less discretion due to increased automation. C Reddick, "Citizen Interaction with E-Government: From the Streets to Servers?", *Government Information Quarterly* 22 (2005).

11 Hood and Margretts, *The Tools of Government in the Digital Age.*

12 Ibid. p3 Such an aim is admittedly difficult to reconcile with many legal philosophies that are based on more idealist or abstract notions.

13 Ibid. p9 Hood and Margretts differentiate between such messages using the terms 'bespoke' and 'broadcast messages'.

14 States can be the source of a number of paternalistic messages that attempt to persuade people that it is morally irresponsible and not socially acceptable to take part in certain activities or lifestyles. These are often linked to public health or anti-social behaviour issues. See J Pykett, "The New Maternal State: The Gendered Politics of Governing through Behaviour Change", *Antipode* 44, no. 1 (2011).

children and send them to school in return for child benefit or to fill out a tax return in the hope of receiving a rebate.[15]

The final category, 'organization', involves the use of state resources in terms of personnel and equipment to achieve policy goals. This could occur, for example, where a state decides to use its medical personnel to offer vaccinations to the public or where it decides to deploy more police to a troubled area. At the extreme end of possible intervention a state is able to use its organizational ability to enforce laws and to curtail potential freedoms through the detention of individuals.[16]

Nodality instruments are often seen as an attractive choice and as something to be opted for in preference to the other types of instruments. Several properties can, for example, be assigned to the use of nodality tools that explain this. First, such tools often have little or no cost. Indeed, in the case of public officials making statements it may actually be difficult to assign any actual cost.[17] This is in contrast to the other categories, which may require the use of more resources, especially those such as treasure and organization. Another important factor is that the state is often seen as justifiably having a free hand in matters of expression given the perception that individuals can simply ignore such activities if they wish to. This is because, in theory at least, individuals can, even if they disagree with the content of such messages, choose to ignore the information they are presented with and act however they wish (section 1c) of this chapter and Chapter 3 will illustrate why such an assumption about SSEs is simplistic given the harm associated with stigmatization).

2 Nodality as the least intrusive type of state tool

In very approximate terms it is possible to state that as one proceeds through the four categories of tools, (i.e. through nodality to treasure to authority and then to organization) there is a potential for greater interference with the personal freedoms and liberties of citizens.[18] This can be illustrated by imagining two contrasting situations. The first where a state seeks to persuade its citizens to obtain vaccinations against an emerging infectious disease by using information campaigns, and the second where the state uses police and healthcare resources to enforce compulsory vaccination or treatment on the population.[19] The second

15 Taxation systems often contain economic incentives which are designed to make being honest an economically rational choice. Such measures have varying effectiveness. See L Book, "Freakonomics and the Tax Gap: An Applied Perspective", *American University Law Review* 56, no. 5. p1167

16 There is, of course, often a synergy between the various domains. Organization will, for example, often be used to support authority, e.g. by the police upholding the laws of the state.

17 Hood and Margretts, *The Tools of Government in the Digital Age*. p22

18 There are, of course, exceptions to the general, constraint free use of nodality instruments. The use of personal data will, for instance, be subject to restrictions. This will be discussed further in Chapter 6.

19 The use of compulsory treatment methods is permitted for a number of conditions, e.g. tuberculosis in a number of Western European jurisdictions. See A Hayward et al., "Epidemiology and Control of Tuberculosis in Western

approach depends primarily on the use of 'organization' and is far more intrusive on the lives of individual citizens than the first which is primarily 'nodality' based. Individuals are free, if they wish to ignore the former but not the latter. As Hood and Margretts write: "In simple terms it could be said that 'nodality' works on your knowledge and attitudes, 'authority' on your rights, status and duties, 'treasure' on your bank balance, and 'organization' on your physical environment or even on your person".[20]

Given this potential difference in the level of impact on citizens' lives, one would naturally expect more legal checks and balances upon the state's freedom of action in the latter scenario and less in the former.[21] In a democratic society, where the idea of checks and balances is central, one would therefore expect to see a greater level of constraint on the state as one moves through the modalities as just described.[22] It would accordingly be logical to expect to see more controls on a state when it attempts to use its organizational abilities to effectuate policy goals than when it seeks to use its nodality given that attempts at persuasion through expressive activities are less imposing than the withdrawal of financial benefits or the use of force.[23] This lack of controls and restraints makes the use of nodality an attractive option in comparison to other modes of action which may be legally restrained or require the use of higher levels of resources in terms of treasure or organization.

Hood and Margretts' expectation of fewer or limited controls on nodality type instruments is important. Most forms of stigmatizing expression (many examples of which will be described in Part 2) could seemingly be categorized as nodality functions. Under Hood and Margretts' vision one would expect a lesser level of legal control on purely expressive activity (even where stigmatizing) than other more 'intrusive' actions, e.g. those related to authority, treasure and organization. Given the potential harm that can be caused by stigmatization, this is an issue of potential concern.

European Cities", *The International Journal of Tuberculosis and Lung Disease* 7, no. 8 (2003).

20 Hood and Margretts, *The Tools of Government in the Digital Age*. p7

21 As will be discussed in Chapter 5 in most Western legal systems one can see such a state of affairs where, in general, acts of expression and public statements by the state are less controlled judicially than acts that compel or prohibit individuals from acting in a certain way.

22 Hood and Margretts, *The Tools of Government in the Digital Age*. Whilst authority may in some respects be thought of as being the most imposing on individuals (by creating law with binding effects upon them) it is important to realize that such laws mean relatively little without the commitment or organization of resources to enforce them. As Hood and Margretts state on page 112), "All governments must be equipped forcibly to arrest their own or other countries' citizens in certain circumstances, if only to enforce the judgments of law courts".

23 This point can, for example, be demonstrated in the difficulty administrative law has in engaging purely administrative acts. This issue is discussed further in Chapter 5. See also A Vermeule, "Our Schmittian Administrative Law", *Harvard Law Review* 122 (2009). For a discussion of these problems in the US context.

3 Nodality instruments – state activities that can bring about stigmatization

The description of nodality instruments is interesting from the point of view of this book because such a categorization would encapsulate the type of activity that this thesis is primarily interested in – stigmatizing state expressions (SSEs). The versatility of Hood and Margretts' description allows it accordingly to embrace those statements or expressions (a number of which will be highlighted in the second part of this chapter) that are capable of causing stigmatization and the negative effects associated with the phenomenon (described further in Chapter 2).[24] Nodality instruments involve the transmission of information to the public in order to obtain a policy objective. This therefore encompasses activities such as public statements (by public employees), messages and information campaigns. An understanding of the importance of nodality instruments, the manner in which they are used and the limitations upon their use will thus be of importance in understanding why SSEs occur and when and why in some circumstances they may arguably be necessary.

Information provided by the state, depending upon its context, can bring about stigmatization. It can do this in two primary ways.

i It can demonstrate to individuals in society that the state holds negative opinions concerning them or a group they are considered to belong to. Given the importance of the state in terms of representing society in general and its perceived moral authority this can be highly stigmatizing.[25]

ii The information released can create a situation where it is likely that individuals in society will draw inferences that lead to the formation of stigmatizing opinions concerning certain categories of people.

The propensity for nodality type instruments to bring about stigmatization is a result of their information based nature. The information that they disseminate can be used by various individuals to discern that they are stigmatized, or in turn, to stigmatize others. Imagine for instance a state health campaign that informs individuals that there is a high prevalence of TB amongst homeless people. Such a campaign may only be informational and not laced with authoritative or

24 There may be some problems with classifying certain 'expressions' that contain limited informational content as nodality. This could be the case with symbolic acts such as statues or other monuments, for example. Such activities have been described as 'government speech' by the US Supreme Court. See *Pleasant Grove City v. Summum* 129 S. Ct. 1125 (2009). See also Chapter 7 where this case is discussed in more detail.

25 The position in which individuals are seen by the groups in which they live is of central importance to stigma. Given that the state in modern society is often seen as representing the views of the society in which we live, the state can be seen as a powerful proxy in terms of representing the views of society in general. See also D Reidpath et al., "'He Hath the French Pox': Stigma, Social Value and Social Exclusion", *Sociology of Health & Illness* 27, no. 4 (2005). The importance of the attitude of the state is further discussed in Chapters 2 and 3.

judgemental statements, but may well be capable of stigmatization.[26] Homeless people may, for example, feel that the provision of such information to the public will lead to their increased stigmatization, as a result of the increased fear people may have of being infected with TB. Such an example demonstrates that nodality type instruments can be stigmatizing, even where the state does not intend them to be.[27]

Where the actual intention of the state is to stigmatize, nodality instruments can be used to show that the state holds stigmatizing views of certain groups of individuals and also to induce private citizens in society to hold such views. Where the state has such an intention, it will often infuse a nodality delivered message with an element of its authority. This may exist in the form of a condemnation of a certain behaviour, lifestyle or characteristic. Such actions by the state can be extremely stigmatizing given its perceived legal or even moral authority (discussed further in Chapter 2). Some of the examples in the second part of this chapter will demonstrate instances of how the line between nodality and authority instruments can easily be crossed, with stigmatizing results. This can be seen where states release messages that have a condemnatory tone, or where they are exhorting individuals to act in a certain way. Imagine, for example, a statement by a head of state where he or she describes the wearing of full-face veils as 'not welcome'.[28] In such instances whilst the state (and its representatives) are not limiting the right of individuals to engage in such acts, their condemnation clearly shows that the state (and arguably society at large) does not approve of such acts. Given the commonly perceived moral authority of the state (and especially those who through the democratic process hold high office) such statements can constitute strong forces which may be capable of inducing individuals to act differently.[29] Not only might such a condemnation induce feelings of guilt or shame in such individuals, but they might also be capable of acting as a signal to other citizens that certain activities are to be condemned as being wrong.[30] In addition, as Part 2 of this chapter discusses prominent figures connected to the state may have the ability to influence the beliefs that individuals hold concerning groups that are vulnerable to stigmatization, beliefs that can result in the accentuation of situations that are already stigmatizing.

26 Quinn, "Crisis Communication in Public Health Emergencies: The Limits of 'Legal Control' and the Risks for Harmful Outcomes in a Digital Age".
27 This is related to the lack of a requirement of intent on behalf of the stigmatizing party. This is discussed in Chapter 2.
28 President Sarkozy made such comments on the suitability of wearing a full face veil in France before such an act was made illegal. http://news.bbc.co.uk/2/hi/europe/8676238.stm
29 In Chapter 2 the ideas of Reidpath are discussed. He was interested in the ability of individuals in a position of authority to spread the existence of stigmatizing beliefs in the population. See Reidpath et al., "'He Hath the French Pox': Stigma, Social Value and Social Exclusion".
30 Researchers in the UK have, for example, shown that those who hold stigmatizing views concerning 'benefit' (social security) claimants often 'take queue' for their views from the government's own aired views on the topic. See B Baumberg Geiger et al., "Benefits Stigma in Britain", See also part 2 of this chapter.

4 Nodality – an instrument that 'does not constrain individuals' – a position that does not take into account the serious psychological effects of stigmatization?

Whilst the state is not the only actor in society that is capable of stigmatization (individuals are of course capable of drawing negative inferences and disseminating negative opinions concerning their fellow citizens), it has, given its perceived moral authority, an enormous potential to stigmatize individuals and groups.[31] It can do so using the provision of information that allows individuals to draw negative conclusions concerning others and treat them differently or act in a stigmatizing manner towards them. Imagine, for example, a public health campaign that identifies a certain community as being the origin of an infectious disease outbreak in a certain country, or another that highlights the lifestyle choices of another community as being largely responsible for an increased prevalence of a certain pathogen amongst that community.[32] Such messages are likely to lead to some level of stigmatization for the groups concerned. In instances however where the state chooses to lend its moral authority to information, perhaps in terms of a command or a condemnation (even if it has no intention of backing up such a command) the possibilities of stigmatization are much greater. This is because in doing so, the state essentially condemns the behavioural characteristics of a group of individuals as being unacceptable. This can be extremely destructive for two reasons. First, the condemnation of the state can be directly stigmatizing to the individuals concerned given that it acts as a 'signal' that they are not accepted by the society in which they live. Second, the perceived moral authority of the state means such actions may have a strong normative affect, signalling to mainstream society that the group in question is a threat and potentially deserving of differential treatment. As Chapter 2 discusses, this is important because the phenomenon of stigmatization relates not only to beliefs and perceptions in the minds of stigmatized individuals but also other members of society.

In contrast to the concept of nodality as an instrument of low constraint, the use of stigmatizing expressions by the state has the possibility of producing significant psychological effects in individuals. These effects can lead to very real consequences for both individuals and society as a whole. The author will argue throughout the book that given the possibility of such consequences, the lack of ability of many legal approaches to engage expressive activity of the state (illustrated in Chapters 4–7) is concerning.

5 Control of nodal governance – a weak spot in terms of individual protection?

Hood and Margretts are correct in stating that the three non-nodal forms of government action i.e. authority, treasure and organization, are capable of

31 Reidpath et al., "'He Hath the French Pox': Stigma, Social Value and Social Exclusion".

32 W Gallagher, "Towards a Sane and Rational Approach to Management of Influenza H1N1 2009", *Virology Journal* 6 (2009). In the H1N1 outbreak, the identification by public authorities of Mexico as the potential source of the outbreak caused the discrimination and stigmatization of people of Mexican descent around the world.

exerting more constraint on individuals than nodality itself. Authority, perhaps being the classic form of control, is often seen as the central hallmark of the state itself.[33] When most people think of what the state is, and what separates it from other organizations they see, they are often likely to invoke the ability of the state to create laws that make certain actions illegal. Another function they may be familiar with is the state's control of many financial aspects of their lives through the use of 'treasure' functions. Individuals may immediately think of taxes or cash benefits they are entitled to by virtue of their citizenship, e.g. pensions or unemployment benefits. With regard to organization, it is that aspect of governance that allows authority to be translated into (i.e. through enforcement) reality. For instance, laws are often given practical power through enforcement by the police and the courts.[34]

Potential misuses of each of these functions are easy to envisage and can have very negative consequences for the individuals involved. Wrongful laws can, for instance, be discriminatory, individuals can suffer financial hardship through restrictive access to funds that others are entitled to and perhaps, most importantly, government agents can wrongfully arrest or even threaten the life of citizens. In times gone by autocratic and absolutist regimes have indeed misused each of these governmental functions on numerous occasions. Since the enlightenment however, there has been a clear tendency to control such powers so as to prevent abuses by the state that could unfairly harm individuals.[35] Systems of controls, checks and balances and a notion of the rule of law have gradually been used in most Western states to control the use of such powers. In most democratic states legal mechanisms exist to prevent the state from misusing such functions with the result that individuals suffer harm. Individuals often have recourse to the judicial system in order to be able to secure compensation or order that the wrongful actions be halted. Thus, if an individual is detained improperly he can ask a court for his immediate release, if he is denied the pension he is entitled to he can apply to the court to have it paid and if he is the subject of a law that blatantly discriminates against him he can even have the law ruled invalid by a constitutional court.[36]

33 Hood and Margretts, *The Tools of Government in the Digital Age*. p6

34 Ibid. p12

35 M Elliot, "Human Rights and the Triumph of the Individual in World Culture", *Cultural Sociology* 1, no. 3 (2007). Many Western philosophers consider the philosophies of human rights to be rooted in ideas such as those described by John Locke in his *Two Treatises on Government* (1689–1690) and the work of the *Enlightenment philosophes* (e.g. Montesquieu, Rousseau, Voltaire) whose notions of individual autonomy and freedom in the face of governmental authority are considered fundamental launching pillars.

36 The US Constitution provides protection against laws that are discriminatory in terms of race through its 'Equal Protection Clause' whilst the European Convention of Human Rights (ECHR) which has legal force in many European jurisdictions (including throughout the EU) offers protection against discriminatory law through Article 14 (discussed further in Chapter 5).

With expressive activities however, states are able to act in a comparatively uninhibited manner in pursuit of whatever objectives they see fit (something that will be illustrated in Chapters 4–7). The reasons for this are numerous and are linked to the historical and contextual development of our societies and also their ideological nature where 'free speech' is cherished as a defining and central virtue of democracy.[37] This includes the ability of many political figures that have links to the state to be able to speak their mind on the issues of the day. This historical and cultural context has led to the formation of legal systems that place extremely limited controls on purely expressive activities, e.g. communication and the release of information. Another important factor can be attributed to the pragmatic need of the government to be able to communicate quickly and in an unhindered manner with the public.[38] As the second part of this chapter will show, states need to respond to a range of complex and often unpredictable situations. Too tight a level of legal control of the ability of the state to express itself might therefore be considered capable of harming its responses to such situations.

6 State expressions – a constraint free way of using authority?

Reasons for the lack of constraints on expressive activity can be found in the development of modern states over recent centuries. One might arguably expect to see greater constraints on government action when authority based tools are utilized in place of, or in combination with, nodality tools than one would see with the use of nodality tools alone. If this were true in the context of expressive activity one might expect to see greater legal constraints upon campaigns that involved the distribution of an authoritative message than ones that distributed merely factual information.[39] This is because such a campaign would be employing authoritative elements by using the authority and standing of the state to condone a particular type of behaviour. Part 2 will present several examples of where states have issued condemnatory messages or information campaigns condemning certain lifestyle choices (e.g. smoking or social security

37 Chapter 4 discusses, for example, the (American) concept of the 'marketplace of ideas'. This concept sees a high level of free speech being necessary in order to allow good ideas to displace bad ones. See R Post, "Racist Speech, Democracy, and the First Amendment", *Faculty Scholarship Series* 208 (1991); A Greene, "Government Speech on Unsettled Issues", *Fordham Law Review* (2001); G Lee, "Persuasion, Transparency, and Government Speech", *Hastings Law Journal* (2005). Whilst Europe does not have as fundamentalist an approach to free speech as the US, it is still a valued concept that will usually take precedent over the feelings of individuals who may, for instance, feel insulted.

38 These factors will be discussed in greater detail in Chapter 6 when the weakness of administrative law in tackling expressive acts of states is discussed.

39 In the Rawlsian conception of justice the neutrality of the state was an important issue. See J Rawls, *A Theory of Justice* (Cambridge, MA: Harvard Press, 1971); "Justice as Fairness: Political Not Metaphysical", *Philosophy and Public Affairs* 14, no. 3 (1985); "The Priority of Right and Ideas of the Good", *Philosophy & Public Affairs* 17, no. 4 (1988); *Political Liberalism* (New York: Columbia University Press, 1993).

dependency).[40] In such instances the state, rather than compelling individuals to take one particular course of action, opts simply to let it be known that it approves of a certain course of action over another. According to Hood and Margretts' analysis such actions do not compel individuals as they are free to ignore such exhortations should they wish to do so. The mixing of nodality and authority instruments can make such an option more difficult for individuals however, given the influence government authority can have on individuals. Where such a course is opted for, over the use of a pure nodality instrument (that informs without the use of authority), one should arguably expect to be able to find the existence of a greater level of constraint upon such state action.[41] As will be shown in the second half of this book however, one is able to observe numerous instances where authoritative figures of the state are able to issue condemnatory and stigmatizing statements concerning behaviour or lifestyles that are perceived as being unacceptable in a manner that is unconstrained by the law.

7 State expressions are becoming more important with the growth of the 'information society'

In centuries past, the state had a far more minimalistic function than its contemporary equivalent. Before the existence of welfare states and public healthcare provision (and the many other functions associated with the modern state) states had relatively few roles in society. The idealized version of the state amongst liberal intellectuals was that described by Locke whereby the state would attempt only to secure public order and security and would leave all other matters to the labour and ingenuity of private individuals.[42] States were often established not for the benefit of individual citizens but for autocratic rulers who often depended on force to maintain his (or sometimes her) grip on power. In such a world the state would, for the average individual, come to represent a source of oppression and wrongdoing as much as that of providing a 'leviathan'. With little in the way of restricting forces, absolute rulers were able to use force arbitrarily, meaning that individuals who fell out of favour with those in power could be subject to

40 See, for example, K Bell et al., "Smoking, Stigma and Tobacco 'Denormalization': Further Reflections on the Use of Stigma as a Public Health Tool. A Commentary on Social Science & Medicine's Stigma, Prejudice, Discrimination and Health Special Issue (67: 3)", *Social Science & Medicine* 70, no. 6 (2010) or S Chapman and B Freeman, "Markers of the Denormalisation of Smoking and the Tobacco Industry", *Tobacco Control* 17, no.2 (2008).

41 Such an expectation is also consistent with the discussion conducted in Chapter 3 where the author discusses the use of condemnatory messages and the restrictive conditions that should apply thereto.

42 See, for example, Locke's First Trieste. Although Locke agreed with the concept of a divine monarchy he felt that it should be limited in terms of its interference with private individuals. This was in contrast to Hobbes, for example, who with his idea of the Leviathan (see *Leviathan or The Matter, Forme and Power of a Common Wealth Ecclesiastical and Civil*) favoured total power for the ruling monarch.

mistreatment at the hands of the state and its machinery.[43] In addition to those at the top, those who occupied key provisions within the state machinery were often able to abuse such positions. The state itself was thus often a feared structure. It had the ability to abuse individuals in terms of their personal integrity and liberty when it desired or to be used to impose duties or taxes on individuals under its power. As the eighteenth and nineteenth centuries progressed the state increased the type and extent of its activities. As a result, the state began to interact with individuals and impose on their lives in an ever increasing number of ways. With the Enlightenment the faith in the benevolence of those who held absolute power was shaken and the need for such powers to be reined in and controlled was postulated. This was seen in the years following the American and French Revolutions, where constitutions were built into states' legal order so as to limit such abuses.[44] In doing so they were primarily concerned with arming individuals with rights that could be used to prevent mistreatment by the state or its officials. The French anarchist Joseph Proudhon described the ever increasing and varying ways government was capable of imposing itself upon individuals in the following way:[45]

> To be governed is to be at every operation, at every transaction, noted, registered, enrolled, taxed, stamped, measured, numbered, assessed, licensed, authorized, admonished, forbidden, reformed, corrected, punished. It is, under pretext of public utility and in the name of the general interest, to be placed under contribution, trained, ransomed, exploited, monopolized, extorted, squeezed, mystified, robbed; then, at the slightest resistance, the first word of complaint, to be repressed, fined, despised, harassed, tracked, abused, clubbed, disarmed, choked, imprisoned, judged, condemned, shot, deported, sacrificed, sold, betrayed; and, to crown all, mocked, ridiculed, outraged, dishonoured. This is government; that is its justice; that is its morality.

As a result of the Enlightenment and the revolutions that followed in its wake, states became frequently based around constitutions and not the whim of a supreme monarch. The notion of the 'rule of law' began to take hold.[46] Constitutional provisions offered protection against various forms of state abuses that involved the enactment of dubious laws, the levying of unfair taxes[47] or unjustified

43 The use of the term 'state' to describe such entities could probably be disputed. Diamond used terms such as 'band', 'tribe', 'chiefdom' and 'state' to describe the evolution of human organizational structures throughout human history in terms of their complexity. Structures such as that described here would probably be termed 'chiefdoms' under his scheme. See J Diamond, *Guns, Germs and Steel: The Fates of Human Societies* (New York: Norton, 1999).

44 C Pierson, *The Modern State* (London: Routledge, 2011). See Chapter 1.

45 Quote from D Miller, *Market, State and Community* (Oxford: Oxford University Publishing, 1989). p6

46 Pierson, *The Modern State*. See Chapters 1 and 2.

47 The cry of 'no representation without taxation' was a rallying call and motivator of those who fought for American independence. The levying of taxes without democratic representation was seen as unjust by American colonists in pre-independence

limitations on personal liberty. In these times when the idea of the modern democratic state began to take form, it was in such domains that individuals feared the activities of the state. Early constitutional and democratic controls thus foresaw protections mainly in terms of the non-nodality mechanisms of government, i.e. authority, treasure and organization.

In comparison with the capacity of the state to cause harm in terms of personal liberties through its organizational structure, the risks posed by the informational functions and risks of the state were limited. Before the rise of the modern information age and associated technologies, the informational capacities of states were much more limited, as accordingly was the abuse that states were able to bring about with such capacities.[48] It is only in modern times that the state has developed the informational capacities needed in terms of processing and dissemination for the use of information by the state to be seen as a threat.[49] Before this time individuals were primarily concerned with abuses of the state in other more 'corporeal' areas where threats were posed to individual integrity, property or financial interests. As a result, where laws have emerged to protect individuals against nodality functions of the state, they have arisen much later, and only as individuals have gradually realized the importance of information to modern life. In many associated areas (e.g. privacy and data protection) the law can be thought of as being in an early stage of development. The late emergence of the use of information as a powerful tool of the state may also represent a further reason why restrictions on its use are limited.[50] Privacy laws (discussed in Chapter 6), for example, are a relatively recent phenomenon and are usually focused on the use of information relating to specific individuals and do not apply to other forms (including many SSEs).

Part 2: Illustrative example of state expressions[51]

This section builds on the preceding discussion about the use of expressions by the state and attempts to provide examples of how and when such nodality competences

America. See G Dorfman, "Founders' Legal Case: No Taxation without Representation Versus Taxation No Tyranny", *Houston Law Review* 44, no. 1377 (2007–2008).

48 There were, of course, some terrible abuses. Most notably the use of lists of Jews' names and addresses by the Nazis in the war.

49 The "transformation of modes of communication for persons, goods and information" is seen as a characteristic of the modern state See Pierson, *The Modern State.* p28

50 There are, of course, exceptions to this. In particular, where information refers to identifiable individuals. Prominent examples include rules relating to informational privacy and data protection. For more see P De Hert and S Gutwirth, "Privacy, Data Protection and Law Enforcement. Opacity of the Individual and Transparency of the Power", in *Privacy and the Criminal Law*, ed. E Claes, A Duff, and S Gutwirth (Antwerp and Oxford: Intersentia, 2006).

51 Stigmatization of those who claim benefit in the UK, for example, has been driven by the media which often bases its stories on statements of government ministers in the policy process see part 2 section 4 and Baumberg Geiger et al., "Benefits Stigma in Britain".

can be used with stigmatizing results. Where this happens various harmful effects may result (see Chapter 2). Such SSEs can occur in a variety of contexts.

Sections 1 and 2 will illustrate how SSEs can be made in order to achieve important objectives such as the handling of a public health or security threat ('functional stigmatization'). Where stigmatization takes place in such cases it is as an unintended side effect caused by action that is taken in order to achieve an important goal. Section 3 will also describe another category which describes instances where the state aims to alter individual behaviour through various forms of communication. The aim may be to reduce unhealthy lifestyle behaviours or to decrease certain types of behaviour that are perceived as being 'anti-social' ('fair criticism'). In such instances the state may cause stigmatization unintentionally, whilst in others stigmatization may be used as a tool to achieve the desired aim in question. A third important category, described in Section 4 can be described as political statements ('statements made for political purposes'). Such statements cannot usually be considered functional, i.e. they are intended to achieve one of the practical goals described above. The point of such statements is rather to allow the public to know what a certain individual who is active in the democratic life of the state (or wishes to be) thinks on a certain issue. Such statements are often made by people who although paid and employed by the state often also have a political function at the same time. As a result such individuals are able to air their views on a variety of subjects in order to garner political favour with the electorate.[52] Such statements can include negative opinions and attitudes concerning certain groups or people, or certain behaviours and can consequently be stigmatizing.[53]

1 Statements made to further important aims of the state ('functional stigmatization')

A Public health campaigns

In all Western societies public health campaigns have become an accepted aspect of public health strategy in general. Such campaigns can be thought of as representing instances where states attempt to catch the attention of individuals and to induce an alteration in their behaviour.[54] The aim of the state may be to protect individuals from potential harmful health factors, to bring about health benefits at the societal level or often both given that the two may well be interconnected.[55]

52 The acceptability of such actions within the context of the democratic state will be discussed in a normative sense in Chapter 3.

53 For more discussion on how apparently functional messages of the state can be infused with political content see Gelders and Oyvind, "Government Communication About Potential Policies: Public Relations, Propaganda or Both?"

54 E Mailbach and R Parrot, *Designing Health Messages: Approaches from Communication Theory and Public Health Practice* (Thousand Oaks, CA and London: SAGE Publications, 1995).

55 W Randolph and K Viswanath, "Lessons Learned from Public Health Mass Media Campaigns: Marketing Health in a Crowded Media World", *Annual Review of Public Health* 25 (2004).

The information released in public health campaigns may come from specialized medical agencies or more general members of municipal, regional or national government such as mayors or ministers.[56] Whilst the aim of such campaigns may be to bring about individual and public health benefits, a negative consequence can be the stigmatization of individuals and groups in a society.[57] Such stigmatization can be both intentional and unintentional. Where stigmatization is intentional it may actually represent a force that the state attempts to harness in order to bring about a public health benefit.[58] Several examples will be presented below in order to illustrate the stigmatizing potential of public health campaigns. In some, the stigmatization caused will represent an unavoidable consequence of such campaigns whilst in others the resultant stigmatization can be seen as a careless or even intentional consequence of such campaigns.

Epidemics of infectious disease can represent crises of international proportions that, apart from the obvious risks to human health involved, pose risks in terms of economic problems, national security issues and community relations.[59] Such crises are categorized initially by a vacuum of relevant information, with individuals and the state not properly understanding the adversary they may be facing. This absence of information can be dangerous in terms of risk to public health and also public order.[60] Populations can, in the absence of information, feel compelled to take irrational measures that may cause more harm than good. Populations may also harbour negative feelings towards governments that they feel have failed to take adequate steps to inform them concerning an emergency situation. As a result, public communication represents a key pillar of public health strategies during the outbreak of an infectious disease. Such efforts can be stigmatizing for various groups as illustrated below.

B The pre-marginalized

Often those at risk of stigmatization by the pronouncements of public officials are those who are already stigmatized. If care is not taken further stigmatization of such individuals can lead to further increases in marginalization and worsen effects such as healthcare avoidance.[61] This can lead to an aggravation of inequality in

56 For a good description of various strategies and approaches to public health information campaigns see "Lessons Learned from Public Health Mass Media Campaigns: Marketing Health in a Crowded Media World," *Annual Review of Public Health* 25.

57 N Guttman and C Salmon, "Guilt, Fear, Stigma and Knowledge Gaps", *Ethical Issues in Public Health Communication* 18 (2004).

58 Bayer, "Stigma and the Ethics of Public Health: Not Can We but Should We".

59 M Meltzer, N Cox, and K Fukuda, "The Economic Impact of Pandemic Influenza in the United States: Priorities for Intervention," *Emerging Infectious Disease* 5, no. 5 (1999); S Davies, "Securitizing Infectious Disease", *International Affairs* 84, no. 2 (2008).

60 T Glass and M Schoch-Spana, "Bioterrorism and the People: How to Vaccinate a City against Panic", *Clinical Infectious Disease* 34 (2002). Inactivity by the state in emergency situations can increase the chances of unnecessary panic and disorder.

61 See Chapter 2 for a discussion of healthcare avoidance as a possible consequence of stigmatization.

society. The danger of stigmatization and its ability to make 'hard to reach communities' even harder to reach is an important consideration that public officials must take into account when releasing information, especially in times of crisis. In such times pre-stigmatized groups are at risk in terms of future stigmatization.[62] This includes for example groups such as the homeless, those who are already ill (and thus thought to have weakened immune systems), homosexuals, the poor in general and individuals from foreign communities. All of these groups are perceived as being at higher risk of disease, even under normal, non-epidemic conditions. Pronouncements by public authorities may therefore under such conditions result in an increase in stigmatization for such groups, even where neither the pronouncement nor the disease is in reality linked to any of these groups.[63] Where such pronouncements link an outbreak of infectious disease to a particular group, the potential for stigmatization is even greater.

Unfortunately, the fear and negative stigmatization that is formed against certain groups within populations during an epidemic can hinder efforts to manage an epidemic of infectious diseases. This has been clearly demonstrated for example with attitudes toward testing and treatment for HIV[64] where black[65] or other groups with a perceived lower socioeconomic status are less likely to seek treatment than other groups. The fact that the stigmatization such groups feel can increase in times of epidemics means that such groups are even less likely than they would be normally to seek treatment if they suspected that they had contracted the illness in question. It is therefore important that public health authorities pay special attention during the early stages of an epidemic to such groups in order to increase the chances that they are likely to avail themselves of treatment and limit where possible harmful healthcare avoidance behaviours that may *inter alia* be induced by stigmatizing beliefs.

C Individuals connected to a perceived origin of an outbreak

During the SARS outbreak of 2004, the Chinese and even the wider Asian community in the US and Canada became the subject of intense stigmatization because they had cultural links with the reported geographic location of the outbreak.[66] Such effects were also observed for the worldwide Mexican community in

62 R Goodwin et al., "Initial Psychological Responses to Influenza a, H1N1 ('Swine Flu')", *BMC Infectious Diseases* 9 (2009).

63 For a good analysis of the potentially stigmatizing effects of Health Information Campaigns see Deliverable D1.6 - "Human Rights, stigmatization and risk of discrimination against specific population segments and target groups" from the TELL ME project. This project is an FP7 project funded by the EU Commission that aims to develop novel communication strategies that can be used in epidemic situations.

64 M Chesney, "Critical Delays in HIV Testing and Care", *American Behavioural Scientist* 42, no. 7 (1999).

65 M Gornik, "Disparities in Medicare Services: Potential Causes, Plausible Explanations, and Recommendations", *Health Care Financing Review* 21, no. 4 (2000).

66 J Williams, Gonzalez-Medina, and L Quan, "Infectious Diseases and Social Stigma", *Infectious Diseases and Social Stigma* 4, no. 1 (2011).

the early weeks of the H1N1 outbreak. The identification of Mexico as ground zero of the emerging pandemic justified many instances of repressive policies against Mexicans in other countries such as the employment of unnecessary quarantine procedures.[67] The very act of naming a country of origin appears to aid individuals and mainstream society in focusing on a group perceived as being outsiders or different than mainstream society. This effect has been also seen more recently with the Ebola crisis whereby numerous African individuals living in the west have faced irrational instances of stigmatization and discrimination. Such a notion is central to many conceptions of what stigmatization entails, corresponding in particular to the tendency for individuals to fear 'out-groups'.[68] The identification of a small minority group that is likely to pose a risk to the other members of a society is therefore likely to lead to stigmatizing effects. Caution should therefore be taken where health communication strategies intend to identify one minority as posing more of a risk than the rest of society as a whole. In reality however one must accept that this will be a difficult task for a public health authority tasked with providing information quickly in the context of a public health crisis. Negative reactions to such identification appear more likely if the group in question is already the subject of stigmatization or discrimination. Even individuals who have no connections with affected areas can find themselves subject to such stigma. This can be the case where an unfamiliar host culture casually groups different minority cultures into one. This occurred in the SARS outbreak for example, where not only the Chinese community felt itself the subject of stigmatizing attitudes but also other south east Asian groups that were present as minorities in Western societies.[69] Epidemic situations can therefore be considered as representing 'tinderbox situations' where careless or even well intentioned statements by the state can start a process of stigmatization for vulnerable groups.

D Vaccination campaigns

It is often more effective to target efforts such as vaccination to certain groups that are at higher risk than the general population. Such groups may for instance be at risk because of lifestyle reasons or other reasons such as health status (e.g. those who are elderly, obese or immune-compromised). Whilst this may make complete sense in terms of an argument based on the limited allocation of resources, it can raise further issues with regard to stigmatization. This is because the targeting of only certain minorities by states for vaccination can increase the risk of stigmatization for such groups.[70] When states target such minorities they must inform the

67 P Perry and F Donini-Lenhoff, "Stigmatization Complicates Infectious Disease Management", *American Medical Association Journal of Ethics* 12 (2010).

68 B Link and J Phelan, "Conceptualizing Stigma", *Annual Review of Sociology* 27 (2001). p370

69 J Schram, "How Popular Perceptions of Risk from Sars Are Fermenting Discrimination.", *British Medical Journal* (2003).

70 A Dawson, "An Ethical Argument in Favour of Routine Hepatitis B Vaccination in Very Low-Incidence Countries", *Lancet Infectious Diseases* 5 (2005).

public which minorities are to be the target for vaccination. The information provided in such a campaign may however provide further information for the stigmatization of minorities.[71] Often this will be accompanied by information detailing why such minorities should be targeted, perhaps highlighting the attributes of such groups in order to attract their attention. Whilst the aims of such efforts may be benevolent, one negative effect is that they may act to distinguish such minorities in a negative light in the eyes of the general population. Such information might for example highlight lifestyle behaviours that are viewed negatively by the population in general.[72] When groups are selected for vaccination because they have vulnerable conditions such as old age or obesity there is also a risk of stigmatization or alienation. Elderly individuals may for instance resent being categorized as a vulnerable group. Such labelling may add to feelings of loss of power and weakness already associated with aging.[73] The elderly form a heterogeneous group; whilst some may be infirm others may, at the same age be relatively healthy. Such individuals may resent such a categorization and feel stigmatized or estranged from the general population as a result.

E Health campaigns against lifestyle habits

Some of the greatest threats to public health come not from emerging pathogens or outbreaks of infectious disease but through the prevalence of certain lifestyle habits that bring with them increased risk of disease. Such habits, in addition to harming those that exhibit them, may also be considered as representing a drain on the public purse as a result of the healthcare resources needed to tackle them.[74] States may therefore be motivated to tackle such problems by both ethical and financial concerns. Two different types of public health campaigns can be identified; (i) those that aim to inform individuals with information relating to the risks of certain lifestyle habits and (ii) those that aim to directly discourage certain types of behaviours through stigmatization. Both types of campaigns are capable of causing stigmatization, though with the second type the stigmatization caused may be greater and also intentional.

One obvious example of a common effort to alter lifestyle habits concerns the dietary habits of individuals. Western nations are currently experiencing an explosion in obesity rates amongst their populations.[75] This is expected to lead to an increase in negative health outcomes for individuals and also an increase in the

71 P Streefland, "Introduction of a HIV Vaccine in Developing Countries: Social and Cultural Dimensions", *Vaccine* 21 (2003).

72 Dawson, "An Ethical Argument in Favour of Routine Hepatitis B Vaccination in Very Low-Incidence Countries".

73 E Mordini and P De Hert, *Ageing and Invisibility* (IOS Press, 2010). p197

74 P Katzmarzyk, N Gledhill, and R Sherpard, "The Economic Burden of Physical Inactivity in Canada", *Canadian Medical Association Journal* 163, no. 11 (2000).

75 L Maclean et al., "Obesity, Stigma and Public Health Planning", *Health Promotion International* 24 (2009).

healthcare costs for most states. As a consequence many states make efforts to tackle obesity through public health messages.[76] This can be encouraged through *inter alia* advice to eat more healthily and exercise more.[77] Given that obesity is becoming more prevalent across all sections of society, public health authorities often employ mass media marketing methods that are aimed at the whole of society. This means that messages aimed at tackling obesity are often targeted at the non-obese as well as the obese. Often a central focus of such campaigns revolves around themes connected to issues of personal responsibility in areas such as overconsumption or lack of exercise. This means that public campaigns against obesity often consist of mass dissemination of the message that obesity is brought about primarily by lack of personal control, with such a message being disseminated to the entire community. It has been argued that such messages are dubious in terms of their effectiveness and are capable of worsening an already serious situation of stigmatization for obese individuals.[78] One negative aspect of such campaigns has been recognized as the promotion of 'thinness' and an increased sense that being overweight is not desirable.[79] This can lead to a strengthening of pre-existing attitudes concerning the undesirability of overweight individuals and also potentially negative psychological effects in those who are, or feel they are, overweight.[80] As will be discussed in Chapter 2 in a more generic manner, the belief that personal responsibility is involved in a stigmatizing trait is often an aggravating factor in terms of the severity of the stigmatization suffered.[81] Such messages may be able not only to create negative beliefs in the general public but also in medical professionals who are involved in the treatment of obese individuals. This can give these health professionals factually incorrect assumptions of personal responsibility.[82] Such ideas can result in different attitudes and even behaviours in the treatment of obese individuals. This can result in negative treatment experiences for obese individuals that further aggravate the stigmatization they suffer and consequently further entrench negative effects such as treatment avoidance (see Chapter 2). A third consequence is the spreading of

76 An example is the 'Choose to Live Better Campaign' launched by the NHS in Northern Ireland. This consists at its core of a website intended to aid people recognize that they are becoming overweight, what they can do to prevent this and the negative consequences of becoming overweight. See http://www.choosetolivebetter.com

77 H Walls et al., "Public Health Campaigns and Obesity – a Critique", *BMC Public Health* 11 (2011).

78 Maclean et al., "Obesity, Stigma and Public Health Planning".

79 S Lewis et al., "I Don't Eat a Hamburger and Large Chips Every Day!" A Qualitative Study of the Impact of Public Health Messages About Obesity in Obese Adults", *BMC Public Health* 10 (2010).

80 R Puhl and C Heur, "The Stigma of Obesity: A Review and Update", *Obesity* 17 (2009).One potential negative effect is that individuals avoid seeking medical help for other problems because they are ashamed of their obesity.

81 See Chapter 2 section 4.

82 Lewis et al., "'I Don't Eat a Hamburger and Large Chips Every Day!' A Qualitative Study of the Impact of Public Health Messages About Obesity in Obese Adults".

negative beliefs regarding obesity throughout the general population. This can result in negative experiences and even discrimination for individuals in a wide variety of contexts in daily life. This can range, for example, from education to employment contexts.[83]

Given that the efficacy of such broad and obesity focused campaigns is questionable, the justifications behind their use has also been questioned in the light of ethical and resource based concerns.[84] It has been suggested that, given the potential for negative stigma related effects, campaigns of this type should as a matter of good practice consider their possible implications in terms of stigmatization.[85] Such an impact analysis should be aware of the potential for the dissemination of negative stereotypes and beliefs concerning stigmatization and also the possible multi-layered context that stigmatization can manifest itself within (e.g. complex issues of power imbalances, issues of intersectional discrimination). It should ensure that negative messages are avoided where appropriate and also allow for a continual analysis of the effects of such campaigns in terms of unforeseen consequences regarding stigmatization.[86]

F Smoking – a special case where stigmatization is acceptable?

Smoking prevention campaigns commonly make use of stigmatization in order to reduce smoking. Unlike the campaigns used to tackle obesity however where stigmatization can usually be seen as an incidental negative effect, anti-smoking campaigns have made more intentional and overt use of the phenomenon of stigmatization to achieve their goals.[87] In the past half century smoking, has, in many Western nations, been making a transition from a *chique* activity that was associated with respectable groups and individuals in society to becoming an activity that is increasingly shunned and marginalized.[88] This has occurred through a multi-pronged approach that includes numerous measures such as selective taxation, laws concerning the permissibility of smoking and also numerous public health campaigns. The combined effect of all these has been to frame smoking as a morally questionable activity that is harmful to the individual that smokes, those surrounding him or her and society in general. Public information campaigns have in particular often adopted attitudes of moral condemnation, for example warning of the harm to the unborn foetus, to children through passive smoking and to others in general. Other campaigns have labelled smokers as being foul smelling, likely to litter, addicts, selfish and over users of public services.[89] The result is that an activity

83 Puhl and Heur, "The Stigma of Obesity: A Review and Update".
84 Walls et al., "Public Health Campaigns and Obesity – a Critique".
85 Maclean et al., "Obesity, Stigma and Public Health Planning".
86 Puhl and Heur, "The Stigma of Obesity: A Review and Update".
87 Bayer, "Stigma and the Ethics of Public Health: Not Can We but Should We".
88 K Bell et al., "Smoking, Stigma and Tobacco 'Denormalization': Further Reflections on the Use of Stigma as a Public Health Tool. A Commentary on Social Science & Medicine's Stigma, Prejudice, Discrimination and Health Special Issue (67: 3)".
89 Chapman and Freeman, "Markers of the Denormalisation of Smoking and the Tobacco Industry".

that was once seen as socially acceptable has been morally tarnished. It has therefore been argued that smoking has been subjected over the decades to a campaign of 'denormalization' in an attempt to remove it as an acceptable activity. Evidence of the success of this policy of denormalization is now becoming omnipresent in society. In 2005, for example, the World Health Organization announced that it would no longer hire smokers in any part of the organization. Bayer argues that the process occurring with smoking is similar to that which has occurred in recent years with drink driving, with mainstream society feeling shame at conducting such acts in public.[90] This has (according to Bayer) led many, who do not wish to have their social position threatened, to relinquish the potentially social harmful activity of smoking. Bayer uses this to argue that success in this area presents an example of where stigmatization can, in appropriate circumstances be acceptable in bringing about public health benefits.[91] There has though been disagreement on whether what exactly is being employed in such situations is indeed stigmatization and whether, if it was, it would be acceptable, even in circumstances such as anti-smoking campaigns.[92] It is notable however that efforts to cause stigmatization in this area have been deemed largely acceptable whereas in other areas, such as drug use for example, the consensus demands that stigmatization is something that is avoided.[93]

G Health campaigns that aim to inform minority groups

Certain health problems may not be spread evenly throughout a population but may be found at higher levels within certain groups in society. This may be for various reasons including genetic distribution within populations, poverty in lower socioeconomic groups and cultural behavioural practices.[94] As a result of this, efforts to tackle such health issues may be directed at minority groups in which they are more prevalent. Health education initiatives that do so can be divided into two categories. On the one hand there are health information campaigns that are intentionally directed at the minority or minorities that may be at the highest risk of developing a condition in question. On the other hand there are initiatives

90 Bayer, "Stigma and the Ethics of Public Health: Not Can We but Should We".
91 Bayer takes the opinion that stigmatization can come in degrees. The stigmatization engendered by anti-smoking campaigns is very moderate in comparison to the stigmatization that those with HIV suffer, for example. In examples such as the former he argues that it is therefore responsible to use such moderate stigmatization in order to achieve a greater social good. See ibid. p470
92 S Burris, "Stigma, Ethics and Policy: A Commentary on Bayer's 'Stigma and the Ethics of Public Health: Not Can We but Should We'".
93 K Bell et al., "Smoking, Stigma and Tobacco 'Denormalization': Further Reflections on the Use of Stigma as a Public Health Tool. A Commentary on Social Science & Medicine's Stigma, Prejudice, Discrimination and Health Special Issue (67: 3)".
94 S. C. Smith, Jr. et al., "Discovering the Full Spectrum of Cardiovascular Disease: Minority Health Summit 2003: Report of the Obesity, Metabolic Syndrome, and Hypertension Writing Group," *Circulation* 111, no. 10 (2005). Cardiovascular disease is, for example, more common in black and other minority groups than in whites in the US.

that do not address minority groups specifically but, given the fact that most sufferers of the condition will emanate from a particular minority group, are likely to have the most significant effects on that group. Given that health campaigns are at their core 'social actions' designed to "influence a large number of individual beliefs, attitudes and behaviours",[95] this means that the social life of individuals in such minority groups may be affected in various ways. Planners of public health campaigns often pay insufficient attention to the unexpected and peripheral social consequences of their campaigns with the consequence that such effects may go unnoticed, especially where campaigns appear successful in achieving their public health outcome.[96] Such possible effects include the stigmatization of individuals belonging to affected groups.

The minority in question can vary according to the particular circumstances of each particular situation. Useful examples can be taken from approaches used during the emergence of HIV as an infectious disease in the 1980s in Europe and North America. At that time many immigrant communities from Africa felt stigmatized by assertions in public messaging that the virus had started in Africa and had spread to the West from there (a similar problem was witnessed in the Ebola crisis in 2015).[97] Individuals from such communities often came to be perceived as both sufferers and originators of the virus. Such messages were often perceived as highly stigmatizing by communities of 'African origin' and also misleading.[98] This was because although some African countries had extremely high rates of infection with HIV this did not translate into an increased prevalence of individuals of African origin in Western countries having HIV. Educational material describing the African origin of the virus was both stigmatizing and conducive of an unjustified sense of unease amongst other population groups in Europe and North America as such messages gave the impression that HIV was primarily a problem for African communities and that it could be avoided by not having interaction with members from such communities. The effects of such measures were predictable, with increased marginalization of already marginalized groups and a perception amongst African communities that they could not trust their local health care infrastructure. Such problems undoubtedly led to treatment avoidance (discussed in Chapter 2) and were therefore questionable in terms of efficacy.

95 H Cho and A Salmon, "Unintended Effects of Health Communication Campaigns", *Journal of Communication* 57 (2007). p1

96 Ibid. p294

97 M Haour-Knipe, "Aids Prevention, Stigma and Migrant Status", *Innovation: The European Journal of Social Science Research* 6, no. 1 (1993).

98 E Lawson et al., "HIV/Aids Stigma, Denial, Fear and Discrimination" (Toronto: The African and Caribbean Council on HIV/AIDS in Ontario (ACCHO), Behavioural and Epidemiological Studies Unit, University of Toronto, 2006). p1 "The racialization of HIV as a Black or African disease by mainstream cultural media and institutions has a detrimental impact on willingness to approach health or support services and on HIV knowledge and awareness."

Even where the condition concerned is not as socially stigmatizing as infection with the HIV virus is, the very act of targeting a minority with public health messages can be stigmatizing for at least some members of the community concerned. Imagine, for example, an immigrant community that was targeted with easy-to-read leaflets due a lack of literacy amongst the population concerned. More literate members of the community who are able to read well and who interact more with the mainstream population might find such messages insulting and stigmatizing.[99] One can also, for instance, imagine a campaign concerned with HIV that aims to target homosexual members of an otherwise conservative immigrant community. The propagation of material in the native language within that community might alert the other members of the community to the existence of a 'sub-minority' and cause their stigmatization. Similar issues have been encountered with campaigns designed to educate adolescents about the benefits of the HPV vaccine.[100] Given that HPV is a virus that is spread through sexual contact, conservative members of some minority groups, e.g. traditional Christian and Muslim groups, have often denounced those who have received the vaccine, leading to the potential for stigmatization of those who opt to receive it.

Such issues highlight the fact that whilst the aims of a public health education initiative may be beneficent,[101] collateral damage for some in the form of unwanted stigmatization is often a byproduct. This is an important factor that public health planners must bear in mind when planning public health education campaigns and messages.[102] When doing so it is important to assess whether the 'collateral damage' brought about warrants the initiative in the first place.[103] Such an assessment requires efforts to be undertaken to understand the groups involved and their sensitivities on the subject and also to monitor the results of the campaign in order to assess stigmatization caused thereby.[104] This dilemma and how to approach it is often at the core of public health ethics which often tends to adopt an approach that leans heavily towards utilitarianism.[105] Whilst this might make sense for physicians and others involved in public health activities it poses problems in terms of its compatibility with non-utilitarian rights based on philosophies of law that are at the heart of many Western legal systems (discussed further in Chapter 3).

99 Guttman and Salmon, "Guilt, Fear, Stigma and Knowledge Gaps". p535

100 L Wong and I Sam, "Current Issues Facing the Introduction of Human Papillomavirus Vaccine in Malaysia", *Malaysian Family Physician* 2, no. 2 (2007).

101 Beneficence is almost universally thought of as an essential principal of medical ethics. Physicians and public health interventions should not act unless their intention is to bring about an improvement in health for individuals. See T Beauchamp and J Childress, *Principles of Biomedical Ethics* (New York: Oxford University Press, 1979).

102 Quinn, "Crisis Communication in Public Health Emergencies: The Limits of 'Legal Control' and the Risks for Harmful Outcomes in a Digital Age".

103 Guttman and Salmon, "Guilt, Fear, Stigma and Knowledge Gaps".

104 See, for example, Maclean et al., "Obesity, Stigma and Public Health Planning".

105 D Callahan and B Jennings, "Ethics and Public Health: Forging a Strong Relationship," *American Journal of Public Health* 92, no. 2 (2002).

2 Security issues – stigmatization in the age of the 'war on terror'

Since the end of the Cold War, threats from non state actors using terrorist means have replaced the threat from other states that existed as the primary concern of national security. This has been reflected in the pronouncements that public figures and security agencies have made on such issues.[106] Since the events of 9/11, many Western states have perceived themselves to be involved in a 'war on terror'. Unlike previous and more conventional wars however this war does not involve large standing armies but small groups of individuals that wish to attack states on their territory and overseas. In the contemporary environment the primary source of such threats is perceived as coming from Islamist extremists, who according to their particular interpretation of Islam are engaged in a holy war with the West. This association of terrorism with Islam has led to unfortunate consequences for the large minorities of individuals in many Western states who are mainstream Muslims. Given this topical context, individuals belonging to such minorities and the mainstream public are exposed to a constant flow of negative information regarding threats from Islamic extremists. Whilst the media amplifies such information in a constant cycle of often sensationalist stories, a primary source of such stories is often public officials or public agencies. Briefings by civil servants, ministers or the police on a potential or intercepted terrorist attack, for example, are common examples.[107] Such information is often seized upon by media outlets and given far more attention than the threat in question actually warrants.[108] The role of immigrant Muslim communities with regard to terrorist threats has come to dominate political and policy discourse, providing a constant flow of stories for the media to concentrate on. The heir to the British throne, Prince Charles stated (following the Charlie Hebdo killings) to great media fanfare that British Muslims should make an effort to adhere to British values.[109] Such stories seem indeed to be a 'hot topic' for the media and have long been given attention far beyond that which the frequency of terrorist attacks in the West would seem to warrant.[110]

Given the stigmatizing potential of such media reports and the receptivity of the media towards such information, public officials have an ability to distribute

106 G Mythen and S Walkate, "British Journal of Criminology", *Criminology and Terrorism* 46 (2006).

107 K Hunt and K Rygiel, *(En)Gendering the War on Terror: War Stories and Camouflaged Politics* (New York: Ashgate Publishing, 2013). Public officials, for example, have been known to peddle myths that support their political view. These include the poor treatment of women in strict Islamic societies in order to discredit Islamic extremism.

108 The attacks of 9/11 killed around 3,000 people. Many times this number die in car accidents each year yet the issue of road safety is by comparison an issue that holds very minor interest for media outlets. For a good discussion of risk and human misunderstanding of it see W Shulze and B Wansik, "Toxics, Toyotas, and Terrorism", *Risk Analysis* 32, no. 678–694 (2012).

109 See http://www.dailymail.co.uk/news/article-2944515/Prince-Charles-alarmed-young-Muslims-searching-adventure-radicalised-frightening-Internet.html

110 A Buonfino, "The Politicization and Securitization of the Discourse of Immigration in Europe", *New Political Science* 26, no. 1 (2004).

information that can lead to the stigmatization of large communities (Chapter 2 discusses the importance of the creation of stigmatizing beliefs or ideas in more detail). Releasing the details of a foiled terrorist plot will, for example, inevitably result in intense media coverage. The information that the police release can often be of dubious quality, especially when it has been released soon after an event has occurred. In 2003, for example, police in Naples arrested 29 Pakistani individuals who were illegal immigrants. The Naples police released information to the national and international press that a major Al Qaida cell had been dismantled and that the cell was planning to assassinate a senior British intelligence official. This information was repeated around the world to great interest and coincided with the visit of the then Italian prime minister, Silvio Berlusconi to Washington. Two weeks later however a judge ordered the release of all of the men citing a lack of evidence.[111] Unfortunately the media are prone to distorting such information and blowing it up out of all proportion.[112] In Belgium the media has in recent years focused heavily on reports of young Belgian Muslims that had gone to fight in the Syrian civil war. Elected officials from left to right made much use of these events, generating numerous stories in the press. Such reactions ranged from statements demanding that identity cards were removed from Muslim youth in danger of going to Syria[113] to a senior member of the Antwerp police stating that the force should "check out young men with long beards".[114] The UK provides another example where suspicion surrounding the British Muslim community has been heighted since the July 2005 bombings that were committed by British born Muslims. Since that event popular discourse and media attention has turned towards British Muslims and the phenomenon of the so-called 'home-grown terrorist' has become a popular theme in the media.[115]

Minorities are, at the best of times, subject to a certain level of stigmatization by virtue of belonging to what is perceived by mainstream society as an 'out-group' (discussed further in Chapter 2). In times of a perceived threat from outside, distrust and stigmatization of such out-groups tends to increase.[116] This means that in contexts such as that which exists at present, where tensions exist between

111 The media reports spoke of explosives and extremist Islamist literature that was seized when in reality the police found sugar that had been sent by relatives in Pakistan and laminated decorative verses from the Koran. See L Fekete, "Anti-Muslim Racism and the European Security State", *Race and Class* 46, no. 1 (2004).

112 Ibid.

113 http://www deredactie.be/cm/vrtnieuws/buitenland/Syrie/130411_Syrie_identiteitskaarten

114 http://www knack.be/nieuws/buitenland/strijders-voor-syrie-antwerpse-politie-zoekt-jongens-met-lange-baarden/article-4000270451472.htm

115 Jef Huysmans and Alessandra Buonfino, "Politics of Exception and Unease: Immigration, Asylum and Terrorism in Parliamentary Debates in the UK", *Political Studies* 56, no. 4 (2008).

116 Link and Phelan, "Conceptualizing Stigma". p370. Throughout the history of the US immigrants have often been blamed for bringing diseases with them. The community that is targeted has changed over time, with recent arrivals usually being the main target.

Western states and a (albeit small) group of Islamic extremists, the Islamic community in such states will be at a higher risk of stigmatization.[117] Public officials, ranging from law enforcement agencies to senior ministers, have a unique role in releasing information that can be easily disseminated and which is capable of causing stigmatization. Careless use of such powers therefore has the potential to stigmatize an already marginalized group in society and create long lasting, negative consequences for society as a whole.

3 Statements made concerning behaviour considered anti-social or dangerous, e.g. drink driving ('fair criticism')

Unhealthy lifestyle patterns (discussed in section A above) are not the only behaviour for which the state attempts to 'persuade' individuals to change their habits. A host of other examples connected to the theme of anti-social behaviour exist. Such habits can range from activities that are illegal and criminalized to those that though not illegal, are considered 'anti-social'. A common example of the former are campaigns aimed at discouraging drink driving.[118] In the latter category one can include the recent examples of campaigns against food wastage.[119] The ability of the state to engage in such persuasive activities is a common use of its nodal competences.

The techniques used in such campaigns can vary from those that contain outright messages of moral condemnation, to those that contain more subtle messages where reason may be the primary tool of persuasion. The potential for stigmatization can vary according to the type of message involved. In the first type of campaign (e.g. anti-drink driving campaigns), the message emanating from the state may describe the irresponsibility of the actions in question and the potential dangers of such actions to the individuals involved and to others that they might come into contact with. In such campaigns the images of children or young people lying dead or injured after being hit by a drink driver are a common theme. Such images can be evoke extremely strong emotions in viewers.[120] Such messages

117 G Mythen, S Walkate, and F Khan, "'I'm a Muslim, but I Am Not a Terrorist': Victimisation, Risk Identities and the Performance of Safety", *British Journal of Criminology* 49 (2009). Huysmans et. al term this the 'politics of exception'. See Huysmans and Buonfino, "Politics of Exception and Unease: Immigration, Asylum and Terrorism in Parliamentary Debates in the UK".

118 R Tay, "The Effectiveness of Enforcement and Publicity Campaigns on Serious Crashes Involving Young Male Drivers: Are Drink Driving and Speeding Similar?", *Accident Analysis and Prevention* 37 (2005).

119 Messages containing moral themes on the virtuosity of reducing food waste are often used, for example. See V Sharp, S Giorgi, and D Wilson, "Delivery and Impact of Household Waste Prevention Intervention Campaigns (at the Local Level)", *Waste Management & Research* 28 (2010).

120 Adds in Northern Ireland have been criticized for showing small children being killed by cars driven by people under the influence of alcohol. Such adverts have been criticized for unnecessarily frightening children who may be viewing them. For a discussion concerning the effectiveness of such campaigns see: A Wall, "Government 'Demarketing' as Viewed by Its Target Audience", *Market Intelligence & Planning* 25, no. 2 (2007).

can be powerfully stigmatizing for those who are associated with the anti-social activity in question. This is because they invoke, in the minds of viewers, potential threats to themselves and their family. They also show those engaging in the activity in question to be selfish and not concerned with the well being of those around them. Drink driving, for instance, has become notably less acceptable in many Western countries in recent decades as the attitude of the public has changed towards those who drink and drive. Such a shift represents a process of 'denormalization' whereby drink driving, once something that anybody might do becomes an activity that only the reckless and irresponsible would engage in. Similar approaches have been used to tackle issues such as gambling and smoking.[121]

Such 'persuasion' campaigns represent the extreme end of state communication. At the other end, there are campaigns that are far less imbued with obvious moral messages from the state. These examples are, however, illustrative of the ability of the state to influence the behaviour of its citizens through the use of persuasive messaging. Persuasion can take an informative form where the state, through its messages, provides individuals with sufficient information so that they can be expected to make 'the right decision'. Other campaigns can aim to persuade by showing that the state (and by extension society at large) finds certain forms of behaviour morally unacceptable.

As Chapter 3 will discuss in further depth, that a state, should in certain circumstances be able to undertake such activities does not seem controversial. It would indeed be difficult to imagine a society where the state was not able to condemn behaviour that was seen as anti-social and which causes negative consequences for other individuals in society. In accepting the normality of such efforts, one also has to accept the normality of the state being able to stigmatize groups of individuals whom it perceives as engaging in lifestyles that are not acceptable. In cases such as those outlined above the state is indeed utilizing the phenomenon of stigmatization as a tool in order to exhort behaviour change amongst citizens. Fear of group disapproval (in such contexts the group is society as a whole) lies at the heart of stigmatization as a phenomenon – discussed further in Chapter 2. Examples such as drink driving demonstrate that stigmatization may not always be an option that is unacceptable. This may go some way to explaining why (as the subsequent chapters of this book will illustrate) the law, in its various guises, may have difficulty in engaging statements that are merely stigmatizing. If the law were to adopt a simple black and white approach to stigmatization, it might make such (often necessary) social interventions by the state impossible.

121 See K Bell, "Legislating Abjection? Secondhand Smoke, Tobacco Control Policy and the Public's Health", *Critical Public Health* 21, no. 1 (2011).and C Messerlian and J Derevensky, "Social Marketing Campaigns for Youth Gambling Prevention: Lessons Learned from Youth," *International Journal of Mental Health and Addiction* 4 (2006).

4 Statements made for political purposes

The previous examples in this section have demonstrated stigmatizing uses of nodality functions, i.e. statements or information releases, that sometimes occur when the state is pursuing an important (and often uncontroversial) objective. All states would likely regard such objectives as being important, if not indispensable, including aims of maintaining public health, public order, maintenance of national security and reducing anti-social behaviour. In such situations stigmatization, where it occurs is usually incidental, or at worst a 'necessary evil' in order to achieve an important goal. Another category relates to expressions of a political nature, made by individuals connected to the state. These types of expressions can bring about stigmatization of a much more dubious kind. Such statements emanate from the political process that lies at the heart of democratic states. They often have no important goal in mind, apart from that of gaining popularity for the individual making the statement.

Such statements may be made by individuals who occupy positions in the state's governing structure. Individuals in this latter category can range from ministers and mayors to local politicians. Such individuals can be thought of as occupying a dual role. On the one hand they are required to act in an executive capacity for the state, with all the connotations of neutrality that come with state roles.[122] On the other hand they also exercise a political function, representing the political grouping they come from.[123] In order to further this they are required to explain their beliefs, the reasons for having taken certain actions and their intentions for future actions. Such information is needed for the public to scrutinize the actions of such figures and ultimately in order to exercise their right to vote.[124] The following section provides a few illustrative examples of how such statements can be stigmatizing.

(i) Stigmatization of the unemployed

Stigmatization in general of those who are unemployed is a common phenomenon. Such stigmatization often rests on the basis that individuals are themselves responsible for their unemployment.[125] In the UK a powerful myth exists

122 State neutrality is an important concept under many theories of good governance. The idea of state neutrality was central to Rawls' theory of justice, for example. See Rawls, *Political Liberalism.* p191 These issues will be discussed in further depth in Chapter 3.

123 Gelders and Oyvind, "Government Communication About Potential Policies: Public Relations, Propaganda or Both?" p61. Elected public officials often use the state apparatus to make political points. This often occurs under the guise of consultation of potential policy changes or changes in legislation.

124 The concept of accountability is important in the American constitution's protection of 'government speech'. Without freedom for the government to 'speak' it would not be possible to understand its motivations for action and not possible to hold it to account. See H Norton and D Keats Citron, "Government Speech 2.0", *Denver University Law Review* 87 (2010). p906

125 G Ho et al., "The Stigma of Unemployment: When Joblessness Leads to Being Jobless", *Institute for Research on Labor and Employment* (2011).

concerning the type of individuals that through economic misfortune claim unemployment and other social security benefits in order to survive.[126] The word 'scrounger' has become a byname for individuals who supposedly are happily living off state resources and who, although they could find work if they wished, have no intention of doing so.[127] In recent years both Labour and Conservative governments have attempted to make political capital by claiming to crack down on such individuals and by attacking their ability to lead such a 'parasitic' life style. Prime Minster David Cameron's government, for example, often stated that it is on the side of 'hard working families' and 'not scroungers'.[128] Such statements have led to and fed off an increasing stigmatization of individuals on benefits in the UK.

The stigmatization of individuals on benefits in the UK is inflamed by the media and in particular the tabloid papers which often publish stories about individual cases of fraud. A main inspiration behind such stories is the policy process that lies behind changes in the UK's complex benefits system. At such times numerous statements are released by "opposition parties, parliamentary committees and organisations".[129] It is also at such times that particularly negative statements can be released by government ministers or those acting on their behalf. The Chancellor of the Exchequer for example exclaimed in a political speech in 2012: "Where is the fairness for the shift worker, leaving home in the morning, who looks up at the closed blinds of the next-door neighbour, sleeping off a life on benefits?"[130] This comment was repeated in numerous outlets in the national press and represents an attempt by the government to characterize those who are out of work as being lazy and choosing their life through fear of hard work. The myth behind the stigma appears to be gaining traction, with an ever larger proportion of the public believing that a large proportion of individuals is on benefits in the UK are 'scroungers'.[131] Often statements made by the government appear be completely lacking in factual reality. Unfortunately, however, this does nothing to diminish the appetite of the media for such stories. On one such occasion

126 Those who claim benefit in Belgium are also stigmatized. A recent article in De Morgen claimed that 50 per cent of Flemings believe that those claiming benefits are 'profiteering'. See http://www.demorgen.be/dm/nl/989/Binnenland/article/detail/1747730/
2013/11/27/1-op-2-Vlamingen-vindt-Wie-uitkering-krijgt-profiteert.dhtml

127 Baumberg Geiger et al., "Benefits Stigma in Britain".

128 http://www.independent.co.uk/news/uk/politics/tories-fear-return-of-nasty-pa rty-in-attacks-on-welfare-scroungers-8442950.html The Conservative Party recently ran an ad-campaign featuring a man lying on his couch and asking the question whether the government should support "hard-working families or people who won't work".

129 Baumberg Geiger et al., "Benefit Stigma in Britain". p7

130 http://www.telegraph.co.uk/news/politics/georgeosborne/9594251/Sketch-Geor ge-Osbornes-nose-for-politics.html The same minister had claimed there were many families taking £100,000 a year in housing benefit. In fact there were only five such families in the UK. See ibid.

131 http://www.comres.co.uk/polls/BBC_Welfare_Poll_November2012.pdf ComRes interviewed 1,001 adults online 16–18 November 2012. Data were weighted to be demographically representative of all British adults aged 18+.

ministers, for example, appeared to brief that 1,360 people had been off work for a decade with "diarrhoea", when in fact they had severe bowel diseases and cancer.[132] Research has shown individuals can be affected by stigmatization surrounding benefits in a number of ways. It can create fear and apprehension, discouraging applicants from applying for benefits they are entitled to. Individuals may fear the hostile negative reactions from others when it becomes known that they are claiming benefit. Additionally, in a certain number of cases, individuals will internalize the stigmatizing stereotypes they are subject to and feel as if they are committing a shameful act by claiming benefits.[133] Stigmatization of benefit claimants can also create a perception that public authorities hold negative opinions of individuals who claim benefits and so discourage stigmatized individuals from interacting with public institutions.[134]

(ii) Immigrants (social, cultural and economic stigma)

The notion of the 'static nation', where the same ethnic group has rested since time immemorial is demonstrably false.[135] Humans as a species have been characterized by migrations and invasions since the species first arose. Despite this, it is a common element of cultural identity across most human cultures to claim attachment to a particular territory that is deemed to belong to the culture in question. Individuals who move to the territory and who may be ethnically different are often perceived as outsiders and so stigmatized. As a result immigrants have, as group in general, been prone to stigmatization and discrimination in most societies throughout human history.[136] Such a tendency can find expression around various issues, some of which have already been touched upon in this analysis. These may include for example ideas that immigrants are loyal to a foreign force that presents a danger to the society in which they now live (i.e. that they are fifth columnists), that they have barbaric or immoral social habits, that they are an economic drain on society, that they are of a criminal disposition and that they may carry disease.[137] Many of these aspects can be found in discourse

132 http://www.guardian.co.uk/society/2012/nov/20/scrounger-stigma-poor-people-benefits
133 This was termed 'personal stigmatization' in a report conducted by the University of Kent. See Baumberg Geiger et al., "Benefits Stigma in Britain".
134 Ibid.
135 M Weal et al., "Y Chromosome Evidence for Anglo-Saxon Mass Migration", *Molecular Biology and Evolution* 19, no. 7 (2002).Even in islands such as the UK cultural changes have been created by numerous waves of immigration from the continent in the last several thousand years.
136 T Brader, N Valentino, and E Suhay, "What Triggers Public Opposition to Immigration? Anxiety, Group Cues, and Immigration Threat", *American Journal of Political Science* 52, no. 4 (2008). The treatment of immigrants as an 'outgroup' is a common feature in all European and American societies.
137 A. Gluszek and J. F. Dovidio, "The Way They Speak: A Social Psychological Perspective on the Stigma of Nonnative Accents in Communication", *Personality and Social Psychology Review* 14, no. 2 (2010). Individuals that speak with non-native accents are, for instance, often perceived of as being less loyal than native speakers.

concerning immigrants and the prejudice relating to them in host societies. Such prejudices are often not only located in the conversations between private citizens but can also exist within discourse at the highest level fed by those holding public office.[138] Politicians are able, through their discourse to act as 'cue points' triggering anxiety concerning 'outgroups' such as immigrants.[139] In France, for example, where public discussion of racial characteristics is taboo,[140] public officials still feel free to criticize foreign cultures that they perceive as being incompatible with the French way of life. Jacques Chirac, for instance, whilst Mayor of Paris, made an infamous speech referring to the 'noise and smell' generated by immigrants in Paris (see below).[141] This was seen as an overt reference to non-European immigration from Africa. Muslims in the UK, including both new arrivals and those who are long settled, have recently found themselves at the centre of a debate concerning 'home-grown terrorists'. A prime source and inspiration behind the media obsession is often the state and executive actors.[142] Many new groups of immigrants are also often stigmatized by virtue of the fact that they have been seen at a greater risk of carrying diseases compared to the general population.

Immigrants are often seen as an economic threat to the native population, either because they are viewed as not willing to work, or willing to work for too little and so undercut the 'population'.[143] Such fears are commonly used not only by far right groups but by mainstream politicians who wish to appeal to public sentiment.[144] In his 'le bruit et l'odeur' (noise and smell) speech Jacques Chirac famously stated:[145]

138 The author wrote a newspaper article in the *Guardian* on these issues in 2013 See http://www.theguardian.com/commentisfree/2013/dec/31/romanian-bulgarian-migration-politicians

139 Brader, Valentino, and Suhay, "What Triggers Public Opposition to Immigration? Anxiety, Group Cues, and Immigration Threat". p960

140 E Bruce-Jones, "Race, Space and the Nation State: Racial Recognition and the Prospects for Anti-Discrimination Law in France and Germany", *Columbia Law Review* 39 (2008).

141 This is often referred to as the 'le bruit et l'odeur' speech. See D Fassin, "The Biopolitics of Otherness", *Anthropology Today* 17, no. 1 (2001).

142 P Statham, "Understanding Anti-Asylum Rhetoric: Restrictive Politics or Racist Publics?", *The Political Quarterly* 74 (163); Brader, Valentino, and Suhay, "What Triggers Public Opposition to Immigration? Anxiety, Group Cues, and Immigration Threat".

143 Over 200 hundred years ago Benjamin Franklin is on record as saying "Already the English begin to quit particular neighbourhoods, surrounded by the Dutch, being made uneasy by the disagreeableness of dissonant manners ... Besides, the Dutch under-live, and are thereby enabled to under-work and under-sell the English who are thereby extremely incommoded and consequently disgusted". See Link and Phelan, "Conceptualizing Stigma". p370

144 The left of centre Labour Party then leader Ed Milliband (and official leader of the opposition) also subscribed to such a view. See http://www.dailymail.co.uk/news/article-2041593/Ed-Miliband-admits-Labours-immigration-policy-DID-drive-wages-living-standards.html

145 http://en.wikipedia.org/wiki/Le_bruit_et_l'odeur

> (Translation) How do you want a French worker who works with his wife, who earn together about 15,000 FF and who sees next to his council house, a piled-up family with a father, three or four spouses and twenty children earning 50,000 FF via benefits naturally without working … If you add to that *the noise and the smell*, well the French worker, he goes crazy. And it is not racist to say this. We no longer have the means of honouring the family regrouping [policy], and we need to finally start the essential debate in this country, as to whether it is moral and normal that foreigners should profit to the same extent as French people, from a national solidarity to which they don't participate, as they pay no income taxes.[146]

In making such a statement Chirac was clearly appealing to anti-outsider, anti-immigrant instincts of the average voter. Such feelings often provide a receptive environment for stigmatization to take root.[147] As Chapter 2 discusses, immigrants represent a group which is always going to be more vulnerable to stigmatization. This situation will exist, even with the best intentions and actions of public authorities. However, the state plays an important role in spreading beliefs and in validating both stereotypes and behaviours for its citizens putting it in a position where its careless use of expressions can make such problems worse.

3 Conclusion

In trying to conceptualize what exactly state expressions are the concept of nodality is useful. It allows most state expressions to be viewed under a single concept, something that no legal approach (at least in Europe) appears able to offer.[148] Nodality describes the ability of the state to act in order to achieve its goals by the collection, organization and provision of information. Such activities include statements, information campaigns and other messages that might be directed at the public in order to effectuate policy goals. Instruments of this type are often favoured because of their perceived low level of impact upon individual citizens. Their impact is considered low because individuals are free, at least in theory, to ignore the provision of information and act however they wish. This stands in contrast to other domains of state activity where through the use of 'authority', 'treasure' or 'organizational measures' the autonomy of individuals may be affected. As a consequence of this limited impact on individuals, there is, in general, an expectation that nodality instruments should be subject to a minimum in terms of restraint (including legal restraint).

The use of nodality functions in reality however often involves more than the mere provision of information. They can often be infused with advice, efforts at

146 The original quote and translation were taken from the English version of the Wikipedia page. See http://en.wikipedia.org/wiki/Le_bruit_et_l'odeur

147 Reidpath et al., "'He Hath the French Pox': Stigma, Social Value and Social Exclusion".

148 As Chapter 7 will discuss the doctrine of 'government speech' developed by the US Supreme Court is an exception to this.

persuasion and implicit or explicit elements of authority (e.g. involving condemnation of certain individuals or activities). The possibility of using such measures to air sensitive information and to air unfavourable opinions on certain groups and lifestyles means that they can be stigmatizing. Given the negative psychological and societal effects that can be invoked by stigmatization (described further in Chapter 2), the contention of Hood and Margretts that nodality instruments are relatively low impact in nature on individuals may be somewhat simplistic. The ability of individuals to simply 'ignore' stigmatizing expressions is in reality questionable.

The potential for harmful psychological and societal effects calls into question the permissibility of the state to use such expressions and in which contexts they may be permitted. In order to illustrate the importance of having such a 'debate', this chapter presented three different ways in which nodality instruments are often used in a stigmatizing manner (i.e. through SSEs).

A 'Functional' stigmatization

Stigmatization can occur as an unintended side-effect of nodality functions that are intended to deal with a pressing need. This could, for example, be in context of public health problems or security issues. In such cases, the public official or organization issuing the statement or releasing the information in question will be preoccupied with the achievement of an important goal (e.g. related to health or security matters). As a result, little attention may be paid to the stigmatizing content of the message and those issuing the message are probably not aware of the negative consequences of such stigmatization.[149] On many occasions, where stigmatization occurs in such a manner, e.g. in public health campaigns, the stigmatization caused can arguably be deemed as minor in comparison to the benefits brought about. Laws preventing states from using SSEs would arguably mean that certain serious issues could not be confronted, having negative consequences for many individuals. In such instances a best approach would probably involve ensuring that stigmatization was avoided when possible and that where stigmatization was caused that it was indeed at an acceptable level given the possible benefits of the measure in question.[150]

B 'Fair criticism'

Rather than being a means to an end, in some circumstances, the goal sought by the public official or institution may be to bring about stigmatization. This may occur, for example, in campaigns designed to reduce behaviour that is considered

149 Guttman and Salmon, "Guilt, Fear, Stigma and Knowledge Gaps".

150 These issues are discussed by the author within the context of the possible application of ECHR Article 8 to stigmatizing statements in P Quinn and P De Hert, "Self Respect—a 'Rawlsian Primary Good' Unprotected by the European Convention on Human Rights and Its Lack of a Coherent Approach to Stigmatization?", *The International Journal of Discrimination and the Law* 14 (2014).

anti-social. Examples of campaigns that could fall into such a strategy include anti-drinking campaigns or some forms of anti-smoking campaigns. In such instances the state may attempt to influence public opinion, in order that a particular activity becomes frowned upon. In making certain activities unpopular, the state effectively places individuals under social pressure to stop the activity in question. Such a process effectively represents a form of stigmatization where people are induced to alter their behaviour through fear of the disapproval of others. In such instances public officials are in reality hoping to induce a common coping response to stigmatization – avoidance of the behaviour that is stigmatized.[151] Most individuals would find it entirely normal that the state is able to condemn behaviour that is seen as anti-social. Given that such condemnation usually consists of a form of stigmatization, simplistic legal restrictions on stigmatization would mean that the state would not be able to condemn such activities (or at least would find it more difficult to do so). Such issues demonstrate why a simple law prohibiting stigmatization would not be suitable as it would be overly broad and would prevent the state from utilizing important nodality functions (discussed further in Chapter 3). In addition, this aspect demonstrates that any legal intervention designed to control stigmatization would have to be flexible in order not to prevent the state from acting in situations where it may need to do so.

C Stigmatization by statements made in the political process

On other occasions stigmatization may result where there is no important objective at stake. Examples include the pseudo-political pronouncements of elected officials holding public office. The very nature of most democratic states means that high public offices are often occupied by individuals who act with a political motive. Such individuals often choose their course of action not only according to their duty as public official but in order to 'curry favour' with potential electorates. As a result, public officials often feel the need to express their 'opinions' on a number of issues, even where they are unable or choose not to take action on such issues themselves. Whilst on the one hand it may seem pointless for public officials to express opinions on areas that in reality lie outside of their competence, the ability of elected officials to express their attitudes and opinions is, on the other hand, seen as an integral aspect of democracy. Voters expect to know the opinions of elected officials on a range of matters and, furthermore, it is difficult to imagine how a democracy would be able to function if elected officials were not allowed to express their views on a number of matters. If such individuals were prevented from airing their views, for fear of stigmatizing certain groups it might make it difficult or impossible for the electorate to inform themselves making it difficult to exercise their electoral right. Given that such views will often take the form of criticism of one group or another, they will often be stigmatizing. The fact that such views emanate from individuals connected to the state will increase their stigmatizing potency.

The aim of this chapter was to show some of the varying ways in which stigmatization can be caused by state expressions. The examples provided demonstrate the

151 See Chapter 2 for a discussion of coping mechanisms.

variety of ways stigmatization can be caused, whether in an intentional or unintentional manner, in order to achieve a vital goal and on other occasions merely for political point scoring. This variety in form and purpose of such expressions demonstrates that the regulation of such statements would need to be a complex and nuanced affair. Outlawing SSEs in all cases would simply not be feasible, most notably because it would prevent the state from acting in numerous cases to protect the vital interests of other citizens and would hinder the democratic process. Given these needs any normative description of when a state may use SSEs would have to be nuanced. This 'normative debate' will take place in Chapter 3, with reference to the notion of self-respect, in particular as described by John Rawls. Before this, however, it is necessary to further explore the phenomenon of stigmatization itself so as to be better able to understand the harm it is capable of producing.

Bibliography

Baumberg Geiger, B, K Bell, D Gaffney. "Benefits Stigma in Britain." (2012) Project report. Elizabeth Finn Care. https://kar.kent.ac.uk/id/eprint/36377

Bayer, R. "Stigma and the Ethics of Public Health: Not Can We but Should We." *Social Science & Medicine* 67 (2008): 463–472.

Beauchamp, T, and J Childress. *Principles of Biomedical Ethics.* New York: Oxford University Press, 1979.

Bell, K. "Legislating Abjection? Secondhand Smoke, Tobacco Control Policy and the Public's Health." *Critical Public Health* 21, no. 1 (2011): 49–62.

Bell, K, ASalmon, MBowers, JBell, and L McCullough. "Smoking, Stigma and Tobacco 'Denormalization': Further Reflections on the Use of Stigma as a Public Health Tool. A Commentary on Social Science & Medicine's Stigma, Prejudice, Discrimination and Health Special Issue (67: 3)." *Social Science & Medicine* 70, no. 6 (2010): 795–799.

Book, L. "Freakonomics and the Tax Gap: An Applied Perspective." *American University Law Review* 56, no. 5: 1163–1185.

Brader, T, N Valentino, and E Suhay. "What Triggers Public Opposition to Immigration? Anxiety, Group Cues, and Immigration Threat." *American Journal of Political Science* 52, no. 4 (2008): 959–978.

Bruce-Jones, E. "Race, Space and the Nation State: Racial Recognition and the Prospects for Anti-Discrimination Law in France and Germany." *Columbia Law Review* 39 (2008): 423–427.

Buonfino, A. "The Politicization and Securitization of the Discourse of Immigration in Europe." *New Political Science* 26, no. 1 (2004): 23–49.

Burris, S. "Stigma, Ethics and Policy: A Commentary on Bayer's 'Stigma and the Ethics of Public Health: Not Can We but Should We'. *Social Science & Medicine* 67 (2008): 473–475.

Callahan, D, and B Jennings. "Ethics and Public Health: Forging a Strong Relationship." *American Journal of Public Health* 92, no. 2 (2002): 169–176.

Chapman, S, and B Freeman. "Markers of the Denormalisation of Smoking and the Tobacco Industry." *Tobacco Control* 17, no. 2 (2008): 25–31.

Chesney, M. "Critical Delays in HIV Testing and Care." *American Behavioural Scientist* 42, no. 7 (1999): 1162–1174.

Cho, H, and A Salmon. "Unintended Effects of Health Communication Campaigns." *Journal of Communication* 57 (2007): 293–317.

Davies, S. "Securitizing Infectious Disease." *International Affairs* 84, no. 2 (2008): 295–313.

Dawson, A. "An Ethical Argument in Favour of Routine Hepatitis B Vaccination in Very Low-Incidence Countries." *Lancet Infectious Diseases* 5 (2005): 120–125.

De Hert, P, and S Gutwirth. "Privacy, Data Protection and Law Enforcement. Opacity of the Individual and Transparency of the Power." In *Privacy and the Criminal Law*, edited by E Claes, A Duff and S Gutwirth, 61–104. Antwerp and Oxford: Intersentia, 2006.

Diamond, J. *Guns, Germs and Steel: The Fates of Human Societies.* New York: Norton, 1999.

Dorfman, G. "Founders' Legal Case: No Taxation without Representation Versus Taxation No Tyranny." *Houston Law Review* 44, no. 1377 (2007–2008): 1377–1440.

Elliot, M. "Human Rights and the Triumph of the Individual in World Culture." *Cultural Sociology* 1, no. 3 (2007) doi:10.1177/1749975507082052

Fassin, D. "The Biopolitics of Otherness." *Anthropology Today* 17, no. 1 (2001): 3–7.

Fekete, L. "Anti-Muslim Racism and the European Security State." *Race and Class* 46, no. 1 (2004): 3–29.

Gallagher, W. "Towards a Sane and Rational Approach to Management of Influenza H1N1 2009." *Virology Journal* 6 (2009) doi:10.1186/1743-422X-6-51

Gelders, D, and I Oyvind. "Government Communication About Potential Policies: Public Relations, Propaganda or Both?" *Public Relations Review* 36 (2010): 59–62.

Glass, T, and M Schoch-Spana. "Bioterrorism and the People: How to Vaccinate a City against Panic." *Clinical Infectious Disease* 34 (2002): 217–223.

Gluszek, A., and J. F. Dovidio. "The Way They Speak: A Social Psychological Perspective on the Stigma of Nonnative Accents in Communication." (In Eng). *Personality and Social Psychology Review* 14, no. 2 (May 2010): 214–237.

Goodsell, C. *The Public Encounter: Where State and Citizen Meet.* Bloomington, IN: Indiana University Press, 1981.

Goodwin, R, S Haque, F Neto, and L Meyers. "Initial Psychological Responses to Influenza A, H1N1 ('Swine Flu')." *BMC Infectious Diseases* 9 (2009) doi:10.1186/1471-2334-9-166

Gornik, M. "Disparities in Medicare Services: Potential Causes, Plausible Explanations, and Recommendations." *Health Care Financing Review* 21, no. 4 (2000): 23–43.

Greene, A. "Government Speech on Unsettled Issues." *Fordham Law Review* (2001): 1667–1688.

Guttman, N, and C Salmon. "Guilt, Fear, Stigma and Knowledge Gaps." *Ethical Issues in Public Health Communication* 18 (2004): 531–552.

Haour-Knipe, M. "Aids Prevention, Stigma and Migrant Status." *Innovation: The European Journal of Social Science Research* 6, no. 1 (1993): 21–37.

Hayward, A, T Darton, N Van-Tam, J Watson, R Coker, and V Schwoebel. "Epidemiology and Control of Tuberculosis in Western European Cities." *The International Journal of Tuberculosis and Lung Disease* 7, no. 8 (2003): 751–757.

Ho, G, M Shih, D Walters, and T Pittinsky. *The Stigma of Unemployment: When Joblessness Leads to Being Jobless.* New York: Institute for Research on Labor and Employment, 2011.

Hood, C, and H Margretts. *The Tools of Government in the Digital Age.* New York: Palgrave Macmillan, 2006.

Hunt, K, and K Rygiel. *(En)Gendering the War on Terror: War Stories and Camouflaged Politics.* New York: Ashgate Publishing, 2013.

Huysmans, Jef, and Alessandra Buonfino. "Politics of Exception and Unease: Immigration, Asylum and Terrorism in Parliamentary Debates in the UK." *Political Studies* 56, no. 4 (2008): 766–788.

Katzmarzyk, P, N Gledhill, and R Sherpard. “The Economic Burden of Physical Inactivity in Canada.” *Canadian Medical Association Journal* 163, no. 11 (2000): 1435–1440.

Lawson, E, F Gardezi, L Calzavara, W Husbands, T Myers, and W Tharao. *HIV/Aids Stigma, Denial, Fear and Discrimination*. Toronto: The African and Caribbean Council on HIV/AIDS in Ontario (ACCHO), Behavioural and Epidemiological Studies Unit, University of Toronto, 2006.

Lee, G. “Persuasion, Transparency, and Government Speech.” *Hastings Law Journal* 65, no 5 (2005): 983–987.

Lewis, S, S Thomas, J Hyde, D Castle, R Warwick, and P Komesaroff. “I Don’t Eat a Hamburger and Large Chips Every Day!” A Qualitative Study of the Impact of Public Health Messages About Obesity in Obese Adults.” *BMC Public Health* 10 (2010): 309–318.

Link, B, and J Phelan. “Conceptualizing Stigma.” *Annual Review of Sociology* 27 (2001): 363–385.

Maclean, L, N Edwards, M Garrard, N Sims-Jones, K Clinton, and L Ashley. “Obesity, Stigma and Public Health Planning.” *Health Promotion International* 24 (2009): 88–93.

Mailbach, E, and R Parrot. *Designing Health Messages: Approaches from Communication Theory and Public Health Practice*. Thousand Oaks, CA and London: SAGE Publications, 1995. doi:10.4135/9781452233451

Meltzer, M, N Cox, and K Fukuda. “The Economic Impact of Pandemic Influenza in the United States: Priorities for Intervention.” *Emerging Infectious Disease* 5, no. 5 (1999): 659–671.

Messerlian, C, and J Derevensky. “Social Marketing Campaigns for Youth Gambling Prevention: Lessons Learned from Youth.” *International Journal of Mental Health and Addiction* 4 (2006): 294–306.

Miller, D. *Market, State and Community*. Oxford: Oxford University Publishing, 1989.

Mordini, E, and P De Hert. *Ageing and Invisibility*. Amsterdam: IOS Press, 2010.

Mythen, G, and S Walkate. “British Journal of Criminology.” *Criminology and Terrorism* 46 (2006): 379–394.

Mythen, G, SWalkate, and F Khan. “‘I’m a Muslim, but I Am Not a Terrorist’: Victimisation, Risk Identities and the Performance of Safety.” *British Journal of Criminology* 49 (2009): 736–754.

Norton, H, and D Keats Citron. “Government Speech 2.0.” *Denver University Law Review* 87 (2010): 899–943.

Perry, P, and F Donini-Lenhoff. “Stigmatization Complicates Infectious Disease Management.” *American Medical Association Journal of Ethics* 12 (2010): 225–230.

Pierson, C. *The Modern State*. London: Routledge, 2011.

Post, R. “Racist Speech, Democracy, and the First Amendment.” *Faculty Scholarship Series* 208 (1991): 267–327.

Puhl, R, and C Heur. “The Stigma of Obesity: A Review and Update.” *Obesity* 17 (2009): 941–964.

Pykett, J. “The New Maternal State: The Gendered Politics of Governing through Behaviour Change.” *Antipode* 44, no. 1 (2011): 217–238.

Quinn, P, and P De Hert. “Self Respect—a ‘Rawlsian Primary Good’ Unprotected by the European Convention on Human Rights and Its Lack of a Coherent Approach to Stigmatization?” *The International Journal of Discrimination and the Law* 14 (2014): 19–53.

Quinn, P. “Crisis Communication in Public Health Emergencies: The Limits of ‘Legal Control’ and the Risks for Harmful Outcomes in a Digital Age.” *Life Sciences, Society and Policy* 14, no. 1 (6 Feb. 2018): 4.

Randolph, W, and K Viswanath. "Lessons Learned from Public Health Mass Media Campaigns: Marketing Health in a Crowded Media World." *Annual Review of Public Health* 25 (2004): 419–437.

Randolph, W, and K Viswanath. "Lessons Learned from Public Health Mass Media Campaigns: Marketing Health in a Crowded Media World." *Annual Review of Public Health* 25: 419–437.

Rawls, J. "Justice as Fairness: Political Not Metaphysical." *Philosophy and Public Affairs* 14, no. 3 (1985): 223–251.

Rawls, J. *Political Liberalism*. New York: Columbia University Press, 1993.

Rawls, J. "The Priority of Right and Ideas of the Good." *Philosophy & Public Affairs* 17, no. 4 (1988): 251–276.

Rawls, J. *A Theory of Justice*. Cambridge, MA: Harvard Press, 1971.

Reddick, C. "Citizen Interaction with E-Government: From the Streets to Servers?" *Government Information Quarterly* 22 (2005): 38–57.

Reidpath, D, K Chan, S Gifford, and P Allotey. "'He Hath the French Pox': Stigma, Social Value and Social Exclusion." *Sociology of Health & Illness* 27, no. 4 (2005): 468–489.

Schram, J. "How Popular Perceptions of Risk from Sars Are Fermenting Discrimination." *British Medical Journal* 326 (2003): 939–900.

Sharp, V, S Giorgi, and D Wilson. "Delivery and Impact of Household Waste Prevention Intervention Campaigns (at the Local Level)." *Waste Management & Research* 28 (2010): 256–268.

Shulze, W, and B Wansik. "Toxics, Toyotas, and Terrorism." *Risk Analysis* 32, no. 1 (2012): 678–694.

Smith, S C, Jr, L T Clark, R S Cooper, S R Daniels, S K Kumanyika, E Ofili, M A Quinones *et al.* "Discovering the Full Spectrum of Cardiovascular Disease: Minority Health Summit 2003: Report of the Obesity, Metabolic Syndrome, and Hypertension Writing Group." (In Eng). *Circulation* 111, no. 10 (15 Mar 2005): e134–139.

Statham, P. "Understanding Anti-Asylum Rhetoric: Restrictive Politics or Racist Publics?" *The Political Quarterly* 74 (163): 163–177.

Streefland, P. "Introduction of a HIV Vaccine in Developing Countries: Social and Cultural Dimensions." *Vaccine* 21 (2003): 1304–1309.

Tay, R. "The Effectiveness of Enforcement and Publicity Campaigns on Serious Crashes Involving Young Male Drivers: Are Drink Driving and Speeding Similar?" *Accident Analysis and Prevention* 37 (2005): 922–929.

Vermeule, A. "Our Schmittian Administrative Law." *Harvard Law Review* 122 (2009): 1096–1149.

Wall, A. "Government 'Demarketing' as Viewed by Its Target Audience." *Market Intelligence & Planning* 25, no. 2 (2007): 123–135.

Walls, H, A Peeters, J Proietto and J McNeil. "Public Health Campaigns and Obesity – a Critique." *BMC Public Health* 11 (2011): 136–143.

Weal, M, D Weiss, R Jager, N Bradman, and M Thomas. "Y Chromosome Evidence for Anglo-Saxon Mass Migration." *Molecular Biology and Evolution* 19, no. 7 (2002): 1008–1021.

Williams, J, Gonzalez-Medina, and L Quan. "Infectious Diseases and Social Stigma." *Infectious Diseases and Social Stigma* 4, no. 1 (2011): 58–70.

Wong, L, and I Sam. "Current Issues Facing the Introduction of Human Papillomavirus Vaccine in Malaysia." *Malaysian Family Physician* 2, no. 2 (2007): 1985–2274.

2 Defining stigma and its potential harm

1 Introduction

> Society is organized on the principle that any individual who possesses certain social characteristics has a moral right to expect that others will value and treat him in an appropriate way.
>
> Erving Goffman[1]

Chapter 1 discussed the concept of state expression and how such expressions are capable of bringing about stigmatization. This chapter will focus on the phenomenon of stigmatization itself. In doing so the author intends to demonstrate both why the creation of stigmatization merits consideration and why it is necessary to consider whether the law can or should be capable of playing any role in constraining stigmatising state expressions (SSEs). At its core stigmatization is a psychological phenomenon that relates to the potential induction of negative psychological states linked to an individual's perception of their place in society. The phenomenon is linked to a range of harmful physical and social effects both at the individual and societal level. Until now, legal scholars have given it limited attention. As the author will argue throughout this book however, this is unfortunate given that the concept of stigmatization can serve as a useful lens in determining the ability of various legal approaches to prevent various forms of harm occurring both to individuals and to society at large. An appreciation of such harm is needed to pave the way for a discussion (in Chapter 3) on when the creation of such harm through SSEs is permissible and when it is not.

In order to provide a broad overview of the concept of stigmatization, this chapter will describe several different approaches that are commonly used in understanding the phenomenon. Each of which is capable of describing important facets of the phenomenon. This begins with section 2 by introducing the work of Erving Goffman, largely considered to be the father of modern academic research on the phenomenon of stigmatization. Section 3 will provide an overview of how the understanding of the concept has greatly expanded since the works of Goffman. Section 4 follows with an overview of theories that focus on stigmatization as

1 E Goffman, *The Presentation of Self in Everyday Life* (Garden City, NY: Doubleday Anchor Books, 1959).

an intra and inter-personal experience (found mostly in psychology-based literature). In particular such approaches allow an appreciation of the manifestation of the phenomenon and its effects on an individual or micro-level. Section 5 will explore stigma from a sociological perspective, demonstrating the effects that the phenomenon can have on society and how society can in turn influence the phenomenon itself (and in particular how those in a position of power can influence it). Such perspectives are useful in highlighting the effects stigmatization can have at the macro or societal level. They are also important in illustrating the importance of beliefs (and those who are able to influence them) to processes of stigmatization. Section 6 will attempt to outline how stigmatization as a concept can be differentiated from other similar concepts that may be found in legal discourse. This includes concepts such as discrimination, stereotyping and marginalization. Such an exercise is important in discerning whether stigmatization as a concept requires a unique legal approach or can be subsumed within other closely related areas. Section 7 will summarize the main negative consequences that can be caused by stigmatization. Finally, section 8 describes a number of important harmful effects associated with stigmatization that (as subsequent chapters will argue) raise questions about the correctness of the use of stigmatizing expressions by the state.

2 Stigmatization – an age old concept that came of age in the twentieth century

Stigmatization is something that most people have an instinctual understanding of, even though they may have given little thought to it. Despite the fact that stigmatizing behaviour has perhaps existed for as long as humanity, academic study of the concept is a recent phenomenon.[2] The term 'stigma' or 'stigmatization' is a term that is heard frequently in everyday parlance. It has been used since ancient Greek times where one would speak of a person possessing a '*stigma*' if he or she possessed a mark or sign that indicated the individual was of inferior moral quality or a lesser being than the average person.[3] A stigma could indicate, for example, that someone was a slave or that they had committed crimes. 'Stigmas' might be applied by way of branding, so as to mark the individual so that others who might encounter him or her would know his or her true moral status and not mistake him or her for a 'normal' individual. Whilst Christianity imbued 'stigma' with another meaning for some time (related to the

2 S Neuberg, D Smith, and T Asher, "Why Do People Stigmatise: Toward a Biocultural Framework", in *The Social Psychology of Stigma*, ed. T Heatherton et al. (New York: Guilford Press, 2000). Behaviour that is analogous to stigmatization has even been observed in chimpanzees. See, for example, J Goodhall, "Social Rejection, Exclusion and Shunning among the Gombe Chimpanzees", *Ethology and Sociobiology* 7 (1986).

3 Jones, "Tattooing and Branding in Graeco-Roman Antiquity", *The Journal of Roman Studies* 77 (1987). Penal tattooing, whether applied to delinquent slaves, to criminals or to prisoners of war was borrowed by the Greeks from Persian culture. The Romans later adopted the practice and it was thus extended throughout the empire.

virtuous wounds of Christ),[4] the modern day use of the word seems to have returned to something similar to the original connotation. In 1895, for example, the French sociologist Émile Durkheim likened the social effects of stigmatization to that of being a convicted criminal.[5]

A Erving Goffman –the starting gun for serious academic study

In the academic world, the notion of 'stigmatization' began to attract significant attention in the 1960s. In his seminal work[6] *Stigma – Notes on a Spoiled Identity,* [7] Goffman attempted to outline exactly what stigmatization involved. To him it involved a process whereby 'normal' individuals discerned or might be able to discern that the stigmatized individual possessed traits that made them different than 'normal individuals'. Goffman's primary focus was therefore on the aspect that an individual might possess that would give rise to his or her stigmatization. The focus was thus, for the most part, on stigmatized individuals themselves and their own thoughts and behaviours. In focusing on the experiences of stigmatized individuals, Goffman proposed several important categories that proved to be very insightful generalizations as to what those who are stigmatized experience. Such ideas have been of use to psychologists in order to anchor their observations of patients in a firm theoretical background. In particular, Goffman gave rise to important concepts such as the 'discredited', the 'discreditable' and 'passing', concepts that would become common parlance when discussing the concept of stigmatization.

According to Goffman, those with stigma can form two groups that experience stigma in different ways, the 'discredited' and the 'discreditable'.[8] For the discredited, the external signs of his or her stigma are strong and unavoidable. Such individuals can be immediately identified as not belonging to the 'normal' class of individuals. Examples of such stigmas might be missing limbs or scarring. As Goffman states, the discredited have a trait that "can obtrude itself upon the attention and turn those of us whom he meets away from him, breaking the claim that his other attributes have upon him".[9] Thus, according to Goffman, others will regard an intelligent individual with a bodily disfigurement primarily as a disfigured individual, not as an intelligent individual.

4 R Ganzevoort, "Scars and Stigma: Trauma, Identity and Theology", *Practical Theology* 1, no. 1 (2008).

5 E Durkheim, *Rules of a Sociological Method*, ed. The Free Press (1895). For a description of Durkheim's ideas on stigmatization see F Mégret, "Law and Contemporary Problems", *Practices of Stigmatization* 76, nos 3 and 4 (2013).

6 Hsin et al., "Culture and Stigma; Adding Moral Experience to Stigma Theory", *Social Science & Medicine* 64 (2007).

7 I Goffman, *Stigma: Notes on a Spoilt Identity* Englewood Cliffs, NJ: Prentice Hall, 1963).

8 Ibid. p14

9 Ibid. p5

Other stigmas however are not so obvious to strangers. They may only reveal themselves after the stigmatized individual reveals certain information or after a 'normal' individual discovers something about the stigmatized individual. Goffman gave such individuals the term of 'discreditable'. Strangers meeting such an individual would not know of his or her difference immediately, rather it would only become apparent after the individual concerned did something to reveal their stigma or decided to release information regarding it in some other way. This could occur, for example, when an individual suffering from a condition decides to self-administer medication in public using a syringe. Once this occurs the individual concerned would move from being a *discreditable* individual to a *discredited* one.[10]

Discredited and discreditable individuals, according to Goffman, face different pressures in dealing with their stigma.[11] The discreditable live under the fear of having their stigma revealed to others. A discreditable individual will seek to avoid becoming a discredited individual. Their thoughts and actions can be preoccupied with hiding evidence of their stigma as much as possible. This can cause anxiety and stress to the individual who may not feel able to act as him or herself.[12] He or she may thus employ a number of coping strategies in order to deal with such stresses (discussed further in section 4).[13] If a discreditable person is in control of information pertaining to their disease he or she can choose between two options. The first, if he or she feels that such actions would be well received in the environment in question, would be to reveal details of his or her condition. The second, if he or she is not so confident of a good reception would be to do what Goffman termed 'passing'. Passing involves attempting to pass oneself off as a 'normal individual' because one fears the consequences of revealing one's true identity. Passing need not solely involve physical traits but can also include cultural and social traits or characteristics.[14] Whilst this might seem disingenuous to an individual who does not possess the stigma in question, the importance of being able to decide whether or not to 'pass' for a discreditable individual should not be underestimated.[15]

10 G Joachim, "Stigma of Visible and Invisible Chronic Conditions", *Journal of Advanced Nursing* 32, no. 1 (2000). p245 Individuals with diabetes will usually fall into such a category for it may not be immediately obvious that an individual is a diabetic to a stranger.

11 S Stefan, "'Discredited' and 'Discreditable:' The Search for Political Identity by People with Psychiatric Diagnoses", *William and Mary Law Review* 44, no. 9 (2003). The discreditable may, for example, have a wider range of interactions than the discredited as they may be able to maintain social contacts that they could not if they were discredited.

12 B Link and J Phelan, "Stigma and Its Public Health Implications", *The Lancet* 367 (2006).

13 Coping strategies are discussed at greater length in section 4.

14 K Leary, "Passing, Posing and 'Keeping It Real'", *Constellations* 6, nos 85–96 (1999).

15 Joachim, "Stigma of Visible and Invisible Chronic Conditions". p245 Passing as a coping mechanism is further discussed in section 4. The relevance of passing on a macro scale (including in reducing societal plurality) is discussed.

However, discredited individuals face a different array of negative emotions. These individuals face immediate recognition upon contact with normal individuals. Thus rejection or the differential treatment of these individuals can be immediate. Discredited individuals as a consequence often feel the need to avoid contact with normal individuals in order to avoid the negative aspects that such interaction can bring about.[16] Discredited individuals are likely to feel that their privacy is invaded by mere interaction with normal individuals, as their different status is apparent to other individuals immediately.[17] The discreditable individual, on the other hand, may feel more comfortable if they are able to carefully manage information pertaining to their status and maintain their ability to keep their status hidden if needs be.[18] For the discreditable individual the ability to carefully manage information regarding their status is important, it allows them to make an informed decision about when and where to disclose information relating to their stigma to other individuals based upon their perception of how such information would be received.

Goffman's work, whilst ground-breaking, has limitations. His approach to stigmatization focused heavily on the stigmatized 'trait' and the response it could evoke. Such an approach places the emphasis on the stigmatized individual (and not on those who stigmatize or society in general), something one could argue is incomplete and unfair.[19] Given that the actions (including as this book shows, SSEs) of society in general are instrumental to processes of stigmatization, the approach offered by Goffman, which focused on the reaction of individuals to stigmatized traits, is insufficient. In addition, whilst Goffman provided a general framework that was very instructive, it is not sufficient to understand the complexities of stigmatization in the many and varied contexts it is capable of manifesting itself within, contexts where a much more specific approach is often needed. Thus, whilst the work of Goffman was eye-opening, it marked the beginning of novel research paths and not the end.

3 The study of stigmatization post-Goffman

A Divergence and complexity

There has, in the decades following Goffman's work, been an enormous expansion in the research conducted on issues of stigmatization, both in terms of conceptual discussion and also empirical investigation.[20] This has led to elaborations,

16 Goffman, *Stigma: Notes on a Spoilt Identity.* p23

17 Ibid. p27

18 Ibid. p57

19 G Scambler, "Health-Related Stigma", *Sociology of Health & Illness* 31, no. 3 (2009). Scambler, for instance, states "what is missing from Goffman's account of the structure of interaction is the causal input of social structures like class, command, gender, ethnicity and so on, more often theorised from outside the symbolic interactionist/ dramaturgical fold".

20 B Link and J Phelan, "Conceptualizing Stigma", *Annual Review of Sociology* 27 (2001). p365

conceptual refinements and, importantly, also to repeated demonstrations of the possible negative effects stigmatization can have on individual lives. Whilst Goffman's work was insightful and provided a cornerstone for the study of stigmatization it represented a very general framework that required adaptation for the many and varying circumstances in which stigmatization has been observed.[21] Contextual adaptation of the concept of stigmatization has allowed it to be applied to numerous circumstances. In the decades that followed Goffman's work this was most notable in two areas. The first was in the domain of psychology. Researchers were able to build upon the framework of Goffman and use it to develop an understanding of numerous behavioural issues in various circumstances. This included much empirical research on the thoughts and behaviour of both those who were stigmatized and those who stigmatize. The second was in the area of psychiatric theory and practice, where the theories that were established by research building on the ideas of Goffman provided a useful way in which to conceive and treat the harmful consequences of the phenomenon.[22] Given the enormous variation in the number and types of contexts in which stigmatization can manifest itself this resulted in numerous different conceptions of stigma emerging, each designed to aid the understanding of the phenomenon in a particular circumstance.

A notable consequence of the multi-contextual approach that has been used to understand stigmatization is that social science provides no one overarching definition of what exactly stigmatization entails.[23] On the contrary, there are many different definitions of what exactly stigmatization is. Link and Phelan provide two explanations for this.[24] The first is due to the vastly different contexts the concept has been applied to. Given that they can vary greatly, differing contexts can often require a different reasoning process in order to allow stigmatization in that context to be conceptualized. Take, for example, the stigmatization of a diabetic that injects insulin in public and a woman who wished to obtain an abortion.[25] In each context stigmatization can manifest itself differently and bring about different effects. The second reason can be attributed to the 'multi-disciplinary' background of the various researchers that work on the concept in its various contexts. Whilst there is often common ground between these disciplines, their varying points of focus often mean that in each case the emphasis in terms of stigmatization is slightly different.

21 Scambler, "Health-Related Stigma". p452
22 P Byrne, "Stigma of Mental Illness and Ways of Diminishing It", *Advances in Psychiatric Treatment* 6 (2000).
23 Burris, "Disease Stigma in U.S. Public Law", *Journal of Law, Medicine and Ethics* 30 (2002).
24 Link and Phelan, "Conceptualizing Stigma". p365
25 See, for example, Joachim, "Stigma of Visible and Invisible Chronic Conditions." p246 The stigma of being diabetic is framed from the perspective of revealing a weakness in public whilst in Kumar, Hessini, Mitchell, 'Conceptualising Abortion Stigma', (2009), *Culture, Health & Sexuality*, 1–15, the stigma of abortion is described as varying in nature and intensity in different cultural settings.

The result of this diverse range of reasoning is that there is a vast body of research on stigmatization that is far from homogenous in terms of background, scope and potential application. This may explain why analysis of the phenomenon of stigmatization in legal literature has thus far been sparse. The lack of a general definition could be seen as something that is not attractive to legal scholars who usually prefer concise definitions.[26]

B Stigmatization – various concepts provided by eclectic approaches

In order to understand the vast body of theories that exist concerning stigmatization one can make conceptual divisions in terms of the aims and approaches of the researchers involved. These concepts will be introduced here but will be dealt with individually in more detail in the following section where there is a relevance for this book. No single one of these approaches is able to explain the complexity of stigmatization as a phenomenon by itself, but each is capable of contributing different insights towards its global understanding or its manifestation in a particular context. In general one can divide the study of stigmatization into three principle areas.[27]

(i) Studies based upon principles of evolutionary psychology

Approaches of this type are primarily concerned with the underlying evolutionary/ sociobiological explanations for the phenomenon. They explore areas such as evolutionary biology, evolutionary psychology and human ecology. Researchers involved in such an approach are often interested in finding explanations for human behaviour and thought processes in our biological nature.[28] Such approaches are often interested in possible influences of human evolution on instances of stigmatization, in particular in the context of a species that has evolved to live in a highly social environment with all the complexities that entails. The three most common proposed bases for a predisposition (on the part of humans in general) to stigmatization are: a) suspicion of outgroups, b) the maintenance of social control (within groups) and c) to avoid disease.[29] By studying the pressures that have shaped human evolution such an approach aims to be able to provide explanations

26 As Burris states "an accepted definition of 'stigma' in social science, and its relationship to law has been generally under-theorized and unsupported by data, reducing our ability to effectively deploy law and other tools in the anti-stigma cause". See Burris, "Disease Stigma in U.S. Public Law".

27 These three areas are well summarized by J Dovidio, B Major, and J Crocker, "Stigma: Introduction and Overview", in *The Social Psychology of Stigma*, ed. T Heatherton et al. (New York: Guilford Press, 2000).

28 See, for example, S Neuberg, D Smith, and T Asher, "Why Do People Stigmatise: Toward a Biocultural Framework"; R Kurzban and M Leary, "Evolutionary Origins of Stigmatization: The Functions of Social Exclusion", *Psychological Bulletin* 127, no. 2 (2001).

29 Neuberg, Smith, and Asher, "Why Do People Stigmatise: Toward a Biocultural Framework", for a general overview of these areas. pp32–48

for the thoughts, motivations and actions of individuals under certain circumstances. In addition a further aim can be to provide potential models based on evolutionary psychology to predict when stigmatization might occur and possible measures that can be taken in order to prevent it or reduce the harm that it can cause.[30] It has been argued that such approaches are useful in explaining why stigmatization is likely to arise in particular contexts.

Whilst such approaches are interesting from an academic perspective and fuel debate they bring with them a number of caveats. First, they offer relatively little in terms of practical value. In particular, their ability to articulate how individuals experience stigmatization and how they may be affected by it is limited. Second, such approaches are too simplistic to fully take into account the impact of culture, ideas and beliefs, all aspects that play a part in stigmatization (see section 3). Third, such theories are often the subject of controversy, being able to incite fierce and impassioned debate (a debate that would likely be distracting in terms of the core message of this book).[31] Fourth, whilst such theories are often plausible, they are difficult if not impossible to prove on a definitive basis.[32] They will not, as a consequence, be dealt with in depth in this chapter. More often than not they represent exercises analogous to theoretical thought experiments that are an attempt to explain empirically observed patterns of behaviour.

Whilst the author certainly does not want to dismiss such theories (and even believes they may have some explanatory merit), they will not (for the reasons given) form a main source of inspiration for this chapter. Thus, whilst it is important to acknowledge that such factors represent an important and valid strand within the literature on stigmatization, they serve little purpose within the context of this book which is more concerned with the practical manifestation of the phenomenon in state expressions and a normative approach towards such issues.

(ii) Attempts to understand the psychological and behavioural manifestations of stigma

Research in this category is usually focused upon the thought processes and behaviour of individuals during instances of stigmatization. Research of this type is motivated by a desire to understand the process of stigmatization from the perspective of the individuals involved. Such an understanding is important in

30 See, for example, D Reidpath et al., "'He Hath the French Pox': Stigma, Social Value and Social Exclusion", *Sociology of Health & Illness* 27, no. 4 (2005); Kurzban and Leary, "Evolutionary Origins of Stigmatization: The Functions of Social Exclusion".

31 For a 'relatively' recent and well informed and impartial discussion of this controversy see U Segerstrale, *Defenders of the Truth: The Battle for Science in the Sociology Debate and Beyond* (Oxford: Oxford University Press, 2001).

32 J Phelan, B Link, and J Dovidio, "Stigma and Prejudice: One Animal or Two?", *Social Science & Medicine* 67 (2008). p363 Link and Phelan in conducting a literature review on various models of stigmatization reflect on this subject. They state that whilst an evolutionary origin may underline stigmatization based on characteristics related to disease, such an origin may or may not be related to other forms of stigmatization, i.e. based on stigmatization of out-groups or stigmatization to achieve social control.

explaining the behaviour of individuals and why, on the individual level, they respond as they do to potentially stigmatizing situations.[33] By understanding how the individual experiences stigmatization one can propose methods that can limit its negative psychological effects. The nature of such an understanding will vary enormously from context to context. Whilst one can easily find studies that may be concerned with the same concept, e.g. 'coping mechanisms', the different contexts they are set in will mean that their approach and findings will differ significantly. Such research makes up the largest part of the body of research available on stigmatization. In each instance, the aim is usually to understand the experience of a particular group of stigmatized individuals in their particular circumstances. Large bodies of literature on issues as diverse as the stigmatization experience of individuals with diabetes,[34] disabled individuals,[35] sufferers of disease[36] and drug addiction[37] exist, all differing in their approach and focus.

(iii) Studies aimed at determining the sociological causes and effects of stigmatization

Another distinct approach to the study of stigmatization focuses on the sociological dimension of the phenomenon. Its aims are usually to study the effects stigmatization can have on society and *vice versa.* [38] Often such research will be focused on efforts to discern how stigmatization, together with other phenomena such as discrimination and stereotyping are connected with problematic issues in society such as inequality and marginalization. Some approaches may, for example, view stigmatization as a by-product of discrimination whilst others may see the former as a driving force behind the latter.[39] Some approaches that could be categorized within this approach will be concerned with the rights of individuals affected by stigmatization and their position in society whilst others will view stigmatization as an phenomenon that exists between powerful and franchised

33 Individuals might, for example, respond with awkwardness or anxiety to those with potentially stigmatizing views or possibly internalize such views and feel negatively about themselves as persons. See, for example, C Miller and B Major, "Coping with Stigma and Prejudice", in *The Social Psychology of Stigmatisation*, ed. T Heatherton et al. (New York: Guilford Press, 2000). and J Crocker, B Major, and C Steel, "Social Stigma", in *Handbook of Social Psychology*, ed. D Gilbert, S Fiske, and G Lindzey (Boston: McGraw-Hill, 1998).

34 See, for example, D Broom and A Whittaker, "Controlling Diabetes, Controlling Diabetics: Moral Language in the Management of Diabetes Type 2", *Social Science & Medicine* 58, nos 2371–2382 (2004).

35 E Cahill and R Eggleston, "Reconsidering the Stigma of Physical Disability: Wheelchair Use and Public Kindness", *The Sociological Quarterly* 36, no. 4 (1995).

36 H Deacon and I Stephney, *HIV/Aids, Stigma and Children. A Literature Review* (Cape Town: HSRC Press, 2007).

37 See, for example, J Dean and F Rud, "The Drug Addict and the Stigma of Addiction", *Substance Use & Misuse* 19, no. 8 (1984).

38 See, for example, Link and Phelan, "Conceptualizing Stigma".

39 . See, for example, L Sayce, "Stigma, Discrimination and Social Exclusion: What's in a Word?", *Journal of Mental Health* 7, no. 4 (1998).

groups in society on the one hand and those who are weak and disenfranchised on the other.[40] Such views tend to regard stigmatization as being closely connected to issues of power and hierarchy within groups and society.[41]

In order to fully understand the stigmatization process in any particular context it may be necessary to combine elements of each approach. This can be briefly illustrated with the case of the stigmatization that individuals who are HIV positive may face. Proponents of 'biosocial' models of stigmatization might, for example, attribute explanatory power to such ideas in explaining why such individuals may be vulnerable to stigmatization.[42] However such an approach may not offer the insight that studies of the cognitive experiences of individuals involved with HIV positive persons do on the potential of educational initiatives to moderate the potentially stigmatizing activities of non-HIV positive individuals.[43] Research into the inter and intra-personal aspects of stigma are most likely to be instructive in such an area. In addition neither of these approaches will be able to describe what stigmatization means for HIV infected persons in terms of their access to jobs and other civil benefits in society, for this the input of sociologists may be required.[44]

The following sections will give a brief overview of the second and third areas described above (i.e. from a psychological and sociological perspective respectively) in an attempt to give the reader a rounded (albeit concise) understanding of the phenomenon. Unfortunately, given the large amount of material available in each of these categories such a description will not be exhaustive but merely indicative. The purpose of the broad description in this chapter is to provide the reader with a firm understanding of the complexities of stigmatization. This understanding will be needed in order to understand that the harm that can be brought about by SSEs is not always desirable in a just and democratic society (discussed further in Chapter 3) and in assessing whether various legal approaches are capable of recognizing and protecting against stigmatization and its harmful effects in its numerous and varied contexts (discussed in Chapters 4–7).

40 The first type of approach can, for example, be seen in: "Social Inclusion and Mental Health", *Psychiatric Bulletin* 2001, no. 25 (2001). The second in Link and Phelan, "Conceptualizing Stigma".

41 See, for example, "Conceptualizing Stigma" or Reidpath et al., "'He Hath the French Pox': Stigma, Social Value and Social Exclusion".

42 Riedpath, for example, posits that stigmatizations of such conditions might serve to prevent the spread of illnesses from high risk populations at the margins of society to low risk, non-marginalized populations. See D Reidpath and K Chan, "HIV, Stigma, and Rates of Infection: A Rumour without Evidence", *PLOS Medicine* 3, no. 10 (2006).

43 See, for example, J Bertand et al., "Systematic Review of the Effectiveness of Mass Communication Programs to Change HIV/Aids Related Behaviors in Developing Countries", *Health Education Research Theory & Practice* 21, no. 4 (2006).

44 R Parker and P Aggleton, "HIV and Aids-Related Stigma and Discrimination: A Conceptual Framework and Implications for Action", *Social Science & Medicine* 57, no. 1 (2003).

4 Stigma as an intra and inter-personal experience

A large and primarily empirical body of research related to stigmatization concerns how it manifests itself on an intra and inter-personal level. Such approaches are usually concerned with the thought process and behavioural aspects of individuals who find themselves in a context where stigmatization takes place.[45] Approaches of this type have allowed a varied and context specific picture of stigma to be generated. It has brought with it an enormous increase in the complexity of the understanding of stigmatization. It describes how the situational or environmental factors at play (e.g. social, cultural, knowledge beliefs etc.), through forming cognitive thought processes, are able to influence affective impulses in order to produce the complex and varied individual experience as it is perceived by individuals involved in varying stigmatizing contexts.[46] Affective processes represent subconscious impulses responsible *inter alia* for the existence of 'basic emotions'. They are largely reflexive in nature. Cognitive thought process however represents the more conscious and reasoned thought processes that are thus capable of being informed by an individual's knowledge and experience whilst affective processes are more impulsive and less 'considered'. Human behaviour can be thought of as a course of action that is influenced by both elements.[47] This second process can make use of elements such as knowledge, beliefs and context. It represents the route by which personal experience and cultural context can impact upon stigmatization in general. This interaction of higher level 'cognitive' thought processes with deeper and more impulsive processes is extremely complex and the result can vary according to the particular circumstances of the case in question. It is here, where individual experience, cultural and social factors are added to the impulsive aspects of stigmatization.[48] The interaction of both cognitive and affective thought processes in processes of stigmatization explain why its manifestation can vary so much from one context to another.[49]

45 Dovidio, Major, and Crocker, "Stigma: Introduction and Overview". p10

46 Ibid. Pages 12–15 provide a concise overview of the cognitive-affective dimension of stigmatization.

47 For a perspective from neurobiology that discusses such aspects in terms of innate and learned elements see A Tierney, "The Evolution of Learned and Innate Behavior: Contributions from Genetics and Neurobiology to a Theory of Behavioural Evolution", *Animal Learning and Behaviour* 14, no. 4 (1986). p340 Tierney states: "I assume that no actual dichotomy exists between innate, or 'instinctive', behavior and learning, but that they operate together to produce many behaviors. The concept of instinct and the classification of behavior into two distinct categories 'instincts' and 'learning' have been repeatedly and justly criticized."

48 A biological explanation for such affective impulses is often put forward. Such explanations see such impulses as having conferred a selection advantage in the context in which humans evolved (i.e. groups with complex social relationships). See, for example, Neuberg, Smith, and Asher, "Why Do People Stigmatise: Toward a Biocultural Framework". Such explanations are, however, difficult to prove definitively and are not universality accepted. Phelan, Link, and Dovidio, "Stigma and Prejudice: One Animal or Two?" p363.

49 Even within Europe, for example, there is a large degree of cultural variation in how stigmas such as being an epileptic manifest themselves. See G Baker et al., "The Stigma of Epilepsy: A European Perspective", *Epilepsia* 41, no. 1 (1999).

Cognitive functions involved in stigma allow input from the social environment in which the individual finds him or herself and also from personal experience. Such input is central to the thought process which lies at the heart of stigmatization and allows it to be linked to the social conditions present in each particular case.[50] The importance of cognitive thought processes provides an input for both group and individual behaviours and beliefs into the stigmatization process. Thus, the situational experience of the individual, in terms of the groups in which he or she exists and the personal beliefs that he or she may hold are able, through the cognitive thought process, to shape the likelihood of inducing stigmatization or being stigmatized by others. Given the ability of the state to communicate and to alter the beliefs and opinions of individuals (including through SSEs) it can be considered as having an important role in affecting these processes (discussed further in section 6).

Research into the individual experience of stigma represents perhaps the largest body of work adding to the understanding of the phenomenon, thanks largely to its application in areas such as psychology and psychotherapy. The following pages represent an illustration of the key areas of study that are important to the ideas in this book. The aim is to produce an appreciation in the reader of the problems stigmatization can produce both on the individual and societal level. In order to facilitate easy understanding it has been divided into different conceptual subcategories which have been chosen so as to provide insight into the various approaches that are available.

A The perceiver and the target

In most instances of stigmatization it is possible to divide individuals into two categories, which can be thought of as the 'perceiver' and the 'target' or sometimes the 'non-stigmatized' and the 'stigmatized.[51] It is the relationship between the two (or more accurately, the perception of that relationship) that is responsible for bringing about stigmatization in any given situation. Both parties undergo different thought processes that are able to bring about stigmatizing behaviour, or the stigmatization of certain individuals. As the following pages in this chapter will show, for stigmatization to exist both categories are required. Individuals cannot become stigmatized unless there are other individuals who are perceived to have stigmatizing views about them. It is this aspect of stigma (i.e. the subjective perception of being stigmatized) that can be used to separate it from other closely related phenomena some of which are prominent in legal thinking, e.g. discrimination and stereotyping (discussed further in section 7).

50 It is this ability to influence the stigmatization through the cognitive thought process that allows initiatives aimed at reducing its manifestation. See, for example, M Heijnders and S Van Der Meij, "The Fight against Stigma: An Overview of Stigma-Reduction Strategies and Interventions", *Psychology, Health & Medicine* 11, no. 3 (2006).

51 Dovidio, Major, and Crocker, "Stigma: Introduction and Overview." Dovidio and colleagues use the terms 'perceiver' and 'target'. See page 10.

(i) The perceiver

The perceiver represents the individuals in any group or society whose actions or opinions (or even perceived opinions) induce a state of stigmatization in others.[52] Perceivers have different 'needs, goals and motivations' than target individuals. It is this difference in roles that brings about different thought processes in individuals and a situation of stigmatization. Such actions or opinions may or may not have the intention causing others to be stigmatized.[53] Indeed, perceivers can intentionally stigmatize individuals by behaving or communicating in a certain way or may do so in a more unconscious manner, behaving in ways that, unbeknown to them, can cause individuals to feel stigmatized.[54] Imagine, for instance, non-disabled individuals who avoid eye contact with disabled individuals who are sitting next to them on the train. The non-disabled individual may or may not be doing this intentionally. He or she may, for instance, reason that avoiding staring is the most considerate thing to do in the circumstances, or may indeed have negative feelings and so choose to avert his or her gaze. Alternatively, the individual concerned may simply have not seen the disabled individual, but because the disabled individual has encountered ambivalent responses in the past, it is assumed to be a negative response. In all these instances the actions of the perceiver may have been able to induce a feeling of self-questioning in the 'targeted' individual whereby he or she may feel that the perceiver is acting in a certain way because of his or her disability. As later chapters of this book will discuss the factors that are demonstrated in this example present difficulties for legal approaches that one might want to use in tackling unwanted instances of stigmatization. The lack of a requirement of intent, for example, creates problems for some legal approaches (e.g. based in criminal law) that depend on the presence of finding a subjective intent, or *mens rea* (discussed in Chapter 4). In addition, the fact that an individual can stigmatize another without actually doing anything to him or her presents problems for several legal approaches that focus on the idea of 'treatment', i.e. where an individual does something that affects the legal rights of another individual (this is discussed further in Chapter 7). In addition the subtlety of stigmatizing actions (including expressions) is likely to be problematic for the laws that often seek to operate over a certain threshold of severity (e.g. hate speech). As the reader will become aware, these problems (which will be discussed in greater depth in subsequent chapters) resurface frequently to bring the application of many legal approaches to stigmatizing activities into doubt.

From the perspective of the stigmatized individual, stigmatization represents a process by which they are judged primarily on the basis of their belonging to some category or group and not on the basis of their personality or individual traits.[55] As

52 Ibid.

53 E Brohan et al., "Experiences of Mental Illness Stigma, Prejudice and Discrimination: A Review of Measures", *BMC Health Services Research* 10 (2010).

54 Neuberg, Smith, and Asher, "Why Do People Stigmatise: Toward a Biocultural Framework". p10. Perceivers may also be known as 'normals' or 'non-stigmatized' depending on the research in question.

55 Ibid.

Goffman stated, stigmatization represents a process whereby a trait of an individual captures the attention of those who interact with him, removing the importance of all other individual qualities.[56] Those who stigmatize, in making such judgements are motivated by notions of group welfare to perceived threats from individuals. Perceptions of individual threats can be based upon affective impulses of revulsion or fear, or they may involve more reasoned thoughts based upon acquired knowledge. They can thus be influenced by experiences, knowledge and beliefs about certain categories of individuals or various groups in society. Such acquired information can act upon affective impulses of disgust or fear in both positive and negative ways. Individuals may, for example, have learned that the conditions that many disabled people possess pose no personal threat in terms of contagion, that the condition is not the fault of the individual or that such individuals are, cognitively speaking, 'normal'.[57] In such instances knowledge and beliefs may allow individuals to temper any response that would otherwise have been more negative.[58] Such beliefs may, for example, in place of hatred, fear or disgust, invoke feelings of ambivalence, pity or empathy.[59] The opposite can also be the case however. Certain individuals may have come across information that they believe renders the individual in question a greater threat to themselves or society at large. Imagine, for example, the classic case of the healthy individual in the 1980s who learns that lesions on an individual's skin are evidence of the onset of AIDS, that AIDS is caused by infection with the HIV virus and that most infections in the Western world are through sexual contact (often homosexual) or intravenous drug use. In such instances a negative affective reaction may be amplified or even provoked by cognitive processes and the beliefs of the individual concerning the situation at hand.[60] In situations such as this reactions of anger, revulsion and blame may be evoked. The difference between reactions of the first kind and the second can be attributed to the beliefs the individual perceiver holds about the stigma in question. Such beliefs can be shaped in many different ways. They can be shaped through cultural ideas handed down from generation to generation, through education or through personal experience with individuals possessing the type of stigma in question.[61] They also provide an important mechanism for the state to influence the manifestation of stigmatization, *inter alia* through the use of SSEs.

56 Goffman, *Stigma: Notes on a Spoilt Identity.*

57 M Deal, "Aversive Disablism: Subtle Prejudice toward Disabled People", *Disability & Society* 22 (2007). Outright negative attitudes to the disabled in the UK are gradually disappearing, but have often been replaced by more ambivalent attitudes. This occurs where individuals learn that 'disablism' is wrong and so supress it but still show ambivalent behaviour subconsciously towards disabled persons.

58 C Crandall and D Moriarty, "Physical Illness Stigma and Social Rejection", *British Journal of Social Psychology* 34 (1995).

59 M Hebl, M Tickle, and T Heatherton, "Awkward Moments in Interactions between Nonstigmatized and Stigmatized Individuals", in *The Social Psychology of Stigma*, ed. T Heatherton et al. (New York: Guilford Press, 2000).

60 B Weiner, R Perry, and J Magnuson, "An Attributional Analysis of Reactions to Stigmas", *Journal of Personality and Social Psychology* 55 (1988). p738

61 E Jones et al., *Social Stigma. The Psychology of Marked Relationships* (New York: W.H. Freeman and Company, 1984). p231 This is in contrast to affective impulses which

(ii) The stigmatized/target group

The 'stigmatized' or the 'target group' is the group of individuals that through their perceptions of the non-stigmatized group's behaviour or opinions feel themselves to be stigmatized. This may, for example, be because stigmatized individuals believe they sense hostility, disgust or ambivalence from non-stigmatized individuals. Even where no particular individual is acting in any way to stigmatize the target group, past experience (real or perceived) may cause the stigmatized individual to feel that he or she is looked down on, disrespected, feared, the subject of disgust or even hatred by others in society.[62] Whether or not individuals are made to feel such a way because of the real or imagined behaviour of others, such feelings are capable of inducing a number of different thought processes, feelings and behaviours. It is these thoughts, feelings and behaviours that most studies on stigmatization focus on. The vast body of literature shows that what each individual thinks, feels and does in an instance of stigmatization can vary enormously. Such variation can occur between individuals in different cultural settings, between individuals that have had different experiences in the past and even between individuals in the same setting on the basis of differing personality. This high level of variation and subjectivity in how individuals in a similar context can respond to stigmatizing forces also presents, as this book will discuss, potential obstacles for the application of certain legal approaches that depend on identifying the negative effects that individuals suffer on an objective basis. In particular, this variability may make it difficult for legal approaches to recognize harm that has been done to an entire group that has been stigmatized as opposed to particular individuals (given that a certain proportion of the group in question may not feel stigmatized at all). This is illustrated in Chapter 6 with the example of privacy approaches that are often likely to have difficulty engaging expressive activity that does not refer to specific persons.

Potential negative responses to stigmatization include anxiety, reduced self-esteem, depression, and social awkwardness. Furthermore these can bring about a number of coping responses that are also associated with negative effects. Some of these issues are described below.

Anxiety – Fear of rejection is often a primary driving force for stigmatized individuals.[63] This explains for instances why many stigmatized individuals choose to 'pass' i.e. to hide the factor that causes their stigmatization.[64] Stigmatized individuals usually aim to be accepted by non-stigmatized individuals and often measure the success of their actions in terms of achieving this goal.[65] As a consequence of this, individuals can become anxious in their contacts with non-stigmatized individuals. This often involves becoming overtly conscious of themselves, their thoughts

represent universal and more 'primitive' and unlearned responses to stigma that can be perceived across all cultures.

62 Crocker, Major, and Steel, "Social Stigma". p516

63 Hebl, Tickle, and Heatherton, "Awkward Moments in Interactions between Non-stigmatized and Stigmatized Individuals".

64 Goffman, *Stigma: Notes on a Spoilt Identity.* (See section 1 of this chapter.)

65 B Wright, *Physical Disability: A Psychological Approach* (New York: Harper, 1983).

and their actions. Given the resultant increased introspection and the possible efforts to hide whatever is causing their stigmatization, such individuals often have the unfortunate experience of feeling that they are the centre of attention in a group environment.[66] When attempting to hide whatever stigmatizes them, individuals can become obsessed with monitoring their conversations and even thoughts for items that may be risky in terms of giving their secret away.[67] This increased anxiety can mean that individuals find that their performance (socially or otherwise) becomes hampered by such preoccupations.

Self-loathing/reduction in self-esteem – In some individuals stigmatization can induce a sense of 'self-loathing'.[68] This process is often termed 'internationalization'.[69] Stigmatization represents not only a process whereby it is communicated to an individual that a trait that he or she possesses is negative, but also by which the individual is made to feel that the trait is undesirable to others. This can lead to a reduction in self-esteem and even the internationalization of negative feelings towards the trait in question and helps to explain why stigmatization can have such corrosive effects.[70] This aspect of stigmatization is interesting from the perspective of this book as it allows the phenomenon to be discussed in the light of a number of ethical and philosophical theories that focus on the need for self-respect (this will be discussed in more depth in Chapter 3 and will be central to the normative argument that the author will attempt to formulate).

The development of a sense of self-loathing is usually associated with a severe reduction in individual self-esteem as a result of the reactions he or she has experienced. A reduction in self-esteem and the onset of a feeling of self-loathing can lead to a feeling of negativity towards oneself, and in particular to those aspects that are connected to the stigma in question. The presence of self-loathing has been accorded an important place in explaining many of the negative outcomes that are associated with stigmatization. The concept of self-loathing/internalization represents the deepest and gravest level of psychological impact from stigmatization.[71] Such a process represents an acceptance of negative evaluations made by other individuals, i.e. the non-stigmatized.[72] This results in a reduced

66 Ibid.

67 J Crocker, "Social Stigma and Self-Esteem: Situational Construction of Self Worth". *Journal of Experimental Social Psychology* 35 (1999). This concept has been described as 'stereotype threat', whereby individuals fear confirming negative stereotypes about themselves to others. A common example is where a black individual fears confirming negative stereotypes of black people to non-black people that he or she may encounter.

68 A Courtwright, "Justice, Stigma, and the New Epidemiology of Health Disparities", *Bioethics* 23, no. 2 (2009).

69 See, for example, M Biernat and J Dovidio, "Stigma and Stereotypes", in *The Social Psychology of Stigma*, ed. T Heatherton et al. (New York: Guilford Press, 2000). p89

70 D Camp, W Finlay, and E Lyons, "Is Low Self-Esteem an Inevitable Consequence of Stigma? An Example from Women with Chronic Mental Health Problems", *Social Science & Medicine* 55 (2002).

71 Crocker, "Social Stigma and Self-Esteem: Situational Construction of Self Worth".

72 Jones et al., *Social Stigma. The Psychology of Marked Relationships*. p131

measure of one's own abilities. An individual who is high in self-esteem feels positively about him or herself, whereas an individual who is low in self-esteem may harbour negative thoughts towards him or herself.

Not all stigmatized individuals will suffer damage to self-esteem however. Because of their personality or personal beliefs some individuals will be better able to resist stigmatizing forces than others.[73] This potential variability adds to the subjective nature of the experience of stigma.[74] Whether or not an individual 'internalizes' the stigma he or she is exposed to can often depend on the personal beliefs they hold. Crocker, for example, showed that black university students who felt they had been treated differently on the basis of their ethnicity may or may not have lowered self-esteem as a result. What seemed important in determining if self-esteem was effected or not was the individual beliefs those affected had.[75] Such beliefs were termed 'collective representations' by Crocker and represent the ideology the individual uses to explain 'how things are as they are'.[76] Thus a black student who is aware of the various socioeconomic and historical reasons for the lower position of black people in society may well (correctly) believe that potential stigmatization or mistreatment is unjustified, as are assumptions that black individuals are less intelligent. This belief can prevent the internalization of negative evaluations that often go with the stigma of being black. By contrast, an individual who is overweight and obese and subscribes to the so-called 'protestant work ethic' is likely to view his or her obesity as his or her fault. This may lead to an internalization of negative perceptions of irresponsibility, greed and laziness.[77] Internalization of a stigma can lead to negative psychological, physical, health and social consequences. With regard to psychological effects, such a situation can result in an increased incidence of anxiety and depression. In physical terms poor mental health has been shown to have a number of direct and indirect effects on physical health. Additionally low self-esteem can lead to social withdrawal. This occurs because social contact for individuals with low self-esteem can be a painful process, especially when such contact is with non-stigmatized individuals. Recognizing the importance of 'beliefs'

73 Ibid.; Crocker, "Social Stigma and Self-Esteem: Situational Construction of Self Worth".

74 "Social Stigma and Self-Esteem: Situational Construction of Self Worth." Historically a reduction in self-esteem as a response to stigmatization has been seen as a central aspect of the response individuals have to being stigmatized. More recent research has shown, however, that not all individuals develop self-loathing. Rather the effect on individual self-esteem is dependent on an individual's personality and the beliefs that he or she possesses regarding the trait that led to his or her stigmatization

75 Ibid. If, for example, individuals had beliefs that a counter party was likely to hold racist views through being ill informed and that such views were false, they usually showed no reduction in their self-esteem. In addition to beliefs about the perceptions of others, individuals may also hold beliefs or ideologies concerning individual responsibility and individual 'blameworthiness' for their situation.

76 Ibid. p102 Crocker discusses the 'protestant work ethic' which is prevalent in many Western democracies and particularly the US. Obese individuals, for example, are more likely to have lower self esteem if they subscribe to the protestant work ethic principle as they are more likely to blame themselves for their predicament.

77 This has been found to occur in relation to stigma. See S Lewis et al., "'I Don't Eat a Hamburger and Large Chips Every Day!' A Qualitative Study of the Impact of Public Health Messages About Obesity in Obese Adults", *BMC Public Health* 10 (2010).

provides another important role for individuals that have informational power in society, including those in the state who are have responsibility for the use of SSEs.

Coping strategies – The notion of feeling devalued in the eyes of others acts as a stressor to stigmatized individuals.[78] Individuals can attempt to cope with such stresses in a number of ways. Strategies may be related to controlling one's own thoughts (i.e. internal coping strategies), or towards one's actions (i.e. external coping strategies). The purpose of the latter type of coping mechanism is to alter the way in which non-stigmatized individuals view the individual. The term 'coping strategies' is very broad and covers a wide range of responses to stigmatization which, depending on the specific strategy, can be positive or negative. The type of coping response that is manifested will depend on the individual, their beliefs and goals and the particular circumstance.[79] Common examples are discussed below.

Internal coping strategies – These are aimed at dealing with stressful thoughts that are provoked by a stigmatizing situation. Such stressful thoughts can bring about a range of negative thoughts and emotions. A primary aim of such strategies is to restrict negative emotions and to protect self-esteem from the damaging effects of stigmatization. One common method of coping of those who are stigmatized is the attribution of the negative outcomes to the unjustified stigmatization of others that the person experiences, and not to the individual him or herself or his or her actions.[80] This may occur, for example, when a person wrongly attributes his or her place of origin as the reason for negative treatment in place of the actual reason that may, for example, be inappropriate behaviour. Whilst such behaviours may act to protect individual self-esteem in stigmatizing situations, it can result in negative social outcomes for individuals. This can occur due to inaccurate attribution of events to 'unfounded stigmatization' rather than their real causes in the social setting and can harm social relationships with other individuals.[81] An example of this might be where individuals project the image of a stigmatizing individual onto individuals who are not actually stigmatizing. Individuals can do this both where stigmatization was in reality to blame for negative outcomes and where it was not.[82] Another coping strategy used by stigmatized individuals to cope is known as 'downward comparison'. This occurs when stigmatized individuals 'look down' on other individuals who possess the stigma in question to a greater extent than they do. This is in order to boost their own perception of their image. Such 'ingroup' comparisons allow stigmatized individuals to boost their self-esteem by feeling comparatively less stigmatized than other individuals in their category.[83]

78 Miller and Major, "Coping with Stigma and Prejudice".
79 Ibid. p251
80 Crocker, Major, and Steel, "Social Stigma".
81 Ibid. p522
82 R Kleck and A Stretna, "Perceptions of the Impact of Negatively Valued Physical Characteristics on Social Interactions", *Journal of Personality and Social Psychology* 39 (1980). Individuals with a physical disfigurement may, for example, falsely attribute negative social outcomes to that disfigurement, even when that is patently not the case.
83 J Crocker and B Major, "Social Stigma and Self-Esteem: The Self-Protective Properties of Stigma", *Psychological Review* 96, no. 4 (1989). p614 This may in part explain the benefits stigmatized individuals can find in socializing with groups of other stigmatized individuals. See Miller and Major, "Coping with Stigma and Prejudice". p258

'Denial' represents another method that stigmatized individuals use to repress negative thoughts and emotions associated with stigmatization. This can involve denial of mistreatment even where it demonstrably existed. This allows individuals to protect self-esteem and continue to function in situations where they need to interact with non-stigmatized individuals. Whilst such responses may be adaptive on an individual scale, on a larger scale they mean that stigmatization may often go unchallenged.[84]

Where the individual is unable to engage in denial the result may be a form of 'psychological disengagement'.[85] Under such a strategy, the stigmatized aspect of the individual in question is removed as something they see as valuable in their personal make-up. Students often disengage, for example, from subjects after doing poorly and adopt an 'it's not my thing' attitude. Such an effect has been used to describe the disengagement of ethnic minority pupils from mainstream education.[86] Doing so allows them to maintain a positive self-image by dis-associating themselves from their negative treatment and achievement in school.[87] Stigmatization in such instances is thus capable of providing serious personal and societal effects through individual efforts designed to cope with it.

External coping strategies – These are aimed at changing the very circumstances surrounding an individual's stigmatization. In instances where the associated stigma is, to a certain extent, 'controllable', the individual involved may attempt to reduce or eradicate whatever property gives rise to the stigma in question.[88] One such example is that of obese or overweight individuals, who on receiving adverse reactions as a consequence of their weight, attempt to reduce their weight through increased exercise or dietary control. Individuals with weight issues (often) fall into a category of individuals where it is possible to do something (though it may be difficult) in order to reduce the factor that gives rise to stigma. Other such categories include individuals who are perceived as being poor. Such individuals will often spend disproportionate amounts on their personal image in terms of clothing or personal transport, etc. This is often an attempt to remove the impression that other people may hold that they are poor.[89]

84 C Miller and C Kaiser, "A Theoretical Perspective on Coping with Stigma", *Journal of Social Issues* 57, no. 1 (2001). pp79–80
85 Crocker, Major, and Steel, "Social Stigma". p528
86 B Major et al., "Coping with Negative Stereotypes About Intellectual Performance: The Role of Psychological Disengagement", *Personality and Social Psychology Bulletin* 24, no. 1 (1998).
87 B Major and T Schmader, "Coping with Stigma through Psychological Disengagement," in *Prejudice: The Target's Perspective*, ed. J Swim, L Chohen, and L Hyers (San Diego: Academic Press, 1998).
88 Miller and Kaiser, "A Theoretical Perspective on Coping with Stigma". Such efforts are known as primary control coping, whereby an individual attempts to exert control over the aspect that gives rise to the stigma in question.
89 G Orwell, *The Road to Wigan Pier* (London: Houghton Mifflin Harcourt, 1972). Orwell provided lengthy examples of the efforts poor people would go to in demonstrating that they were not poor. Often this would involve spending essential resources in order to create a façade of wealth. This could have negative consequences in terms of reducing the money that such individuals had to spend on food and heating.

Where the aspect that gives rise to the stigma in question cannot be removed or reduced individuals may opt to conceal it, or 'to pass' as Goffman described it. Individuals are able to pass with a wide range of potential 'stigmatizable' aspects including various diseases or illnesses, sexual orientation, religion, criminal history, etc. The classic example is the gay man who hides his sexuality from others and lives outwardly as a heterosexual. By taking such action the individual may increase his chances of successful participation in the group or the society in which he lives and access to the benefits that brings.[90] Such behaviour provides avenues for group pressure to change the behaviour of individuals. Essentially the wider group, using stigmatization, threatens individuals perceived as having 'deviant' aspects with a reduced social interaction. As a result, individuals, if they are able to, may be persuaded to reduce the existence or visibility of whatever characteristic is at issue. It is this mechanism that various forms of propaganda and information campaign try to use. One can, for example, envisage a governmental campaign against drink driving or an anti-smoking campaign (examples of which were discussed in Chapter 1).[91] In the first instance the aim of the propaganda may be to shame individuals in to stopping drink driving. The second may intend to shame smokers into not smoking in public places in order to reduce harm to other individuals caused by passive smoking. In both these cases, the aim is to induce a certain amount of 'shame' into individuals in order to encourage them to desist from their actions and to make it socially unacceptable to continue with such actions.

Passing, however, is not something that is cost free for individuals. Those who conceal their stigmas and so are capable of passing are, according to Goffman's framework, categorized as the 'discreditable'.[92] The discreditable live under the fear of having their stigma revealed to others. A discreditable individual will seek to avoid becoming a 'discredited' individual. His or her thoughts and actions can be preoccupied with hiding evidence of his or her stigma as much as possible. This can cause anxiety and stress to the individual who may not feel able to act as him or herself.[93] It can also result in healthcare avoidance strategies whereby a sufferer of a condition does not seek medical treatment in order to keep his or her condition hidden (discussed further in section 6).[94]

In other instances, however, individuals may find it difficult or impossible to conceal the characteristic that gives rise to their stigmatization (discredited individuals in the language of Goffman). One can imagine a range of stigmatizing characteristics that would be impossible to avoid. These include gross disfigurations, not being able

90 See section 6 on the importance of seeming able to act reciprocally in terms of being accepted by one's group.

91 R Bayer, "Stigma and the Ethics of Public Health: Not Can We but Should We", *Social Science & Medicine* 67 (2008).

92 Goffman, *Stigma: Notes on a Spoilt Identity.* p5

93 Link and Phelan, "Stigma and Its Public Health Implications".

94 M Chesney, "Critical Delays in HIV Testing and Care", *American Behavioural Scientist* 42, no. 7 (1999). Individuals, for instance, avoid seeking HIV testing for fear of being revealed to others as HIV positive.

to walk, missing limbs, gender and aspects connected to ethnicity. In such instances the possibility of reducing whatever aspect gives rise to the prevailing stigma does not exist. Consequently individuals are presented with less options in order to 'cope' with their stigma. Where this occurs individuals may make efforts to convince non-stigmatized individuals that the aspect that gives rise to their stigma does not merit it.[95] In doing so individuals attempt to change the beliefs that individuals hold and so moderate their response to the aspect that is being stigmatized. They may do so by intensifying efforts, working harder to socialize with non-stigmatized people in order to show their worth as an individual person.[96] Such positive exposure may act to show non-stigmatized individuals that the aspect that gives rise to their stigma does not justify doing so. In today's society gay people have been trying and succeeding in doing this for some time, gaining acceptance and equality in terms of legal rights with heterosexual individuals. The ability to influence the belief systems of society is an important route for oppressed minorities.[97] The aim of such efforts will often be to show that there is no element of personal responsibility involved in the aspect that has been stigmatized.[98]

In contrast to attempting to change the perceptions of those who are not stigmatized, some individuals may choose to avoid situations and individuals they find to be stigmatizing. They may, for instance, try to avoid individuals they know are stigmatizing or situations that could provoke a stigmatizing response.[99] Such avoidance measures can serve to perpetuate stereotypes or stigmas.[100] Women in the workplace may, for example, seek to avoid potentially stigmatizing situations such as social events, ethnic minorities may stay away from cultural events known to be safe havens for prejudicial ideas, or individuals with certain diseases may seek to avoid seeking medical attention given prior experience with judgemental medical professionals. This may result in unjustified prejudices and stigmas going unchallenged. This type of coping mechanism can result in serious consequences for both individuals and society in general and will be dealt with in greater detail in section 6.

95 Miller and Kaiser, "A Theoretical Perspective on Coping with Stigma". p84 When stigmatized people have positive expectations regarding society and its prospects for change they are more likely to engage in 'normative' efforts to change the opinions of those who stigmatize. This may include action through legal channels or political lobbying.

96 Miller and Major, "Coping with Stigma and Prejudice".

97 Such efforts will often take the form of 'educational and persuasion' campaigns. Examples in the US include the 'Black is Beautiful' movement and the "National Association for the Advancement of Fat Acceptance". See ibid. page 256.

98 J Crocker and B Major, "Reactions to Stigma: The Moderating Effect of Justifications", in *The Psychology of Prejudice: The Ontario Symposium: Vol 7*, ed. M Zanna and Olson (Hillsdale, NJ: Erlbaum, 1994).

99 Miller and Kaiser, "A Theoretical Perspective on Coping with Stigma". Women, for instance, are known to make efforts to avoid interaction with men (if possible) that are known to be sexist.

100 Major and Schmader, "Coping with Stigma through Psychological Disengagement". p255

Where individuals are unable to avoid such situations whilst carrying on with their daily life, more extreme avoidance measures may be opted for such as withdrawal from social life in general. This may allow hurtful comparisons with non-stigmatized individuals to be avoided and also the social rejection that may ensue.[101] This can act to protect personal self-esteem. One strategy employed to avoid interaction with non-stigmatized individuals is to affiliate primarily with other stigmatized individuals and limit socialization to that group. In addition to avoiding negative interaction with non-stigmatizing individuals such association may allow downward comparison which often boosts self-esteem. Unfortunately this may have negative societal consequences tending towards ghettoization. This may leave a particular stigma intact or even strengthen it as it may reduce the familiarity non-stigmatized have with those who are stigmatized, thus increasing the potential anxiety of such encounters, when they do occur for both parties.

B The importance of context and the individual

The above pages represent as concise a summary as possible of a broad range of coping mechanisms for individuals that feel stigmatized. They demonstrate the wide variety of ways in which individuals can react when they are stigmatized. Some can be considered positive, for example where individuals attempt to change the opinion of stigmatizing individuals, or where (in some situations) individuals attempt to remove the aspect that is stigmatizing them (e.g. by losing weight or adopting a healthier lifestyle) where the stigmatized trait in question can be harmful to the individual concerned (e.g. obesity or anti-social behaviour).[102] Others can be considered negative, including the potential for self-loathing, anxiety, treatment avoidance and social isolation. It is clear that individuals vary in terms of their reaction to stigma and which one of these mechanism they may exhibit. Such variation can be found between cultures, between types of stigmatization and even between different individuals who experience the same stigmatization in the same context. Important factors in deciding which coping strategies will primarily manifest themselves include the attitudes of the surrounding society, the personal beliefs (often affected by the level of education and the experience) of the individuals involved, the innate personality characteristics of the individual concerned and also the actual practical possibilities available (i.e. the prevailing social, legal or economic situation may simply make some options impossible to choose). These factors mean that the phenomenon of stigmatization, with its highly subjective nature sits ill at ease with related concepts in law that depend upon more objective concepts, e.g. discrimination. This may in part explain why study by legal scholars of the phenomenon has hitherto been largely limited.[103]

101 Crocker and Major, "Social Stigma and Self-Esteem: The Self-Protective Properties of Stigma",
102 M Leary et al., "Self-Esteem as an Interpersonal Monitor: The Sociometer Hypothesis", *Journal of Personality and Social Psychology* 68, no. 3 (1995).
103 For an exception see I Solanke, *Discrimination as Stigma* (Oxford: Hart, 2017).

5 Stigmatization from a sociological perspective

A The need for more than just an 'individual-centric' approach to stigmatization

As the reader will gauge from the above discussion, the main body of stigmatization related research focuses on psychological processes that occur in stigmatized and non-stigmatized individuals at the individual level and, by the same token, interaction between individuals.[104] Such approaches are often highly empirical in nature. Scambler described the psychological research that followed in the decades post Goffman as a "synthesis of micro-analyses".[105] Such a 'micro scale' approach was started by Goffman and followed by numerous researchers, especially in the domain of psychology thereafter. Stigmatization presented a valuable concept for academics and professionals (e.g. psychologists) involved in such roles to describe the day-to-day interaction that individuals with a stigmatized trait undergo in their interaction with others (both stigmatized and non-stigmatized). The product of such research has been (negatively) likened to a 'script', which sets out the roles that individuals play in incidences of stigmatization.[106] Whilst this literature provides an essential insight into the manifestation of stigmatization on an individual level, it is limited in terms of the knowledge it provides in terms of the effects of stigma on society as a whole.

Restricting the study of stigma to the individual level experience (as was mainly the case until the 1990s) proved insufficient for two reasons. First, such approaches fail to capture the real social bases that lie behind instances of stigmatization. Stigmatization is not only a phenomenon that occurs between one or two people but also in terms of individual or group interaction with society as a whole. Second, an overly individualistic approach to the understanding of stigma fails to catch the phenomenon in the greater societal context it finds itself in. In such a macro-context stigmatization is closely linked to other processes such as discrimination and prejudice and is influenced by the economic and hierarchical nature of our societies.[107] Stigmatization in reality represents an integral part of the divisions that exist in all societies between the rich and powerful, on the one hand, and the poor and weak, on the other.[108] An overly individualistic approach fails to catch the 'material realities' of the many effects that come with stigmatization. Stigmatization

104 M Oliver, *The Politics of Disablement* (Basingstoke: Macmillan, 1992).
105 Scambler, "Health-Related Stigma". p444
106 Ibid.
107 Sayce, "Stigma, Discrimination and Social Exclusion: What's in a Word?"
108 Foucault, for instance, was interested in the use of stigma and normalization by society in order to control individuals. He considered, for example, that mental health approaches in the law were designed to control those perceived as deviant. See Lewis et al., "'I Don't Eat a Hamburger and Large Chips Every Day!' A Qualitative Study of the Impact of Public Health Messages About Obesity in Obese Adults". See also: Reidpath et al., "'He Hath the French Pox': Stigma, Social Value and Social Exclusion" (discussed further in section 7). Marx also saw stigma as connected to power, finding that stigmas were formed through the ideas of the ruling class. K Marx, "Ideology. Part I: Feuerbach. Opposition of the Materialist and Idealist Outlook" (1848).

often goes hand in hand with the social and economic exclusion of minority groups in society.[109] When one views the effects of stigmatization on a macro-scale different types of issues become more readily apparent. Such research does not invalidate that of Goffman and his followers but rather builds upon it.[110]

The motivation for new approaches to understanding the phenomenon was primarily that the principal body of research available on stigmatization was largely descriptive and lacked explanatory or predictive power.[111] Such problems were the result of a focus on the interaction between individuals whilst neglecting the 'macro-sociological perspective' that might exist. This has resulted in a failure to integrate potential contributions from other relevant areas such as biology, politics, economics and even history. In addition, such models tend to focus more on the stigmatized than the non-stigmatized individual. This arguably has had the effect of placing the 'blame' at the feet of the stigmatized individual. Such an approach ignored the role of non-stigmatized individuals (including society as a whole) in forming a stigmatizing scenario and the societal beliefs that often drive them to do so. Indeed such societal 'beliefs' often serve to maintain the prevailing structure of power and division of material wealth. The overly individualistic focus of stigmatization studies has led to disability and minority rights movements; for example relying more on concepts such as 'discrimination' and 'oppression' which have seemingly been able to give a much higher degree of attention to salient sociological and legal issues.[112] This led *inter alia* to frustration amongst disability theorists who felt that the post-Goffman era of micro-analysis failed to take into account the dynamic of stigmatization within the "social structure of political economy".[113]

For these reasons, research on the sociological impact of stigmatization is very useful. Whilst such research exists, it is smaller in comparison to the body of research concerned with psychological issues that occur on the individual level. The author of this book will argue that such approaches are nonetheless helpful in developing a conceptual understanding of how the state, through its expressions (as illustrated in Chapter 1), can affect processes of stigmatization, in particular through influencing collective beliefs that may fuel incidences of it.

B A descriptive approach

In an attempt to respond to the type of criticism described above, Link and Phelan attempted to frame stigmatization from a more sociological perspective. Their aim was to be more attentive to the nature and consequences of stigma than its

109 Sayce, "Stigma, Discrimination and Social Exclusion: What's in a Word?"

110 Scambler, "Health-Related Stigma". p442 As Scambler says, "it is not so much that Goffman was wrong as that there were questions which he didn't ask".

111 D Reidpath et al., "'He Hath the French Pox': Stigma, Social Value and Social Exclusion".

112 Sayce, "Social Inclusion and Mental Health"; "Stigma, Discrimination and Social Exclusion: What's in a Word?"

113 Scambler, "Health-Related Stigma". p442

sources.[114] For them stigma can be seen to have four common aspects. First, stigmatization requires that an individual or a group of individuals possess a differing trait that identifies them as being part of a group in society.[115] A second necessary component is that the trait in question allows individuals to be clearly separated, conceptually speaking, from other members of society. Individuals who suffer from various diseases provide such an example, where those who have contracted or developed diseases can be easily separated in conceptual terms from those that do not. Third, the linking of the individual's trait in question to a negative attribute allows the stigmatized group to be thought of as of being of a lower quality than other individuals that do not possess the label.[116] An example of such an assumption would be that individuals who are HIV positive are more promiscuous than other individuals. The fact that individuals who have such traits that can so easily lead to devaluation and a lower position in social hierarchies can lead to very real disadvantages for such individuals in day-to-day life including an increased risk of discrimination in numerous contexts. The fourth is that for stigmatization to occur there needs to be a pre-existing imbalance in power relations.[117] Imbalances in power relations can result in negative consequences for individuals that are prone to stigmatization. Individuals with more power have the ability to affect the lives of those without power in negative ways. In such instances, stigmatized individuals can be subjected to discrimination by those with more power in social relationships. This imbalance in power is fundamental in allowing stigmatization to lead to a lowering of position in the social hierarchy. Given that an individual's relative position in society is important for securing both economic and social resources, stigmatization can therefore lead to both social and economic marginalization.

Link and Phelan's concept represents an advance in terms of understanding how the concept of stigmatization, is at the societal level, closely linked to other phenomena such as stereotyping and discrimination (phenomena that are often incidentally recognized as legal concepts). Indeed they suggest a close relationship between the two, with discrimination being conducive to stigmatization. They present a very loose and expansive definition stating that stigmatization exists when "elements of labelling, stereotyping, separation, status loss and discrimination occur together in a power situation that allows them".[118] Stigmatization for them is therefore a very broad label that can be applied when all of these are occurring together to a group in society. Indeed for Link and Phelan it was the convergence of these phenomena that signalled the existence of stigma.[119] Status loss and discrimination, for example, were identified as a component of

114 Link and Phelan, "Conceptualizing Stigma". p366
115 For example, Link and Phelan contrast having curly hair and having black skin. In most societies possessing curly hair is not seen as denoting membership of a group whereas having black skin is. Ibid. p367
116 Ibid. p370
117 Ibid, p375
118 Link and Phelan, "Conceptualizing Stigma". p377
119 Ibid. p367

stigmatization. The link between stigmatization and discrimination was also something emphasized by Sayce.[120] Speaking primarily from her experience with sufferers of mental health disorders she also viewed stigmatization and discrimination as being closely related. For her it was necessary to tackle stigmatization in order to reduce instances of discrimination against people experiencing or with a history of mental illness. Link and Phelan surmised that the purpose of labelling individuals and setting them apart from society was to justify their differential treatment, i.e. discrimination.

C A concept centred on access to resources – stigmatization as a 'tool'

The last of Link and Phelan's descriptive points described above, i.e. that stigma usually occurs in a situation of power imbalances is particularly interesting in the context of this book. It suggests that stigmatization may often be used as a tool by those who are in a more powerful position in society to justify unfair arrangements or treatment of those in a weaker position. Such an analysis is something that has been supported by other researchers who have described stigmatization as something that can be used by those who have access to or control power, resources or other advantages to marginalize those that do not. Reidpath and colleagues, for instance, attempted to build a framework that sees stigmatization as something that is used to marginalize those with limited access to resources.[121] At the heart of this concept is the fact that in our society social position and access to certain social groups are very closely linked to distribution of various resources. Membership of such groups denotes a right of access to certain resources whilst a lack of membership denotes exclusion.[122] Resources are, by their nature, limited and thus the subject of control. The limited availability of resources in all societies throughout history has led to social inequality with some individuals in society having less than others. It has been argued that, in this omnipresent human context, stigmatization has been used as a tool by groups and societies in restricting the flow of social resources to those deemed not deserving of them.[123]

120 Sayce, "Social Inclusion and Mental Health".

121 For a similar perspective see L Molm, N Takahashi, and G Peterson, "Risk and Trust in Social Exchange: An Experimental Test of a Classical Proposition", *American Journal of Sociology* 105, no. 5 (2000).

122 Reidpath et al., "'He Hath the French Pox': Stigma, Social Value and Social Exclusion". Link and Phelan's description has been described as 'synthetic' by Reidpath and colleagues in that it provides guidelines for assessing when stigmatization may exist but does not really provide an adequate understanding (in terms of the societal level) of why it occurs. Whilst Reidpath bases many of his arguments on the concept of sociobiology, his conclusions, in terms of how stigmatization may be often be used, are similar to those (e.g. Link and Phelan) who do not attempt to root their ideas in such a way.

123 R Goodin, *Protecting the Vulnerable: A Reanalysis of Our Social Responsibilities* (Chicago: The University of Chicago Press, 1985); R Trivers, *Social Evolution* (Menlo Park, CA: The Benjamin/Cummings Publishing Company, 1985). For more see Reidpath et al., "'He Hath the French Pox': Stigma, Social Value and Social Exclusion." p481

At the heart of such processes of stigmatization lies the creation of negative stereotypes (see section B above). Such stereotypes can be used to convey negative assumptions concerning a particular group, assumptions that may be used to justify negative forms of treatment including social and economic exclusion. The development of negative stereotypes can allow groups that share a common trait in society to be labelled in a negative manner (one which will usually take little account of shared characteristics)[124] allowing and even justifying negative treatment of the group concerned. In this way the development of such stereotypes and their deployment in processes of stigmatization often go hand in hand with discrimination and other forms of ill treatment that worsen the plight of disadvantaged groups in society.

D Those who are able to influence categorizations or stereotypes

The above idea, which could be described as a 'stigmatization as tool', also allows one to envisage important roles for other institutions or individuals that may be outside the traditional range of characters in terms of the perceiver/target model at the heart of most stigmatization research. Importantly for this book this arguably includes the various organs of the state and those connected to them. The stigmatization as tool idea sees an important, if not crucial, role for those who are able to influence the existing categorizations (or create new ones) at the societal level, including through the use of SSEs. Such categorizations are used by individuals to decide how they should treat certain groups of people.[125] When made at the macro level by those in prominent positions of influence they can be important in the creation of stereotypes which may inform individual decisions on whether or not to discriminate on the micro or individual level.[126] The types of individuals and institutions that are able to influence such categorizations are numerous. Principal amongst them are the individuals and institutions connected to the state. Such individuals, by virtue of the resources they possess, the competences they have, their ability to affect the lives of individuals in society and also by virtue of their authority which, in modern societies often extends from a democratic mandate, have enormous power to generate categories or stereotypes capable of producing stigmatization. Drawing on reasoning by Link and Phelan,[127] Scambler[128] poses several questions that can be asked in order to help determine which individuals might have the power to bring about stigmatization against groups on a large scale. Where such questions are answered in the positive Scambler suggests that it is necessary to be concerned with the possibility of creating stigmatizing stereotypes that have the potential to pervade throughout society. These questions are:

124 "'He Hath the French Pox': Stigma, Social Value and Social Exclusion".
125 S Andersen and R Klatzky, "Traits and Social Stereotypes: Levels of Categorization in Person Perception", *Journal of Personality and Social Psychology* 53, no. 2 (1987)..
126 Reidpath et al., "'He Hath the French Pox': Stigma, Social Value and Social Exclusion".
127 Link and Phelan, "Conceptualizing Stigma".
128 G Scambler, "Health-Related Stigma",

i Do those who might stigmatize have sufficient power to ensure the human difference they recognize and label resonates in the public culture?
ii Do those who might confer stigma have the power to ensure that the culture 'deeply accepts' the stereotypes they connect to labelled differences?
iii Do those who might stigmatize possess enough power to underwrite and maintain a separation of 'us' from 'them'?
iv Do those who might confer stigma have the power to control access to core institutions like schooling, job markets, housing and healthcare in order to 'put really consequential teeth into the distinctions they draw'?

Scambler's observation resonates with the importance of 'beliefs' discussed in section 4. Such beliefs were important because they are capable of amplifying or moderating affective urges to act in a stigmatizing way. In contrast to those such as Crocker (who look at beliefs from the intra-personal perspective), Scambler is concerned with the potential for key players in society to influence such beliefs. Such potential is central to the theme of this book, given as Chapter 1 illustrated, the state and range of actors connected to it have an unparalleled ability to disseminate stigmatizing the categorizations and stereotypes through SSEs. Public officials or institutions have the authority and resources to reach large parts of the population.[129] Their ability to use official channels or access the media to spread messages are unmatched by almost all other actors in society. Consequently, if such officials or institutions wish to form categorizations or stereotypes that are capable of creating or reinforcing stigmatizing attitudes amongst the public, they have an almost unique potential to do so. The potential for prominent figures (including those connected to the state) to create stigmatizing stereotypes gives rise to legitimate questions in terms of the regulation they are subjected to under the law.

6 Differentiating stigmatization from similar concepts

A Discrimination

At various points in the forgoing analysis it has become apparent that stigmatization is very closely related to other processes such as discrimination, stereotyping and marginalization. This raises the question of whether stigmatization is a significantly different concept to merit the effort of individual definition both in a 'legal' and 'sociological' sense.[130] From a legal scholar's point of view it is important to answer such questions in order to be able to discern what stigma is, how it

129 Chapter 2 presents examples of public officials who have with their expressions stigmatized vast groups of individuals based on medical conditions they possessed, their religion, their origin or even their socioeconomic status.

130 Both the concepts of stereotyping and discrimination have, for example, received a great deal of attention in terms of their legal definition. See R O'Connell, "Cinderella Comes to the Ball: Art 14 and the Right to Non-Discrimination in the ECHR", *Legal Studies* 29, no. 2 (2009) and A Timmer, "Toward an Anti-Stereotyping Approach for the European Court of Human Rights", *Human Rights Law Review* 11, no. 4 (2011).

differs from discrimination and what points should legal systems recognize? These problems pose important questions as to the suitability of stigmatization as a concept in discussing the plight of minorities and vulnerable groups. What does such a concept mean? Does it describe the effects on the stigmatized and their behaviour, the actions of those non-stigmatized, or both? In addition, one may pose the question as to whether stigmatization as a 'legal concept' (discussed further in section 7) is superfluous given the availability of several other related concepts (most notably that of discrimination, which as Sayce described is a favoured concept of disability movements)?[131]

Given the primarily legally orientated aims of this book, a key aim is to discern both *should* and *does* the law protect against stigmatization?[132] A key requirement in answering these questions will be looking at the relationship between stigmatization and other concepts that the law does clearly recognize. If one is not able to show that there is a significant distinction between stigmatization and other similar concepts, one could argue that it is arguably unnecessary to be concerned with the specific recognition of stigmatization as a phenomenon by the law. The following pages will therefore be devoted to a close comparison between stigmatization and similar concepts in an effort to see if there is indeed 'clear water' between them.

(i) A clear relationship between the two concepts

The words 'stigmatization' and 'discrimination' are familiar to most people in most countries and societies.[133] They are used in day-to-day language by the media, politicians and often normal citizens.[134] If one was to ask the average person what either word meant they would however often be unable to offer a reasonable concise definition. Both individuals and representatives of groups will often use both words to describe their own or others' mistreatment in society. If one were to examine thoroughly what individuals actually mean when using these words, one would see that there is often little effort made in defining what each constitutes. This reflects the difficulty academic scholars from various disciplines have had when tackling the subject.[135] Rather,

131 Sayce, "Social Inclusion and Mental Health".

132 As the Introduction to this book discussed, Chapter 3 will attempt to build a normative position on the use of stigmatizing statements by the state whilst Chapters 4–7 will present illustrative examples of problems key approaches may have in impacting upon stigmatizing statements.

133 P Quinn and P De Hert, "Self Respect—a 'Rawlsian Primary Good' Unprotected by the European Convention on Human Rights and Its Lack of a Coherent Approach to Stigmatization?", *The International Journal of Discrimination and the Law* 14 (2014).

134 See, for example, the paper commissioned by Health Scotland entitled "Stigma: An International Briefing Paper – Tackling the Discrimination, Stigma and Social Exclusion Experienced by People with Mental Health Problems and Those Close to Them" concerning mental health stigma. This report used all of these terms frequently. It is available at: http://ec.europa.eu/health/mental_health/eu_compass/reports_studies/stigma_paper.pdf

135 Burris, "Disease Stigma in U.S. Public Law". p179

individuals appear to use such words without giving ample thought to defining them. It is not just lay people but academics, legal scholars and even the judiciary that employ such practices.[136] For example, in the discourse above, one can clearly see a kind of chicken-and-egg debate being played out. Link and Phelan assert that discrimination is a part of stigmatization[137] whereas Sayce appears to believe that stigmatization causes discrimination and that by stopping the former one should be able to reduce the latter. Both positions could be used to support the 'stigma as tool' concept discussed above whereby stigmatization is often used in order to justify discriminatory patterns of behaviour by those in a position of relative power.

Unfortunately Link and Phelan do not offer a definition of what they consider discrimination to be. Sayce, however, does. She recognizes that discrimination can mean either "unfair treatment", or "treating people differently".[138] Though they do not go to the effort of making such a distinction, Link and Phelan appear to operating under a similar notion. They discuss examples such as black individuals being overlooked by potential white employers and unfair and unfounded attitudes that individuals might have towards individuals with a history of a mental condition or history thereof.[139] Unlike Sayce, however, Link and Phelan view discrimination as only part of the problem involved in instances of stigmatization. This is because their analysis appears to recognize the perceiver/target axis proposed by Dovidio (see section 4) and colleagues (a predominantly psychology based concept).[140] For they assert that whilst discrimination can be induced by collectively held negative stereotypes concerning individuals this is only part of the problem that brings about the harm that is caused in instances of stigmatization. The other side of the stigmatization coin is the beliefs that stigmatized individuals themselves hold concerning their position in society. Such beliefs can induce fear, apprehension or the utilization of one (or more) of the coping mechanisms discussed in section 4.[141] These affects can be triggered by fear or apprehension in stigmatized individuals over possible encounters with those who might be potential 'stigmatizers'.[142] Thus, in the Dovidio/Link and Phelan conception, stigmatization represents a large and complex framework which involves a sort of

136 Quinn and De Hert, "Self Respect—a 'Rawlsian Primary Good' Unprotected by the European Convention on Human Rights and Its Lack of a Coherent Approach to Stigmatization?"
137 Link and Phelan, "Conceptualizing Stigma".
138 Sayce, "Stigma, Discrimination and Social Exclusion: What's in a Word?" Sayce's definition of discrimination was not intended to define it as a legal concept. A discussion of discrimination as a legal concept is conducted in Chapter 5. See also P Quinn, "The Problem of Stigmatizing Expressions – the Limits of Anti-Discrimination Approaches", *International Journal of Discrimination and the Law* 17, no. 1 (2017).
139 Link and Phelan, "Conceptualizing Stigma". p372
140 Dovidio, Major, and Crocker, "Stigma: Introduction and Overview".
141 As discussed in section 4 these include avoidance, downward comparison and passing as a non-stigmatized individual. See, for example, M Biernat and J Dovidio, "Stigma and Stereotypes" (New: York: Guilford Press, 2000).
142 Link and Phelan, "Conceptualizing Stigma". p374

psychological dance between perceivers and targets. This process can include various other well recognized concepts such as stereotyping and discrimination.

(ii) The induction of psychological changes lies at the heart of stigmatization but not of discrimination

It is important to distinguish between stigmatization and discrimination as concepts. Despite the fact that such concepts may be used (erroneously) in an interchangeable manner, the foregoing analysis indicates that they do in fact have different meanings. Whether one takes the first or second description of discrimination offered by Sayce above, it becomes apparent that the concept relates only to one side of this psychological and social dance, i.e. between the perceiver and target as described by Dovidio in the stigmatization framework.[143] Both refer to the concept of 'treatment' of a weaker party by a stronger party. Whilst in each of the two definitions the type of treatment may change (i.e. unfair or differential treatment), the one sided nature of the concept remains. In an act of potential discrimination the weaker party has no influence on whether an act of discrimination actually occurs. It is only through action (or inaction) by the stronger party that discrimination can occur. Conversely, the weaker party is not able to alter this. With stigmatization however, according to Link and Phelan, it is necessary to pay attention to both parties. The thoughts, attitudes and behaviours of both parties are significant and all play a part in determining whether, in a particular instance stigmatization is taking place. This is because depending on the context, personality and beliefs of the individual involved, people can react differently to potentially stigmatizing forces. Some may be badly affected by stigmatizing attitudes whilst others, due to personality factors or beliefs that they possess, may have a greater capacity to resist and so avoid negative effects.[144]

In addition to the one sided nature of Sayce's discrimination definitions, one can also distinguish them from stigmatization by the way they pivot on the notion of 'treatment' by another party (i.e. some form of corporeal or tangible imposition). With stigmatization however, the key factor is the psychological state and consequent behaviour of the stigmatized individual. This can be influenced by numerous factors, including but not limited to the way they are 'treated' by other individuals. Other factors include the personal beliefs of the individual concerned and the severity of the stigmatizing aspect in question. Even where no differential or negative 'treatment' occurs stigmatization can induce negative psychological or even physiological outcomes for stigmatized individuals. It is the potential for such changes to be induced in individuals that is a requisite for 'stigmatization' (discussed in section 4). They include anxiety, harm to self-esteem, internationalization, the employment of internal and external coping strategies, etc.

143 For more see: Dovidio, Major, and Crocker, "Stigma: Introduction and Overview". p12

144 Crocker, "Social Stigma and Self-Esteem: Situational Construction of Self Worth". p91 Crocker termed this a 'situational construction of self-worth'.

Whilst one would normally expect discrimination to induce such psychological effects this need not always be the case. Where discrimination occurs, the discriminating party may well view the discriminated party in a negative light and treat that person unfairly. The discriminating party need not however intend that the individual perceives him or herself in a negative manner and may take steps to ensure that the individual discriminated against does not learn the true reason for his decision. A good example of this is where a potential employer refuses to employ someone because of his or her ethnic origin but hides from the individual concerned that this was the reason for his decision. In such a context one could say that whilst the individual has suffered discrimination he has not been stigmatized. With stigmatization however, the stigmatizing individual brings about a situation where the individual or group concerned becomes aware of negative views concerning them held by stigmatizing individuals.[145] In this situation, the stigmatizing individual may not be intending to deny the individual a legal right and therefore is not acting to discriminate as in the first example. An example of such a relationship between two private individuals would be where an individual mocks a homosexual individual in the street for being promiscuous or immoral, causing that person to feel that he or she should hide his or her sexual orientation from others in the future.[146] Similarly (as Chapter 1 illustrated) the state or linked institutions can issue statements or release information whereby the result is that certain individuals view themselves in a negative light. In such instances the stigmatizing party may neither possess nor exercise the power to alter legal rights or deny access to rights to resources to individual(s) (and so is not able to discriminate) but can still bring about stigmatization.[147] This difference between the two concepts is important as it creates significant doubts in the ability of anti-discrimination approaches to tackle instances that are brought about through expressions or statements.[148] This will be discussed further in Chapter 5.

(iii) 'Treatment' is not a prerequisite for stigmatization but is for discrimination

The negative effects described above can be induced without any particular 'mistreatment' by non-stigmatized individuals. 'Stigmatizers' (i.e. those who hold stigmatizing views) need not even be present for the inducement of such psychological states to occur.[149] What is needed to induce psychological states and certain beliefs amongst stigmatized individuals is the perception of negative opinions

145 Courtwright, "Justice, Stigma, and the New Epidemiology of Health Disparities."
146 Whilst such a statement may not constitute discrimination it may, according to the jurisdiction in question constitute hate speech. This is discussed further in Chapter 4.
147 Quinn and De Hert, "Self Respect—a 'Rawlsian Primary Good' Unprotected by the European Convention on Human Rights and Its Lack of a Coherent Approach to Stigmatization?" p24
148 Quinn, "The Problem of Stigmatizing Expressions -the Limits of Anti-Discrimination Approaches".
149 Crocker, "Social Stigma and Self-Esteem: Situational Construction of Self Worth". p103

of non-stigmatized people towards them, beliefs concerning the validity of such opinions and the presence of a context in which such beliefs would apply. In the context of African American students described in section 4, for example, such a situation existed where they were being tested for intelligence. The possibility that their scores would be looked at in the light of a supposed stereotype of lesser intellectual ability by those who conducted the test was enough to induce the phenomenon of 'stereotype threat'. The presence of individuals holding stigmatizing views, let alone individuals who treated them badly was not necessary, nor was any tangible form of mistreatment. As Chapter 5 will discuss in further detail, most definitions of discrimination centre around the concept of 'treatment'.[150] This usually involves the imposition of binding changes on certain individuals by others. Where such 'treatment' does not occur (as is the case with most SSEs) one would usually not be able to describe a particular situation as being one of 'discrimination'.

This situation means prohibiting discrimination is not sufficient to prevent stigmatization from occurring, given that it can take place without any form of 'treatment'. Indeed in many such cases discrimination is indeed prohibited but stigmatization and its effects persist.[151] An African American student may not have personally encountered discrimination him or herself, but through life experience may have formed the belief that white individuals perceive African Americans to have a lower level of intelligence than their white counterparts.[152] Such beliefs may have been formed *inter alia* by collective experiences, by stories, by subconscious perceptions, through contact with a small number of individuals, through negative stereotypes perpetuated in the media concerning black people, from within the black community and also importantly the perceived attitudes of the state.[153] The presence of discrimination can no doubt make such situations worse.[154] Discrimination *can* cause stigmatization, both for those who are discriminated against and also other members of that community. Discrimination need not exist however for stigmatization to occur. The possibility to have stigmatization even in the absence or prohibition of discrimination clearly demonstrates that the two concepts are not the same and that there is a need for society to take measures to deal with both. Hoping simply that an anti-discrimination approach will be enough to remove stigmatization from society is therefore misplaced.[155] There is thus a need to maintain separate

150 Quinn, "The Problem of Stigmatizing Expressions – the Limits of Anti-Discrimination Approaches".
151 Burris, "Disease Stigma in U.S. Public Law".
152 Crocker, "Social Stigma and Self-Esteem: Situational Construction of Self Worth".
153 H Stevenson et al., "Influence of Perceived Neighborhood Diversity and Racism Experience on the Racial Socialization of Black Youth", *The Journal of Black Psychology* 31, no. 3 (2005). Black youth in the US have been shown to be influenced in their beliefs concerning the racism of others by both family and community, for example.
154 Link and Phelan, "Conceptualizing Stigma".
155 Burris, "Disease Stigma in U.S. Public Law".

concepts in order to be aware of and address the two distinct, but related problems that individuals face in society.

B Stigmatization and stereotyping

(i) Stereotyping does not depend on the induction of negative psychological states

Stereotypes are beliefs about the characteristics of groups of people.[156] It has been theorized that the ability to stereotype is advantageous in that it allows individuals to categorize others and make rapid judgements in a complex world.[157] The price of such a short cut is often however an unfair 'pigeon-holing' of individuals into neat categories based on little or no consideration of their individual characteristics.[158] Stereotyping can be separated from stigmatization through several differing properties. First, stereotypes can be good or bad.[159] Consider, for example, the age-old stereotypes of 'German efficiency' or 'British politeness'. These are clearly examples of stereotypes concerning positive attributes of certain groups of people.[160] It would, however, be a misnomer to speak of a positive stigma. Such a concept would not meet the requirement identified by Link and Phelan that a trait be capable of being linked to a negative characteristic.[161] Second, the establishment of stereotypes is not dependent upon the possible inducement of negative effects such as the internalization of negative feelings towards oneself or other harmful coping mechanisms. When the negative effects of stereotyping are described however, 'negative psychological effects' are often highlighted as negative consequence and are often cited as a reason by psychologists and courts to avoid harmful stereotyping (i.e. stereotype threat).[162] The author of this book contends that such situations represent a conflation of the concepts of stigmatization and stereotyping. A negative stereotype can, of course, be capable of inducing negative psychological states, e.g. the induction of coping responses or the internalization of negative emotions towards oneself. Once again however such an operation is not necessary for stereotyping to occur. As discussed above, people can be the subject of positive stereotypes. If psychological harm does occur as a result of stereotyping a better description would arguably be 'stigmatization due to

156 C Stangor, "Overview" in *Stereotypes and Prejudice: Essential Readings,* ed. C Stangor (Philadelphia, PA: Psychology Press, 2000). p5
157 See, for example, W Lippmann, *Public Opinion* (Miami, FL: BN Publishing, 2007 (first published 1922)). p36
158 Biernat and Dovidio, "Stigma and Stereotypes".
159 Ibid. p108
160 For another view that argues that stereotypes are always negative (even when they are 'positive') see http://www.theguardian.com/commentisfree/oliver-burkemans-blog/2012/dec/12/stereotypes-bad-even-when-good
161 Link and Phelan, "Conceptualizing Stigma" p368
162 Timmer, "Toward an Anti-Stereotyping Approach for the European Court of Human Rights". p716 C Steele and J Aronson, "Stereotype Threat and the Intellectual Test Performance of African Americans", *Journal of Personality and Social Psychology* 69 (1995). p809

negative stereotyping'.[163] The fact that stigmatization can be created by negative stereotypes demonstrates the close links between the two concepts.[164]

(ii) Stereotyping is less important in some forms of stigmatization

Stereotyping plays a lesser role in some types of stigmatization than others. Where there is great heterogeneity between individuals who suffer a certain stigma type, the role of stereotyping is less. This can be the case, for example, when one speaks of stigmas involved in congenital or other disfigurement.[165] Amongst such individuals there is great variation in the actual disfigurement they possess and the social stigma that it may bring.[166] Compare, for example, the disfigurements and social implications for a person with a missing limb and extreme facial disfigurement. Given the heterogeneity in such stigmas, the average non-stigmatized individuals will not likely have encountered many individuals possessing such attributes and, as a consequence, will not possess enough information to form a stereotype. If one compares this to other groups that suffer stigma in societies such as ethnic minorities there is a very different picture. The attribute that stigmatizes such individuals manifests itself much more homogeneously in such individuals. Given this, and the larger number of such individuals in society (in comparison to people with disfigurements), there is a greater chance that the average non-stigmatized individual will have encountered individuals from an ethnic minority and so will have at least some information with which to form a stereotype. In cases of the first type stereotyping will play a minor role in stigmatization, a stigmatizing response of individuals will primarily be guided primarily by affective (i.e. subconscious, impulsive) thought processes.[167] In cases of the second type, stereotyping is likely to play a greater role, with the stereotype in question informing the individuals cognitive (i.e. reasoned thought process) and driving the stigmatization process.

(iii) Stereotyping is closely linked to the concept of 'stigmatizing beliefs'

Stereotypes seem closely connected, if not analogous to, the concepts of belief and ideology discussed above (see section 6). Such aspects play a very important role in many forms of stigmatization and are capable of inducing, accentuating or

163 This is also discussed in Quinn and De Hert, "Self Respect—a 'Rawlsian Primary Good' Unprotected by the European Convention on Human Rights and Its Lack of a Coherent Approach to Stigmatization?"

164 Steele and Aronson, "Stereotype Threat and the Intellectual Test Performance of African Americans".

165 Biernat and Dovidio, "Stigma and Stereotypes".

166 D Hamilton and S Sherman, "Perceiving Persons and Groups", *Psychological Review* 103 (1996). Such groups are low in 'entitivity', meaning they are difficult to group by shared characteristics.

167 For more on the difference between affective and cognitive thought processes see section 4 of this chapter. See also Dovidio, Major, and Crocker, "Stigma: Introduction and Overview". p13

moderating stigmatization.[168] In the context of stigmatization they can represent a part of the cognitive component that acts upon the affective thought process that underlies stigma.[169] In this way stereotypes can be used to justify stigmatization by giving reasonable justification to the urge to differentiate in the quality and good intentions amongst one's own group and other groups in society (i.e. outgroups).[170] Thus people may look for, and cling to, negative stereotypes concerning a stigmatized minority. The numerous stereotypes of 'lazy' and 'dirty' immigrants may be an example of this.[171] In terms of the focus of this book, it is the very power of public officials and public bodies to spread such negative stereotypes through SSEs that raises questions as to what legal controls should be available to prevent them.

Beliefs can however be positive. Collectively we are able to use complex ethical reasoning to show that individuals deserve equal respect to ourselves. We attempt to instil such beliefs in our children in school and through other channels in society.[172] Such beliefs are aimed at tempering affective impulses to stigmatize and to discriminate. These positive beliefs can often also take the form of stereotypes. In the UK, for example, concepts such as 'hard working Poles' have been used to compare Polish immigrants in a positive light to working class British workers. Such concepts are often used by anti-racism campaigners in an effort to reduce racism against such individuals. Another example of such a stereotype concerns the happy and gentle nature of those individuals with Down's Syndrome. Research indicates that such positive beliefs or stereotypes are able to temper potential negative reactions towards individuals with a severe form of handicap.[173] Whilst this may not be able to remove the stigmatization that such individuals feel, it can reduce the negative consequences that can flow from it.[174]

168 See section 6.

169 Dovidio, Major, and Crocker, "Stigma: Introduction and Overview". It is the higher level cognitive thought process that gives the variation found in stigmatization across cultures and contexts. It acts upon basal affective impulses that are less informed by knowledge and experience.

170 See section 4 for a proposed biocultural basis underpinning discrimination against out groups. See also Reidpath et al., "'He Hath the French Pox': Stigma, Social Value and Social Exclusion".

171 Chapter 1, for example, uses the example of a speech where the then mayor of Paris criticized the 'noise and the smell' of African immigrants.

172 Neuberg, Smith, and Asher, "Why Do People Stigmatise: Toward a Biocultural Framework".

173 A Simon, "The Relationship between Stereotypes of and Attitudes toward Lesbians and Gays", in *Stigma and Sexual Orientation: Understanding Prejudice against Lesbians, Gay Men, and Bisexuals. Psychological Perspectives on Lesbian and Gay Issues*, ed. G Herek (Thousand Oaks, CA: Sage Publications, 1998).

174 I Katz, *Stigma: A Social-Psychological Perspective* (Hillsdale, NJ: Erlbaum, 1981). Often such positive beliefs or stereotypes can result in hostile reactions being replaced with attitudes of ambivalence. Whilst ambivalence in itself may well be preferable to hostility it still brings with it feelings of rejection and can add to the stigmatization that stigmatized individuals feel.

C Stigmatization and marginalization

Like stereotyping, marginalization is a concept that is very closely connected to that of stigmatization. Marginalization as a term has been used with differing meanings. A sociologist might define a marginalized group as a group that is 'not completely integrated'.[175] As with stigmatization, common understandings of the word may be different, with the *Oxford New English Dictionary* stating that a marginalized group is "a group that has links to two different societies but is not completely integrated in either".[176] The term is often used to refer to very different notions, with one referring to economic marginalization where individuals are excluded from sharing in the economic benefits of society and a social meaning where individuals are deemed to be outside socially acceptable society.[177] The terms 'social exclusion' and 'economic exclusion' are often used synonymously for these concepts in modern political discourse. Such concepts were originally more prominent in French political discourse but gained use in English in the 1990s.[178]

Marginalization and stigmatization may often be viewed as having a cause-and-effect relationship with each other. Individuals may, for example, become socially marginalized through stigmatization because they are perceived to be a threat to the group they live in, possibly because they have not followed the social rules or traditions of that group.[179] In such instances stigmatization is used to economically and socially marginalize individuals so that they are unable to share in the social and economic benefits that come with participation in group life. Marginalization often manifests itself as a result of stigmatization. Another perspective that views a perceived ability or willingness to reciprocate with other members of the groups tends to see economic and social marginalization as a process that will lead to stigmatization.[180] Where this has been shown to occur, individuals stigmatize those who are

175 W Koschnick, *Standard Dictionary of the Social Sciences* (Munich: K. G. Saur, 1993). p1237

176 L Brown, *New Shorter Oxford Dictionary* (Oxford: Oxford University Press, 1993) p 696.

177 A good description (in Dutch) of the variation in contemporary and middle ages use of the word marginalization can be found in Dupont, "'Qu'est-ce que la marginalité? Marginale groepen in de stedelijke samenlevingen in de Late Middeleeuwen: definities en problemen", in *Van oud en nieuw recht*, ed. D. Heirbaut and D. Lambrecht, pp219–240 (Antwerp: Kluwer, 1998).

178 D Byrne, *Social Exclusion* (Maidenhead and New York: McGraw-Hill Education, 2005). See pages 1–10.

179 Neuberg, Smith, and Asher, "Why Do People Stigmatise: Toward a Biocultural Framework".

180 Reidpath et al., "'He Hath the French Pox': Stigma, Social Value and Social Exclusion". Riedpath takes such a viewpoint from a biosocial perspective. Others such as Link and Phelan seem to come to the same conclusion without resorting to biosocial explanations. They see a role of stigmatization as being the justification of mistreatment by those in a position of power of those in a weaker position. This will inevitably result in marginalization and exclusion. See Link and Phelan, "Conceptualizing Stigma". On pages 370–371 the authors state, "In our reasoning, when people are labeled, set apart, and linked to undesirable characteristics, a rationale is constructed for devaluing, rejecting, and excluding them".

perceived as being unable to contribute economically or socially to group life. Stigmatization results through the perception that further engagement with such individuals would be a wasted investment and so should be avoided. Stigmatization acts therefore as a sign that due to the social and economic marginalization of the individual he or she is to be avoided in terms of further social and economic engagement. Once again there is, at least to a certain extent, something of a chicken-and-egg aspect at play. This is because the stigmatization that such individuals suffer is likely to lead to yet further marginalization and therefore consequently a greater susceptibility to further stigmatization.

For the purposes of this discussion it is clear that though more distant from stigmatization than the concept of stereotyping, the concept of marginalization can be separated on the same basis, i.e. by the lack of a requirement of the induction of negative psychological states, for example, an internalization of negative emotions, harm to self-esteem or through the deployment of coping mechanisms. Such effects need not be present for marginalization to occur. Marginalization as a social concept appears to be associated more with the attitudes of others and not the marginalized themselves, i.e. society in general which refuses to see the marginalized as part of the mainstream or share with them the economic benefits of society. Another conceptual difference is that marginalization as an economic term is concerned more with practical realities than mental or psychological states. In this context the term is more concerned with the end result than the mechanism by which negative effects can occur. In this way one can state that discrimination, stereotyping or stigmatization can lead to marginalization, i.e. the being on the margins of society. Being marginalized however does not necessarily mean that one is stigmatized. An individual may have chosen or be happy with his or her existence at the 'margins of society'. The term marginalization it is therefore argued is best used to describe a possible result of the processes described above.

7 The main negative consequences that can be produced from stigmatization

Stigmatization (including where brought about by SSEs) can cause a range of negative outcomes for individuals and society as a whole. The following section will attempt to catalogue some of these effects in a concise manner. What follows below is a general description and not an exhaustive review of all the negative effects of stigmatization which can vary enormously from context to context.[181] The need to categorize such effects is twofold. First, stigmatization is capable of producing a number of effects that are not immediately apparent. Without a sound understanding of the phenomenon and its ability to produce such effects it is difficult to understand why activities such as SSEs can be harmful. This knowledge allows causational links between stigmatization and other negative phenomenon in

181 As "Conceptualizing Stigma". p365 "[T]he stigma concept has been applied to an enormous array of circumstances. Each one of these is unique, and each one is likely to lead investigators to conceptualize stigma in a somewhat different way."

society to be understood. Without such knowledge it would be difficult to see where an instance of stigmatization was capable of having negative effects, and of what magnitude they might be. Second, given the aims of this book, it will be necessary to be aware of such effects when examining the law so as to see whether it does actually offer protection against the phenomenon. Given that some of the effects that can occur as a result of stigmatization are not immediately apparent, a lack of awareness of such effects would therefore render an analysis of a legal system's ability to protect against the phenomenon incomplete.

A Effects on the individual level

(i) Internal effects

Stigmatization is capable of producing numerous negative effects in individuals.[182] Some of these have already been described in section 4. The phenomenon is capable of producing negative effects whether individuals subscribe to the ideas that those who stigmatize hold or not.[183] These include effects such as stress, anxiety and paranoia, harm to self-esteem and even 'internalization' (discussed further in section 4). Most research on stigmatization focuses on these micro-level or individual aspects of the phenomenon. As a result, the emotional experiences of those subjected to stigma are well documented. It is not only these negative emotions themselves, but also many of the coping behaviours that individuals experiencing stigmatization employ that can produce harmful effects. A large part of the research conducted on stigmatization has been devoted to contextual analyses of the phenomenon in different contexts. Thus, the manifestation of these generic concepts is likely to differ from context to context depending on the circumstances in question. Again, we can take, for example, the stigmatization of a diabetic who injects insulin in public and a woman who wished to have an abortion.[184] Given the completely different contexts that exist in each situation the effects of anxiety, stress, avoidance, etc. are likely to manifest themselves in different ways.

(ii) Stress effects – physical responses

There is evidence to show that individuals who perceive themselves to be of a lower social position or group often undergo a chronic physiological stress response.[185] Given that stigmatization can induce or reinforce the belief that one occupies a lower rank in the social order,[186] stigmatzing forces can exacerbate

182 Burris, "Disease Stigma in U.S. Public Law".
183 Steele and Aronson, "Stereotype Threat and the Intellectual Test Performance of African Americans".
184 See, for example, Joachim, "Stigma of Visible and Invisible Chronic Conditions", *Journal of Advanced Nursing*, 32, no. 1. (2000). p246 See note 25.
185 M Marmot, *The Status Syndrome: How Social Standing Affects Our Health and Longevity* (New York: NY Times Books, 2004). pp104–137
186 Link and Phelan, "Conceptualizing Stigma".

such problems.[187] This effect has been shown to be more prevalent in more unequal societies. This response is associated with an increase in the production of stress hormones that induce various physical effects associated with a response to stress.[188] The most prominent example of such a negative physical effect of stress is a poorer level of cardiovascular health.[189] This has been used to partially attribute poorer states of physical health to individuals in disadvantaged sections of society such as lower socioeconomic groups, individuals with lower levels of education, minority groups and immigrants.[190] The effect of long term stress on the body provides a mechanism by which psycho-social phenomena can have an effect on an individual's physical health. Another possible negative of such chronic stigmatization is depression which is harmful in itself but which can also increase the likelihood of substance abuse and other harmful behaviour.[191]

B Societal effects

(i) A reduced desire to seek healthcare – the risks of healthcare avoidance

Stigmatized groups have been observed to engage in harmful healthcare avoidance behaviours as a result of lower expectations of how they will be received. Behaviour of this type is a particular manifestation of the avoidance coping mechanisms that stigmatized individuals use to protect individual self-esteem (see section 4). Such groups can range from the classic examples that are prone to stigmatization and discriminatory behaviour (e.g. racial, religious, sexual orientation, age) to more specific groups that only arise in certain healthcare contexts. This latter group might include individuals who choose to lead unusual lifestyles, individuals that utilize alternative forms of medicine and a host of others. Whatever the group in question, individuals that form part of these groups can feel that in attempting to obtain healthcare they are the subject of stigmatization.[192] Black individuals in the US (who often perceive themselves to have a lower socioeconomic status) are slower to seek treatment, for example, than their white peers, even in conditions where such treatment is equally available. It has been argued this is because they feel they are more likely to be judged responsible for their condition as a result of irresponsible behaviour than their white peers.[193] The same logic also applies to

187 Courtwright, "Justice, Stigma, and the New Epidemiology of Health Disparities". p92

188 This concept of the power of relative social positioning to directly induce health problems has also been used to explain why more equal societies do better in terms of health outcomes in the book *The Spirit Level*. See R Wilkinson and K Pickett, *The Spirit Level: Why Equality Is Better for Everyone* (New York: Bloomsbury Press, 2010).

189 Marmot, *The Status Syndrome: How Social Standing Affects Our Health and Longevity*.

190 Wilkinson and Pickett, *The Spirit Level: Why Equality Is Better for Everyone*.

191 H Deacon, "Towards a Sustainable Theory of Health-Related Stigma: Lessons from the HIV/Aids Literature", *Journal of Community & Applied Social Psychology* 16 (2006).

192 M Gornik, "Disparities in Medicare Services: Potential Causes, Plausible Explanations, and Recommendations", *Health Care Financing Review* 21, no. 4 (2000).

193 Chesney, "Critical Delays in HIV Testing and Care".

other groups who feel that the fact they belong to an already stigmatized group might be used in order to attribute blame to them for having contracted their condition. This may explain why homosexual and intravenous drug injecting individuals are slower to be tested and seek treatment for HIV than heterosexual individuals or individuals who have contracted the virus through a blood transfusion.[194] The initial poor response of society and public health planners to the emergence of HIV in the 1980s has been described as a classic example of the devastation unnecessary stigmatization can bring about. Unnecessary stigmatization in that situation has been blamed for driving the condition underground and aggravating the spread of the disease.[195] As a consequence it is extremely important for public individuals to be aware of the potentially devastating effects that both intentional and unintentional stigmatization can have on individuals, groups and even the whole of society. Individuals in the black community in the US, for example, often have mistrustful attitudes towards public service providers, including healthcare providers that are offering potential vaccination services.[196] The same logic may also apply to individuals in poor socioeconomic subgroups such as certain immigrant groups. Individuals in such subgroups may have a more fatalistic attitude towards health issues than those who come from more advantaged subgroups and who, as a consequence, have been more used to securing beneficial healthcare in the past. Given the difficulty in tackling such issues once they exist, it is extremely important that public entities avoid creating or cementing such problems by stigmatizing groups inadvertently, including through SSEs.[197] This unfortunately is something that (as Chapter 1 illustrated) is not always the case.

(ii) A reduced general motivation to seek the necessary goods in life

Individuals that are the subjects of stigmatization often possess a lesser motivation to secure the important resources (or goods) needed to have a successful life. This lesser motivation stems from the negative experiences such individuals (or members of their cohort) have had in attempting to secure such goods in the past.[198] This produces a desire to avoid similar negative and judgemental responses in the future. This can manifest itself, not only in a reduced desire to socialize with potential 'stigmatizers' but, also, in a reduced desire to secure important resources such as public services which are supposed to be available to all on an equal basis.

194 Scambler, "'Sociology, Social Structure and Health-Related Stigma", *Psychology, Health & Medicine*, 11, 3 (2006.

195 J Mann, "Health and Human Rights: If Not Now, When?", *Health and Human Rights* 2, no. 3 (2007).

196 Chesney, "Critical Delays in HIV Testing and Care". p35

197 Pre-stigmatized groups have, for instance, been shown to be at an increased risk of stigmatization during public health crisis such as epidemics. See R Goodwin et al., "Initial Psychological Responses to Influenza A, H1N1 ('Swine Flu')", *BMC Infectious Diseases* 9 (2009).

198 Gornik, "Disparities in Medicare Services: Potential Causes, Plausible Explanations, and Recommendations".

This can include aspects such as education, healthcare and employment opportunities.[199] This reduced motivation means that stigmatized groups will secure fewer of the resources in life that are needed than those groups that are not stigmatized, often meaning they have a lower standard of living than non-stigmatized groups.

This can produce a consequent reduction in health status for such individuals and also entrench social and economic inequalities.[200] This concept, whereby an individual lowers his or her expectations in life as a result of his or her social position in society has been termed 'adaptive preferences' in economics.[201] Individuals from stigmatized groups often demand (and therefore receive) lower levels of public services and other goods than their non-stigmatized peers. This is an important factor that may help in explaining why, even in societies that create systems of equal access to public services (e.g. healthcare or education), one does not always see the same levels of utilization for the various groups that make up that society. It also demonstrates why anti-discrimination approaches (i.e. in terms of access) are unlikely by themselves to be sufficient to deal with the problems of access faced by vulnerable groups.[202] This will be discussed further from the perspective of SSEs in Chapter 5.

(iii) Negative effects on a society's democratic vitality

The preservation of the pluralistic character of societies is often regarded as an element of essential importance in the health of a democracy. Such pluralism depends on the ability of individuals to live their own version of the 'good life', free (as much as is possible) from unwanted steering from outside forces.[203] In order to do this, individuals need to have 'self-respect', a concept that represents the power to resist outside forces and opinions and to pursue one's own conception of the good life.[204] Stigmatization is capable of corroding individual self-respect and is therefore damaging to the ability of individuals to live their desired life (the relationship between, self-respect and self-esteem will be discussed in more depth in Chapter 3).[205] Given that stigmatization may prevent people from living their preferred lifestyle choice unchecked, stigmatization may result in a

199 Courtwright, "Justice, Stigma, and the New Epidemiology of Health Disparities".

200 Ibid. p92 This is also something the author discusses in: P. Quinn, "Crisis Communication in Public Health Emergencies: The Limits of 'Legal Control' and the Risks for Harmful Outcomes in a Digital Age", *Life Sciences, Society and Policy* 14, no. 1 (2018).

201 See, for example, J Elster, *Sour Grapes: Studies in the Subversion of Rationality* (Cambridge: Cambridge University Press, 1985).

202 Quinn, "The Problem of Stigmatizing Expressions – the Limits of Anti-Discrimination Approaches".

203 S Gutwirth, *Privacy and the Information Age* (New York: Rowman & Littlefield, 2002).

204 J Rawls, *A Theory of Justice. Revised Edition* (Cambridge, MA: Harvard University Press, 1999). p155

205 J Rawls, *A Theory of Justice* (Cambridge, MA: Harvard Press, 1971). p386 Rawls describes the importance of self-respect in preserving an individual's ability to pursue his or her desired path in life.

reduction in societal plurality.[206] This may especially be the case where lifestyles or ideas that are marginal and outside of the mainstream are the subject of stigmatization. Given that (as was discussed in section 4 above) one common coping response to stigmatization is to 'pass', i.e. to hide the stigmatized trait in question, there is the possibility that certain people will opt to pass in order to give the impression of having a mainstream lifestyle or culture.[207] Where this occurs on a macro scale the result can be that certain groups feel pressured into seeming to prefer the ideas or lifestyle choices of the mainstream or the majority in society. Such behaviour was a near universal occurrence in the past for members of the gay community.[208]

7 Conclusion

Stigmatization is a complex and multifaceted phenomenon. The concept only began to attract serious academic study in the second half of the twentieth century, with the work of Goffman. Since then, research on matters of stigmatization have expanded into various domains. Research into the psychological processes that occur in individuals (by far the most expansive concerning the phenomenon) who are being stigmatized (or sometimes who stigmatize) allows the harm that has been experienced by stigmatization on an individual or micro level to be visualized. In addition to this, attempts to understand the effects of stigmatization in sociological terms have improved the understanding of how the phenomenon can manifest itself on a macro level allowing the potential effects at the societal level to be visualized. An appreciation of this harm (i.e. on both on the micro and macro levels) is important in order to develop a normative position on the use of SSEs (as will occur in Chapter 3) and to look at the ability of the law in its various guises to meet this normative approach (Chapters 4–7). In particular, this chapter has looked at aspects of stigmatization that are relevant to this book. They include the following effects.

(i) The negative effects of stigmatization

In terms of individual effects, these can include a reduction in self-esteem, the internalization of the negative opinions of others and the deployment of a range of coping mechanisms. All of these can have negative effects on individuals. These can range from stress and anxiety (on an acute]or chronic basis), to hiding aspects of oneself that are thought to be stigmatized and even acceptance that one is of lower value as a result of the stigmatized trait that one possesses (i.e. internalization). On the macro scale these effects can accumulate to produce problems for groups that are the target of stigmatization, especially those that are in an already vulnerable and marginalized position. These include problems in terms of

206 Quinn and De Hert, "Self Respect—a 'Rawlsian Primary Good' Unprotected by the European Convention on Human Rights and Its Lack of a Coherent Approach to Stigmatization?" p28

207 For more on passing see section 1 and the discussion concerning the ideas of Goffman.

208 S Siedman, *Beyond the Closet: The Transformation of Gay and Lesbian Life* (New York: Psychology Press, 2002). p38

healthcare avoidance, a reduced desire to seek the necessary goods that one may require in order to prosper (e.g. education, employment, etc.) and also a potential reduction in societal plurality (with negative consequences for the democratic vitality of the society in question).

(ii) The importance of beliefs/stereotypes to the process of stigmatization

In terms of contributory factors there are both 'affective' and 'cognitive' aspects. Affective aspects of stigmatization relate to lower level impulsive urges to negatively think of or react to individuals who for one reason or another may be stigmatized. Such sentiments could include feelings of disgust, fear, hatred, ambivalence, etc. Human behaviour is also however influenced by higher level cognitive impulses. It is through such processes that knowledge, experiences and beliefs are able to impact upon the manifestation of stigmatization. Whilst such processes can be used to accentuate potentially stigmatizing responses, they can also be used to temper them. The ability of experiences and beliefs to influence the manifestation of stigmatization means that it is therefore important to consider the role of those who have a role at a societal level to influence or formulate such beliefs, including through SSES. In modern societies this includes the state and individuals connected to it. As Chapter 3 will discuss, such individuals and institutions have a prominent role to play in influencing the attitudes and beliefs of society, including towards groups that may be vulnerable to stigmatization.

(iii) Aspects of stigma that may be problematic for the law

The recognition of stigmatization as a phenomenon and its engagement by the law may not be straightforward given some of the properties that define it. It is closely linked to other similar concepts such as discrimination and stereotyping. It has a number of properties however that raise questions about the ability of legal approaches to recognize the harm it might produce or to provide redress for them.

First, it can be differentiated on a number of aspects, of which the most important is that stigmatization is defined by its ability to induce particular psychological states in the mind of the target. This central aspect of stigmatization, i.e. the induction of psychological changes, is not something that is often the focus of legal approaches. As Chapter 5 will discuss, this may, for example, be the case with anti-discrimination approaches which often focus upon (and require) the presence of treatment (i.e. an action that imposes binding changes), something that is not necessary in incidences of stigmatization which can be triggered merely by the perception (accurate or not) that others hold negative views concerning oneself.[209] This lack of a requirement for treatment was illustrated repeatedly in Chapter 1 which highlighted numerous examples of SSEs that are capable of stigmatizing without imposing any binding effects on individuals.

209 A similar problem also exists concerning the potential application of administrative law approaches (discussed in Chapter 6) and privacy approaches (discussed in Chapter 7).

Second, the way in which individuals react to stigmatization is also extremely subjective. This means that it is not possible to speak of uniform harm that is experienced by all individuals in a stigmatized group. This may make it difficult for legal approaches that depend upon establishing that objective harm has been experienced by individuals. This will be illustrated further in Chapter 5 with the example of administrative law which often depends upon the imposition of binding changes (usually in terms of legal rights or obligations) upon individuals in order to be able to challenge acts by public bodies.

Third, stigmatization does not require intent on the part of stigmatizing individuals. Such individuals may, as this chapter has shown, stigmatize unintentionally (or may even be mistaken for having stigmatizing opinions). This is likely to create problems for legal approaches that depend upon establishing intent, e.g. criminal law approaches to hate speech (discussed in Chapter 4). Further problems are created by the sheer variety of expressions that may be considered stigmatizing. This can include relatively mild and seemingly innocuous gestures. Whilst such expressions can be responsible for stigmatization they may often fall far below the definition of what may be considered hate speech.

Bibliography

Andersen, S, and R Klatzky. "Traits and Social Stereotypes: Levels of Categorization in Person Perception." *Journal of Personality and Social Psychology* 53, no. 2 (1987): 235–246.

Baker, G, J Brooks, D Buck, and A Jacoby. "The Stigma of Epilepsy: A European Perspective." *Epilepsia* 41, no. 1 (1999): 98–104.

Bayer, R. "Stigma and the Ethics of Public Health: Not Can We but Should We." *Social Science & Medicine* 67 (2008): 463–472.

Bertand, J, K O'Reilly, J Denison, R Anhang, and M Sweat. "Systematic Review of the Effectiveness of Mass Communication Programs to Change HIV/Aids Related Behaviors in Developing Countries." *Health Education Research Theory & Practice* 21, no. 4 (2006): 567–597.

Biernat, M, and J Dovidio. "Stigma and Stereotypes." In *The Social Psychology of Stigma*, edited by T Heatherton, R Kleck, M Hebl and J Hull, 88–125. New York: Guilford Press, 2000.

Brohan, E, M Slade, S Clement, and G Thornicroft. "Experiences of Mental Illness Stigma, Prejudice and Discrimination: A Review of Measures." *BMC Health Services Research* 10 (2010): 80–92.

Broom, D, and A Whittaker. "Controlling Diabetes, Controlling Diabetics: Moral Language in the Management of Diabetes Type 2." *Social Science & Medicine* 58 (2004): 2371–2382.

Brown, L. *New Shorter Oxford Dictionary*. Oxford: Oxford University Press, 1993.

Burris, S. "Disease Stigma in U.S. Public Law." *Journal of Law, Medicine and Ethics* 30 (2002): 179–190.

Byrne, D. *Social Exclusion*. Buckingham: McGraw-Hill Education, 2005.

Byrne, P. "Stigma of Mental Illness and Ways of Diminishing It." *Advances in Psychiatric Treatment* 6 (2000): 65–72.

Cahill, E, and REggleston. "Reconsidering the Stigma of Physical Disability: Wheelchair Use and Public Kindness." *The Sociological Quarterly* 36, no. 4 (1995): 681–698.

Camp, D, W Finlay, and E Lyons. "Is Low Self-Esteem an Inevitable Consequence of Stigma? An Example from Women with Chronic Mental Health Problems." *Social Science & Medicine* 55 (2002): 823–834.

Chesney, M. "Critical Delays in HIV Testing and Care." *American Behavioural Scientist* 42, no. 7 (1999): 1162–1174.

Courtwright, A. "Justice, Stigma, and the New Epidemiology of Health Disparities." *Bioethics* 23, no. 2 (2009): 90–96.

Crandall, C, and D Moriarty. "Physical Illness Stigma and Social Rejection." *British Journal of Social Psychology* 34 (1995): 67–83.

Crocker, J. "Social Stigma and Self-Esteem: Situational Construction of Self Worth." *Journal of Experimental Social Psychology* 35 (1999): 89–107.

Crocker, J, and B Major. "Social Stigma and Self-Esteem: The Self-Protective Properties of Stigma." *Psychological Review* 96, no. 4 (1989): 608–630.

Crocker, J, and B Major. "Reactions to Stigma: The Moderating Effect of Justifications." In *The Psychology of Prejudice: The Ontario Symposium, Vol 7*, edited by M Zanna and J Olson, 289–314. Hillsdale, NJ: Erlbaum, 1994.

Crocker, J, B Major, and C Steel. "Social Stigma." In *Handbook of Social Psychology*, edited by D Gilbert, S Fiske and G Lindzey, 504–553. Boston: McGraw-Hill, 1998.

Deacon, H. "Towards a Sustainable Theory of Health-Related Stigma: Lessons from the Hiv/Aids Literature." *Journal of Community & Applied Social Psychology* 16 (2006): 418–425.

Deacon, H, and I Stephney. *HIV/Aids, Stigma and Children. A Literature Review*. Cape Town: HSRC Press, 2007.

Deal, M. "Aversive Disablism: Subtle Prejudice toward Disabled People." *Disability & Society* 22 (2007): 93–107.

Dean, J, and F Rud. "The Drug Addict and the Stigma of Addiction." *Substance Use & Misuse* 19, no. 8 (1984): 859–869.

Dovidio, J, B Major, and J Crocker. "Stigma: Introduction and Overview." In *The Social Psychology of Stigma*, edited by T Heatherton, R Kleck, M Hebl and J Hull, 1–30. New York: Guilford Press, 2000.

Durkheim, E. *Rules of a Sociological Method*. The Free Press, 1895.

Elster, J. *Sour Grapes: Studies in the Subversion of Rationality*. Cambridge: Cambridge University Press, 1985.

Ganzevoort, R. "Scars and Stigma: Trauma, Identity and Theology." *Practical Theology* 1, no. 1 (2008): 19–31.

Goffman, E. *The Presentation of Self in Everyday Life*. Garden City, NY: Doubleday Anchor Books, 1959.

Goffman, I. *Stigma: Notes on a Spoilt Identity*. Englewood Cliffs, NJ: Prentice Hall, 1963.

Goodhall, J. "Social Rejection, Exclusion and Shunning among the Gombe Chimpanzees." *Ethology and Sociobiology* 7 (1986): 227–236.

Goodin, R. *Protecting the Vulnerable: A Reanalysis of Our Social Responsibilities*. Chicago: The University of Chicago Press, 1985.

Goodwin, R, S Haque, F Neto, and L Meyers. "Initial Psychological Responses to Influenza A, H1N1 ('Swine Flu')." *BMC Infectious Diseases* 9 (2009) doi:10.1186/1471-2334-9-166

Gornik, M. "Disparities in Medicare Services: Potential Causes, Plausible Explanations, and Recommendations." *Health Care Financing Review* 21, no. 4 (2000): 23–43.

Gutwirth, S. *Privacy and the Information Age*. New York: Rowman & Littlefield, 2002.

Hamilton, D, and S Sherman. "Perceiving Persons and Groups." *Psychological Review* 103 (1996): 336–355.

Hebl, M, M Tickle, and T Heatherton. "Awkward Moments in Interactions between Non-stigmatized and Stigmatized Individuals." In *The Social Psychology of Stigma*, edited by T Heatherton, R Kleck, M Hebl and J Hull, 275–306. New York: Guilford Press, 2000.

Heijnders, M, and S Van Der Meij. "The Fight against Stigma: An Overview of Stigma-Reduction Strategies and Interventions." *Psychology, Health & Medicine* 11, no. 3 (2006): 353–363.

Hsin, Klienman, Link, Lee, and Good. "Culture and Stigma; Adding Moral Experience to Stigma Theory." *Social Science & Medicine* 64 (2007): 1524–1535.

Joachim, G. "Stigma of Visible and Invisible Chronic Conditions." *Journal of Advanced Nursing* 32, no. 1 (2000): 243–248.

Jones, C. "Tattooing and Branding in Graeco-Roman Antiquity." *The Journal of Roman Studies* 77 (1987): 139–155.

Jones, E, A Farina, A Hastorf, H Markus, D Miller, and R Scott. *Social Stigma. The Psychology of Marked Relationships*. New York: W.H. Freeman and Company, 1984.

Katz, I. *Stigma: A Social-Psychological Perspective*. Hillsdale, NJ: Erlbaum, 1981.

Kleck, R, and A Stretna. "Perceptions of the Impact of Negatively Valued Physical Characteristics on Social Interactions." *Journal of Personality and Social Psychology* 39 (1980): 861–873.

W Koschnick, *Standard Dictionary of the Social Sciences*. Munich: K. G. Saur, 1993.

Kumar, A, L Hessini, and E Mitchell. "Conceptualising Abortion Stigma." *Culture Health and Sexuality* 11, 6 (2009): 1–15.

Kurzban, R, and M Leary. "Evolutionary Origins of Stigmatization: The Functions of Social Exclusion." *Psychological Bulletin* 127, no. 2 (2001): 187–208.

Leary, K. "Passing, Posing and "Keeping It Real." *Constellations* 6, no. 1 (1999): 85–96.

Leary, M, E Tambor, S Terdal, and D Downs. "Self-Esteem as an Interpersonal Monitor: The Sociometer Hypothesis." *Journal of Personality and Social Psychology* 68, no. 3 (1995): 518–530.

Lewis, S, S Thomas, J Hyde, D Castle, R Warwick, and P Komesaroff. "'I Don't Eat a Hamburger and Large Chips Every Day!' A Qualitative Study of the Impact of Public Health Messages About Obesity in Obese Adults." *BMC Public Health* 10 (2010): 309–318.

Link, B, and J Phelan. "Conceptualizing Stigma." *Annual Review of Sociology* 27 (2001): 363–385.

Link, B, and J Phelan. "Stigma and Its Public Health Implications." *The Lancet* 367 (2006): 528–529.

Major, B, and T Schmader. "Coping with Stigma through Psychological Disengagement." In *Prejudice: The Target's Perspective*, edited by J Swim, L Chohen and L Hyers, 37–60. San Diego: Academic Press, 1998.

Major, B, S Spencer, T Schmader, C Wolfe, and J Crocker. "Coping with Negative Stereotypes About Intellectual Performance: The Role of Psychological Disengagement." *Personality and Social Psychology Bulletin* 24, no. 1 (1998): 34–50.

Mann, J. "Health and Human Rights: If Not Now, When." *Health and Human Rights* 2, no. 3 (2007): 113–120.

Marmot, M. *The Status Syndrome: How Social Standing Affects Our Health and Longevity*. New York: NY Times Books, 2004.

Marx, K.*Ideology. Part I: Feuerbach. Opposition of the Materialist and Idealist Outlook*. (1848).

Mégret, F. "Law and Contemporary Problems." *Practices of Stigmatization* 76, nos 3 and 4 (2013): 287–318.

Miller, C, and C Kaiser. "A Theoretical Perspective on Coping with Stigma." *Journal of Social Issues* 57, no. 1 (2001): 73–92.

Miller, C, and B Major. "Coping with Stigma and Prejudice." In *The Social Psychology of Stigmatisation*, edited by T Heatherton, R Kleck, M Hebl and J Hull, 243–272 New York: Guilford Press, 2000.

Molm, L, N Takahashi, and G Peterson. "Risk and Trust in Social Exchange: An Experimental Test of a Classical Proposition." *American Journal of Sociology* 105, no. 5 (2000): 1396–1427.

Neuberg, S, D Smith, and T Asher. "Why Do People Stigmatise: Toward a Biocultural Framework." In *The Social Psychology of Stigma*, edited by T Heatherton, R Kleck, M Hebl and J Hull, 31–61. New York: Guilford Press, 2000.

O'Connell, R. "Cinderella Comes to the Ball: Art 14 and the Right to Non-Discrimination in the ECHR." *Legal Studies* 29, no. 2 (2009): 211–229.

Oliver, M. *The Politics of Disablement*. Basingstoke: Macmillan, 1992.

Orwell, G. *The Road to Wigan Pier*. London: Houghton Mifflin Harcourt, 1972.

Parker, R, and P Aggleton. "HIV and Aids-Related Stigma and Discrimination: A Conceptual Framework and Implications for Action." *Social Science & Medicine* 57, no. 1 (2003): 13–24.

Phelan, J, B Link, and J Dovidio. "Stigma and Prejudice: One Animal or Two?" *Social Science & Medicine* 67 (2008): 358–367.

Quinn, P. "The Problem of Stigmatizing Expressions -the Limits of Anti-Discrimination Approaches." *International Journal of Discrimination and the Law* 17, no. 1 (2017): 23–50.

Quinn, P, and P De Hert. "Self Respect—a "Rawlsian Primary Good" Unprotected by the European Convention on Human Rights and Its Lack of a Coherent Approach to Stigmatization?" *The International Journal of Discrimination and the Law* 14 (2014): 19–53.

Quinn, P. "Crisis Communication in Public Health Emergencies: The Limits of 'Legal Control' and the Risks for Harmful Outcomes in a Digital Age." *Life Sciences, Society and Policy* 14, no. 1 (6 Feb. 2018). doi: doi:10.1186/s40504-018-0067-0

Rawls, J. *A Theory of Justice*. Cambridge, MA: Harvard Press, 1971.

Rawls, J. *A Theory of Justice. Revised Edition*. Cambridge, MA: Harvard University Press, 1999.

Reidpath, D, and K Chan. "HIV, Stigma, and Rates of Infection: A Rumour without Evidence." *PLOS Medicine* 3, no. 10 (2006): 1708–1710.

Reidpath, D, K Chan, S Gifford, and P Allotey. "'He Hath the French Pox': Stigma, Social Value and Social Exclusion." *Sociology of Health & Illness* 27, no. 4 (2005): 468–489.

Sayce, L. "Social Inclusion and Mental Health." *Psychiatric Bulletin* 25, no. 4 (2001): 121–123.

Sayce, L. "Stigma, Discrimination and Social Exclusion: What's in a Word?" *Journal of Mental Health* 7, no. 4 (1998): 331.

Scambler, G. "Health-Related Stigma." *Sociology of Health & Illness* 31, no. 3 (2009): 441–455.

Segerstrale, U. *Defenders of the Truth: The Battle for Science in the Sociology Debate and Beyond*. Oxford: Oxford University Press, 2001.

Siedman, S. *Beyond the Closet: The Transformation of Gay and Lesbian Life*. New York: Psychology Press, 2002.

Simon, A. "The Relationship between Stereotypes of and Attitudes toward Lesbians and Gays." In *Stigma and Sexual Orientation: Understanding Prejudice against Lesbians, Gay Men, and Bisexuals. Psychological Perspectives on Lesbian and Gay Issues*, edited by G Herek, 62–81. Thousand Oaks, CA: Sage Publications, 1998.

Solanke, I. *Discrimination as Stigma*. Oxford: Hart, 2017.

Stangor, C. "Overview." In *Stereotypes and Prejudice: Essential Readings*, edited by C Stangor. Philadelphia, PA: Psychology Press, 2000.

Steele, C, and J Aronson. "Stereotype Threat and the Intellectual Test Performance of African Americans." *Journal of Personality and Social Psychology* 69 (1995): 797–811.

Stefan, S. "'Discredited' and 'Discreditable:' The Search for Political Identity by People with Psychiatric Diagnoses." *William and Mary Law Review* 44, no. 9 (2003): 1341–1383.

Stevenson, H, J Derek McNeil, T Herrero-Taylor, and G Davis. "Influence of Perceived Neighborhood Diversity and Racism Experience on the Racial Socialization of Black Youth." *The Journal of Black Psychology* 31, no. 3 (2005): 273–290.

Tierney, A. "The Evolution of Learned and Innate Behavior: Contributions from Genetics and Neurobiology to a Theory of Behavioural Evolution." *Animal Learning and Behaviour* 14, no. 4 (1986): 339–348.

Timmer, A. "Toward an Anti-Stereotyping Approach for the European Court of Human Rights." *Human Rights Law Review* 11, no. 4 (2011): 707–738.

Trivers, R. *Social Evolution*. Menlo Park, CA: The Benjamin/Cummings Publishing Company, 1985.

Weiner, B, R Perry, and J Magnuson. "An Attributional Analysis of Reactions to Stigmas." *Journal of Personality and Social Psychology* 55 (1988): 738–7448.

Wilkinson, R, and K Pickett. *The Spirit Level: Why Equality Is Better for Everyone*. New York: Bloomsbury Press, 2010.

Wright, B. *Physical Disability: A Psychological Approach*. New York: Harper, 1983.

3 Developing a normative approach towards the use of stigmatizing state expressions

1 Introduction

> Justice is the first virtue of social institutions, as truth is of systems of thought.
>
> John Rawls[1]

This chapter attempts to develop a normative argument for when it is acceptable for a state to use stigmatizing state expressions (SSEs). In doing so it will make use of the concept of self-respect, which is found in a number of moral and philosophical theories on how a just society should be organized. The author of this book will discuss the link between this concept and the potential negative effects of stigmatization such as harm to self–esteem and internalization that were discussed in Chapter 2. This allows the formulation of a number of normative principles which the author will argue can be used to analyse whether laws and legal systems are capable of protecting individual self-respect as one might expect in a just society.

As section 2 will show, the concept of self-respect has been linked to stigmatization as a factor that can allow one to resist the phenomenon and its associated negative effects. Rawls considered the ability of self-respect to allow individuals to resist outside forces and opinions so important that he termed it the "most important primary good" (section 3). As section 4 will show, the importance of self-respect is also associated with a number of other legal theorists such as Sen and Nussbaum. The weight such thinkers give to the possession of self-respect is important in the context of this book because, as section 5 will discuss, it has an important relationship with the concept of self-esteem, a term that is commonly used in literature on stigmatization when discussing the negative effects that the phenomenon can bring about. This relationship means that legal theories that relate to the need to support self-respect will have important implications for the use of stigmatizing expressions by the state (discussed in section 6). Rawls attributed a particularly important role to the state in terms of showing equal respect to the various conceptions of 'the good' that exist in society, i.e. amongst the various religious, moral and philosophical persuasions that exist in life. This, taken

1 J Rawls, *A Theory of Justice* (Cambridge, MA: Harvard Press, 1971).

together with Rawls's concept of 'lexical priority' (which the author will argue allows the state to stigmatize in certain contexts, e.g. to protect the rights of others) means that a state should only criticize individual conceptions of the good in certain limited circumstances (discussed in section 6 and 7). This allows a number of normative principles concerning the use of SSEs to be formulated (sections 8–13).

2 Stigmatization as a force capable of harming individual self-respect

The preservation of the pluralistic character of societies is often regarded as an element of essential importance in the health of a democracy. Such pluralism depends *inter alia* on the ability of individuals to live their own version of the good life, free (as much as possible) from unwanted steering from outside forces.[2] In order to do this, individuals need to have self-respect, a concept that represents the power to resist outside forces and opinions.[3] The concept of self-respect has been linked to stigmatization by describing self-respect as something that allows individuals to 'resist' stigmatizing forces and lead their lives in the manner in which they would wish.[4] In what can represent a symbiotic relationship, self-respect has also been described as something that can be harmed by damage to self-esteem,[5] which can be caused *inter alia* by stigmatization.[6] This ability to connect the concept of self-respect to the harmful effects that stigmatization can bring about, through harm to self-esteem, negative coping mechanisms or internalization (see Chapter 3 for a description of these) is significant because the protection of individual self-respect is important to a number of theories concerning the organization of society on a just basis.[7]

Stigmatization and self-respect are related in two ways. First, self-respect is a concept that allows individuals to resist the forces of stigmatization, i.e. to continue to value themselves and their ideas as being valid, despite outside criticism. Second, as Courtwright argues, stigmatization can itself, under certain

2 S Gutwirth, *Privacy and the Information Age* (Lanham, MD, Boulder, CO, New York and Oxford: Rowman & Littlefield Publishers, 2002).

3 Rawls, *A Theory of Justice* (Cambridge, MA: Harvard University Press, 1999), p155 Rawls states, "A sense of their own worth is necessary if they are to pursue their conception of the good with satisfaction and to take pleasure in its fulfilment. Self-respect is not so much a part of any rational plan of life as the sense that one's plan is worth carrying out."

4 A Courtwright, "Justice, Stigma, and the New Epidemiology of Health Disparities", *Bioethics* 23, no. 2 (2009). p94

5 M Leary et al., "Self-Esteem as an Interpersonal Monitor: The Sociometer Hypothesis", *Journal of Personality and Social Psychology* 68, no. 3 (1995).

6 D Camp, W Finlay, and E Lyons, "Is Low Self-Esteem an Inevitable Consequence of Stigma? An Example from Women with Chronic Mental Health Problems", *Social Science & Medicine* 55 (2002). See also Chapter 2, section 4 for a description of the effects of stigmatization on self-esteem.

7 C Stark, "Rawlsian Self-Respect", in *Oxford Studies in Normative Ethics*, ed. M Timmons (Oxford: Oxford University Press, 2012). Rawls saw the two concepts (i.e. self-respect and self-esteem) as being so interconnected that he often used the terms interchangeably.

circumstances, harm an individual's self-respect.[8] Roland and Foxx, for instance, suggested that severe stigmatization is capable of harming individual self-respect.[9] Self-respect can therefore act as a buttress to stigmatizing forces allowing individuals to resist them, but in certain instances where the stigmatization is severe enough it is able to damage self-esteem. There is thus an important need to foster self-respect in society. As the author will illustrate in this chapter this includes considering the permissibility of negative stigmatizing statements by the state. The notion of self-respect and the ability of societies to foster it within individuals is an important concept in a number of theories concerning the just organization of societies and consequently the legal institutions regulating them (see section 3). The following section will commence with a focus on Rawls' notion of self-respect given his extensive writings on the subject and the centrality of the concept to his *Theory of Justice* and subsequent works.

3 Rawls – self-respect as the primary social good

A Rawls' principles of justice

In *A Theory of Justice*, [10] Rawls aimed to create principles that he felt would form the foundations of a just society.[11] For Rawls, fairness was the foundational principle behind what should constitute justice. At the heart of his vision was the notion that all individuals should be treated equally and be shown equal respect by the state. Rawls reasoned this through the use of a theoretical concept of 'the original position'. This original position was to be constructed behind a supposed veil of ignorance.[12] Under such a concept the individuals choosing the rules that would be applied to the society in which they would live would not know the position they would occupy in such a society or the personal properties they might possess. Free of such encumbrances, Rawls argued individuals would be able to act in a rational manner in deciding what would be the best principles by which a society would be run. They would also have a rational interest in ensuring that the lowliest individuals were treated in a fair and just manner (for there is every chance that they too would occupy such a position). Rawls postulated that, acting from such a position, rational individuals would be able to agree on two key principles that would ensure that a society would be fair.[13] These principles are:[14]

8 Courtwright, "Justice, Stigma, and the New Epidemiology of Health Disparities", pp94–95
9 C Roland and R Foxx, "Self-Respect: A Neglected Concept," *Philosophical Psychology* 16 (2003).
10 Rawls, *A Theory of Justice*.
11 P Lehning, *John Rawls: An Introduction* (Cambridge: Cambridge University Press, 2006). See preface.
12 Rawls, *A Theory of Justice*. p118
13 N Daniels, "Democratic Equality: Rawls' Complex Egalitarianism", in *The Cambridge Companion to Rawls*, ed. S Freeman (Cambridge: Cambridge University Press, 2002).
14 Rawls, *A Theory of Justice*. p53

1 Each person is to have an equal right to the most extensive scheme of equal basic liberties compatible with a similar scheme of liberties for others;
2 Social and economic inequalities are to be arranged so that they are both (a) reasonably expected to be to everyone's advantage, and (b) attached to positions and offices open to all.

Rawls therefore theorized that there were two categories of benefits that would need to be regulated in order to allow a just society. These were liberties (described in point 1) and goods (described in point 2). Liberties, according to Rawls, must be protected for everyone to the same extent. Inequality in terms of personal liberties may not be permitted in a just society. Rawls described liberties as taking the following form: "this or that person (or persons) is free (or not free) from this or that constraint (or set of constraints) to do (or not to do) so and so on".[15] Rawls stated that in terms of constraints, the protection of liberties may "range from duties and prohibitions as defined by law to the coercive indulgences arising from public opinion and social pressure". Rawls envisaged that liberties would be protected by law, to the same extent for all, whether rich or poor, old or young, strong or weak. Such liberties can be thought of as corresponding to the legal rights that individuals possess according to laws and constitutions. Such rights cannot (according to Rawls) be removed or interfered with unless it is to protect the rights of another.

Rawls' second rule does not relate to personal liberties but to social and economic goods. Unlike rights and liberties, Rawls supposed that rational individuals, might from their original position, behind a "veil of ignorance" agree that social and economic goods might not be provided absolutely equally for everyone. Rawls subscribed to the idea that inequality in such aspects was permissible if such inequality was to the benefit of the least fortunate in society.[16] In this manner Rawls reasoned that inequality may be able to bring benefits to the least fortunate through the fruitful results of innovation of certain individuals This poses an essential condition that stipulates where and how inequality is permitted to exist. Where inequality of a particular good was not to the advantage of everybody, inequality should not, according to Rawls, be permitted. Given this, Rawls postulated that his second principle of justice would be the resultant rational conclusion. This rule would allow measures that would reduce the possession of such goods only if the goods of the least fortunate were not adversely affected. Rawls called this the 'difference principle'.[17] The other key part of the second principle is the notion of 'equal opportunity' (described in part (b) of point 2 above). This idea demands that all individuals in society should have the potential to improve their situation with regard to their possession of such goods. This means that whilst

15 Ibid. p177
16 Ibid. pp53, 266 This was because a system of absolute equality would be both impossible to achieve (especially for social aspects) and would prevent individuals from striving to fulfil their individual goals in life.
17 Ibid. p65

inequalities may be permitted (e.g. in wealth, property, etc.), individuals should have access to the possibility of improving the level of such goods they possess.

B Primary goods – self-respect as first amongst equals

At the core of Rawls's conception was the idea of 'primary goods'. These are the goods that everybody would require irrelevant of their aims and desires in life.[18] A greater level of possession of these goods translates into a greater chance of success in achieving one's aims, whatever they might be. In other words such goods correspond to the things that are needed to strive for any conceivable version of the 'good life'. Whilst Rawls could accept inequality of social goods in general, he reasoned that a course of action that resulted in a state of inequality in terms of a primary good could not be just. This distinction is important because it explains where and when a just society might allow inequalities in terms of a social good.[19]

Whilst there has been considerable debate amongst scholars about which items can be considered primary goods, Rawls did at least clearly outline what for him was the "most important primary good". This was the primary good of having a sense of one's own worth, also described as 'self-respect'.[20] Rawls considered self-respect to be so important as to amount to perhaps the most important primary good in life.[21] Self-respect is not so much a rational plan of life but rather the sense that one's plan of life, whatever it might be, is "worth carrying out". Without self-respect one may be plagued with failure and "self-doubt" and find it difficult to continue with one's endeavours as one might have otherwise wished. Without self-respect all desires and activities become futile aims, allowing one to sink into "apathy and cynicism".[22] Thus, self-respect for Rawls is something that all must possess if they are to be able to have any chance of striving for their own version of the good life, whatever that might be.

4 *Sen, Nussbaum and self-respect in terms of capability*

A Self-respect as an important capability

Rawls has not been the only legal philosopher to highlight the role of self-respect. Proposed alternative ideas also give a significance to the notion. Sen, for example, criticized Rawls' 'goods focused approach' as being too materialistic and focused on utility.[23] In particular he pointed to the concept of 'adaptive preferences' to

18 Ibid. p79

19 A Gibbard, "Disparate Goods and Rawls' Difference Principle: A Social Choice Theoretic Treatment", *Theory and Decision* 11 (1979). "Rawls's difference principle asserts that a basic economic structure is just if it makes the worst of people as well off as is feasible. How well off someone is is measured by an 'index' of 'primary goods'."

20 Rawls, *A Theory of Justice.* p387

21 Ibid. p348

22 Ibid. p386

23 A Sen, *Inequality Reexamined* (Cambridge, MA: Harvard University Press, 1995).

explain why utility can be a poor measure of justice in society. The concept of adaptive preferences has been used to explain why people who are in perceived lower positions in society often alter their expectations and desires as a result. A man from a slum in a poor country may, for example, feel privileged and contented because he has a mundane job that provides just enough to feed his family whereas an individual with the same level of intelligence but with a more privileged upbringing would likely not be so happy in finding himself in such a job.[24] The concept of adaptive preferences means one cannot measure whether a society is just simply by questioning people about their level of utility, i.e. are they living life the way they find gives them the greatest satisfaction? Such a measure according to Sen ignores the ability of the human mind to adjust his or her horizons and expectations to the position in which he or she finds him or herself in life. It therefore acts to preserve the status quo, even if unjust.[25] Sen proposed that rather than focusing on goods as Rawls does (i.e. wealth, level of education, etc.), it would be better to focus on 'capabilities'. His 'capabilities approach' accordingly looks at the possibilities that each individual has in society to achieve various things. According to Sen the presence of equal liberties as Rawls called for is necessary but is not sufficient. What is also required in a just society is to ask whether, given the material and social realities that are present, is it possible for an individual to do certain things, or to have certain capabilities as Sen puts it.[26] The benefits of such an approach can be demonstrated by a simple example. Imagine a country where under the constitution women are entitled to vote. This right becomes little more than a theoretical possibility if the prevailing social structures and attitudes that constitute a woman's living environment actively seek to prevent political engagement.[27]

Nussbaum has led a lengthy discussion on the works of Sen and has sought to build upon his effort.[28] She has compiled an extended list of capabilities that she sees as being omnipresent in terms of being required the world over in order to allow individuals to be able lead their version of the good life. Her work also retained a central place for self-respect. She states, for example, that one must be capable of "the social bases of self-respect and non-humiliation; being able to be treated as a dignified being whose worth is equal to that of others".[29] Thus, associating stigmatization with possible effects on individual self-respect allows the concept to be discussed in light of not only the ideas of Rawls (as Courtwright proposes),[30] but also others such as Sen and Nussbaum who propose alternative approaches for the creation of just societies.

24 For a good description of adaptive preferences see J Elster, *Sour Grapes: Studies in the Subversion of Rationality* (Cambridge: Cambridge University Press, 1985).
25 M Nussbaum, "Capabilities as Fundamental Entitlements: Sen and Social Justice", *Feminist Economics* 9, nos 2–3 (2003). p34
26 A Sen, *Equality of What? The Tanner Lecture on Human Values* (Cambridge: Cambridge University Press, 1980). p205
27 Nussbaum, "Capabilities as Fundamental Entitlements: Sen and Social Justice". p38
28 A Sen, *Inequality Rexamined* (Cambridge, MA: Harvard University Press, 1973). p39
29 Nussbaum, "Capabilities as Fundamental Entitlements: Sen and Social Justice". p42
30 Courtwright, "Justice, Stigma, and the New Epidemiology of Health Disparities".

This arguably demonstrates a potential support for the control of stigmatization caused by the state from a variety of different (and even opposing) moral theories concerned with the just arrangement of society.

B Objective and subjective conceptions of the good life both united in the importance to which they give self-respect

One can draw a distinction between conceptualizations of the good life, in terms of their objective or subjective approach, as described by Rawls on the one hand and Sen and Nussbaum on the other.[31] The first category subscribes to an almost completely subjective view of what constitutes the good life. Such a conception sees it as impossible to describe what activities a person must be able to perform in order to be capable of leading the 'good life' but rather interests itself in the availability of economic and social goods that may be needed to lead his or her version of the good life, whatever that might be. It is autonomy, together with a fair distribution of the goods in society, that allows individuals to select whatever version of the good life they wish. Thinkers such as Rawls usually focus on the procedural rules society operates under so as to ensure all individuals are treated (as far as possible) in the same fair manner by the state. Such neutrality constitutes an important way of promoting self-respect, because it allows individuals to see that they are valued as equal beings by the state.

This primarily subjective approach can however be contrasted with thinkers such as Sen and Nussbaum who subscribe to a concept of the good life that can, at least in part, be described objectively.[32] Such ideas rest on the notion that all humans share common capabilities that they must possess in order to be able to lead their version of the good life. Such capabilities must not be exactly specified but can refer to general concepts that, according to Sen and Nussbaum must be present for individuals to lead a fulfilling life. Such ideas convey the assumption that an individual must possess certain capabilities (i.e. he or she must be able to do certain things) in order to be able to lead his or her version of the good life whatever that is. For both thinkers one such capability is the capability of having self-respect.[33]

It is worth highlighting two points here that are very salient in terms of the need for self-respect and its fundamental importance in a just society. First, despite the different nature of the approaches of Rawls and Sen and Nussbaum, each holds self-respect as being a requisite for individuals to be able to struggle for their version of the good life.[34] Without it both sets of ideas see the good life as being unattainable. One can thus say that there is a certain unity amongst thinkers from both subjective and objective schools concerning the importance of self-respect in a

31 R Sugden, "Welfare, Resources, and Capabilities: A Review of Inequality Reexamined by Amartya Sen", *Journal of Economic Literature* 31 (1993).

32 Ibid. p1961

33 See Sen, *Inequality Rexamined*, p39 and Nussbaum, "Capabilities as Fundamental Entitlements: Sen and Social Justice". p42

34 D Clark, "Sen's Capability Approach and the Many Spaces of Human Well Being", *The Journal of Development Studies* 41, no. 8 (2005).

just society. Second, the fact that subjective based approaches (such as Rawls' approach) maintain the need for self-respect, is a remarkable testament to its general importance in a just society. This is because even in an otherwise subjectively based conception of the good life, where one holds that it is not possible to say what items an individual must possess or what acts he or she must be able to do in order to lead the good life, Rawls still feels it necessary to classify self-respect as being objectively required in all cases. Accordingly, Rawls places self-respect not only in the important category of 'primary goods', but states that it is perhaps the 'most important primary good'.[35] Thus one might go as far as saying that Rawls saw self-respect to be so important that he considered it to be objectively required in all instances.

5 The relationship between self-respect and self-esteem (harmed by stigma)

A Linking self-respect to self-esteem

The astute reader will probably have noticed an important semantic discrepancy in the tone of this chapter's discussion compared to that of the previous chapter. This chapter has focused thus far largely on the importance given to self-respect. However, if we look back to the second chapter, a large part of the discussion on the potential negative effects of stigmatization concerned the possible detrimental effects on self-esteem. It is therefore important to pose the question of whether the concepts of self-respect and self-esteem are indeed similar, related or even identical?

When making the link between stigmatization and self-respect, Courtwright treats the concepts as related, stating that self-respect can protect self-esteem.[36] An 'intuitive' understanding of the two terms might suggest that they are synonymous. The following section will attempt to establish the similarities, differences and relationship between the two. Doing this will allow the ideas generated by theorists such as Rawls to be applied to the phenomenon of stigmatization. The aim behind doing this is to attempt to establish principles that will help to determine where SSEs are acceptable in a just society and where they are not. Establishing a connection between the two concepts serves an important purpose because doing so brings the psychological concept of stigmatization and its known harm to self-esteem within the realms of self-respect and moral theories such as those of Rawls.

B Self-esteem and self-respect comparing apples and pears?

The term 'self-esteem' is one that is found frequently in the literature on stigmatization and its effects on the intra and inter-personal sphere (see Chapter 2).[37]

35 Rawls, *A Theory of Justice.* p348

36 Courtwright, "Justice, Stigma, and the New Epidemiology of Health Disparities".

37 See, for example, Camp, Finlay, and Lyons, "Is Low Self-Esteem an Inevitable Consequence of Stigma? An Example from Women with Chronic Mental Health Problems" and C Miller and B Major, "Coping with Stigma and Prejudice", in *The Social*

For psychologists and psychiatrists, a reduction in individual self-esteem has often been described as a negative effect of stigmatization and one that can allow the internalization of negative emotions.[38] Self-respect as a concept however finds its most natural home, not in psychological literature, but in literature concerned with philosophy and morals.[39] The concept is closely related to the Kantian notion of human dignity, that humans are special and unique entities that deserve respect in all instances because of their supposed unique rational nature.[40] The following paragraphs will attempt to summarize this conceptual difference.

(i) Self-respect

The notion of human dignity has often been used to justify moral codes and philosophies that lie at the centre of liberal democracies.[41] The justification for the concept of human dignity, that humans are uniquely rational, has been described as the successor to the pre-Renaissance idea in Christianity that all humans deserved a certain level of respect because they were created in God's image.[42] Since the Enlightenment the justification for the concept has shifted to the notion that humans possess a unique capacity for rational thought and decision making. Human dignity, according to Kant, demands that all individuals are treated with a minimum of respect, no matter their level in society or the deeds that they have committed. Additionally, the concept of human dignity has often been used to argue that human beings are obliged to treat themselves with a certain level of respect, i.e. to have self-respect.[43] To not do so, would be to not respect the dignity of him or herself and of human beings in general. Self-respect is the internal component of the concept of respect for others because of the human dignity all human beings possess. Since its inception, the idea of human dignity and its associated requirement for self-respect has been routed in ideas of philosophy rather than psychology. Indeed, part of its rationale is to distinguish humans from other animals, even those species that are our closest relative by proclaiming our uniqueness. This has given rise to criticism that trying to use the concept to explain human behaviour is "too philosophical" and in particular too detached from empirical "psychological research and theory".[44] Such a lofty philosophical notion has been described as ignoring the psychological peculiarities that humans

Psychology of Stigmatisation, ed. T Heatherton et al. (New York: Guilford Press, 2000).

38 For a more in-depth analysis of the potential negative consequences of stigmatization see Chapter 2.

39 Roland and Foxx, "Self-Respect: A Neglected Concept". p250

40 Stark, "Rawlsian Self-Respect". pp258–260, 240

41 M Elliot, "Human Rights and the Triumph of the Individual in World Culture,, *Cultural Sociology* 1, no. 3 (2007). p359

42 C McCrudden, "Human Dignity and Judicial Interpretation of Human Rights", *The European Journal of International Law* 19, no. 4 (2008). See page 658.

43 Roland and Foxx, "Self-Respect: A Neglected Concept".

44 D Statman, "Humiliation, Dignity and Self-Respect", *Philosophical Psychology* 13, no. 4 (2000).

exhibit. Given, however, that a fundamental aim of civilized society is to prevent individuals from acting solely according to their impulsive desires and fears, this is not surprising. In this regard, one can think of self-respect as an ethical or spiritual belief that prompts us to treat individuals (including ourselves) in a way that may be different from the way our more 'animalistic' impulses may direct us to do.

(ii) Self-esteem

Self-esteem on the other hand represents no great philosophical concept, nor does it possess any moral or philosophical connotation. As the term indicates, it involves an estimation of one's self-worth or value. Psychological experimentation has for decades shown that an individual's level of self-esteem is a closely connected acceptance by his or her peers. As has been shown with experiments concerned with stigmatization, perceived rejections or negative assessments from those with whom one interacts can often have a negative effect on self-esteem.[45] Some have argued that this is because in the environment we as a species evolved in, it was advantageous to be aware of the opinions and attitudes of others around us.[46] This would, it is reasoned, allow us to avoid alienation or ostracization which could have severe consequences. Unfortunately this set of social antennae (called a 'sociometer' by some)[47] with which we are equipped is sensitive to all forms of social rejection, whether they are justified or not. As a consequence rejection is painful, even if the action and expressions of our peers are not justified. This occurs daily for diverse reasons such as race, gender or sexual orientation. Where this occurs, individuals will experience the same pain related to the harm that is occurring to their self-esteem. Unfortunately, in attempting to avoid such painful feelings individuals may attempt to avoid contact with potential stigmatizers or engage in other coping responses that are associated with negative consequences on both the individual and the societal level (see Chapter 2 section 4 for more on coping responses).[48] Whilst our social antennae may therefore often be able to help us to maintain our social position, they also have the ability to leave us open to the effects of unjust stigmatization based on factors that have no link to immoral or anti-social behaviour.

45 J Crocker and B Major, "Social Stigma and Self-Esteem: The Self-Protective Properties of Stigma", *Psychological Review* 96, no. 4 (1989).

46 M Leary, "The Social and Psychological Importance of Self-Esteem", in *The Social Psychology of Emotional and Behavioral Problems*, ed. R Kowalski and M Leary (Washington, DC: APA, 1999).

47 M Leary and D Downs, "Interpersonal Functions of the Self-Esteem Motive: The Self-Esteem System as a Sociometer", in *Efficacy, Agency and Self-Esteem*, ed. M Kernis (New York: Plenum Press, 1995). pp123–144

48 For a description of coping responses, including how they can bring about harmful behaviour, see Chapter 1 sections 4. See also Miller and Major, "Coping with Stigma and Prejudice", and B Major et al., "Coping with Negative Stereotypes About Intellectual Performance: The Role of Psychological Disengagement", *Personality and Social Psychology Bulletin* 24, no. 1 (1998).

C The interaction of psychological concepts (self-esteem) with rational ethical principles (self-respect)

The principal location of the concept of self-esteem in psychological theories and concepts such as the sociometer, is in stark contrast to the philosophical and moral basis that underlies the concept of self-respect. The former represents self-evaluations that are performed to largely subjective criteria and largely on the affective level. It relates to more impulsive sentiments concerning one's perception of acceptance by others. The latter represents more rationally performed evaluation according to more objective criteria.[49]

(i) The symbiotic relationship of self-respect and self-esteem – self-respect as a belief capable of protecting against harm to self-esteem

Despite the two concepts being demonstrably quite different they may well be linked and capable of influencing each other.[50] Whilst self-esteem may represent a mechanism to conform behaviour to that desired by one's peers or group this does not mean that one should view such a result as being morally appropriate in many circumstances. Whereas sometimes it may be capable of bringing about an appropriate response, e.g. allowing someone to moderate their behaviour when their actions are being perceived as being unjustifiably arrogant or anti-social, on other occasions it may allow immoral and unjust stigmatization to have harmful consequences. This may be the case, for instance, where a group oppresses a minority because it sees them as being deviant. In doing so it attempts to stifle behaviour it does not see as acceptable.[51] This may simply be for reasons of asserting the dominance of one larger group over a smaller one. However, it may result in harm to the self-esteem of the persecuted group and perhaps a consequent change in behaviour as a coping strategy.[52] Whilst such an outcome may be explicable from a psychological viewpoint, it cannot be said to be ethically acceptable.

In looking for a possible moral or ethical counterweight the notion of self-respect presents itself as a suitable candidate. Courtwright, for example, maintains that self-respect is something that allows stigmatization to be resisted.[53] This is a concept that Roland and colleagues also subscribe to.[54] For them the concept

49 Roland and Foxx, "Self-Respect: A Neglected Concept".

50 D Sachs, "How to Distinguish Self-Respect from Self-Esteem", *Philosophy and Public Affairs* 10 (1981). p352

51 B Mullen and R Brown, "Ingroup Bias as a Function of Salience, Relevance, and Status: An Integration", *European Journal of Social Psychology* 22 (1992) and Tiane L. Lee and Susan T. Fiske, "Not an Outgroup, Not yet an Ingroup: Immigrants in the Stereotype Content Model", *International Journal of Intercultural Relations* 30, no. 6 (2006).

52 See Chapter 1 section 5 for a description of coping strategies. See also C Miller and C Kaiser, "A Theoretical Perspective on Coping with Stigma", *Journal of Social Issues* 57, no. 1 (2001).

53 See Courtwright, "Justice, Stigma, and the New Epidemiology of Health Disparities". p93

54 Roland and Foxx, "Self-Respect: A Neglected Concept". p272

of self-respect reflects a higher level, cognitive based thought process that could be used to put a brake on the otherwise likely responses to threats to self-esteem. Although Roland was not referring specifically to stigmatization, he appears to be subscribing to a common theme that has been described throughout the literature on the concept (and in Chapter 2 of this book). That is the idea that within the context of processes of stigmatization, beliefs that individuals hold can be used to temper the basic affective emotive responses they are feeling.[55] Self-respect may therefore be thought to represent the philosophical and moral equivalent of the notion of a 'protective belief', found frequently throughout the literature on stigmatization. Beliefs can of course be positive and negative in terms of the individuals concerned. What of course would set the concept of self-respect apart from many negative beliefs is its human dignity centred, Kantian potency for upholding the dignity of each and every individual.[56] This fits well with the concept of self-respect as described by Rawls – as a property that allows one to strive for one's own desired version of the good irrespective of the potentially negative views of others.

In a rare use of the term self-respect in the psychological context, Roland and colleagues argue that self-respect is a notion that can allow individuals to resist the negative emotions associated with a reduction in self-esteem. They seem to agree with Courtwright's idea that self-respect can be used by individuals to resist the harmful effects of attacks on self-esteem.[57] Under such a notion, possession of self-respect allows individuals, upon suffering a lowered sense of esteem, to not "abandon self respecting behaviours in order to meet inclusionary needs".[58]

Self-respect as a positive belief appears therefore to have the potential to both aid individuals in reducing their potentially stigmatizing behaviour and to allow potentially stigmatized individuals to resist the negative effects of stigmatization. The notion that self-respect may represent a belief (in the concept of human dignity) that is capable of both moderating stigmatizing behaviour and allowing affected individuals to resist it is interesting given the importance that self-respect is given in many theories, most notably in Rawls' concept of 'justice as fairness'. Given that severe stigmatization is capable of harming individual self-respect, i.e. where internalization occurs (see Chapter 2), this raises the question of whether societies should take steps to limit such stigmatization, especially where it emanates from the state or those who are connected to it. Using this perspective the remaining part of this chapter will consider what obligations may be incumbent upon the state in terms of its potential use of stigmatizing expressions.

55 J Crocker, "Social Stigma and Self-Esteem: Situational Construction of Self Worth", *Journal of Experimental Social Psychology* 35 (1999).
56 Roland and Foxx, "Self-Respect: A Neglected Concept". p248
57 Courtwright, "Justice, Stigma, and the New Epidemiology of Health Disparities".
58 Roland and Foxx, "Self-Respect: A Neglected Concept". p271

6 The duties of a society to foster self-respect - the concept of Rawlsian neutrality and the difficulties of distribution of self-respect

If self-respect represents an idea that can reduce instances of stigmatization, one can say that increasing the prevalence of self-respect and the awareness of it will help in reducing stigmatization. Conversely, harming self-respect is likely to worsen incidences of stigmatization and its associated effects. As Rawls stated, as the most important primary good it allows individuals to commit to their desired choice in life and ignore outside opinions that do not approve.[59] The state has an important duty to promote self-respect and to avoid activities that intentionally harm the self-respect of individuals. This is discussed in further detail below.

A A general duty upon the state to provide self-respect through equal treatment

Rawls proposed that an important and simple way in which the state could promote individual self-respect was to demonstrate full and equal respect for the liberties of all members of society. By protecting the liberties of all citizens equally, irrespective of their wealth, importance or position in society the state would be sending out a message that all individuals are of the same moral worth even if some, by good fortune or through their own innovation, enjoy a greater proportion of goods than others.[60] The visibility of such equal treatment should act to reinforce a sense of both mutual (i.e. respect for others) and self-respect. This would emanate from the belief that all citizens are entitled to an equal protection of individual liberties (i.e. equality before the law) by the state irrespective of whether they are rich or poor, strong or weak, etc. Equal treatment fosters the self-respect of each citizen through the state demonstrating that they are valued as full and equal human beings and citizens irrespective of their personal qualities or failings. Acting in such a manner is consistent with the concept of treating individuals with dignity, i.e. showing that solely by virtue of being human, all people are entitled to certain rights, rights which they possess to the same extent as all other individuals in society.

B Self-respect as no ordinary good – a good where inequalities are not advantageous to those with the least

However, even if one accepts in principle that the state should therefore foster and protect self-respect, it is not readily apparent how this might be achieved in reality. Does the state need to go beyond the provision of fundamental rights and liberties on an egalitarian basis? Questions remain, for example, as to whether the state is capable of 'distributing' self-respect and whether different individuals can possess it in unequal amounts. The distribution of goods (of which self-respect is one) is the primary concern of Rawls' second principle of justice. The second principle

59 Rawls, *A Theory of Justice*. p386
60 *A Theory of Justice* (Cambridge MA: Harvard University Press, 1999). p477

itself allows for an unequal distribution to be acceptable so long as any measure that proposed a change resulted in a benefit for those that had the least of such goods.[61] This principle was however a more specialized statement of the more general 'difference' principle being that "All social primary goods – liberty and opportunity, income and wealth, and the bases of self-respect – are to be distributed equally unless an unequal distribution of any or all of these goods is to the advantage of the least favoured".[62] In simple language this means that inequalities are only permitted if inequality in a particular good would be to the advantage of those with the least.[63]

In many cases inequality would allow entrepreneurial types to become richer but with the result that there is an overall increase in the level of economic activity, benefitting all. Rawls postulates, for example, that an unequal distribution of certain economic goods may be acceptable because it will allow innovation and entrepreneurship in society as, in order to become richer, those at the top will have to engage in economic activity. With a quality such as self-respect however this is arguably not the case. As Rawls described, this good is of a 'primary nature'. For such a good it is not possible to conceive of a person in the worst position with regard to self-respect as being able to prefer "his prospects with inequality to his prospects without it".[64] This is because a primary good is something that everybody needs in order to pursue their desired path in life, no matter what that might be. Without self-respect an individual lacks the belief that he or she has the worth to overcome obstacles in his or her way, and the ability to ignore the disapproving opinions of others.[65]

In addition, at the very core of self-respect lies the concept of equality. Self-respect poses the idea that all humans are equal because of their unique property as a species for rationality.[66] Given that one cannot be more human than another, one cannot have more self-respect than another (unlike self-esteem). Self-respect is therefore arguably an all or nothing, black or white, quality. One cannot have too much of it (unlike self-esteem).[67] In not having self-respect one has not lost one's dignity as a human being, but may have lost one's realization of it. Unlike the case for economic resources, it is difficult to conceive of possible arguments for why it would be beneficial for some individuals with no self-respect to live in a society with others who do possess it.[68] Not possessing self-respect means not possessing

61 *A Theory of Justice.* p302 Additionally the second principle mandated that all must have equal access to the systems that distribute such goods.

62 Rawls' second principle also contains the criteria of equality of opportunity. This is referred to as a third principle by some commentators. See Chapter 3 section 3.

63 Rawls, *A Theory of Justice.* p92

64 Ibid. p56 This 'difference test' determines when inequality in a particular group may be permitted.

65 Statman, "Humiliation, Dignity and Self-Respect".

66 McCrudden, "Human Dignity and Judicial Interpretation of Human Rights".

67 Sachs, "How to Distinguish Self-Respect from Self-Esteem".

68 Whilst the author does not subscribe to this point of view, there exists a potentially interesting debate on whether people can have 'damaged' self-respect or 'threatened' self-respect. This is connected to the concept just described concerning the possibility of having less self-respect than others. For a good discussion on this concept see ibid.

a primary good and therefore not being able to strive effectively for one's path in life no matter what that might be. There is no associated benefit that can make such an inequality worthwhile. Even if one would accept that it was possible to have partial self-respect (which this author does not), individuals with less (i.e. those not able to properly maintain self-respect), or none, would be at a permanent disadvantage in achieving whatever goals they might have in life. Given this one can argue that the state should take measures to avoid such an unequal distribution occurring, from aggravating it and, where possible, to reduce such inequalities.

The foregoing analysis allows the formation of a primary normative principle that may be applied to potential instances of stigmatization brought about by public statements:

Normative principle (i)
There are no instances where states need to intentionally damage an individual's self-respect.

This provides a hard and fast rule with no exceptions.[69] It is important however at this juncture to state that the principle described above does not mean that states are not able to engage in criticisms of acts they do not approve of. As will be discussed in more detail in section 12, whilst criticism may be capable of impacting upon self-esteem, it need not necessarily harm individual self-respect (i.e. that an individual can see him or herself as a valid and equal member of society capable of carrying out his or her desired plan in life). Measured criticisms of an individual's actions can, in certain contexts, be needed, for example, to reduce certain forms of behaviour that are perceived as anti-social. Such criticism need not amount to attacks that are capable of harming self-respect (e.g. attacks upon the dignity of particular individuals). The principle here rather seeks to mandate that when engaging in such criticisms states should not intentionally engage in attacks that are likely to harm individual self-respect, e.g. intensely stigmatizing attacks that demonize certain groups, calling in to question their validity as citizens or human beings. In terms of the potential types of legal approaches that might be most suitable in seeing that this principlle is adhered to, criminal law approaches to hate speech represent one likely example. One reason for this is that this principle represents a clear black and white line that should not be crossed in any circumstances. There may therefore be a role to play here for the criminal law in the form of hate speech law (discussed in Chapter 4).

7 Harming self-esteem with stigmatizing expressions – the relevance for self-respect

Given the fact that most forms of criticism will not take the form of direct attacks on self-respect (e.g. serious attacks on the human dignity of individuals such as hate

69 This is similar to the core concept described by Kant whereby the state should in no circumstances do anything that is contrary to the human dignity of individuals. See also Roland and Foxx, "Self-Respect: A Neglected Concept".

speech) but rather harm to self-esteem through criticism or the provision of information that is judged stigmatizing, it is important to discern what obligations are incumbent upon states (given the duty to foster self-respect) in terms of expressions that may affect self-esteem (i.e. moderately stigmatizing expressions or statements).

A Do Rawls' principles of justice seem, in practical terms, to be primarily concerned with the protection of self-esteem?

Whilst Rawls emphasized the importance of self-respect, there has been some debate over what exactly it entails and how it should be fostered. This debate arose because many of those who have studied Rawls have argued that the concept of self-respect as he described it, would not be protected by the principles of justice he outlined (despite that being his stated aim). Stark, for example, identifies three potential statements that could be used to describe individuals with self-respect:

a Individuals believe that their activities have intrinsic self-worth.
b Individuals find their own activities to be self-benefitting (e.g. they derive some form of pleasure or utility from their acts).
c Individuals believe their chosen activities to be valued by society as a whole.[70]

Self-respect, as Rawls outlined it in a *Theory of Justice*, involved individuals valuing their own chosen activities intrinsically, i.e. (a) above, that they were worthwhile.[71] Rawls' principles of justice, however (through their emphasis on the neutrality of the state), appeared more concerned with fostering an environment where an individual felt that his or her chosen version of the good life was valued by others or more specifically the state which is seen as existing at the centre of society, i.e. (c) above. It is admittedly difficult to conceive of how a society or state would go about directly achieving the version of self-respect that Rawls outlined in *A Theory of Justice* as such a concept exists on a subjective basis, i.e. in the thoughts and beliefs of individuals. This means that in order to provide self-respect directly the state would effectively have to control the minds of individuals to ensure they had self-respect. Whilst Rawls' conception of self-respect focuses on the perceptions that individuals hold concerning their conception of the good life, the principles of justice that he elaborated, however, appear to be more concerned with engineering society so that it demonstrably respects the individual's chosen path in life. It could therefore be argued that Rawls' principles are more concerned with protecting *self-esteem* than *self-respect*. This invokes a responsibility on society to ensure that it acts in a manner that is respectful of the choices that individuals make. This raises the question as to whether Rawls really intended this or, had he perhaps confused the concepts of self-esteem and self-respect?[72]

70 Stark, "Rawlsian Self-Respect". p243
71 Rawls, *A Theory of Justice.* pp386–387
72 For a theory on the differences between the two concepts see Sachs, "How to Distinguish Self-Respect from Self-Esteem".

B Protecting self-esteem in order to protect self-respect?

One possible conclusion is that although Rawls' goal was to protect self-respect, he wanted to achieve this in practical terms *vis-à-vis* the protection of self-esteem, primarily, through the principle of state neutrality. In attempting to explain how this might be, Stark states that Rawls' self-respect would be protected by a society's political arrangements ensuring option (c) above was respected. Although accepting option (c) above equates to protecting self–esteem and not the notion of self-respect as Rawls described it, she argued that this would lead to a situation where individual self-respect was ultimately fostered. This, she argues, is primarily down to the social nature of human beings. In deciding whether their desired path in life is of value and worth pursuing, they draw not only upon their own reasoning but on the perceptions of others.[73] Where humans are told by all around them that their activities are without value or are morally wrong, they are likely to incorporate such ideas in making their own decisions, even if their plans may make objective sense. This concept, is at the heart of the notion of internalization, which is described as one of the most corrosive outcomes of stigmatization (see Chapter 2 section 4).[74] Rawls appears to recognize the importance of social perception; identifying the link between the power of outside perceptions and the importance they have to individuals in assessing the validity of their preferred way of life when he discusses the need for individuals to find that their deeds are appreciated by society and those around them.[75] For Rawls, recognition by others was also important in protecting individual self-respect. In *Political Liberalism*, Rawls states that self-respect involves not only having "a secure sense of our own value … [and a] firm conviction that our determinate conception of the good life is worth carrying out" but is also rooted in "our self confidence as a fully cooperating member of society capable of pursuing a worthwhile conception of the good".[76] Stark uses such declarations to argue that whilst for Rawls the power of self-respect was in allowing the individual to believe that his own desired version of the good life was worth striving for, such self-respect could be pragmatically provided for by showing individuals that their choices were respected by other individuals and society at large, i.e. (c) as described above. If Stark is correct about Rawls, he was appreciating that although self-respect and self-esteem are different conceptions, self-esteem has the power to influence self-respect, particularly if it is harmed through the dismissive opinions of other individuals and society in general. Although Rawls did not state so explicitly, he seems to have appreciated the ability of more subjective processes linked to stigmatization (and the harm they can inflict on self-esteem) to affect the ability of individuals being able to 'possess' the rational concept of self-respect.

73 Rejection by other groups in society can, for example, be harmful to individual self-respect. See C McKinnon, "Exclusion Rules and Self-Respec", *Journal of Value Enquiry* 34 (2000).
74 See Chapter 1 section 4 where the concept of internalization is discussed. See also Miller and Major, "Coping with Stigma and Prejudice".
75 Rawls, *A Theory of Justice*. p440
76 *Political Liberalism* (New York: Columbia University Press, 1993). p318

The foregoing analysis. if correct, suggests that the primary role a state can play in ensuring that individuals have self-respect (and therefore the personal belief that one's plan for the good life is valid) is to show respect to individuals and their plan for life. This is supported by the manner in which Rawls describes a society's duty to provide the 'social bases for self-respect' suggesting that whilst the state cannot be expected to provide self-respect directly, it can provide a basis for it by valuing the choice of life of its citizens (i.e. supporting their self-esteem). How a state should go about doing this is discussed further below.

8 A positive or negative duty towards self-esteem?

A A positive duty is not feasible

Proponents of the existence of a positive duty on the state to boost the self-esteem of its citizens are hard to find. Some have argued positive actions by the state to boost self-esteem raise new risks of inequality driven by the innate human need to feel superior to others.[77] In particular there exists the risk that a state would find it impossible to boost individual self-esteem equally and, as a result, some individuals would lose out.[78] This would lead to the risk of having first and second class citizens where those who are actively praised by the state come to be accepted as being superior to those who have not, leading to a flawed type of meritocracy in line with the Nietzschean vision of 'the power of the noble'.[79] The utilization of such a 'politics of esteem' approach would therefore run the risk of harming the notion of self-respect that holds equality at its core. This would arise when certain individuals found themselves to be less esteemed by the state (and, by association, society in general), leading them to the conclusion that they are perceived as lesser citizens. Individuals from different cultures may, for example, value different traits and require different types of praise to have their esteem boosted.[80] This is in contrast to self-respect which revolves around equality in terms of being a rational human being, a concept that entails subscribing to a value that can be objectively defined.[81] Furthermore, it is difficult to measure individual or group self-esteem

77 See F Fukuyama, *The End of History and the Last Man* (New York: Free Press, 1992). p182

78 Such positions are similar to those used in favour of a state being strictly secular. See, for example: M Friedman and V Sarogiou, "Religiosity, Psychological Acculturation to the Host Culture, Self-Esteem and Depressive Symptoms among Stigmatized and Nonstigmatized Religious Immigrant Groups in Western Europe", *Basic and Applied Social Psychology* 32, no. 2 (2010).

79 A Laitinen, "Social Bases of Self-Esteem: Rawls, Honneth and Beyond", *Conference Paper* (2012). Available at http://nome.unak.is/nm-marzo-2012/vol-7-n-2-2012/45-conference-paper/307-social-bases-of-self-esteem-rawls-honneth-and-beyond

80 Even individuals within the same culture react differently in terms of changes to self-esteem resulting from stigmatizing stimuli. This may be down to a range of factors such as life experiences, personal beliefs and possibly even genetics. See Crocker and Major, "Social Stigma and Self-Esteem: The Self-Protective Properties of Stigma".

81 Roland and Foxx, "Self-Respect: A Neglected Concept".

empirically, especially in different contexts. This would make it difficult for the state to assess how its efforts of self-esteem boosting were progressing with different groups and different individuals.[82] In addition, constant efforts by the state to boost the esteem of its citizens might be seen as false or not genuine leading such efforts to be ignored and therefore wasteful.

B A negative duty to avoid damage to self-esteem? – Potential implications?

Given the problems identified above, it might be reasonable to conclude that rather than being responsible for boosting the self-esteem of individuals, a more realistic alternative would be for the state to have a duty not to harm the self-esteem of individual citizens. Whilst perhaps being less fantastical and infeasible than the option of a positive duty (discussed above), there are also important issues of feasibility with regard to a negative duty. One might ask, for example, in the course of reasonable activity is it actually possible for a state to avoid reducing the self-esteem of all of its citizens all of the time? The functioning of a state requires various pronouncements and releases of information on a day-to-day basis. These actions may be required to secure rights that citizens view as essential and may be of constitutional importance. Sometimes the provision of such information may result in stigmatization. Not releasing various types of information in such contexts might however constitute a failure to meet other duties and obligations that apply to the state in question. Such obligations may relate to duties like keeping citizens secure physically, providing healthcare, providing security, providing material needs and also duties related to the release of information in order to provide transparency of the functioning of government to its citizens. These relate to the concepts of 'functional stigmatization', 'fair criticism' and stigmatization through statements 'made for political reasons' described in Chapter 1 part 2. Given that such functions are, to a certain extent, unavoidable (and arguably necessary) in a functioning democratic society, any normative position must be able to accommodate them. In deciding when and in what contexts a state may be permitted to use such expressions, Rawls' concept of 'lexical priority' (discussed below) is useful.

9 The importance of Rawls' lexical priority

The Rawlsian conception of justice foresaw a hierarchy in terms of the priorities a just society should commit itself to (see section 3 above). First are the fundamental liberties, which under all circumstances must be guaranteed for all individuals, followed by the protection of the equal opportunities principle, and then, finally, comes respect for the difference principle in terms of the distribution of social goods. In the event of a conflict, according to Rawls, a just society should give priority to protecting the first and second principle for some individuals over protecting the third for others. Rawls would thus see it as permissible to act in a

82 Laitinen, "Social Bases of Self-Esteem: Rawls, Honneth and Beyond".

way that reduced an individual's holding of a particular social good if it was required to protect the personal liberties or equal opportunity of others. States would therefore, under a Rawlsian scheme, have the right to take action that risked an unfair distribution of goods if it had to do so to protect the essential liberties of certain individuals. Imagine, for instance, a situation where certain individuals were trying to enrich themselves whilst violating the personal liberties of others. A state would be justified in taking action in such instances to protect the personal liberties of the latter group even if it risked preserving or creating an unjust distribution of goods *vis-à-vis* the former group.[83] However, where action is not required to ensure that the first or second principles are upheld, it would be unjust to allow a distribution of social goods that was not in line with Rawls' 'difference principle'. This means that if a society were to take action that resulted in an unfair distribution of social goods in a situation where such action was not required to protect the personal liberties or equal opportunity of others, it would not be acting in a just manner.

In the context of this book the good that we are interested in is the primary good of self-respect. States are arguably able to affect the distribution of this good with various forms of SSE, including *inter alia*, public acts of condemnation of a particular group or minority. This may occur on some occasions because the acts of the group in question are perceived as a threat to the liberties of society in general (i.e. 'functional stigmatization' or 'fair criticism' as described in Chapter 1). On other occasions, however, the purpose of such condemnation may be less noble, with the aim being primarily to boost political appeal to mainstream society (i.e. statements 'made for political purposes'). Rawls's concept of lexical priority suggests the state would not be justified in using language loaded with moral condemnation where it is not needed in order to protect the fundamental liberties or equal opportunities of other individuals. The use of morally condemning language in a public announcement by the state may only be acceptable where such efforts are needed to protect the liberties or equal opportunities of others. In such a category one can, for example, imagine instances where the actions of some individuals were threating the rights of others, e.g. smoking next to children, drink driving or the commission of other crimes. Such condemnation would not however be acceptable where such aims were not sought. This could be the case where public statements are issued by those in public office condemning the actions of a group in society merely because they are distasteful to the majority of individuals in society. This would include condemnation of the cultural habits of minorities solely because they were different, as was the case with the *le bruit et l'odeur* (noise and smell) speech by the then mayor of Paris, Jacques Chiraq (see Chapter 1 part B).[84]

10 'Functional stigmatization'

As Chapter 1 described, on certain occasions efforts may be made to provide information specifically to a certain community so that it can protect itself. This

83 R Taylor, "Rawls's Defense of the Priority of Liberty: A Kantian Reconstruction", *Philosophy & Public Affairs* 31, no. 3 (2003).

84 D Fassin, "The Biopolitics of Otherness", *Anthropology Today* 17, no. 1 (2001).

may, for example, occur where a particular ethnic group is at a heightened risk by virtue of lifestyle habits or genetic factors to developing a particular condition.[85] In such instances the provision of relevant information to the community in question may allow the individuals within that community to take measures to protect themselves. Without such measures the state may be seen as failing in terms of the obligations it might have towards citizens in terms of taking measures to protect their health.[86] Even where such measures have positive aims and even results in terms of individual health, some members of the community may feel stigmatized by the provision of information to the public that highlights their increased risk of the condition in question. Such measures may, for example, make previously unknown knowledge available to the general public, allowing it to form potentially harmful stereotypes of the community in question and therefore also the possibility of stigmatization. This may result in harm to the self-esteem of certain individuals. This may occur where public health campaigns state that certain immigrants (e.g. from Sub-Saharan Africa) may be considered as having a higher chance of being HIV positive (discussed in Chapter 1 'part B).

On many occasions the provision of information in such a manner by public authorities may appear justifiable even though there is a risk that the self-esteem of certain citizens may be harmed in doing so. For whilst a harm to individual self-esteem may be occurring, such harm is occurring in order to prevent another arguably greater harm, e.g. threats to individual health. In the example provided above concerning public health, were the government not to provide relevant information to individuals in the community concerned, it might mean that individuals become sick or die from afflictions that otherwise could have been prevented. In such situations there are two factors available that can be used to defend the state in its choice to release potentially stigmatizing information concerned. First, the harm that can be prevented may be arguably more serious than the potential harm to self-esteem that may occur to certain individuals. Second, it is important to recall that self-esteem does not equate to self-respect (see section 5). Whilst one's self-respect can potentially be harmed by low self-esteem, this need not always be the case. Research conducted by various specialists in stigma has shown that individuals who hold strong personal beliefs about their individual worth can resist threats to self-esteem and their potentially negative effect on self-worth.[87] In addition, in the context of state efforts in such areas as public health or security, individuals are likely to take note of the aim behind the expressions in question, e.g. protecting public health or safety. Where this occurs, the provision

85 S C Smith, Jr et al., "Discovering the Full Spectrum of Cardiovascular Disease: Minority Health Summit 2003: Report of the Obesity, Metabolic Syndrome, and Hypertension Writing Group", *Circulation* 111, no. 10 (2005).

86 See N Daniels, "Justice, Health and Healthcare", *American Journal of Bioethics* 1, no. 2 (2001).

87 See, for example, Crocker, "Social Stigma and Self-Esteem: Situational Construction of Self Worth". Black students in the US have been found to be able to resist potential harm to self-esteem where they hold positive beliefs that are capable of explaining acts of stigmatization as irrational. See also Chapter 2 section 4

of such information, even where it has the potential to be stigmatizing is likely to be seen as being made in order to achieve important aims and not with the intention of purely stigmatizing. In attempting to assess the potential harmful effects of a threat to self-esteem it should be remembered that whilst serious and sustained assaults on individual self-esteem may bring about harm to individual self-respect, this need not be the case where the potential threat to self-esteem is short lived and of a moderate nature.[88]

One might thus argue that the harm to self-esteem that may be incidentally caused in such cases can be considered 'proportional' when related to the potential benefits that may be achieved. One can also make the argument that a failure to prevent suffering (in both physical and social terms) that is preventable would in any event result in harm to the self-esteem of the individuals affected. In such circumstances the actions of the state may, if successful, even be considered self-esteem neutral. Both of these possible defences would however depend upon the context in question. Where the potential benefits of the information release in question are major, such arguments will be stronger. Where the potential benefits are weaker such arguments will also be weaker.

Support for this reasoning may also be found applying Rawls' principle of 'equality of opportunity'.[89] This relates to a supposed duty upon society to provide what it can in order to allow individuals to maintain normal functioning and to participate in the life of society. For Rawls, the purpose of such a principle was that individuals should not only have a right to access the offices and positions that are associated with the distribution of goods but also an effective chance of obtaining them. Daniels, for instance, has argued that the duty to provide healthcare can be envisaged within such a requirement. This is because fair and equal provision of healthcare is required in order to correct inequalities that occur merely by chance for many individuals in terms of illness and disability. Daniels reasons that the provision of healthcare in a just and fair manner is able to make a contribution to Rawls' principle of equality of opportunity.[90] Such fair provision entails not only equality of access to healthcare services for all, but also access to the necessary information needed to maintain health. Without such access numerous individuals would be left to the mercy of various conditions that would render their societal participation difficult, and thus limit their access to the various positions that provide access to the social goods required to achieve one's aims in life.[91]

Furthermore, if one were to take Rawls' principle of 'lexical ordering' into account,[92] the protection of equality of opportunity is placed second, after the protection of basic liberties and before the distribution of social goods. Therefore, if one was to analogize the above example in terms of Rawlsian theory and also

88 Roland and Foxx, "Self-Respect: A Neglected Concept".
89 Daniels, "Justice, Health and Healthcare".
90 N Daniels, *Just Healthcare* (New York: Cambridge University Press, 1985).
91 N Daniels and J Sabin, "Limits to Healthcare: Fair Procedures, Democratic Deliberation, and the Legitimacy Problem for Insurers", *Philosophy and Public Affairs* 26, no. 4 (1997). fn9
92 Rawls, *A Theory of Justice*. See pages 37–40.

accept Daniels' contention that healthcare falls under Rawls' second principle, equality of fair opportunity, it would seem to imply that the state has a primary duty (once essential liberties are protected) to ensure the equality of opportunity principle. This would seem to mean the state would have an obligation to consider the equality of its citizens (in terms of healthcare) as taking priority over its obligations to fairly distribute social goods including self-respect.[93]

The same reasoning could also apply to other types of situations where the provision of certain information that was stigmatizing to certain groups would be capable of meeting important goals. In such cases the provision of certain types of information might be stigmatizing to some groups but may allow for the protection of important fundamental liberties of other citizens (i.e. the protection of life, limb or property). The foregoing analysis provides another important potential principle in the regulation of SSEs. That is:

Normative principle (ii)
The state should use SSEs that may harm individual self-esteem only where doing so would secure the individual liberties or equal opportunities of others.

These requirements suggest that legal approaches that allow a necessity/proportionality balancing exercise may be suitable for such functions. Chapters 5 and 6 will accordingly discuss (the limited) applicability Articles 8 (in terms of privacy) and 14 (in terms of an anti-discrimination approach) of the European Convention on Human Rights to regulate SSEs. The central role of the concepts of necessity and proportionality in case law linked to these articles makes them interesting as candidate legal approaches that can allow actions by public bodies that produce harm in certain contexts but not in others.

11 Harming self-esteem with public statements based on inaccurate information

Given the need to respond quickly to many situations, there are, in certain areas, risks that information released is not verified as being accurate before it is released. This means that such information may contain inaccurate aspects that may be capable of stigmatization. An example could be where the security services of a state name several members of an ethnic minority as being suspected of planning or committing terrorist acts.[94] Another may be a public health agency that has erroneously attributed the origin of an infectious disease outbreak to a particular community.[95] Often in such instances, a state may be acting in order to protect important interests of its

93 See ibid. p477
94 L Fekete, "Anti-Muslim Racism and the European Security State", *Race and Class* 46, no. 1 (2004).
95 See Chapter 1 section 2A for examples of where stigmatization has occurred through the release of inaccurate information by the state.

citizens. In other instances, states may intentionally emit disinformation where it is felt that the provision of such incorrect information will further their aims.[96] It is possible, however, that such information may lead to the formation of negative stereotypes. The existence of such stereotypes may increase the possibility of stigmatization of the group and therefore a reduction in the self-esteem of its members.[97]

Such instances present a situation, unlike that described in section 4 above, in which the harm brought about to individual self-esteem seems difficult to defend. Where information is factually dubious it is difficult to argue that the state is pursuing an objective that could achieve aims that would warrant potential harm to self-esteem. This is because it is difficult to see how the potential harm produced by the provision of stigmatizing information that is factually incorrect can bring about any positive outcomes that could justify its provision in the first place. Incorrect information by its very nature does not allow individuals to alter their behaviour successfully to achieve something. The harm brought about to self-esteem would thus be difficult to justify in terms of the proportional benefit it would bring in terms of fulfilling other important obligations. This lack of utility allows us to state a further potential principle that should be applied to SSEs, i.e. that:

Normative principle (iii)
There is a duty upon states not to harm individual or group self-esteem through the release of incorrect information.

In terms of legal approaches that may be able to ensure adherence to this principle, one could envisage the application of administrative law approaches to check that the expressive activities of the state are performed correctly, reducing the potential for mistakes. As Chapter 5 will however illustrate, administrative law approaches may often have difficulty in engaging expressive acts as a result of the way such legal approaches envisage the concept of an 'administrative act'.

12 Harming the self-esteem of groups considered to be undertaking unacceptable activities (i.e. fair criticism)

On an intuitive level, most individuals would probably feel that the ability of the state to condemn individuals and activities it does not approve of is a natural function of the democratic state. We elect our politicians to occupy the highest executive posts within the state, as a result we may expect them to represent our

96 During the conflict in Northern Ireland, for example, the British state was responsible for the emission of a constant stream of misinformation, whereby it falsely attributed some of its covert activities to certain groups in society. See A Briggs and P Cobley, *The Media: An Introduction* (London: Pearson Education, 2002). Chapter 6

97 For a good analysis of the potentially stigmatizing effects of health information campaigns see Deliverable D1.6 – "Human Rights, Stigmatization and Risk of Discrimination Against Specific Population Segments and Target Groups" from the TELL ME project, an FP7 project funded by the EU Commission that aims to develop novel communication strategies that can be used in epidemic situations.

views and express them accordingly. If, however, we think of such matters from a Rawlsian perspective (especially with its emphasis on the original position), such activities may present challenges. Problems exist around Rawls' requirement of state neutrality in terms of expressing opinions on an individual's chosen lifestyle and his or her version of the good life. Indeed, for Rawls the equal respect that the state would show to all citizens is indispensable in providing for the social conditions needed for individuals to have self-respect.

Does the requirement of state neutrality mean that the state is not allowed to condemn individuals, even when their lifestyle choices or behaviour are obviously anti-social or posing a threat to others? This question appeared to be unanswered by Rawls in the original version of *A Theory of Justice.* [98] As a result some concluded that Rawls' vision was too simplistic because it would not allow a state to condemn anti-social positions, including attitudes that were intolerant, e.g. advocating a theocratic or intolerant society where the rights of others would not be respected. However, Rawls later refined his stance on such issues.[99] In doing so he stated that the state did not have to show neutrality in terms of all possible forms of the good. Such a stance would obviously be ridiculous and impractical. Indeed, given that a state is capable of enacting laws that criminalize certain behaviours, it would seem bizarre if the state was not able to criticize ideas and behaviours it found unsuitable. Such an extreme requirement would not allow a state to express its preference for more peaceful and tolerant options over those that advocated conflict and intolerance in society. Accordingly, states should be allowed to show their disapproval of ideas or ways of life that do not wish to show tolerance to others or respect the rights and equal opportunities of others. As Rawls stated, "it is neither possible nor just to allow all conceptions of the good to be pursued (as some involve violation of basic rights and liberties)".[100] A state may therefore, for example, express its disapproval of ideas espoused by extreme religious groups that wish to see women's rights restricted or people discriminated against on the basis of their ethnicity or other similar characteristics. Criticism of such groups by the state would therefore not be inconsistent with Rawls' conception of justice as fairness even though it would show that the state did not have equal respect for the version of the good concerned. This is because such groups wish to advance ideas or practices that would see the fundamental freedoms or equal opportunities of others being harmed. As a consequence, the potential harm to individual self-esteem produced by condemnation may be justified. Interestingly, Rawls pointed out that the criticisms of such groups need not necessarily harm their self-respect. This was because in criticizing such groups the state does not deny their validity as human beings, nor state that they should have less rights or opportunities than others. Rather the state is condemning their desire to usurp the rights and equal opportunities of others. As Rawls states, "admissible ideas of the good must

98 Rawls, *A Theory of Justice.*

99 "The Priority of Right and Ideas of the Good", *Philosophy & Public Affairs* 17, no. 4 (1988).

100 Ibid. p258

respect the limits of, and serve a role within, the political conception of justice".[101] Where activities do not threaten the fundamental rights and liberties of others criticism would not be justified.

Examples of such instances could include individuals who choose to lead alternative lifestyles and those who wish to live at a distance from society. The fact that other members of society might not find the choices and ideas of such groups to their taste does not mean that they can be considered harmful. In order to be considered so in the Rawlsian sense, such groups must advocate views or commit acts that threaten the rights of others or limit equal opportunities. This division of potential criticisms of perceived anti-social behaviour into acceptable and non-acceptable categories allows us to add a further principle that can be applied to stigmatizing statements made by the state:

Normative principle (iv)
The state should not criticize individuals for their ideas or lifestyle choices unless they threaten the fundamental rights or the equality of opportunity of others.

As Chapter 4 will discuss, criminal laws related to hate speech could serve an important role in ensuring that such a line is not overstepped by the state in its criticism of particular groups in society. 'Fair criticism' is unlike situations where direct attacks are made on minority groups for political purposes (see the discussion below), which may imply that certain groups or minorities are less worthy or respectable than other citizens. Such attacks produce levels of stigmatization that go far beyond fair criticism.

13 Statements or expressions made for political reasons

The political process represents an integral component of all democratic societies. The actors involved in this process are many and varied. Rawls recognized in *Political Liberalism* that a just society founded on his principles of justice would be made up of diverse groups with competing interests and diverging views of both how society should be run and life in general.[102] In such a world it is not just likely, but inevitable that individuals will differ in terms of their conception of the good, perhaps even holding the conception of certain other individuals in society in contempt. Whilst such views can be stigmatizing for those concerned, resulting in harm to self-esteem, Rawls contended that his vision of the neutral state would help to protect individuals from the worst excesses of such stigmatization – a corrosion of their self-respect. This is because through showing the same respect for the rights and equal opportunities of all individuals the state would be

101 Ibid. p253
102 *Political Liberalism*. Rawls states, " Political liberalism assumes that, for political purposes, a plurality of reasonable yet incompatible comprehensive doctrines is the normal result of the exercise of human reason within the framework of the free institutions of a constitutional democratic regime". (pxvi)

affirming to all that they are equal citizens having the same value (i.e. through providing equality before the law in terms of equal liberties). Such a demonstration, given the perceived importance of the state, is important in providing the social bases for self-respect.[103] In maintaining self-respect in this way, the state would strengthen the ability of individuals to resist the stigmatizing opinions of other non-state actors in society.[104]

A Political figures can represent factional interests

In modern democratic societies the opinions of the many and various groups in society are given a voice through political representatives. Such representatives are able to run for election and, if successful, occupy positions in the legislative or even executive structures of states. Whilst such a process may be indispensable in terms of providing representation, problems will arise given the dual nature of such elected representatives. Many will occupy positions that are 'connected to the state' (see discussion concerning President Trump in the Introduction). As a consequence, when such individuals make statements, they may use the resources or the authority of the state to make their message resonate (see Chapter 1).[105] Such individuals will often be members of political parties. They will, as a result, also have an interest in furthering the appeal of their political grouping in order to boost both their personal chances and the chances of their faction in future elections. This means that, in addition to making statements that further the general aims of the state, such individuals will make statements and engage in public discussions in order to further their political interest.

B Political figures can use the state as a platform to stigmatize

As many examples in Chapter 1 demonstrated, such political statements will often represent condemnations of certain groups and their choices in life. This may, for example, occur when a minister states that he wants to reduce the number of a certain type of immigrant coming into the country because of a certain behaviour they exhibit. Such statements may harm the self-esteem or even self-respect of the groups concerned in extreme circumstances As, for example, when such figures question the validity of certain groups of individuals as citizens of their country.[106]

103 *A Theory of Justice*. p82
104 Courtwright, "Justice, Stigma, and the New Epidemiology of Health Disparities", and "Stigmatization and Public Health Ethics", *Bioethics* 27, no. 2 (2013).
105 D Gelders and I Oyvind, "Government Communication About Potential Policies: Public Relations, Propaganda or Both?", *Public Relations Review* 36 (2010).
106 See examples in Chapter 1 section 2C concerning certain migrant groups. See also the report B Baumberg Geiger et al., "Benefits Stigma in Britain" Project report. Elizabeth Finn Care (2012). Available at: https://kar.kent.ac.uk/id/eprint/36377 For more concerning hostility to immigrants throughout history by majoritarian groups in society see Lee and Fiske, "Not an Outgroup, Not yet an Ingroup: Immigrants in the Stereotype Content Model".

The fact that those issuing such statements occupy state or quasi-state positions means that their statements can have a greater impact on individuals given that they can be associated with the authority of the state itself.

One prominent example of where such issues come to the fore is the process of policy formation that occurs at the heart of all democratic states. When ministers make statements announcing potential new policies (perhaps at the commencement of a consultation processes), the statements may have a simultaneous role, pertaining both to their political functions (in an attempt to rally political support) and also to the state function (by signalling that a period of official consultation is beginning).[107] Such statements bring into question Rawls' concept of state neutrality given that debate, criticism and condemnation are often at the core of politics. Whilst it may be difficult or impossible to envisage a democracy that does not permit such political debate, even amongst those who occupy important positions within the state, it is important to recognize the ability of such individuals, given their positions, to negatively affect the self-esteem or self-respect of individuals through their statements.

Stigmatizing statements of this type are both similar and different in some regards to those discussed in section 12 above. They differ in that they are not made by the state in order to change behaviour that is perceived as anti-social, but rather in order to curry political favour with certain individuals. Such statements do not find justification in the fact that they can be used to prevent uncivil behaviour or intolerant attitudes, i.e. conceptions of the good that are not permissible according to Rawls' principles of justice, but in the fact that they are a practical necessity in the democratic process. This is because most systems presuppose that officials seeking (and holding) elected positions are entitled or even are duty bound to air their views on topics of contention in society. The need for the availability of such information finds justification in creating the conditions necessary for an informed electorate.[108]

C *Confusion over the identity of the messenger?*

At the heart of this issue lies a potential oversimplification in Rawls' analysis of what constitutes a just society in a pluralistic world. Whilst Rawls accepts that society will probably be made up of diverse groups that may have vastly different conceptions of what constitutes the good, he envisages in the midst of this a set of institutions (i.e. the state) that is capable of demonstrating equal respect for all individuals and their respective conceptions of it. Even if we could assume that such institutions might be theoretically neutral, i.e. that the state and its institutions are created by and operate under law that meets Rawls' conception of justice, it is necessary to remember that such institutions

107 Gelders and Oyvind, "Government Communication About Potential Policies: Public Relations, Propaganda or Both?"

108 H Norton and D Keats Citron, "Government Speech 2.0", *Denver University Law Review* 87 (2010).

can often be represented or even personified by individuals with a political motive. When a prime minster or mayor of an important city launches an attack on a certain group in society, is he or she speaking as an office holder, or as a member of a political group? Given this ambiguity the potential recipients of this message – the electorate – might find it difficult to deduce whether such opinions are reflective of the attitude of the state in general or simply represent the political views of one group in society

Given the potential implications of stigmatization (Chapter 2 section 7), the frequency with which politicians engage in such outbursts, and the potential harm that such statements, when perceived to come from the state, can engender for self-respect, one might expect that such statements would face some level of legal restraint in a just society. However, this could be seen to place constraints on the democratic activity of the state, where a deference to freedom of speech is often seen as an essential component (discussed in Chapter 7).

D The need for clarification

Does the discussion above mean that there should be yet another exception for allowing stigmatizing statements by political figures connected to the state, i.e. where it is needed, perhaps a so-called 'democratic exception'? Whilst such an exception would allow an unstifled democratic debate it would open the door to almost unlimited stigmatization through SSEs in the name of democracy, something that seems intuitively bizarre. Given that some level of free speech is necessary in a democratic society, especially between senior political figures, a compromise solution might be more favourable. Such a solution would seek to allow freedom of speech, but at the same time dissociate the state from expressions that would indicate a stigmatizing bias. In particular, one might expect that individuals who are vested with important positions within the state to be prevented from making stigmatizing attacks on groups within society and their version of the good. This could be the case, for example, where certain key players are prevented from making such statements whilst they occupy important office, e.g. presidents, prime ministers, mayors, etc. Such an option is likely too simplistic, however, given the need for such individuals to be able to express themselves in order to ensure accountability. Another possibility is a requirement that individuals who occupy such positions are compelled to identify with which hat they speak with, i.e. to state whether they speak as a politician or on behalf of the state. Such a requirement could be applicable where political individuals choose to criticize particular groups in a society for political reasons (and not for reasons of 'fair criticism' as discussed above in section 12). It would make it clear to individuals who feel stigmatized that they are being stigmatized by the individual concerned for political reasons and not the state itself. In terms of a principle that could be used to assess potential legal systems one can therefore say that:

Normative principle (v)
Stigmatizing statements made during the political process should be clearly identified as neither emanating from, nor representing the opinion of the state itself but of an individual or group with political motives.

In terms of a particular area of law, one can perhaps look to approaches that may be categorized under administrative law (see Chapter 5). Such approaches are often concerned with matters of legality (i.e. whether the decision maker has the authority) and form (i.e. whether the correct forms have been used in the administrative act in question). Given the important role administrative law plays in most states to regulate the acts of public bodies it represents a prominent candidate in terms of a legal approach that one might reason could fulfil a role in this area with regard to SSEs. As Chapter 5 will discuss further however, the ability of most administrative law approaches to engage SSEs is likely to be limited.

14 Conclusion

This chapter developed five normative principles that the author argues can be used to discern whether the law is able to prevent SSEs in a way that would be consistent with the need to project self-respect. The reasoning behind these principles was deduced from the relationship of the primarily psychological concept of self-esteem and the primarily moral and philosophical concept of self-respect to the phenomenon of stigmatization. As Rawls contended, the important nature of self-respect as a primary good demonstrates that it is vital for individuals in terms of giving them the ability to strive for whatever version of the good life they see fit, irrespective of the possible disapproving opinions of others that they may be exposed to. Individuals who do not possess self-respect are not able to pursue their desired path in life nor do they possess the motivation needed to obtain the other goods necessary for such a life. Rawls argued that states have a duty to protect individual self-respect where possible, in particular by not showing disapproval for the proffered version of the good life of the various groups and individuals that exist in society. States may however be confronted with numerous situations where they are required to make certain statements or release information that are capable of stigmatizing certain individuals or groups. The normative principles proposed in this chapter were designed to allow a state to carry out these functions whilst at the same time ensuring that the self-respect of individuals and groups was not unnecessarily harmed. These principles are:

> Normative principle (i)
> There are no instances where states should, using SSEs, intentionally damage an individual's self-respect.
> Normative principle (ii)
> The state should use SSEs that may harm individual self-esteem only where doing so would secure the individual liberties or equal opportunities of others.
> Normative principle (iii)

There is a duty upon states not to harm individual or group self-esteem through the release of incorrect information.

Normative principle (iv)

The state should not criticize individuals for their ideas or lifestyle choices unless they threaten the fundamental rights or the equality of opportunity of others.

Normative principle (v)

Stigmatizing statements made during the political process should be clearly identified as neither emanating from, nor representing the opinion of the state itself but of an individual or group with political motives.

Chapters 4–7 of this book will illustrate how some of the legal approaches that have been suggested in this chapter may be likely to apply to stigmatizing expressions, including those that have been made by the state. As will become clear, however, it may be difficult to identify legal approaches that can ensure that these normative principles are met. This is especially the case for principles (ii)–(v). As Chapters 4–7 show this is because of the difficulty many legal approaches have in engaging purely expressive acts.

Bibliography

Baumberg Geiger, B, K Bell, D Gaffney. "Benefits Stigma in Britain." Project report. Elizabeth Finn Care (2012). Available at: https://kar.kent.ac.uk/id/eprint/36377

Briggs, A, and P Cobley. *The Media: An Introduction*. London: Pearson Education, 2002.

Camp, D, W Finlay, and E Lyons. "Is Low Self-Esteem an Inevitable Consequence of Stigma? An Example from Women with Chronic Mental Health Problems." *Social Science & Medicine* 55 (2002): 823–834.

Clark, D. "Sen's Capability Approach and the Many Spaces of Human Well Being." *The Journal of Development Studies* 41, no. 8 (2005): 1339–1368.

Courtwright, A. "Justice, Stigma, and the New Epidemiology of Health Disparities." *Bioethics* 23, no. 2 (2009): 90–96.

Courtwright, A. "Stigmatization and Public Health Ethics." *Bioethics* 23, no. 2 (2013): 90–96.

Crocker, J. "Social Stigma and Self-Esteem: Situational Construction of Self Worth." *Journal of Experimental Social Psychology* 35 (1999): 89–107.

Crocker, J, and B Major. "Social Stigma and Self-Esteem: The Self-Protective Properties of Stigma." *Psychological Review* 96, no. 4 (1989): 608–630.

Daniels, N. *Just Healthcare*. New York: Cambridge University Press, 1985.

Daniels, N. "Justice, Health and Healthcare." *American Journal of Bioethics* 1, no. 2 (2001): 2–16.

Daniels, N. "Democratic Equality: Rawls' Complex Egalitarianism." In *The Cambridge Companion to Rawls*, edited by S Freeman, 241–276. Cambridge: Cambridge University Press, 2002.

Daniels, N, and J Sabin. "Limits to Healthcare: Fair Procedures, Democratic Deliberation, and the Legitimacy Problem for Insurers." *Philosophy and Public Affairs* 26, no. 4 (1997): 303–350.

Elliot, M. "Human Rights and the Triumph of the Individual in World Culture." *Cultural Sociology* 1, no. 3 (2007): 343–363.

Elster, J. *Sour Grapes: Studies in the Subversion of Rationality*. Cambridge: Cambridge University Press, 1985.

Fassin, D. "The Biopolitics of Otherness." *Anthropology Today* 17, no. 1 (2001): 3–7.

Fekete, L. "Anti-Muslim Racism and the European Security State." *Race and Class* 46, no. 1 (2004): 3–29.

Friedman, M, and V Sarogiou. "Religiosity, Psychological Acculturation to the Host Culture, Self-Esteem and Depressive Symptoms among Stigmatized and Nonstigmatized Religious Immigrant Groups in Western Europe." *Basic and Applied Social Psychology* 32, no. 2 (2010): 185–195.

Fukuyama, F. *The End of History and the Last Man*. New York: Free Press, 1992.

Gelders, D, and I Oyvind. "Government Communication About Potential Policies: Public Relations, Propaganda or Both?" *Public Relations Review* 36 (2010): 59–62.

Gibbard, A. "Disparate Goods and Rawls' Difference Principle: A Social Choice Theoretic Treatment." *Theory and Decision* 11 (1979): 267–288.

Gutwirth, S. *Privacy and the Information Age*. Lanham, MD, Boulder, CO, New York and Oxford: Rowman & Littlefield Publishers, 2002.

Laitinen, A. "Social Bases of Self-Esteem: Rawls, Honneth and Beyond." *Conference Paper* (2012). *Available at*http://nome.unak.is/nm-marzo-2012/vol-7-n-2-2012/45-conference-paper/307-social-bases-of-self-esteem-rawls-honneth-and-beyond

Leary, M. "The Social and Psychological Importance of Self-Esteem." In *The Social Psychology of Emotional and Behavioral Problems*, edited by R Kowalski and M Leary, 197–221. Washington, DC: APA, 1999.

Leary, M, and D Downs. "Interpersonal Functions of the Self-Esteem Motive: The Self-Esteem System as a Sociometer." In *Efficacy, Agency and Self-Esteem*, edited by M Kernis, 123–144. New York: Plenum Press, 1995.

Leary, M, E Tambor, S Terdal, and D Downs. "Self-Esteem as an Interpersonal Monitor: The Sociometer Hypothesis." *Journal of Personality and Social Psychology* 68, no. 3 (1995): 518–530.

Lee, Tiane L., and Susan T. Fiske. "Not an Outgroup, Not yet an Ingroup: Immigrants in the Stereotype Content Model." *International Journal of Intercultural Relations* 30, no. 6 (2006): 751–768.

Lehning, P. *John Rawls: An Introduction*. Cambridge: Cambridge University Press, 2006.

Major, B, S Spencer, T Schmader, C Wolfe, and J Crocker. "Coping with Negative Stereotypes About Intellectual Performance: The Role of Psychological Disengagement." *Personality and Social Psychology Bulletin* 24, no. 1 (1998): 34–50.

McCrudden, C. "Human Dignity and Judicial Interpretation of Human Rights." *The European Journal of International Law* 19, no. 4 (2008): 655–724.

McKinnon, C. "Exclusion Rules and Self-Respect." *Journal of Value Enquiry* 34 (2000): 491–505.

Miller, C, and C Kaiser. "A Theoretical Perspective on Coping with Stigma." *Journal of Social Issues* 57, no. 1 (2001): 73–92.

Miller, C, and B Major. "Coping with Stigma and Prejudice." In *The Social Psychology of Stigmatisation*, edited by T Heatherton, R Kleck, M Hebl and J Hull, 243–272. New York: Guilford Press, 2000.

Mullen, B, and R Brown. "Ingroup Bias as a Function of Salience, Relevance, and Status: An Integration." *European Journal of Social Psychology* 22 (1992): 103–122.

Norton, H, and D Keats Citron. "Government Speech 2.0." *Denver University Law Review* 87 (2010): 899–943.

Nussbaum, M. "Capabilities as Fundamental Entitlements: Sen and Social Justice." *Feminist Economics* 9, nos 2–3(2003): 33–59.
Rawls, J. *A Theory of Justice (First edition)*. Cambridge, MA: Harvard Press, 1971.
Rawls, J. "The Priority of Right and Ideas of the Good." *Philosophy & Public Affairs* 17, no. 4 (1988): 251–276.
Rawls, J. *Political Liberalism*. New York: Columbia University Press, 1993.
Rawls, J. *A Theory of Justice (Revised edition)*. Cambridge MA: Harvard University Press, 1999.
Roland, C, and R Foxx. "Self-Respect: A Neglected Concept." *Philosophical Psychology* 16 (2003): 247–287.
Sachs, D. "How to Distinguish Self-Respect from Self-Esteem." *Philosophy and Public Affairs* 10 (1981): 346–360.
Sen, A. *Inequality Reexamined*. Cambridge, MA: Harvard University Press, 1973/1995.
Sen, A. *Equality of What? The Tanner Lecture on Human Values*. Cambridge: Cambridge University Press, 1980.
Sen, A. *Inequality Reexamined*. Cambridge, MA: Harvard University Press, 1995.
Smith, S. C., Jr., L. T. Clark, R. S. Cooper, S. R. Daniels, S. K. Kumanyika, E. Ofili, M. A. Quinones, et al. "Discovering the Full Spectrum of Cardiovascular Disease: Minority Health Summit 2003: Report of the Obesity, Metabolic Syndrome, and Hypertension Writing Group." (In Eng). *Circulation* 111, no. 10 (2005): e134–139.
Stark, C. "Rawlsian Self-Respect." In *Oxford Studies in Normative Ethics*, edited by M Timmons, 238–261. Oxford: Oxford University Press, 2012.
Statman, D. "Humiliation, Dignity and Self-Respect." *Philosophical Psychology* 13, no. 4 (2000): 523–540.
Sugden, R. "Welfare, Resources, and Capabilities: A Review of Inequality Reexamined by Amartya Sen." *Journal of Economic Literature* 31 (1993): 1947–1962.
Taylor, R. "Rawls's Defense of the Priority of Liberty: A Kantian Reconstruction." *Philosophy & Public Affairs* 31, no. 3 (2003): 256–271.

4 Stigmatizing state expression as hate speech

1 Introduction

> [The] defamation of a minority group, through hate speech, undermines a public good that can and should be protected: the basic assurance of inclusion in society for all members. A social environment polluted by anti-gay leaflets, Nazi banners, and burning crosses sends an implicit message to the targets of such hatred: your security is uncertain and you can expect to face humiliation and discrimination when you leave your home.
>
> Jeremy Waldron[1]

Criminal law arguably has a potential role to play in regulating some forms of stigmatizing expressions. Whilst the demand for legal certainty and its consequent rigidity mean that criminal law will be unlikely to play a major role in upholding all the normative principles (discussed in Chapter 3), it is perhaps uniquely suited to upholding normative principle (i). This requires that states never engage in expressions that are intended to harm the self-respect (linked closely to human dignity) of individuals in society. This principle demands a hard and fast approach (whereby all such expressions are forbidden). This chapter will examine the existence of potentially relevant criminal law and the possibility of applying it to figures connected to the state. In doing so it will look at varying approaches that are taken in different jurisdictions towards harmful speech. This will include a 'libertarian approach' as exemplified by the US (i.e. where very little speech law exists), a 'pragmatic approach' found in most other Western states (where certain expressions against specific categories of people are forbidden) and a 'dignity centred approach' most notability illustrated by Germany (where insulting remarks against unspecified groups may be criminalized). This chapter will also look at the effect rules on immunity for public figures are likely to have in instances where hate speech law might be applicable to certain stigmatizing state expressions (SSEs).

1 J Waldron, *The Harm in Hate Speech* (Cambridge, MA: Harvard University Press, 2012).

2 Criminal law is only suitable for preventing extreme expressions

A Expressions that are unintentional or mildly stigmatizing are not suitable for criminalization

Those with a familiarity with hate speech laws will see immediately that they are likely to be of limited application to many if not most forms of SSE. Whilst hate speech law varies from state to state a number of important initial observations can be made concerning its potential applicability to SSEs. Perhaps most important is that hate speech laws are usually only targeted at expressions that are considered as being seriously harmful. This usually involves serious attacks or insults, often against specifically defined vulnerable groups and minorities (discussed further in section 4). Such laws are not normally aimed at mildly stigmatizing remarks or expressions that cause mild offence but usually target more serious expressions that are perceived as threats to public order or assaults on human dignity (see section B below). Most states do not criminalize simple insults and very few states have laws against harmful expressions made against unspecified groups in society. This means that the vast majority of the SSEs described in Chapter 1 are unlikely to be considered as amounting to hate speech.

When describing the concept of 'stigmatizing expressions' it is furthermore important to remember (as Chapters 1–3 discussed) that not all expressive activities that are capable of leading to stigmatization are unavoidable or even undesirable. Even those that are considered undesirable or immoral may not be suitable for criminalization. Simple reactions of ambivalence, for example, to those who may have unsightly deformations may well be upsetting for those involved, but may in reality be a response that is deeply rooted in instinct and something that is to a large extent impossible to prevent.[2] Individuals may, for example, avert their eyes when a disfigured person enters the room to avoid staring. Whilst this may be done with a positive intention, the result may be stigmatizing to such a person who may be all too familiar with such a response.

In some circumstances individuals may not be aware that their expressive acts may be stigmatizing. Take, for example, an individual who states he or she "doesn't like to eat in restaurants in a particular area". In doing so he or she may offend someone from a minority that predominates in that area. Such a statement might be taken by a listener with a knowledge of the area as evidence of the individual's dislike for the people who live in that area and may cause offence. An individual may make such a statement with the intention of expressing such sentiments or they may be an unintentional result. The individual may, for example, not frequent such restaurants because he or she finds the prices too high, or because he or she is allergic to the food in question. He or she may not even know that a certain minority lives there. Despite the lack of culpability such expressive

2 M Hebl, M Tickle, and T Heatherton, "Awkward Moments in Interactions between Nonstigmatized and Stigmatized Individuals", in *The Social Psychology of Stigma*, ed. T Heatherton, et al. (New York: Guilford Press, 2000). Individuals can learn to suppress such reactions with education and increased familiarity with such individuals.

acts may still be capable of offence and stigmatization. A world that would criminalize such offensive expression would therefore not only require that individuals limited what they said, but would require such individuals to be on permanent alert to the possibility that their expressive acts might be offensive to others. Such a situation would be both impracticable and undesirable in terms of personal liberty.

B Criminal law is suitable only in order to prohibit serious expressive harm that can be defined in an objective manner

Given that the criminal law is not generally suitable for combatting unintentional, minor or useful stigmatization, one should perhaps only expect to see its deployment in order to tackle those forms of stigmatization that can be considered as serious. This expectation is reflected in many systems of criminal law that are designed to combat hate speech. When one looks at the criminal laws that exist from state to state one sees that for the most part states usually enact laws that are intended to target only those offensive expressive acts that are considered very harmful.[3] The term stigmatization is not invoked in legal provisions. The wording of the offence in question is often selected so that harmful expressions over a particular threshold are criminalized. In looking at the laws that exist, one can observe that one of the two approaches below are used.

(i) Laws aimed at protecting the dignity of individuals and groups

Laws in this category aim to prohibit insulting or offensive remarks that are considered serious enough to be capable of harming the dignity of the person or group involved. Such remarks or expressions go beyond those that may be offensive on a subjective basis depending on the context. Laws of this type are unlikely to apply to expressions that may be mildly insulting (even on an objective basis) but will usually only apply to expressions that are deemed serious enough to be capable of harming the dignity of the individual(s) involved (though this is not always how a law may be explicitly formulated). Human dignity (as will be discussed in section 5) is, however, a concept that invokes different things depending upon the cultural and legal situation it is invoked in. Its meaning has been interpreted differently across various legal systems.[4] Germany is notable in having developed a relatively communitarian conception of dignity and for invoking it *inter alia* in laws concerning harmful expression (see section 5). This approach in Germany is used to criminalize insults against individuals and groups that represent attacks on the dignity of the individuals concerned. Such attacks involve

3 Germany and the US are the main exceptions to this. The US (see section 4) is at one extreme, where the criminalization of almost no expression is permitted by the Constitution, whereas Germany (at the other end of the spectrum) has criminal provisions for insult (see section 5).

4 C McCrudden, "Human Dignity and Judicial Interpretation of Human Rights", *The European Journal of International Law* 19, no. 4 (2008).

assertions that the individual(s) or groups concerned are, for one reason or another, less than human, less capable of rational thought and, as a consequence, should be viewed as deserving less respect than one would normally attribute to a human being. As a German court once aptly stated, dignity is harmed where "the subject quality of the human being is being negated in principle".[5]

(ii) Laws aimed at maintaining public order

A second, much more common type of criminal offence can be seen in those laws that have a more pragmatic goal than the protection of human dignity, the aim usually being the maintenance of public order or the protection of individual rights. These types of criminal offences are usually concerned with the ability of certain types of expression to induce individuals to act in a way that would bring about harmful outcomes for the individuals concerned. Such outcomes may involve the threat of physical violence, intimidation to a level that individuals no longer have the autonomy to conduct their affairs as they would wish and the fostering of an environment that is conductive to discrimination against the group in question. Approaches of this type often take the form of the promulgation of criminal laws that prohibit expressions that are likely to trigger specific harm against certain groups. The most common is related to 'inciting hatred' related to race or ethnicity. One can refer to such offences as 'incitation type' offences. The justification for such laws is often that inflammatory racist speech can encourage people to commit crimes or discriminate against individuals of a different racial or ethnic origin.[6]

The following sections of this chapter will illustrate three different approaches towards dealing with harmful expression such as hate speech. Whilst these approaches vary in the breadth and intensity of stigmatizing expression they are able to engage, one constant is that in all types of approach there will be a vast amount of stigmatizing expression that will not be engaged, including many of the examples shown in Chapter 1.

3 The libertarian approach as exemplified by the American First Amendment

A The overarching role of the First Amendment

The US has been described by some commentators as essentially being in a 'minority of one' in terms of its approach to harmful expression.[7] Through the

5 Decision of the Federal Constitutional Court (Entscheidungen des BVergGE) Vol. 30, 1 (25 f.); Vol. 109, 279 (312f.). Quote taken from T Hornle, "Criminalizing Human Behaviour to Protect Human Dignity", *Criminal Law and Philosophy* 6 (2012). p318

6 A Tsesis, "Dignity and Speech: The Regulation of Hate Speech in a Democracy", *Wake Forrest Law Review* 44 (2009). p505

7 R O'Neil, "Hate Speech, Fighting Words, and Beyond – Why American Law Is Unique", *Albany Law Review* 76, no. 1 (2013). J Downing, "'Hate Speech' and

Supreme Court's judicial interpretation of its First Amendment, it has positioned itself at the more fundamentalist end of the spectrum in terms of its protection for individual free speech. The First Amendment enshrines protection of free speech in the Constitution. It reads:

> Congress shall make no law respecting an establishment of religion, or prohibiting the free exercise thereof; or abridging the freedom of speech, or of the press; or the right of the people peaceably to assemble, and to petition the Government for a redress of grievances.[8]

The existence of the First Amendment in the US Constitution, and its subsequent interpretation by the Supreme Court gives it an extreme civil libertarian character in terms of its ability to restrict harmful forms of expression. In this context the content of speech is generally viewed as being indivisible, with the state (and consequently the criminal law at federal or state level) not being able to draw a distinction between speech that is harmful or degrading and that which is not.[9] Whilst the US Constitution allows the federal and state governments to protect their citizens from physical harm caused by other citizens, the First Amendment clearly prevents intervention in nearly all expressive acts, even if they are capable of causing psychological harm. The US legal system therefore draws a general distinction between speech and conduct, with the former being largely free from government intervention.[10] As a consequence, the states of the US have very little criminal law that forbids insulting or degrading expressions or even expressions that are targeted at vulnerable groups. The Supreme Court has created some limited exceptions that are listed below.

(i) Obscenity

The Supreme Court has held that certain forms of obscenity can be prevented without running afoul of the First Amendment. Rather than focusing upon all obscenities, the court has been more sympathetic to controls where the obscene expression in question "taken as a whole, lacks serious literary, artistic, political or scientific value".[11] In other words the court is describing expressions that are obscene or lewd for the sake of it, expression that is devoid of any significant meaning. Where there is some significant meaning attached, be it political, cultural, artistic, etc., the court is much less sympathetic to the prospect of a ban (even if such content represents a racist idea). In one case, for example, the

'First Amendment Absolutism' Discourses in the US", *Discourse & Society* 10, no. 2 (1999). See concluding remarks.

8 This extract also contains what is known as the establishment clause which prevents the US government from supporting or interfering with religious practice.

9 N Strossen, "Regulating Racist Speech on Campus? A Modest Proposal?", *Duke Law ournal* 484 (1990).

10 C Taylor, "Hate Speech and Government Speech", *Journal of Constitutional Law* 12, no. 4 (2010).

11 *Miller v. California* 413 U.S. 15, 24 (1973). p24

Supreme Court ruled against the prosecution of an individual for obscenity because he wore a t-shirt saying "Fuck the draft" in court.[12] In this instance the inclusion of the word "draft" was considered as being able to give such commentary a political meaning. Given the limitations of the concept of 'obscenity' as outlined by the Supreme Court it is likely to be of little relevance in terms of SSEs given that (as Chapter 1 illustrated) they usually possess more substantive content (e.g. stereotypes relating to particular groups in society).

(ii) Harassment

In addition to obscenity, the US Supreme Court has stated that the First Amendment rights of some citizens must not be allowed to violate the constitutional rights of others through harassment. The constitutional right to privacy in one's own home will, for example, trump another's First Amendment rights. In the case of *Frisby v. Schultz* [13] the court, for example, ruled that the First Amendment did not entitle pro-life supporters to be allowed to make noisy protests and picket doctors at their own homes. In that case, the right of the individual doctors to enjoy privacy in their own homes was given precedence over the right of protestors to attempt to transmit loud anti-abortion messages inside from the street. In that case the court stated: "there simply is no right to force speech into the home of an unwilling listener". Similarly, individuals have the right to be protected from harmful forms of speech in the workplace. An important element of such cases also is that the individuals involved are effectively captive audiences, individuals cannot simply leave their home or workplace.[14] There is no constitutional right against being offended (outside the home at least) or against being exposed to insulting messages in public. One should therefore not read such cases in an overly expansive manner. When no other such constitutional rights exist (such as privacy in the home), the First Amendment rights of others (i.e. to speak freely) cannot be challenged in such a way.[15]

(iii) Fighting words

The Supreme Court also recognized, in a case that now seems somewhat dated, the concept of certain types of expression that may be criminalized because they are likely to result in an imminent breach of the peace. In the case of *Chaplinsky v. New Hampshire*,[16] a man issued insults to a police officer who was attempting to arrest him. His words were reputed to have been something along the lines of

12 *Cohen v. California*, 403 U.S. 15, 16 (1971).

13 *Frisby v. Schultz*, 487, 487–488 (1988).

14 Similar arguments apply to places of education. See N Strossen, "Regulating Workplace Sexual Harassment and Upholding the First Amendment – Avoiding a Collision", *Villanova Law Review* 37, no. 4 (1992). p760

15 H Nissenbaum, "Privacy as Contextual Integrity", *Washington Law Review* 79 (2004). p108

16 *Chaplinsky v. New Hampshire*, 315 U.S. 568, 571–573 (1942).

"[you are] a damned fascist" and a "god dammed racketeer". In a ruling on the case the Supreme Court stated that First Amendment protection did not apply to expressions uttered in a face-to face manner that were "likely to cause a breach of the peace". The *Chaplinsky* precedent is now over 70 years old. Whilst it has never directly been overturned by the Supreme Court, it has been suggested that its validity in terms of a precedent is now dubious, especially given the developments of the Supreme Court in favour of a more extreme protection of free speech (see below).[17]

B A raging debate over the criminalization of hate speech

The limitations imposed by the US Constitution resonate at the centre of a decades long debate in the US concerning the permissibility of hate speech legislation.[18] Free speech fundamentalists have constantly maintained that the Constitution, supporting a free 'marketplace of ideas'[19] allows no place to regulate hate speech no matter how vitriolic or harmful.[20] Supporters of laws criminalizing hate speech had hoped the limited exceptions described above would be enough to provide cover for states to criminalize certain forms of hate speech.[21] However, since the 1990s the Supreme Court has shown itself to be very unreceptive in terms of the infringement upon individual expression that may be permitted even where the speech in question is clearly hate speech. In the case of *R.A.V. v City of Saint Paul*[22] the US Supreme Court struck down a Minnesota law that prohibited the placing of racist symbols, including burning crosses (and swastikas) on public or private property with the aim of "arousing anger, alarm or resentment in others on the basis of race, color, creed, religion or gender". The Supreme Court ruled that the law represented "content differentiation" by the state because it purported to ban only types of expression that were directed towards "race, color, creed, religion or gender".

This hardline position was moderated, albeit slightly, in the Supreme Court case of *Virginia v. Black.*[23] That case concerned a Virginia law that prohibited cross burning that had the intention of "intimidating any person or group of persons". Unlike *R.A.V.*, where restrictions on intimidating racist speech were prohibited, the Supreme Court agreed that certain expressions could be limited, where there

17 G Gard, "Fighting Words as Free Speech", *Washington University Law Quarterly* 58 (1980). As far back as 1980 scholars have viewed Chaplinksy as an unreliable precedent.

18 O'Neil, "Hate Speech, Fighting Words, and Beyond – Why American Law Is Unique".

19 M Reddish and G Lippman, "Freedom of Expression and the Civic Republican Revival in Constitutional Theory: The Ominous Implications", *California Law Review* 79, no. 2 (1991).

20 R Post, "Racist Speech, Democracy, and the First Amendment", *Faculty Scholarship Series* 208 (1991).

21 S Heyman, *Free Speech and Human Dignity* (Chicago, IL: Faculty Scholarship Commons, 2008).

22 *R.A.V. v. City of Saint Paul*, 505 U.S. 377, 397, 415 (1992).

23 *Virginia v. Black*, 538 U.S. 343 (2003).

was a clear intent to intimidate. The court, however, limited the potential applicability of this ruling by explicitly referring to historically recognized hate symbols such as the burning cross. In justifying its decision the court stated:

> The First Amendment permits Virginia to outlaw cross burnings done with the intent to intimidate because burning a cross is a particularly virulent form of intimidation. Instead of prohibiting all intimidating messages, Virginia may choose to regulate this subset of intimidating messages in light of cross burning's long and pernicious history as a signal of impending violence.[24]

In terms of preventing stigmatizing expressions, the libertarian approach as espoused by the US Supreme Court's reading of the Constitution is extremely limited. This means that the ability of the criminal law to make a contribution, in terms of the regulation of stigmatizing statements, is limited. This even includes laws that might play a part in upholding normative principle (i), i.e. that SSEs should not be used to directly attack self-respect. US law makers are only able to enact laws that are capable of restricting the most serious and extreme forms of stigmatization, i.e. where the expression concerned is tantamount to a threat of physical violence against a certain community, and then only where it takes the form of a culturally recognized hate symbol. In terms of possible stigmatizing expressions this represents only a small category of the most intensely stigmatizing type. As Chapter 1 illustrated stigmatizing expression can exist in an almost unlimited range of contexts beyond that recognized by the Supreme Court in *Black*. This largely limits or even prevents the creation of hate speech laws in the US that are likely to have an effect on SSEs.

4 The pragmatic approach

Most countries, including those of Western Europe, Australia and Canada[25] adopt more interventionist and nuanced approaches to expressive acts perceived as harmful. Many of these are capable of impacting upon speech (including SSEs) that is stigmatizing. The types of criminal offences that exist in these states can be divided into two groups. The first are general offences concerning acts of defamation or insult. The second (and more important) type is usually employed to tackle hate speech targeted against certain sensitive groups. Crimes of this type are often based around a similar template that, though with variations, is replicated in numerous legal systems. The template could be read as follows, "It is illegal to commit expressive act X against groups W, Y. Z". This basic structure is repeated across numerous states, including (but not limited to) the UK, Australia, Belgium, the Netherlands and France (examples of which will be presented in this chapter).

24 *Black*, 538 U.S. at 363. Quote taken directly from O' Neil, "Hate Speech, Fighting Words, and Beyond – Why American Law Is Unique". p489

25 The author does not claim that this list is exhaustive. An exhaustive review of the law in every state pertaining to harmful expression would be beyond the scope of this book.

Each applies this basic structure to a number of expressive acts. What can vary in each state, however, is the definition of the actual acts that are illegal and also the groups that are protected

A Laws relating to insult or defamation

Many states in the civil law world have a wide variety of laws that criminalize various forms of defamatory or insulting expression. These are usually related to expressive acts against specific individuals, although some states do recognize insults against groups (e.g. France).[26] This limits the potential applicability to many forms of SSE, which as Chapter 1 illustrated often refer to groups and not specific individuals. Stigmatization at its heart is not related to the honour or reputation of individuals, but to the negative perception held by some about groups of individuals with certain traits in society.[27] Accordingly, when an individual is stigmatized, one is not usually speaking of an aspect that is unique to that individual but of an assertion that the individual concerned possesses a trait that denotes his or her membership of a category which is perceived as undesirable. As a consequence, when an individual is stigmatized, rather than being attacked on the basis of his or her individuality, the individual concerned is usually being 'de-individualized' through a form of negative stereotyping that is usually entailed in the process of stigmatization (see Chapter 2 section 3). Most of the laws concerning insult in this category of states, however, relate to attacks on an individual's honour,[28] where an individual is alleged to be something that he or she is not (e.g. defamation). Whilst such attacks may involve the application of a stigmatized stereotype (imagine, for example, an allegation that a male politician wore women's clothes in secret), what is central to such offences is the attack on the individual's honour, and not the stigmatization of the group in question (e.g. men who wear female clothing). This aspect is demonstrated by the fact that most of the insult laws in this category apply only where identifiable individuals have been targeted. Where somebody merely attacks the trait that is stigmatized (by saying, for example, that men who wear female clothing are perverts) such laws do not apply. As a consequence, such laws have relatively little (in both aim and effect) to do with reducing the impact of stigmatizing expressions in society. The situation may, however, be different where insult or defamation laws are also able to be applied to groups. The following sections discuss, with a number of illustrations, how such laws are capable of impacting upon stigmatizing expressions.

26 See Article 32 de la loi du 29 juillet 1881.

27 B Link and J Phelan, "Conceptualizing Stigma", *Annual Review of Sociology* 27 (2001); J Dovidio, B Major, and J Crocker, "Stigma: Introduction and Overview", in *The Social Psychology of Stigma*, ed. T Heatherton et al. (New York: Guilford Press, 2000).

28 An exception to this may include crimes such as the Belgian offence of 'divulgation' – a form of insult that can even involve the publication of true facts.

B Negative expressive acts targeted at certain sensitive groups

The second category of criminal offences is more concerned with attacks on groups in society than attacks upon the honour of specific individuals. Such laws have often been created in order to tackle problematic hate speech. They usually focus on targeted expressive acts, i.e. the 'X' in the above template. Despite the common aim, of reducing harmful hate speech, there is a large variation in what is described in the law of different states. Criminal offences within this template are capable of covering varying types of expression that are capable of being stigmatizing. The following paragraphs will discuss how such laws may be able to contribute to the regulation of stigmatizing statements.

(i) Threatening, abusive or insulting words to stir up hatred – inciting hatred

This formulation is used in a number of criminal offences. In the UK this type of format represents the core of the approach to hate speech. There, the compulsory requirement is 'stirring up hatred'[29] whilst 'inciting hatred' is common in continental European jurisdictions (e.g. Belgium and The Netherlands).[30] The term 'stirring up' connotes creating hatred in others. If the requirement is that an expression be capable of stirring up hatred in others, one would expect that comments are made in public, i.e. in the presence of others, as in order to stir something up, others must necessarily be exposed to the idea in question.[31] Although not explicitly invoking the idea of stigmatization, such an offence covers aspects that are closely associated with the phenomenon. Most notably, an important facet of stigmatization often involves the (even if only perceived) conveyance of stigmatizing views to individuals who interact with the individual or group that is being stigmatized (see Chapter 2 section 4). Whilst hatred need not be required in all forms of stigmatization (many forms of stigmatization can be based on more subtle forms of disgust, scorn of fear, for example),[32] it can be an important factor in many forms of severe stigmatization, especially those which are likely to lead individuals to act in a violent way.[33]

The requirement of having to 'stir up hatred' will not, however, catch many forms of stigmatization that fall below the 'hatred' threshold. When one speaks of hating a group, one is speaking of detesting whatever characteristic defines that

29 Section 23 of the Public Order Act (1985).

30 For Belgium see Article 453 of the *Code pénal*. For the Netherlands see Wetboek van Strafrecht Article 137(d).

31 For further discussion on the concept of 'stirring up hatred' (in the context of religious hatred) see A Jeremy, "Practical Implications of the Enactment of the Racial and Religious Hatred Act 2006", *Ecclesiastical Law Journal* 9, no. 3 (2007).

32 Hebl, Tickle, and Heatherton, "Awkward Moments in Interactions between Non-stigmatized and Stigmatized Individuals". p226

33 R Kurzban and M Leary, "Evolutionary Origins of Stigmatization: The Functions of Social Exclusion", *Psychological Bulletin* 127, no. 2 (2001); D Reidpath et al., "'He Hath the French Pox': Stigma, Social Value and Social Exclusion", *Sociology of Health & Illness* 27, no. 4 (2005).

group. A common desire is that hated groups leave the city, region or country where they are hated. Such intense feelings are stigmatizing because they are apparent to the group in question that is the subject of such hatred. Hatred is, however, an extreme state. One can envisage states other than hatred which could also be stigmatizing. Disrespect, apathy, dislike, ridicule, etc. are all of a lower intensity than hatred, for example, but are still stigmatizing. 'Insulting words' that threaten merely to stir up one of these states would not, for example, be an offence under UK law even if they are made against protected groups (though Australian law in contrast seems to offer some level of protection to expressions of a lesser intensity).[34] As a result, there is in effect no prohibition on mild insults or offence to sensitive groups (even where they may be stigmatizing) if the result merely threatens to stir up ridicule or dislike but not hatred. It would be difficult to argue, for example, that individuals who publicly state that a certain group is ''boring', 'odd' or 'tight with their money' was attempting to stir up hatred. Whilst such assertions may be stigmatizing, they are not notions easily associated with 'hatred'.

(ii) Inciting discrimination

The criminalization of the 'incitation of discrimination' is conceptually different from 'incitation to hatred'. This is because the former involves calling for actions whereas the latter involves the creation of a state of mind in others. In the case of (direct) discrimination,[35] one calls for the differential treatment of two categories of people where there is no reasonable and objective justification.[36] A call to treat members of a particular ethnic group differently from other individuals in a society would be an example, as would a call not to serve gay people in shops. 'Incitement to discrimination' provisions are extremely wide-ranging and have the potential to catch a large amount of stigmatizing expression. On a simple reading such offences would apply to almost any call for (unjustified) differential treatment of a protected category. These range from the obviously racist or homophobic calls described above, to calls for women to be kept out of the armed forces or not to be allowed to join the Catholic priesthood. In countries such as Belgium that have a very large number of protected categories (including *inter alia* health status and wealth) the possibility to infringe such laws is even higher and may include what in other states would be considered acceptable territory for a debate on public policy. This breadth of potential application means that a systematic application of such laws would likely result in a severe limitation of free speech that would be both

34 See, for example, Crown Prosecution Service, "Sexual Orientation: CPS Guidance on Stirring up Hatred on Grounds of Sexual Orientation" (Mar 2010), https://www.cps.gov.uk/legal/s_to_u/sexual_orientation

35 For more consideration of the relationship between stigmatizing expressions and anti-discrimination approaches see Chapter 5.

36 This is the definition used by the Belgian Centre pour l'égalité des chances et la lutte contre le racisme which often acts as a partie civile in criminal cases of this type. Available at https://www.unia.be/files/Z_ARCHIEF/CGKR_JV_discriminatie_FR.pdf

infeasible (in terms of police and court power) and undesirable from a democratic perspective. It seems that in order to prevent such laws from being overused, prosecutors may apply them in a restricted manner, as has been the case in Belgium where it is often reserved for egregious and high profile examples.[37] Despite this reticence, there have been a number of high profile prosecutions against individuals in Belgium and the Netherlands for incitation to discrimination. One such example included Fouad Belkacem, a prominent figure in the Sharia4Belgium organization who called for an Islamic state to be introduced in Belgium and as a result a state of illegality for many groups and the potential death penalty for homosexuals.[38] Another Belgian incident involved the conviction of a Wallonian far right politician, Daniel Féret for *inter alia* incitation to discrimination. He called for the rejection of asylum seekers and the closure of facilities intended to deal with them.[39] As the European Court of Human Rights recognized, Féret had called for differential treatment (e.g. with regard to social security) for on the one hand Belgians and Europeans, and on the other hand all other groups.[40] Demanding the denial of rights on such a basis would be plainly discriminatory.

As Chapter 2 discussed stigmatization and discrimination whilst not identical are closely related phenomena. Discrimination (and thus also incitement to discrimination) is in many cases likely to lead to the stigmatization of those involved. Prohibiting calls to discriminate against certain groups will, therefore, prevent some stigmatizing expressions against those groups. Such an offence will not, however, catch the vast range of stigmatizing expressions that fall outside the definition of incitation to discrimination, even where such expressions are made against vulnerable groups that may be prone to both stigmatization and discrimination

C The use of protected categories in the pragmatic approach

(i) Membership of a specific category determines whether or not protection of the law applies

In this pragmatic group of countries, the type and number of protected categories are important. Using the template described above, one can see that they are of equal importance in deciding whether certain types of expression constitute criminal offences. Historically in most countries, the first categories to be recognized as

37 Ibid. See also B Van Stokkhom, H Sackers, and J Wils, "Godslastering, Discriminerende Uitingen Wegens Godsdienst En Haatuitingen", in *Onderzoek en beleid* (Wetenschappelijk Onderzoeken Documentatiecentrum, 2007). The imposition of hate speech laws in the Netherlands has been described as a 'paper tiger'.

38 http://www.standaard.be/cnt/dmf20121130_018

39 Mr Feret made an appeal to the European Court of Rights in Strasbourg but his appeal was rejected. See *Féret v. Belgium* (Application no. 15615/07). This case is discussed at greater length in section 4.

40 *Féret* para 6.

deserving of special protection were those such as race, ethnic origin or country of origin. The creation of these special categories was needed to make a special type of criminal offence, one that covered hateful and negative expression (and also violent acts) towards individuals in these groups. The creation of criminal offences involving these groups often came about as a response to the racism that occurred between 'native' populations and large numbers of recently arrived immigrants in the 1960s, 1970s and 1980s.[41] With time other categories came to be added such as 'religious grouping' and 'sexual preference'. The first of these came in a wave that largely started after the September 2001 attacks where followers of Islam were increasingly becoming the subject of verbal and physical attacks because of their religion.[42] The second came with the gradual increase in the openness of gay people and the ever increasing acceptance by mainstream society of such individuals. These basic categories are now protected in most democratic states.[43]

In addition to these familiar categories, some states have gone further in specifying additional protected categories that form part of criminal law. This is most notably the case for Belgium where a vast array of additional categories is recognized. These include "family ascendance", "national or ethnic origin", "gender", "civil state", "birth", "age", "personal wealth", "philosophical convictions", "health status" (present or future), "disability", "language", "membership of a union", "physical characteristics", "genetic characteristics" or "social origin".[44] France and the Netherlands lie somewhere in between, protecting a larger number of categories than the UK and Australia but less than Belgium. The effect of having such categories extends the potential range of the existing criminal offences. In Belgium, for example, it is a criminal offence to incite hatred or discrimination against 16 different categorizations. Such a range of categories represents, at least in theory, a potentially heavy impediment to free speech in general. In order to avoid this, states that have such provisions often apply them very infrequently and for exceptional cases.[45]

This can be contrasted with the UK, where the promulgation of hate speech laws has been reserved for serious cases deemed in the public interest.[46] The use of wide definitions of groups can also create issues in terms of an application that is too broad. Take, for example, the category of 'sexual orientation'. Some states,

41 L Ray and D Smith, "Racist Offenders and the Politics of 'Hate Crime'", *Law and Critique* 12, no. 3 (2001). p209

42 This included, for example, the Racial and Religious Hatred Act of 2006 in the UK and La loi du 10 mai 2007. Loi tendant à lutter contre la discrimination entre les femmes et les hommes' in Belgium.

43 In Australia, the categories relating to religious groups and sexual orientation are not protected throughout Australia but only in some of its component states.

44 La loi du 10 mai 2007 –. Loi tendant à lutter contre la discrimination entre les femmes et les hommes Article 22 (2).

45 "Discrimination en diversité. Rapport annuel 2011 – Centre pour l'égalité des chances et la lutte contre le racisme."

46 "Law Commission Consultation Paper No 213: Hate Crime: The Case for Extending Offences. Appendix A: Hate Crime and Freedom of Expression under the European Convention on Human Rights." Available at http://www.lawcom.gov.uk/app/uploads/2015/03/cp213_hate_crime_amended.pdf

such as France[47] and Belgium,[48] have a category that criminalizes harmful speech concerning 'sexual orientation' whereas others, such as the Netherlands, have more precisely defined provisions, speaking of harmful speech to individuals because of his or her 'hetero or homosexuality'.[49]

The use of broad terms, however, presents problems in terms of their potential impact on individual free speech and may call into question rights connected under freedom of speech including *inter alia* article 10 of the European Convention on Human Rights (ECHR) (discussed further in Chapters 5 and 6).[50] This was highlighted in the *Vanneste* case where the French *Cour de Cassation* overturned Mr Vanneste's conviction to incite hatred against gay people by virtue of their sexual orientation.[51] In that case the point was made that the proposed offence was so overly broad that it could be used to cover sexual activities (or proclinations) that are in fact criminal offences, such as paedophilia. As a consequence, it was argued that such a provision represented an unjustifiable imposition on freedom of political speech.

(ii) The selection of protected groups – protecting groups already accepted by mainstream society?

Given the existence of categories of sensitive groups deemed deserving of special legal protection, one might ask why such groups have been chosen for inclusion and why others have not? Why, for instance, does sexual orientation usually find protection, but not an urge to commit acts of paedophilia (accepting of course the important distinction between those who feel paedophilic impulses and those who act upon them)?[52] Why does race usually exist as a protected category, but not being poor or homeless? It is not difficult to think of numerous groups of individuals that are vulnerable and are subject to negative speech on a regular basis but which fall outside the groups mentioned above (even with the unusually wide formulations adopted in Belgian law). Such groups will often as a result be highly vulnerable to stigmatization. Imagine, for instance, groups such as the homeless, drug addicts,[53] smokers, alcoholics, people considered unattractive, the overweight, those with low intelligence, the eccentric, etc. This list is of course by no means exhaustive. Why is it, one might ask, that such groups do not usually find protection in laws designed to cover negative speech, whilst the familiar categories described above do? The level of

47 Article 32 de la loi du 29 juillet 1881.

48 *Code pénal belge* Article 453. Ibid.

49 *Strafwetboek* Article 137(d).

50 The relevance of Article 10 ECHR to the potential restriction of SSEs is considered further in Chapters 5 and 6 (concerning privacy approaches under Articles 8 and 14 ECHR).

51 *Vanneste, Christian*. Chambre criminelle de la Cour de cassation française12 novem bre 2008, pourvoi n° 07-83398.

52 J Morgon, "US Hate Crime Legislation: A Legal Model to Avoid in Australia". Morgon discusses the lack of protection for paedophiles in hate protection legislation.

53 R Room, "Stigma, Social Inequality and Alcohol and Drug Use", *Drug and Alcohol Review* 24 (2005).

stigmatization and hateful speech may well be higher for sensitive groups of individuals who fall outside the protection of the law than for those that are protected.[54] Compare, for example, the stigma of being black with that of being a drug addict. Whilst there is no doubt still prejudice and stigmatization of black people in most Western societies one would probably not agree that they face the same level of stigmatization as a drug addict does.[55] The same goes for an obese person or a person who may be considered unattractive.[56] Why is it then that most states choose not to criminalize hateful speech against such groups, whereas they ubiquitously do so on the basis of race?

One possible response to the question posed above might be that many (but not all) of the groups that do not find protection described in the common categories used in criminal law can be defined in terms of behaviours and not innate characteristics.[57] As a result they bring into play issues of personal responsibility with the result that many individuals would feel that they should be allowed to criticize such behaviours if they bring about negative consequences for society.[58] In addition, some of these categories may encompass individuals that partake in behaviours that may have themselves been criminalized. It would be, at the very least, unintuitive if the state made it illegal for people to direct harsh criticism and even hatred towards such people given that the state itself had chosen to criminalize such behaviour. Whilst this line of reasoning might be logical in terms of those behaviours that happen to be illegal (e.g. acts of paedophilia) it does not apply to many other groups for which hate speech is seemingly permitted.

Other individuals may be the subject of harmful speech as a result of aspects that are not related to behaviour or activities that are not generally condemned or illegal. Take, for example, people who are considered as unattractive, those who have red hair or those who have a lower than average intelligence.[59] Such individuals are no more in a position to control their characteristics than a person can their ethnicity or sexuality.

54 S Janke and J Hoyer, "Stigmatization of People with Pedophilia: A Blind Spot in Stigma Research", *International Journal of Sexual Health* (2013).

55 R. Room, "Stigma, Social Inequality and Alcohol and Drug Use". Drug use and addiction carries with it significant stigmatization, which is often intensified by the criminalization of drug use.

56 R Puhl and D Brownell, "Psychosocial Origins of Obesity Stigma", *Obesity Reviews* 4 (2003). p213

57 E Janssen, *Faith in Public Debate. On Freedom of Expression, Hate Speech and Religion in France & the Netherlands* (Cambridge: Interstentia, 2015). Discussing this concept in the context of the ECHR and Article 10.

58 This is the idea behind the concept of the sociometer, see M Leary et al., "Self-Esteem as an Interpersonal Monitor: The Sociometer Hypothesis", *Journal of Personality and Social Psychology* 68, no. 3 (1995).

59 F Whittington-Walsh, "The Broken Mirror – Young Women, Beauty & Facial Difference", *Women's Health and Urban Life* 5, no. 2 (2006). "People perceived as possessing an 'unattractive' face are stigmatized with undesirable social qualities and if seen as exceptionally 'different' from desirable faces could, until recently, be legally punished if out in public." D Heckert and A Best, "Ugly Duckling to Swan: Labelling Theory and the Stigmatization of Red Hair", *Symbiotic Interaction* 20, no. 4 (2011). Red headed individuals face stigmatization in many societies.

One way of conceptualizing this state of affairs is to see states in this intermediate group as making a 'pragmatic compromise' about where it is necessary to inhibit free speech in order to prevent certain types of hateful expression that can have corrosive effects upon society. This choice involves only offering protection to a few categories of people. There is no firm consensus as to why certain groups are deserving of protection whilst others are not. Some may justify it on a pragmatic basis where categories relate to large vulnerable minorities that have a history of suffering abuse. Others might argue that the categories that are used in reality represent groups that have become strong enough to advocate for their own protection.[60] Whatever the reason, the existence of such categories in most hate speech law acts to limit its potential applicability to stigmatizing expressions.

5 The dignity centred approach' as exemplified by Germany

A Dignity centred constitution

Hate speech was instrumental in allowing the demonization of minority political, cultural and ethnic groups leading to horrors such as the Holocaust for which Germany has since had to shoulder responsibility.[61] Those involved in the formation of the postwar German state were conscious of the need to go to great lengths to distinguish it from the Nazi state that had perpetrated such horrors.[62] Certain rights were thus mandated in the constitution, the 'Basic Law' (*Grudgesetz*). Notable constitutional provisions convey the need to value human dignity,[63] personal honour[64] and respect for democratic principles. Unlike many other constitutions, the German constitution (in Article 1) requires that the dignity of individuals be protected in an absolute manner. This is in contrast to the right to 'freedom of communication' which, though protected by the constitution, is not given such an absolute value.[65] This latter right may be limited in appropriate circumstances in order to protect other constitutional rights whilst the right to individual dignity may not.[66] In balancing rights of communication with other rights the German legal system differentiates between different types of speech, with favoured and more protected types (sometimes described as 'speech plus') enjoying more protection in comparison to unfavoured and unprotected types of speech (sometimes described as 'speech minus').

60 Morgon, "US Hate Crime Legislation: A Legal Model to Avoid in Australia". p31
61 Tsesis, "Dignity and Speech: The Regulation of Hate Speech in a Democracy".
62 J Whitman, "The Two Western Cultures of Privacy – Dignity Versus Liberty". *Faculty Scholarship Series* 649 (2004).
63 Basic Law Article 1.
64 Article 5(2).
65 Basic Law Article 5.
66 For a good description of the German laws that can be used to restrict freedom of speech see W Brugger, "The Treatment of Hate Speech in German Constitutional Law (Part I)", *German Law Journal* 3 (2002).

B Individual and collective criminal defamation or insult in German law

The German Federal Penal Code criminalizes both individual and collective versions of defamation and insult.[67] An insult can be defined as an "attack on the honour of another person by intentionally showing disrespect or no respect at all". Such an offence is punishable by a prison sentence of up to one year. Where attacks are more than just a mere insult and go beyond simple lack of respect, German law foresees a more serious offence of using defamatory assertions to attack a person's "honour".[68] This offence is concerned with public expressions. A further offence of using defamation, i.e. spreading untruths to harm an "individual's public esteem", also exists.[69] Factual incorrectness is not a prerequisite in order for a criminal offence to exist. Section 192 of the Penal Code states that attacks on the honour of a person can occur even in cases where the assertion is essentially true (i.e. through insults).[70] What is important is the form in which the assertion arises. Thus, a truthful assertion can represent an attack on one's honour if it is made in a certain way. The protection of individual dignity, honour and social standing is thus at the heart of the German approach to regulating hateful or insulting speech.[71]

In addition to expressive attacks on individuals, German law also criminalizes expressions that are capable of defaming groups. The courts have recognized both the existence of defamatory attacks on collective bodies or organizations (*Kollektivbeleidigung*) and also insults against less cohesive groups that merely represent individuals with a shared characteristic (*Beleidigung von Einzelpersonen unter einer Kollektivbezeichnung*). The first type will share a common organizational structure (e.g. a charity or business organizations). The second, however, could represent much more loosely connected groups that share a characteristic that renders them vulnerable to insult. This goes beyond the approach used in most other countries (i.e. those adopting the pragmatic approach) where the focus is on an exhaustively defined set of categories. In contrast, under the German system there is no exhaustive definition. The notion of a group is rather left open, being able, for example, to represent 'disabled people' or all the 'Turks in Germany', for example.

C The Federal Constitutional Court and its treatment of group insults

The German Federal Constitutional Court has stated that for an insult to be capable of affecting a group it must pertain to an aspect that is:

> present in all members of the collective, whereas association with features applying to some but obviously not all members does not…diminish the

67 Part 14 Sections 185–200.
68 Section 187.
69 Section 186
70 Whitman, "Enforcing Civility and Respect: Three Societies".
71 For a discussion of the historical and contemporary importance of the concept of dignity to German law see Whitman, "The Two Western Cultures of Privacy – Dignity Versus Liberty".

> personal honour of each individual member. Since [to] every addressee of such a statement [it] is clear that not all can be meant but particular persons are not named, no one is defamed by such a statement.[72]

In addition, the court has held that "[t]he larger the collective to which a disparaging statement relates, the weaker the personal involvement of the individual member can be ...".[73] A court is more likely to find that a group insult occurred the smaller the size of the group was. As a consequence, minorities are more likely to be able to avail themselves of this provision than majoritarian groups. In addition, where the insult in question contains material that is commonly associated with hate speech, i.e. regarding race, ethnicity or physical and mental characteristics, the court is more likely to find that the insult is capable of harming the dignity of all members of the group. Brugger identifies several conditions that increase the likelihood of a group insult being declared under the Penal Code:[74]

1 a small, rather than a large, group is attacked;
2 the group's characteristics differ from those of the general public;
3 the defamatory statement assaults all members of the group rather than single or typical members; and
4 the criticism is based on unalterable criteria or on criteria that are attributed to the group by the larger society around them instead of by the group itself.

The criteria described above were developed in the *Soldiers are Murderers Case.* This case involved the distribution of leaflets by several peace activists that alleged that "solders are murderers". After receiving complaints concerning the leaflets the police charged the activists involved with their distribution with collective insult under Article 185 of the Penal Code. In that case, although a criminal court had convicted those involved in the distribution of the leaflets, the Federal Court overturned the conviction as it found that the alleged insult was too imprecise. This was because the insult in the leaflet had not specified which soldiers it referred to. It was not possible to know whether the leaflet was referring to certain German soldiers, all German solders or all soldiers in general (i.e. all soldiers from all countries). As a result, the leaflets were considered not to refer to a group that was clearly definable. Another indicative case involved a poem entitled "The fraudulent asylum seeker".[75] In that case, the author of the poem accused asylum seekers of taking advantage of the German asylum system and of "bringing AIDS to Germany". Even though the poem, as a form of cultural expression, was protected under Article 5(3) of the basic law, the court found that the unfounded

72 .BVerfGE 93, 266, 300, Decision of 10 October 1995, Soldiers are Murderers = Decisions 659, at 685. Quote taken from W Brugger, "The Treatment of Hate Speech in German Constitutional Law (Part II)", *German Law Journal* 4, no. 1 (2002). p26

73 Ibid., 301 = Decisions, at 686.

74 Brugger, "The Treatment of Hate Speech in German Constitutional Law (Part II)". p26

75 For an analysis of this and the *Soldiers are Murderers Case* see ibid.

accusations were serious enough to amount to a group insult against asylum seekers and as a result attacked the human dignity of asylum seekers.[76]

D The German dignity centric approach – casting a wider net for stigmatizing expression?

The German approach can be contrasted with that used by most other states that intervene in matters of harmful expression. Its focus is not on the harm brought about to public order or other societal issues such as discrimination but the protection of individual dignity. In this regard it is more conceptually similar to the concept of stigmatization which concerns the psychological effects that can be brought about at an individual level. Individual dignity is also closely connected to the concept of self-respect and internationalization (see Chapters 2 and 3). Another result of this focus (and not a more public order orientated approach) is that it is not only the usual protected categories that find protection but potentially all (minority) groups within society. An approach of this type is thus far more likely to catch a wider range of stigmatizing expression than a pragmatic type approach.

Whilst dignity centred expressive offences may be capable of catching many types of stigmatizing expression, in particular those of an extremely stigmatizing nature, they do not prevent all types of stigmatizing expression. There are a wide range of expressions that are capable of being stigmatizing, but which cannot be considered as attacks upon individual dignity. Such expressions can be made both intentionally and unintentionally.[77] Imagine someone who unconsciously shows that he or she does not enjoy the company of a certain individual, or even someone who explicitly states that he or she does not like someone. Imagine also someone who states that he or she doesn't find people with a certain physical appearance sexually attractive, e.g. because they are tall or short, have a certain hair colour or not much hair, or because they appear to come from a particular ethnic group. All of these expressions may be offensive and stigmatizing. They do not, however, constitute an attack on the dignity of the individual concerned. These comments represent a wholly subjective valuation on the part of the 'speaker' that are made according to wholly subjective criteria. They do not deny the objective value of the individuals to which they refer in terms of ability for rationality or equality as human beings (see Chapter 3 for a discussion on the objective nature of the concept of human dignity). In the words of the German court, the 'subject quality' of the individual concerned (as a human being) is not being negated in principle.[78] As a consequence, many forms of stigmatizing speech are still permitted under a dignity centred regime, though such forms are mild in comparison to the graver forms that may be permitted elsewhere and not

76 Bayerisches Oberstes Landesgericht (BayObLG), Decision of 31 January 1994, Neue Juristische Wochenschrift 1994. pp.952, 953

77 See Chapter 2 section 4, see also Hebl, Tickle, and Heatherton, "Awkward Moments in Interactions between Nonstigmatized and Stigmatized Individuals".

78 Decision of the Federal Constitutional Court (Entscheidungen des BVergGE) Vol. 30, 1 (25 f.); Vol. 109, 279 (312f.).

deemed capable of harming human dignity (i.e. under the libertarian or pragmatic approaches). In addition, the use of such a 'dignity centred provision' would allow for the potential offence that may be caused in the context of normal democratic debate (at least if it remained within civilized boundaries, which in most Western states is admittedly often not the case). This means that the state and those who work for or are associated with it would be permitted to carry out important functions that are necessary in all democratic societies, even where this involves the inevitable stigmatization of certain individuals or groups.

E Dignity as an uncertain concept – problems associated with its use

Whilst the German approach seems to have the most potential in meeting normative principle (i) (see Chapter 3), it is important to recognize that the use of the concept of dignity would present its own problems in a number of jurisdictions. These problems are apparent when one observes the debate amongst scholars that has raged concerning the legal meaning of dignity.[79] In particular, there is no one consensus about what dignity is or what it demands in terms of legal systems. Whilst one will be able to find a near consensus that individuals should be treated with dignity by virtue of being human, one finds completely differing interpretations amongst legal scholars of exactly what such dignity demands.[80] Some see dignity as being the justification of important legal rights such as human rights and the explanation for their existence,[81] but not as a legal right that can realistically be enforced by itself.[82] Scholars or judges holding such a position may or may not feel the principle of human dignity is useful in interpreting legal rights when there are doubts. In addition, the concept of human dignity has been used to justify varying philosophical approaches to the application of the law including diverse conceptions from positions that are motivated by the maximization of autonomy (e.g. Hungary) communitarian (e.g. Germany), individualistic (e.g. the US). or even, Christian or socialist principles.[83]

As a consequence, the deployment of the dignity based approach in legal disputes is highly contextual and each approach contains idiosyncrasies typical of the particular legal context concerned. This is something that is important to bear in mind when looking at the legal concept of dignity as used in the German context. Germany has a

79 For a good review of dignity as a legal concept and the confusion that surrounds its exact meaning, see McCrudden, "Human Dignity and Judicial Interpretation of Human Rights".

80 This differing interpretation also extends to the legal systems of various jurisdictions. As ibid. points out on page 699, "the German Constitutional Court adopts a more communitarian approach, whilst the predominant approach to dignity in the US Supreme Court, the Canadian Supreme Court, and the Hungarian Constitutional Court is more individualistic. The South African Constitutional Court appears to be significantly split on the issue."

81 The Universal Declaration of Human Rights, for example, invokes dignity in its preamble in such a justificatory sense.

82 See, for example, Heyman, *Free Speech and Human Dignity.*

83 McCrudden, "Human Dignity and Judicial Interpretation of Human Rights".

history that is atypical amongst most western states. Most other states do not share such a history and as a consequence are likely to view the concept of human dignity differently. Given this, the existence of a requirement to protect human dignity within hate speech law may not produce the same results as it has in Germany.

Another problem for the potential implementation of criminal law based upon a German style conception of dignity might be that such laws could be considered too broad to be acceptable under human rights obligations designed to protect freedom of expression. One notable potential problem may come from Article 10 of the ECHR (such issues will be discussed in greater detail in Chapters 5 and 6). Such a problem was highlighted earlier in this chapter in the *Vanneste* case in France where the *Cour de Cassation* ruled that a law that criminalized incitation of hatred against people because of their sexual orientation was too broad to be considered acceptable under Article 10 ECHR.[84] If the French court was correct this would mean that even if a German style communitarian concept of dignity were to be imported into other legal systems, criminal laws targeting expression would still nonetheless be restricted due to the existence of rights concerning freedom of expression. The introduction of laws criminalizing insults against unspecified groups in society may therefore represent a step too far for most legal systems where dignity is not given an absolute weight in constitutional terms.

7 Using the criminal law against the state

A The criminal liability of the state is often limited

The state for many purposes also has a legal identity. It can own property, employ individuals, engage in contract, etc. The modern state is also subject to legal action in many instances where it causes harm to individuals.[85] Most[86] modern states have removed historical immunities they may have possessed for tortious or contractual faults.[87] As a result of this it is generally accepted that private

84 *Vanneste, Christian*. In that case the court raised the point that a ban on criticism of people for their sexual orientation was so wide that it would, for example, prevent individuals from criticizing acts of paedophilia.

85 Historically, most Western states had a blanket immunity against civil (non-criminal) suit. This meant that the state could not be pursued in court, even where it had committed a wrong (e.g. a tort in a common law jurisdiction) that, if it had been committed by a private individual, would give rise to a legal right of action. In France until the ninteenth century it was, for instance, forbidden to commence a civil legal action against a civil servant unless permission from the *Conseil d'état* had been obtained This position was originally provided by the Napoleonic *Constitution du 22 Frimaire An VIII*. This position was, however, modified with a decree by *Le Tribunal des Conflits* in 1873.

86 The US has preserved a higher level civil (non-criminal) immunity than Europe. These immunities apply to state and federal government. See S Waxman, and Morrison, T, "What Kind of Immunity? Federal Officers, State Criminal Law, and the Supremacy Clause", *Yale Law Journal* 112 (2003).

87 P Aalto, *Public Liability in EU Law: Brasserie, Bergaderm and Beyond* (Oxford: Hart Publishing, 2011). In Europe a division can be made between states that have created a special liability regime for themselves, e.g. Finland, France and Germany, and states

individuals can undertake (non-criminal) legal action against the state when they have been harmed by its actions.[88] This raises questions as to whether hate speech laws can be used against individuals working for the state or connected to it (by occupying a political function).

This general openness to liability does not, however, always extend to criminal liability. Most states possess (with some notable exceptions) a general immunity from criminal prosecution.[89] As a result it is not possible in many jurisdictions to bring a criminal case against the state itself. This is the case in the UK, for example, where the immunity of the Crown to criminal prosecution is generally accepted,[90] as it is in other common law countries.[91] The picture may be more nuanced in civil law states where in some jurisdictions (e.g. France) it has been reasoned that the state can in theory be held liable for criminal sanction and may have to pay fines where a court determines that this is necessary.[92] In other civil law jurisdictions, e.g. Belgium, a position similar to that of the common law states may be adopted where the state and its bodies (e.g. devolved parts of the state such as regional governments and local government) are not criminally liable, though individual civil servants may be.[93]

Even in jurisdictions where the criminal liability of the state may in theory be considered possible (e.g. in France) it is seldom if ever invoked.[94] Given that the state in many jurisdictions also possesses a monopoly on prosecution this seems logical as otherwise the state would be required to consider prosecuting itself. This general immunity of the state means that in order to bring the force of criminal sanction to bear upon severely stigmatizing expressions (such as hate speech) it is necessary to conceive of the target of such proceedings in a different manner.

such as the UK that foresee state liability as being treated the same in legal terms as private liability. Although this may mean that such liability can be conceived of differently in legal terms, the practical results are often similar.

88 G Dari-Mattiacci, N Garoupa, and F Gomez-Pomar, "State Liability", *Gomez-Pomar, F State Liability* 18, no. 4 (2010).

89 H Roelvink et al., "Strafrechtelijke Aansprakelijkheid Van De Staat" (2002). Available at http://www.recht.nl/doc/rapport_strafrechtelijke_aansprakelijkheid_staat.pdf In most states in Europe the state cannot be held criminally responsible. Denmark, Ireland and Norway form exceptions to this where the state can be held criminally responsible.

90 M Sunkin, "Crown Immunity from Criminal Liability in English Law", *Public Law* Winter (2003).

91 For a similar description of criminal immunity of both federal and state governments in the US see Waxman and Morrison, "What Kind of Immunity? Federal Officers, State Criminal Law, and the Supremacy Clause".

92 See the report of the *Conseil d'État* in 1996, "La responsabilité pénale des décideurs et des personnes morales" by Philippe Raimbault. This matter was also discussed in the French *Sénat* in 2002 (where this quote has been taken from. Available at http://www.senat.fr/questions/base/2000/qSEQ000323478.html

93 M Nihoull, "La responsabilité pénale des personnes morales en Belgique", *La Charte* (2005). Article 5 of the *Code pénal*, brought in by la loi du 4 mai 1999 which applies to private bodies such as companies, does not apply to the state.

94 Roelvink et al., "Strafrechtelijke Aansprakelijkheid Van De Staat".

Given that the state as an abstract entity is usually immune from prosecution the use of the criminal law will likely be more effective where it is used against the 'human component' of the state (discussed further below).

B A state can also be restrained by restraining its 'human component'

Whilst it may be difficult to restrain the state itself (as an abstract entity) using criminal law, it may be possible to achieve the same practical result by applying the criminal law to the 'human component' of the state (see Introduction section 5C). The abstract notion of 'the state' is of little practical meaning without the various individuals that make it function.[95] In all of the activities that it undertakes, the state is dependent upon this human component to decide a particular course of action and to carry it out. This includes the expressive activities of the state. If one looks at all of the examples of stigmatizing expressions in Chapter 1, for example, it is evident that all require some form of input from the human component of the state.

Agents of the state were often historically immune from criminal prosecution for crimes that were committed in the course of their duty.[96] However, such immunities have been gradually removed in many jurisdictions. With regard to individuals occupying roles within the state's organization, the general rule of thumb is that individuals working for the state who commit crimes will be liable for criminal prosecution.[97] The legal framework regulating such liability differs from state to state however (as is discussed below).

C Common and civil law examples

In UK law there is a presumption that "[g]enerally, a person will not be acting in the course of his official duties as a servant of the Crown when doing something that is prohibited by the general law".[98] This state of affairs exemplifies an assumption of 'non-immunity' whereby actions of public officials that are contrary to the

95 For more on this 'abstract notion of the state' and its importance to European political traditions see K Dyson, *The State Tradition in Western Europe* (Oxford: ECPR Press, 2010).

96 Waxman and Morrison, "What Kind of Immunity? Federal Officers, State Criminal Law, and the Supremacy Clause". p2209

97 Exceptions exist, however, for individuals occupying certain executive posts, e.g. president, prime ministers, etc. Many states also have immunities for ceremonial heads of state such as monarchs. For a description of how the concept of immunity emerged from the immunity of the Crown in the common law see S Sunkin and S Payne, *The Nature of the Crown: A Legal and Political Analysis* (Oxford: Oxford University Press, 1999).

98 This quote is taken from a pamphlet prepared for Members of the Office of the UK Parliamentary Council. Available at https://www.gov.uk/government/uploads/system/uploads/attachment_data/file/193143/Crown_Application_pamphlet_12-03-13.pdf This topic in UK law is discussed at greater length in *Craies on Legislation: A Practitioner's Guide to the Nature, Process, Effect and Interpretation of Legislation (10th edition)* (Sweet & Maxwell, 2012) 11.5.6–11.5.7 and 11.5.16–11.5.21.

requirements of the criminal law will likely be deemed as not being in the 'course of official duties'. In such cases the individual conducting such actions is likely to be held responsible in place of the state. This is important as it means that hate speech legislation will often apply to public servants and that they will face prosecution if they are in contravention of the relevant laws. A similar situation exists in other common law states such as New Zealand where the law clearly demonstrates that individuals employed by the government are subject to criminal prosecution.[99] The US in comparison recognizes a greater range of immunities for public employees. Whilst no general system of immunity from criminal prosecution for public employees exists, immunity may be available under certain circumstances.[100] However, given the lack of room under the US Supreme Court's libertarian approach for hate speech laws the existence of various immunities has little material effect on the ability of state employees to use stigmatizing expressions.

In France, despite the existence of a parallel system of *droit administratif* that is applicable to decisions of the state (discussed further in Chapter 5), public employees are also subject to criminal prosecution where they have violated the criminal code (*Code pénal*). That French civil servants are subject to the same criminal laws as ordinary citizens is highlighted by the fact that the state, as employer, is expected to undertake the financial and administrative burdens of defending the civil servant in question if he or she is to face criminal charges for conduct committed in the course of duty.[101] This includes laws on speech to incite hatred and certain forms of insulting speech. A similar state of affairs exists in many other European countries. In Belgium and the Netherlands, the state and its constituent elements are immune from criminal prosecution but individual civil servants can be held criminally responsible for their actions.[102] Local government bodies are responsible for paying for any criminal fines imposed on the mayor or locally elected officials.

8 The immunity of political figures linked to the state

A Parliamentary privilege

The concept of parliamentary immunity can be traced back to the then English Parliament of 1397. At that time the House of Commons had criticized the

99 Section 11 of the Crown Immunity Act (2002), for example, states that immunities that apply to the state under section 6(2) of the Act dot not apply to those who are employed by the Crown.

100 P Larkin, "'Sauce for the Goose Is Sauce for the Gander': Treating Private Parties and Government Officials Alike under the Criminal Law", *Legal Memorandum*. Some protections do, however, exist for public employees that do not exist for those in comparable private sector employment.

101 La loi n° 83–634 du 13 juillet 1983 Article 11. See also Aricle 29.

102 Article 5 of the Belgian Criminal Code. The lower level structures of *gemeente* (municipality) and *provincie* (province) are, however, open to civil action where damage has been caused.

actions of the monarch, King Richard II, and the excessive waste of resources by members of his court. As a response a leading parliamentary critic was sentenced to death for treason. Despite the power of the king, the Parliament was able to secure his pardon and release. The 1689 Bill of Rights enshrined in law the ability of Members of Parliament to be able to discuss all matters freely within Parliament without interference from outside. In France, such a concept began to crystallize after the 1789 Revolution where the decree of 23 June guaranteed members of parliament freedom from outside restrictions whereby the parliament would need to agree to any legal charges against one of its members.[103] Today most Western democracies have some form of immunity for individuals who are elected to high office, e.g. the head of state or parliament (including members of the executive). In contemporary Europe there broadly exist two systems of parliamentary privilege which more or less fall along the lines that divide common law Europe from civil law Europe. The first type is based on the traditions established in the UK centuries ago whilst the latter are mostly based on the principles that were created during the French Revolution to protect democratic debate.

(i) Parliamentary privilege in civil law countries

The systems of immunity for France and Belgium typify that used in Europe in general. These systems foresee two types of immunity. The first concerns immunity for acts that are committed in the course of duties as a parliamentarian. The second concerns restrictions on the ability of the state to commence criminal (or civil actions) against parliamentarians for acts that are committed outside the confines of such duties. The first type of immunity is usually absolute,[104] whilst the second usually can be waived by a majority vote of the parliament in question. In order to minimize the all-embracing nature of this immunity, the concept of what exactly falls within 'parliamentary functions' is often interpreted restrictively. Interviews given to the media, for example, in France are not seen as being in the course of parliamentary duties.[105] This meant that as a result of an interview given by the French politician Christian Vanneste to French TV in which he stated that homosexuality was an "inferior lifestyle choice" and "a danger to humanity" his parliamentary immunity could be lifted. A similar situation exists in Germany where approval from the *Bundestag* is needed in order to allow the prosecution of a member of parliament to proceed. In addition to most of the parliaments in continental Europe, the European Parliament follows this system, with the EU treaties demanding that Member States apply the same rules of immunity to MEPs as

103 This description is largely taken from the Report for the European Parliament by the Directorate-General for Research, 'Parliamentary Immunity in the Member States of the European Union and in the European Parliament Legal Affairs Series W8 Ref', (European Parliament)". p2

104 Germany is an exception to this as it does not provide for immunity for defamation. See ibid. p25

105 Ibid. p144

they would to parliamentarians in their own legal systems.[106] The European Parliament has however shown itself to be willing to revoke the immunity of its members including for incidences of racially motivated hate speech. This occurred in 2013 when the European Parliament revoked the immunity of Marine Le Pen, the leader of the French *Front Nationale*, for comments she made analogizing the activities of the Islamic community in France to that of the Nazi occupation in the 1940s.[107]

(ii) Parliamentary privilege in common law countries

The systems of parliamentary immunity in UK and Ireland (and one civil law country – the Netherlands) are less extensive than those found in other EU states. The UK parliamentary system, for example, foresees immunity from civil actions for those engaged in the debates and proceedings of Parliament. This protects individuals from being sued under the UK's relatively strict defamation laws when they might, for example, accidently or even intentionally slander individuals. Unlike most European states however the UK does not foresee any immunity from criminal prosecutions for acts committed by Members of Parliament, even when participating in the debates and proceedings of Parliament. This means that MPs in the UK could face prosecution for committing an act of hate speech as recognized in the UK, even if it were made on the floor of Parliament.

B Members of the executive

In addition to elected parliamentarians, it is common to find that members of a state's executive may also enjoy a certain level of immunity from criminal prosecution. Depending on a particular state's constitutional arrangements, such individuals may also be elected or members of the parliament (e.g. the UK). Blanket immunities (where they exist) are usually greater for heads of state than for heads of government, with the US president, for example, enjoying totally immunity from criminal prosecution whilst he or she is in office and considerable protection thereafter for acts that were committed during his or her presidency.[108] In France, the president can only be held accountable for acts of treason, and then only with the consent of both houses of parliament.[109] Correspondingly, many European monarchs[110] (as head of state) receive a similar or greater level of immunity. As a consequence, such individuals are free (at least legally speaking) to make whatever expressions they wish without fear of being charged with a criminal offence. For

106 *Protocol on the Privileges and Immunities of the European Union*, Chapter III, Articles 7, 8 and 9.

107 http://www.bbc.co.uk/news/world-europe-23142984

108 Memorandum of the Attorney General, "A Sitting President's Amenability to Indictment and Criminal Prosecution", 24 Op. Off. Legal Counsel 222 2000.

109 Article 68 of the French Constitution.

110 In the Dutch Constitution, for example, Article 42 provides that the king or queen is inviolable. The same is provided for by Article 15 of the Belgian Constitution.

heads of government such as prime ministers there is usually a lower level of absolute protection available.[111] The UK prime minster, for example, enjoys no higher legal protection than others in his or her cabinet, but as a Member of Parliament he or she enjoys the same rights and privileges as other parliamentarians (discussed above). Given that a prime minster (or other heads of government) and their ministers are usually able to command a majority of their respective parliament it may be difficult in reality to envisage such immunity being lifted.

The result of these provisions is that senior members of the executive enjoy important immunities from prosecution meaning that they can effectively be free from the threat of prosecution under laws concerning harmful expression (if they exist in the jurisdiction in question).[112]As Chapter 1 illustrated it is often members of the executive that have access to the communicational machinery of the state, allowing them to disseminate SSEs widely. Given the requirement to protect human dignity and self-respect by the state that Chapter 3 posed (see normative principle (i)), the ability of such political figures to engage in hate speech may appear excessive, because such types of expression are arguably superfluous to democratic debate (given that such speech is often gratuitously offensive and usually contains few abstract or practical ideas).

9 Conclusion

Given that SSEs are expressions, it is natural to look towards hate speech laws. In societies where they exist hate speech laws have been created in order to limit expressions that are considered harmful. The creation of such offences represents exceptions to the usual norms of free expression that exist in most democratic societies. This chapter has shown that, whilst hate speech laws may prevent a limited range of stigmatizing expressions, they are unlikely to be able to engage the majority. The extent to which stigmatizing expression will be engaged depends upon the jurisdiction in question and the way in which hate speech law is formulated within it.

Most Western states have (to varying extents) forged laws that target selected types of expression against certain exhaustively defined protected categories of people. Common examples of the type of expression involved are ‘incitement to hatred’ and ‘incitement to discrimination’. Common examples of protected categories involve ‘ethnicity’, ‘race’, ‘sexuality’, etc. Whilst offences of this type will

111 T Hoppe, “Public Corruption: Limiting Criminal Immunity of Legislative, Executive and Judicial Officials in Europe”, *Vienna Journal on International Constitutional Law* 5 (2011).

112 The effect of such entitlements in common law jurisdictions such as the UK will, however, be minimal given that UK parliamentarians do not enjoy immunity from criminal prosecution. Given that members of the UK executive (including the prime minster) are essentially Members of Parliament, this state of affairs applies to them also. See S Boylan and C Newcombe, “Parliamentary Immunity: A Comparison between Established Democracies and Russia: A Crisis of Democratic Legitimacy for Russia”, *Journal of International Legal Studies* 3 (1997).

protect some groups against certain expressions that may be considered stigmatizing, the range of potential stigmatizing expressions that can be created goes far beyond these categories (as was illustrated in Chapter 1). Certain countries have forms of hate speech law that have a potentially far wider reach. This was exemplified by Germany where hate speech law is predicated on the need to protect individual dignity. This allows hate speech against groups that are not defined in law to be prosecuted. Such an approach arguably comes closest to meeting normative principle (i) (discussed in Chapter 3). It may not, however, be realistic to expect such an approach to be deployed in other countries that do not have the same historical experience as Germany. In such countries the concept of dignity is likely to be understood differently and a consensus on the need to constrain freedom of expression to such an extent may not exist.

When discussing SSEs, it is also important to consider the applicability of hate speech law (when it is indeed applicable to a stigmatizing expression) to the state. In many (but not all) jurisdictions there is an assumption that the state itself cannot be held criminally liable. It is often possible, however, to hold those employed by the state criminally liable. This is because where employees who work for the state break the criminal law they are often regarded as acting outside the course of their duty and acting alone. Given that the human component that works for the state is central to its communicational activities the potential application of the criminal law may act as a deterrent to state employees from engaging in SSEs (where hate speech legislation is applicable to the stigmatizing expression in question).

The situation concerning important figures with a political function is more complicated. For members of the executive (again depending upon the state in question) immunities may apply that prevent criminal prosecution. Whilst such immunities serve an important purpose, allowing those involved in the political and higher functioning of the state to function freely, they also act to allow a number of high profile individuals to express themselves (often with the authority of the state) in ways that may be stigmatizing. This is concerning because as Chapter 1 discusses, it is precisely those individuals, often with ready access to the state's communicational machinery, who can disseminate SSEs most effectively.

Bibliography

Aalto, P. *Public Liability in EU Law: Brasserie, Bergaderm and Beyond. Oxford: Hart* Publishing, 2011.

Affaire Féret C. Belgique (2009).

Allen, M C, Directorate-General for Research Division for Social, Legal and Cultural Affairs. *Parliamentary Immunity in the Member States of the European Union and in the European Parliament Legal Affairs Series W8 Ref.* Luxemburg: European Parliament L-2929, 1999.

Anderson, E, and R Pildes. "Expressive Theories of Law: A General Restatement." *University of Pennsylvania Law Review* 148, no. 5 (2000): 1503–1575.

Bayer, R. "Stigma and the Ethics of Public Health: Not Can We but Should We." *Social Science & Medicine* 67 (2008): 463–472.

Biernat, M, and J Dovidio. "Stigma and Stereotypes." In *The Social Psychology of Stigma*, edited by T Heatherton, R Kleck, M Hebl and J Hull, 88–125. New York: Guilford Press, 2000.

Bowles, R, M Faure, and N Garoupa. "The Scope of Criminal Law." *Journal of Law ad Society* 35, no. 3 (2008): 389–416.

Boylan, S, and C Newcombe. "Parliamentary Immunity: A Comparison between Established Democracies and Russia: A Crisis of Democratic Legitimacy for Russia." *Journal of International Legal Studies* 3 (1997): 205–235.

Brugger, W. "The Treatment of Hate Speech in German Constitutional Law (Part I)." *German Law Journal* 4, no. 1 (2002).

Brugger, W. "The Treatment of Hate Speech in German Constitutional Law (Part II)." *German Law Journal* 4, no. 1 (2002).

Bruns, A. "Access to Media Sources in Defamation Litigation in the United States and Germany." *Duke Journal of Comparative & International Law* 10 (2000): 283–305.

Burris, S. "Stigma, Ethics and Policy: A Commentary on Bayer's 'Stigma and the Ethics of Public Health: Not Can We but Should We'." *Social Science & Medicine* 67 (2008): 473–475.

Carmi, G. "Dignity Versus Liberty: The Two Western Cultures of Free Speech." (22 August 2008). Available at SSRN:https://ssrn.com/abstract=1246700orhttp://dx.doi.org/10.2139/ssrn.1246700Congdon, A. "Burned Out: The Supreme Court Strikes Down Virginia's Cross Burning Statute in Virginia V. Black." *University of Chicago Law Review* 35, no. 4 (2004): 1049–1116.

Dari-Mattiacci, G, N Garoupa, and F Gomez-Pomar. "State Liability." *Gomez-Pomar, F State Liability* 18, no. 4 (2010): 773–811.

Dean, J, and F Rud. "The Drug Addict and the Stigma of Addiction." *Substance Use & Misuse* 19, no. 8 (1984): 859–869.

"Discrimination en diversité. Rapport annuel 2011 – Centre pour l'égalité des chances et la lutte contre le racisme."

Donoghue, K. "Casualties of War – Criminal Drug Law Enforcement and Its Special Costs for the Poor." *New York University Law Review* 77 (2002): 1778–1804.

Dovidio, J, B Major, and J Crocker. "Stigma: Introduction and Overview." In *The Social Psychology of Stigma*, edited by T Heatherton, R Kleck, M Hebl and J Hull, 1–28. New York: Guilford Press, 2000.

Downing, J. "'Hate Speech' and 'First Amendment Absolutism' Discourses in the US." *Discourse & Society* 10, no. 2 (1999): 175–189.

Duff, A. *Theories of Criminal Law, the Stanford Encyclopedia of Philosophy. E Zalta, 2013. Available at*http://plato.stanford.edu/Entries/Criminal-Law..

Dyson, K. *The State Tradition in Western Europe*. Oxford: ECPR Press, 2010.

European Union Agency for Fundamental Rights. *Handbook on European Non-Discrimination Law*. (2010).

Franklin, K. "Good Intentions: The Enforcement of Hate Crime Penalty-Enhancement Statutes." *The American Behavioral Scientist* 46, no. 1 (2002): 154–172.

Gard, G. "Fighting Words as Free Speech." *Washington University Law Quarterly* 58 (1980): 531–581.

Gelders, D, and I Oyvind. "Government Communication About Potential Policies: Public Relations, Propaganda or Both?" *Public Relations Review* 36 (2010): 59–62.

Memorandum of the Attorney General. "A Sitting President's Amenability to Indictment and Criminal Prosecution." 24 Op. Off. Legal Counsel 222 2000.

Goffman, I. *Stigma: Notes on a Spoilt Identity*. Englewood Cliffs, NJ: Prentice Hall, 1963.

Hart, H. "The Aims of the Criminal Law." *Law and Contemporary Problems* 23 (1958): 401–441.

Hebl, M, M Tickle, and T Heatherton. "Awkward Moments in Interactions between Nonstigmatized and Stigmatized Individuals." In *The Social Psychology of Stigma*, edited by T Heatherton, R Kleck, M Hebl and J Hull, 275–306. New York: Guilford Press, 2000.

Heckert, D, and A Best. "Ugly Duckling to Swan: Labelling Theory and the Stigmatization of Red Hair." *Symbiotic Interaction* 20, no. 4 (2011): 365–384.

Heyman, S. *Free Speech and Human Dignity*. Chicago, IL: Faculty Scholarship Commons, 2008.

Hood, C, and H Margretts. *The Tools of Government in the Digital Age*. New York: Palgrave Macmillan, 2006.

Hoppe, T. "Public Corruption: Limiting Criminal Immunity of Legislative, Executive and Judicial Officials in Europe." *Vienna Journal on International Constitutional Law* 5 (2011): 538–549.

Hornle, T. "Criminalizing Human Behaviour to Protect Human Dignity." *Criminal Law and Philosophy* 6 (2012): 307–325.

Janke, S, and J Hoyer. "Stigmatization of People with Pedophilia: A Blind Spot in Stigma Research." *International Journal of Sexual Health* 25, no. 3 (2013): 169–184.

Janssen, E. *Faith in Public Debate. On Freedom of Expression, Hate Speech and Religion in France & the Netherlands*. Cambridge: Interstentia, 2015.

Jenness, V, and R Grattet. "The Criminalizing of Hate: A Comparison of Structural and Polity Influences on the Passage of 'Bias-Crime' Legislation in the United States." *Sociological Perspectives* 39, no. 1 (1996): 129–154.

Jeremy, A. "Practical Implications of the Enactment of the Racial and Religious Hatred Act 2006." *Ecclesiastical Law Journal* 9, no. 3 (2007): 187–201.

Kurzban, R, and M Leary. "Evolutionary Origins of Stigmatization: The Functions of Social Exclusion." *Psychological Bulletin* 127, no. 2 (2001): 187–208.

Larkin, P. "'Sauce for the Goose Is Sauce for the Gander': Treating Private Parties and Government Officials Alike under the Criminal Law." *Legal Memorandum* (31 July 2013).

"Law Commission Consultation Paper No 213: Hate Crime: The Case for Extending Offences. Appendix A: Hate Crime and Freedom of Expression under the European Convention on Human Rights." Available at http://www.lawcom.gov.uk/app/uploads/2015/03/cp213_hate_crime_amended.pdf

Lawrence, F. *Punishing Hate: Bias Crimes under American Law*. Cambridge MA: Harvard University Press, 1999.

Leary, M, E Tambor, S Terdal, and D Downs. "Self-Esteem as an Interpersonal Monitor: The Sociometer Hypothesis." *Journal of Personality and Social Psychology* 68, no. 3 (1995): 518–530.

Link, B, and J Phelan. "Conceptualizing Stigma." *Annual Review of Sociology* 27 (2001): 363–385.

Major, B, and T Schmader. "Coping with Stigma through Psychological Disengagement." In *Prejudice: The Target's Perspective*, edited by J Swim, L Chohen and L Hyers, 37–60. San Diego: Academic Press, 1998.

Major, B, S Spencer, T Schmader, C Wolfe, and J Crocker. "Coping with Negative Stereotypes About Intellectual Performance: The Role of Psychological Disengagement." *Personality and Social Psychology Bulletin* 24, no. 1 (1998): 34–50.

McCrudden, C. "Human Dignity and Judicial Interpretation of Human Rights." *The European Journal of International Law* 19, no. 4 (2008): 655–724.

Miller, C, and C Kaiser. "A Theoretical Perspective on Coping with Stigma." *Journal of Social Issues* 57, no. 1 (2001): 73–92.

Miller, C, and B Major. "Coping with Stigma and Prejudice." In *The Social Psychology of Stigmatisation*, edited by T Heatherton, R Kleck, M Hebl and J Hull, 243–272 (New York: Guilford Press 2000).

Mitchell, Timothy. "The Limits of the State: Beyond Statist Approaches and Their Critics." *American Political Science Review* 85, no. 1 (2014): 77–96.

Morgon, J. "US Hate Crime Legislation: A Legal Model to Avoid in Australia." *Journal of Sociology* 38, no. 1 (2002): 25–48.

Nihoull, M (Ed.), Misonne, A, Leroux, O, Coisne, S, Fagnart, J-L, Vandermeersch, D, Hamer, I, Renard, C, De Pauw, W and Waeterinckx, P, "La responsabilité pénale des personnes morales en Belgique: une évaluation de la loi du 4 mai 1999 instaurant la responsabilité pénale des personnes morales en Belgique après cinq années d'application." Projucit, *La Charte*, Bruxelles.

Nissenbaum, H. "Privacy as Contextual Integrity." *Washington Law Review* 79 (2004): 104–139.

Norrie, A. *Crime, Reason and History: A Critical Introduction to Criminal Law*. Cambridge: Cambridge University Press, 2001.

Oellers-Frahm, K. "Italy and France: Immunity for the Prime Minister of Italy and the President of the French Republic." *International Journal of Constitutional Law* 3, no. 1 (2005): 107–115.

O'Neil, R. "Hate Speech, Fighting Words, and Beyond – Why American Law Is Unique." *Albany Law Review* 76, no. 1 (2013): 467–498.

Organisation for Economic Co-operation and Development, The Representative on Freedom of Media. *Libel Laws and Insult Laws: A Matrix on Where We Stand and What We Would Like to Achieve* Representative on Freedom of Media OECD. OECD, 2005.

Post, R. "Racist Speech, Democracy, and the First Amendment." *Faculty Scholarship Series* 208 (1991).

Puhl, R, and D Brownell. "Psychosocial Origins of Obesity Stigma." *Obesity Reviews* 4 (2003): 212–227.

Quinn, P, and P De Hert. "Self Respect—a 'Rawlsian Primary Good' Unprotected by the European Convention on Human Rights and Its Lack of a Coherent Approach to Stigmatization?" *The International Journal of Discrimination and the Law* 14 (2014): 19–53.

Rawls, J. *A Theory of Justice (First edition)*. Cambridge, MA: Harvard Press, 1971.

Rawls, J. "Justice as Fairness: Political Not Metaphysical." *Philosophy and Public Affairs* 14, no. 3 (1985): 223–251.

Rawls, J. *Political Liberalism*. New York: Columbia University Press, 1993.

Rawls, J. "The Priority of Right and Ideas of the Good." *Philosophy & Public Affairs* 17, no. 4 (1988): 251–276.

Rawls, J. *A Theory of Justice (Revised edition)*. Cambridge, MA: Harvard Press, 1999.

Ray, L, and D Smith. "Racist Offenders and the Politics of 'Hate Crime'." *Law and Critique* 12, no. 3 (2001): 203–221.

Reddish, M, and G Lippman. "Freedom of Expression and the Civic Republican Revival in Constitutional Theory: The Ominous Implications." *California Law Review* 79, no. 2 (1991): 267–311.

Reidpath, D, K Chan, S Gifford, and P Allotey. "'He Hath the French Pox': Stigma, Social Value and Social Exclusion." *Sociology of Health & Illness* 27, no. 4 (2005): 468–489.

Robinson, P, and J Darley. "Does Criminal Law Deter? A Behavioural Science Investigation." *Oxford Journal of Legal Studies 24*, no. 2(2004):173–205.

Roelvink, H, M Bovens, G Knigge, and H Kummeling. "Strafrechtelijke Aansprakelijkheid Van De Staat." (2002). Available at http://www.recht.nl/doc/rapport_strafrechtelijke_aansprakelijkheid_staat.pdf

Room, R. "Stigma, Social Inequality and Alcohol and Drug Use." *Drug and Alcohol Review* 24 (2005): 143–155.

Runciman, D. *Pluralism and the Personality of the State*. Cambridge: Cambridge University Press, 1997.

Strossen, N. "Regulating Racist Speech on Campus? A Modest Proposal?" *Duke Law Journal* 484 (1990): 533–553.

Strossen, N. "Regulating Workplace Sexual Harassment and Upholding the First Amendment – Avoiding a Collision." *Villanova Law Review* 37, no. 4 (1992): 757–785.

Strudler, A. "The Power of Expressive Theories of Law." *Maryland Law Review* 60 (2001): 492–505.

Sunkin, M. "Crown Immunity from Criminal Liability in English Law." *Public Law* Winter (2003): 716–729.

Sunkin, S, and S Payne. *The Nature of the Crown: A Legal and Political Analysis*. Oxford: Oxford University Press, 1999.

Taylor, C. "Hate Speech and Government Speech." *Journal of Constitutional Law* 12, no. 4 (2010): 1115–1189.

Tsesis, A. "Dignity and Speech: The Regulation of Hate Speech in a Democracy." *Wake Forrest Law Review* 44 (2009): 497–534.

Van Stokkhom, B, H Sackers, and J Wils. *Godslastering, Discriminerende Uitingen Wegens Godsdienst En Haatuitingen: Een Inventariserende Studie*. Meppel: Boom Juridische uitgevers en Justitie WODC, 2007.

Vanneste, Christian (2008). Chambre criminelle de la Cour de cassation française12 novem bre 2008, pourvoi n° 07-83398.

Waldron, J. "Dignity and Defamation – the Visibility of Hate." *Harvard Law Review* 123 (2009): 1596–1657.

Waldron, J. *The Harm in Hate Speech*. Cambridge, MA: Harvard University Press, 2012.

Waxman, S, and Morrison, T. "What Kind of Immunity? Federal Officers, State Criminal Law, and the Supremacy Clause." *Yale Law Journal* 112 (2003): 2195–2259.

Whitman, J. "Enforcing Civility and Respect: Three Societies." *Faculty Scholarship Series* 646 (2000).

Whitman, J. "The Two Western Cultures of Privacy – Dignity Versus Liberty." *Faculty Scholarship Series* 649 (2004): 1153–1221.

Whittington-Walsh, F. "The Broken Mirror – Young Women, Beauty & Facial Difference." *Women's Health and Urban Life* 5, no. 2 (2006): 7–24.

Zick, T. "Cross Burning, Cockfighting, and Symbolic Meaning: Toward a First Amendment Ethnography." *William and Mary Law Review* 45, no. 5 (2004): 2263–2398.

5 The importance of the lack of binding effects produced by SSEs

1 Introduction

> The imposition of stigma is the commonest form of violence used in democratic societies ... Stigmatization is a highly sophisticated form of violence in so far as it is rarely associated with physical attacks or threats. It can be best compared to those forms of psychological torture in which the victim is broken psychically and physically but left to all outward appearances unmarked.
>
> Robert Pinker[1]

The reader of this book will no doubt be aware a major and re-occurring theme is the inability of the law (in terms of various legal approaches) to be able, in many instances, to engage with potentially harmful stigmatizing expressions. This chapter will focus on a common reason for this: that such expressions often produce a lack of binding effects upon specific individuals (at least in terms of effects that the law is willing to recognize as binding effects). The creation of such binding effects often represents a 'trigger event' which is needed in order to allow the application of an important legal approach. Without the existence of such a trigger event many legal approaches are not able to engage SSEs.

This chapter will demonstrate the importance of this issue using the illustrative examples of anti-discrimination and administrative law. These two examples are useful because although very different in terms of underlying purpose, scope and intended application, they are both seemingly often unable to engage a wide range of SSEs. The primary reason for this is that SSEs usually do not produce binding effects for individuals. Although stigmatizing state expressions are capable (as Chapter 2 discussed) of bringing about a range of psychological harm and associated effects (e.g. harmful coping behaviours), such aspects are often not recognized by a number of legal approaches that one would intuitively expect to apply in such circumstances.

1 R Pinker, *Social Theory and Social Policy* (London: Heinemann Educational Books, 1971). Quote taken directly from M Cusack, J Gavin, and D Kavanagh, "Dancing with Discrimination: Managing Stigma and Identity", *Culture and Organization*, 9, no. 4 (2003).

Part 1 of this chapter will look at the example of anti-discrimination approaches. Given the similarities and links between the phenomenon of discrimination and stigmatization (discussed in Chapter 2), anti-discrimination approaches represent a likely first port of call for those who feel they have been harmed by SSE. This chapter illustrates the problems that such approaches may have by discussing the potential application (to SSEs) of Article 14 of the European Convention of Human Rights (ECHR) and the EU's equality directives.[2] Part 2 will look at the potential application of administrative law to SSEs. This type of law, in many states, allows individuals and other entities to challenge actions of the state that may affect their interests. Many systems of administrative law are not, however, likely to recognize purely expressive activates as an administrative act, with the consequence that they are not likely to be of application. Again the reason is because such activities are not likely to be seen as producing binding effects.

The lack of binding effects brought about by many types of SSE means that important examples of both approaches may often be of little use to individuals who feel that have been harmed by SSEs. This means that both types of approaches are usually able to contribute little in terms of meeting the normative position outlined in Chapter 3. This is notable given that both types of approaches are highly adaptable to particular contexts, *inter alia* allowing acts to be analysed for their necessity and proportionality. Given this, they could have been suitable in playing a role in meeting normative principles (ii)–(iv) if they were to be applicable.

Part 1: Anti-discrimination law and SSEs

2 Discrimination and stigmatization are common bed fellows

Anti-discrimination approaches are probably the first type of legal approach that will come to mind for individuals looking for relief from SSEs. The words 'stigmatization' and 'discrimination' are familiar to most people in most countries and societies.[3] The words are often used in an analogous manner and in the same contexts. Both individuals and representatives of groups will often use both words to describe their own or others' mistreatment in society. If one were to examine thoroughly what individuals actually mean when using these words one would see that there is often little effort made in defining what each constitutes.[4] Rather,

2 More specifically this article focuses on Council Directive 2000/43/EC of 29 June 2000 implementing the principle of equal treatment between persons irrespective of racial and ethnic origin (the RED) and Council Directive 2000/78/EC of 27 November 2000 establishing a general framework for equal treatment in employment and occupation (the EED).

3 P Quinn and P De Hert, "Self Respect—a 'Rawlsian Primary Good' Unprotected by the European Convention on Human Rights and Its Lack of a Coherent Approach to Stigmatization?", *The International Journal of Discrimination and the Law* 14 (2014).

4 S Burris, "Disease Stigma in U.S. Public Law", *Journal of Law, Medicine and Ethics* 30 (2002). p179

individuals appear to use such words without giving ample thought to defining them. It is not just lay people but academics, legal scholars and even the judiciary that employ such practices. A casual glance at many legal writings and judgments often show that the terms are often used to describe similar phenomena, even sometimes being used interchangeably.[5] Little effort is furthermore often given to defining each of these respective concepts.[6] Individuals or groups in vulnerable positions often suffer both stigmatization and discrimination simultaneously, and in a manner that makes separating them difficult.[7] There is without doubt a certain symbiosis between the two concepts. These factors may partly explain why the two concepts are used synonymously. This situation could lead individuals to assume that anti-discrimination approaches may be suitable for preventing the harm associated stigmatization. This is not, however, the case, in particular with regard to stigmatizing expressions. This is because in many instances expressive activity does not bring about binding effects, something that is required in order for many anti-discrimination approaches to be applicable.

Stigmatization can occur in the absence of 'discriminatory treatment' (and the consequent existence of binding effects) including instances involving gestures or expressions such as SSEs. This is because these are activities which individuals can (in theory at least) simply ignore if they so wish. Chapter 1 discussed numerous types of state expressive activity that can be stigmatizing without at the same time being discriminatory (at least from a traditional legal perspective). One can draw a distinction between the two phenomena in that stigmatization is primarily concerned with the potential induction of harmful psychological effects whilst discrimination is usually concerned with the actual tangible treatment of individuals. An important consequence of this is often that where such 'treatment' does not occur one would usually not be able to describe a particular situation as being one of 'discrimination'. This situation is reflected in a number of important legal approaches to problems of discrimination. This is particularly notable for generalized anti-discrimination approaches such as that developed by the European Court of Human Rights (ECtHR) under Article 14 of the ECHR.[8]

This situation often means that prohibiting discrimination is not sufficient to prevent stigmatization from occurring, given that it can take place without any form of treatment. Indeed in many cases discriminatory treatment is indeed prohibited but stigmatization and its effects persist.[9] Stigmatizing expressions (including those made by the state) often represent good illustrations as to the limits of anti-discrimination approaches. As Chapter 2 discussed individuals can

5 I Solanke, *Discrimination as Stigma* (Oxford: Hart, 2017).

6 In the ECHR discrimination case of *Kiyutin v. Russia* [2011] ECHR 439, for example, the court used the terms frequently together. At no point did it make the effort, however, to define stigmatization or separate it conceptually from the concept of discrimination.

7 B Link and J Phelan, "Stigma and Its Public Health Implications", *The Lancet* 367 (2006).

8 P Quinn, "The Problem of Stigmatizing Expressions – the Limits of Anti-Discrimination Approaches", *International Journal of Discrimination and the Law* 17, no. 1 (2017).

9 Burris, "Disease Stigma in U.S. Public Law".

feel stigmatized by the expressive activity (including by the state) without having suffered any discriminatory act. The presence of discrimination can no doubt make such situations worse, but is nonetheless only one potential source of stigmatization.[10] Discrimination *can* cause stigmatization, both for those who are discriminated against and also other members of that community. Discrimination need not exist, however, for stigmatization to occur. The possibility of having stigmatization (including from state expressions) even in the absence or prohibition of discrimination clearly demonstrates that the two concepts are not the same and that there are limits as to what anti-discrimination approaches can do to prevent stigmatizing expressions, including where they are made by the state.

The remaining sections of Part A will discuss the limitations of anti-discrimination approaches in being able to engage with such expressions. This will include (in section 3) the generalized approach adopted by the ECtHR under Article 14 of the ECHR. Sections 4–5 will highlight the less general and more focused approach adopted under the EU's anti-discrimination directives. These approaches have been selected because they demonstrate that the wider the potential application of an anti-discrimination approach is, the more likely it is to be dependent upon the concept of treatment, limiting its potential application to stigmatizing expressions, including by the state.[11]

3 The ECHR and its anti-discrimination directives

There are several factors (discussed in sections (A)–(C) below) that would seemingly make the ECHR, and its anti-discrimination approach under Article 14 of the Convention potentially interesting *vis-à-vis* stigmatizing expressions. Perhaps most importantly, the application of Article 14 has been widened considerably in recent years. Furthermore, it is capable of applying to discriminatory acts against a non-exhaustively defined list of categories. These factors can be considered as making Article 14 not of universal but of broad and general application. Taken together with the fact that the ECtHR has shown itself to be aware of the phenomena of stigmatization (*inter alia* in its concept of 'indirect discrimination'), they raise the question of whether Article 14 could be considered capable of application to stigmatizing expressions. The reality, however, (discussed in section D) is that ECtHR has not yet recognized an instance of purely expressive activity to be capable of constituting discrimination. As the paragraphs below discuss this is because its discrimination approach is firmly based on the concept of treatment.

10 B Link and J Phelan, "Conceptualizing Stigma", *Annual Review of Sociology* 27 (2001). Discrimination can worsen stigmatization or, alternatively, be an outcome from stigmatization.

11 For a good discussion concerning the limitation of these directives from the perspective of intersectionality, see T Degener, "Intersections between Disability, Race and Gender in Discrimination Law", in *European Union Non-Discrimination Law and Intersectionality: Investigating the Triangle of Racial, Gender and Disability Discrimination*, in *European Union Non-Discrimination Law and Intersectionality: Investigating the Triangle of Racial, Gender and Disability Discrimination,* ed. D Schiek and A Lawson (Farnham: Ashgate Publishing, 2011).

A Article 14 provides broad protection against discrimination related to Convention rights

The wording of Article 14 demonstrates clearly what for a long time was considered a fundamental weakness of what the ECHR was able to offer in terms of an anti-discrimination approach, i.e. that it only appears to apply to discrimination in terms of the rights delineated in the ECHR, given the explicit reference "enjoyment of the rights and freedoms set forth in this Convention". Such a potential weakness had allowed Article 14 to be coined the 'Cinderella provision'.[12] This weakness has, however, been shown to be somewhat overstated for two reasons. First, the ECtHR has been extremely active in expanding the scope of the rights described in the ECHR.[13] This means *inter alia* that many types of stigmatizing activity may be capable of engaging various ECHR provisions. This most noticeably includes the court's case law on Article 8 – the right to a private and family life (discussed further in Chapter 6).[14] This article has been interpreted extremely widely, offering protection against a wide range of actions that affect the ability of individuals to live their lives as they wish and with sufficient privacy.[15] Second, the ECHR has interpreted the term "enjoyment of the rights and freedoms set forth in this Convention" in such a way as to catch any discrimination in an area falling 'within the ambit' of a Convention right. The concept of 'within the ambit' created by the court acted to greatly expand the potential applicability of Article 14.[16] This non-onerous requirement requires simply that the alleged discrimination falls 'within the sphere of another convention right'. Such a test has a lower threshold than that which would be needed for engagement of the right in question (i.e. alone without Article 14). The non-demanding nature of the under the ambit requirement was, for example, demonstrated in the *Belgian Linguistic* case.[17] That case concerned discrimination in terms of particular entitlements in terms of education that were not themselves protected by Article 8 of the convention. However, the court pointed out that the within the ambit requirement allowed the case to fall within the sphere of Article 8. The court, therefore, clearly demarcated that the protective scope of Article 14 (in terms of non-discrimination) is able to go beyond rights strictly protected under Article 8 (or any other

12 R O'Connell, "Cinderella Comes to the Ball: Art 14 and the Right to Non-Discrimination in the ECHR", *Legal Studies* 29, no. 2 (2009). p229

13 A Stone Sweet and T Burnell, "Trustee Courts and the Judicialization of International Regimes: The Politics of Majoritarian Activism in the European Convention on Human Rights, the European Union, and the World Trade Organization", *Journal of Law and Courts* 1, no. 1 (2012).

14 See also Quinn and De Hert, "Self Respect—a 'Rawlsian Primary Good' Unprotected by the European Convention on Human Rights and Its Lack of a Coherent Approach to Stigmatization?"

15 For a broad overview consult R White and C Ovey, *The European Convention on Human Rights* (Oxford: Oxford University Press, 2009). See Chapters 15 and 16.

16 A Baker, "The Enjoyment of Rights and Freedoms: A New Conception of the 'Ambit' under Article 14 ECHR", *Modern Law Review* 69, no. 5 (2006).

17 *Belgian Linguistics* (1968) 1 EHRR 252, 283.

article for that matter).[18] Although Article 14 cannot therefore be invoked in a standalone manner the limitations that it has traditionally been associated with have been reduced through the case law of the ECtHR in recent decades. This makes its potential application to SSEs interesting given the wide variety of forms they can take.

B Article 14 ECHR has a non-exhaustive list of categories to which it applies

Article 14 ECHR not only explicitly names a wide selection of categories (sex, race, colour, language, religion, political or other opinion, national or social origin, association with a national minority, property, birth) but also contains the phrase "other status". As the ECtHR has shown on numerous occasions it is willing to use this as a means to consider other types of category that are not explicitly described in Article 14, therefore expanding its potential range of applicability. These even include categories that had not been envisaged when the convention was drafted.[19] As O'Connell points out, the use of the wording "other status" has allowed Article 14 to include "unenumerated grounds such as sexual orientation, health,[20] marital status,[21] or others that would not necessarily be considered under domestic anti-discrimination laws".[22] The non-exhaustive description of the potential categories to which it may apply can be seen as denoting a broad and general application in terms of the types of groups Article 14 ECHR may cover. This can, for example, be contrasted with most hate speech laws (discussed in Chapter 4) which usually apply only to an exhaustively defined list of categories. This flexibility is important in terms of the potential effect on discriminatory activities, allowing the ECHR's anti-discrimination approach to be applied to a wide range of categories (including some that may not as yet have been envisaged). Again this makes the potential application of Article 14 to stigmatizing expressions worth investigating given that such expressions can be made against a wide variety of groups in many different contexts (see Chapter 1).

C The ECtHR has recognized problems associated with stigmatization

Whilst for some time the ECtHR was only willing to view discrimination from a classic 'direct' perspective it has shown an increasing openness to the concept of

18 Baker, "The Enjoyment of Rights and Freedoms: A New Conception of the 'Ambit' under Article 14 ECHR". p727

19 O'Connell, "Cinderella Comes to the Ball: Art 14 and the Right to Non-Discrimination in the ECHR". See page 221.

20 *Salguero da Silva Mouta v. Portugal* (2001) 31 EHRR 1055.

21 See, for example, *Re P* [2008] UKHL 38, [2008] 3 WLR 76.

22 The ECtHR considered a case during 2007 on language policy, concerning the 'Ukrainization' of Russian names in official Ukrainian documents. The ECtHR ultimately found the policy did not violate Article 14, largely because the policy preserved a role for individual choice as to how an individual's names should appear. See *Bulgakov v. Ukraine* (Application No 59894/00) 11 September 2007.

'indirect discrimination'.[23] Since the *Thlimmenos* [24] case in 2000, the court has shown itself to be willing to consider cases where, due to different situations related to historic disadvantage, etc., it may be necessary to take a different approach between *prima facie* similar cases. Perhaps the most important case, in terms of demonstrating the court's willingness to look at indirect discrimination, is the case of *D.H. and Others v. Czech Republic.* [25] This case concerned the decision by the Czech state to place Roma children who had not mastered the Czech language into the country's system of special schools for children with severe learning difficulties. Such treatment was not only reserved for the Roma, but also for children of other origins who had not yet mastered the national language. In that case the Grand Chamber stated that it was not necessary to show any intention to discriminate, and that *prima facie* discriminatory treatment could be found where the results of a measure disproportionately affected a group (in this case the Roma) in a negative way.[26] In such cases the burden would shift to the state, creating a need for it to show it was justified in not opting for alternative measures to correct the situation.

The recent sympathy the ECtHR has shown towards a wide notion of indirect discrimination represents an important widening of the potential reach of the anti-discrimination protection offered by the ECHR, creating what can be considered a 'second generation' approach to problems of discrimination. It demonstrates that the ECtHR is receptive to taking into account a wider range of factors (i.e. beyond those which it traditionally considered in the concept of 'treatment') when discerning whether an act of discrimination has occurred. This includes effects that may occur at the group level, that may be created even in the absence of a discriminatory motivation and that may not be clear without further investigation.[27] Importantly the court has, in describing such unintended or indirect effects, considered the importance of stigmatization as a phenomenon and has used the presence of the phenomenon to help justify a finding of indirect discrimination.[28] In the case of *D.H.*, for example, the court was concerned with the stigmatizing effects that the potential segregation of children who could not speak the national language could have on Roma children (given that a disproportionate number of Roma would be involved).[29] This demonstrates that, although the court has not

23 O'Connell, "Cinderella Comes to the Ball: Art 14 and the Right to Non-Discrimination in the ECHR". p220
24 *Thlimmenos v. Greece*, 34369/97.
25 *D.H. and Others v. Czech Republic* (Application No 57325/00).
26 See *D.H.* para 175.
27 O'Connell, "Cinderella Comes to the Ball: Art 14 and the Right to Non-Discrimination in the ECHR".
28 In (not an indirect discrimination case) *Kiyutin* (*Kiyutin v. Russia* [2011] ECHR 439), for example, the court was also seemingly influenced by the potential stigmatization that could be caused by the deportation of non-Russian nationals from the Russian Federation if they were found to be HIV positive.
29 *D.H.* para 50. The court quoted a report that stated, "Being subjected to special schools or classes often means that these children follow a curriculum inferior to those of mainstream classes, which diminishes their opportunities for further education and for finding employment in the future. The automatic placement of Roma children in

explored the concept of stigmatization in depth, it is open to including the concept as a possible 'indirect effect' within its conception of indirect discrimination.[30] The openness that the court has shown to indirect effects and the sensitivity it has shown to group harm gives the impression that it could be open to seeing the existence of SSEs as a form of discrimination (though as section D below will discuss this hope may well be misplaced).

D Are expressions alone capable of engaging Article 14?

Despite the more extensive nature of the anti-discrimination approach offered by the ECtHR and its apparent receptivity to issues of stigmatization (including effects that exist at a group level), there is little in the court's case law to suggest that it would be willing to find 'expressive acts' that do not have binding effects as being capable of engaging Article 14. As a consequence, those seeking protection from the ECtHR because of stigmatization occurring from purely expressive acts may have difficulty in using Article 14. If this is indeed correct, it seems to neutralize the flexibility provided by the within the ambit concept and the non-exhaustive list of categories described in Article 14, at least in terms of expressive activities or statements. It also represents an important limit on how far the court will go in recognizing the existence of 'group harm'. This is because whilst Article 14 may allow individuals to invoke other articles without engagement (e.g. Article 8), they still have to show an engagement of Article 14, that is that a *prima facie* act of discriminatory treatment occurred. While the ECtHR has not expressly stated that treatment is a *sina qua non* in order for discrimination to exist under Article 14, it has said little to indicate otherwise. There are furthermore indications in the reasoning of the court in a number of judgments that seemingly imply the importance of the concept and help in outlining what it involves.[31] These are discussed below.

(i) The court has never found Article 14 to be engaged without 'treatment' existing

While the ECtHR has found certain categories of expressive activity (see section E) to be capable of infringing convention rights, it has never been presented with a case where it found an expression in the absence of treatment to be discriminatory under Article 14. Expressions that are merely stigmatizing (i.e. are not accompanied by a form of treatment) do not produce any binding effects on individuals (if one ignores the psychological issues that are associated with stigmatization – see Chapter 2). This is because in theory individuals are able to ignore expressions and continue to act as they wish. Correspondingly, no example of 'stigmatization alone' (i.e. not

classes for children with special needs is likely to increase the stigma by labeling the Roma children as less intelligent and less capable."

30 Quinn and De Hert, "Self Respect—a 'Rawlsian Primary Good' Unprotected by the European Convention on Human Rights and Its Lack of a Coherent Approach to Stigmatization?"

31 Ibid.

accompanying some other kind of act) has been dealt with by the ECtHR *vis-à-vis* Article 14 (or any other article for that matter).[32] There is, therefore, no support in terms of case law to suggest that the ECtHR would be willing to hear a stigma alone case (i.e. stigmatization brought about by an expression) under Article 14.[33] The same distinction applies when considering whether stigmatization has been dealt with by the ECtHR under its 'anti-stereotyping' strategy. Stereotypes are very closely related to stigmatization, with a negative stereotype having the potential to stigmatize. However, it is important to note that when the ECtHR has acted to prevent stereotyping, it has done so under the guise of Article 14, that is, treating it as a form of discrimination.[34] The 'stereotyping' cases which the court has heard have always involved some form of treatment. Where instances of stereotyping are manifested merely as statements or expressive acts and do not involve the imposition of binding changes (i.e. treatment), there is nothing under the ECtHR's current case law to suggest that Article 14 will be engaged.

While the ECtHR has demonstrated that it is receptive to the concept of stigmatization, in particular considering it as a factor in deciding whether the engagement of a particular right was justified (see, e.g., *Kiyutin v. Russia* [2011] ECHR 439, S & *Marper v. United Kingdom* [2008] ECHR 1581, *A, B and C v. Ireland* [2010] ECHR 2032 and *D.H. and Others v. Czech Republic* (number 57325/00)), this has always occurred where an engaging factor existed that clearly constituted treatment. This is because in all such cases, this occurred where the court had already established the existence of an act that demonstrably altered individuals' legal rights (e.g. not allowing them to reside on a state's territory as in *Kiyutin* or not allowing them to attend a mainstream class in school, e.g. *D.H.*). Whilst the ECtHR has shown that it is open to at least recognizing the concept of stigmatization, it has never found expressions that are merely stigmatizing to be capable of engaging convention rights in the absence of treatment. What it did find was that such factors can be taken into account in determining whether another engaging factor is justified and therefore permissible. Whilst it is of course conceivable that the court could decide differently if the right case was to be put before it (imagine, for instance, extremely stigmatizing expressions made about certain minorities by a public official in the absence of treatment), the case law as it is presently available suggests that such expressions would not, by themselves, be capable of engaging Article 14.

32 Some forms of pure expression have been considered by the court. Examples of this might include hate speech cases that have been heard under Article 8. See, for example, *AKSU* (see section (ii) below). In such cases, however, the ECtHR did not explicitly invoke the concept of stigmatization, though there are of course stigmatizing effects from hate speech.

33 Quinn, "The Problem of Stigmatizing Expressions – the Limits of Anti-Discrimination Approaches".

34 A Timmer, "Toward an Anti-Stereotyping Approach for the European Court of Human Rights", *Human Rights Law Review* 11, no. 4 (2011).

(ii) The ECtHR's implicit references to treatment

In terms of what the court has itself said, the strongest support for the treatment concept comes from the case of *Baczkowski & Others v. Poland* [2007] ECHR 1543/06. In that case, the court reiterated that there was limited scope (giving due consideration to Article 10 and its requirement for freedom of speech) under Article 14 to limit the political speech of public officials such as mayors.[35] This case involved homophobic remarks made by a mayor prior to the cancellation of a gay pride march, supposedly on grounds of traffic safety. Severe negative expressions could according to the court be understood as instructions in the context of a particular decision (or treatment) that was taking place. Such remarks appear to indicate that the court sees expressive activity as not constituting treatment itself but only capable of providing additional evidential value as to the correctness of treatment that may have occurred.[36] Expressions in the absence of such treatment would, therefore, not seem to be able to constitute acts of discrimination.

Further support for this reading of *Baczkowski* comes from the Grand Chamber ruling in the case of *AKSU v. Turkey* (application numbers 4149/04 and 41029/04). That case concerned both an academic publication and a common dictionary that had been partially funded by the Turkish state. The complainant alleged that both contained insulting expressions. The first included assertions that some Roma were involved in theft and other criminality; the second included common insulting metaphors in the Turkish language that used the word 'Gypsy'. The complainant alleged that such expressions were discriminatory and served to increase the problems of discrimination for the already vulnerable Roma community in Turkey and beyond. The Grand Chamber, however, refused to see *AKSU* as a discrimination case because it did not involve a 'difference in treatment'. The court stated that this was because the complainant had not shown that the publications had 'a discriminatory intent or effect'. The court said that this differentiated the case from other cases where discrimination under Article 14 had been found to be applicable, citing, for example, the cases *Chapman v. the United Kingdom* (application number 27238/95) and *Sejdic´ and Finci v. Bosnia and Herzegovina* (application numbers 27996/06 and 34836/06). These cases involved instances where the discriminatory treatment involved clear effects on the legal rights of the individual involved. *Sejdic´ and Finci,* for instance, involved a constitutional provision barring non-ethnic Bosnians from holding certain offices. *Chapman* involved a refusal of planning permission. The reference to these cases in terms of what actually constitutes 'a desire to create differential treatment or effects' appears to indicate that the court was concerned with a desire to bring about such treatment through the imposition of legally binding changes (e.g. laws or practices that have legal effects for individuals such as planning permission). This is something expressions by themselves (including those made by the state) are arguably not able to do (given that they can in theory be ignored).

35 *Baczkowski* para 98.

36 O'Connell, "Cinderella Comes to the Ball: Art 14 and the Right to Non-Discrimination in the ECHR". On page 220, O'Connell states, 'Even if there is a specific example of a racist comment by a public official, the ECtHR will not necessarily conclude this demonstrates that treatment of a victim has been motivated by a discriminatory purpose".

E Differentiating stigmatizing expressions and hate speech

In discussing the position of the ECtHR concerning expressive acts, it is necessary to also consider its position on hate speech (for which the ECtHR has found a positive duty requiring states to prevent it).[37] As Chapter 2 discussed expressive acts of this type are not only deeply stigmatizing but also target specific vulnerable groups in society. The ECtHR has without doubt recognized that such types of expression can be limited, even in the absence of the kind of binding effects or treatment that have been discussed thus far. Upon analysis of the case law of the court, several important factors quickly become apparent that will limit its likely impact om SSEs.[38]

First, the court has not looked at the hate speech cases that have come before it using Article 14. Whilst one might assume that the court has not done so because it does not look at hate speech as representing a discriminatory act, such a presumption would, however, in reality be too strong. The real reason that most cases have been heard on other grounds is because of the way they have been brought before the court. The vast majority of cases represent appeals against the application of national laws on hate speech to particular acts of expression (e.g. notable cases include *Leroy v. France* (application number 36109/03), *Jerslid v. Denmark* (application number 15890/89), *Vejdeland and Others v. Sweden* (application number 1813/07) and *Feret v. Belgium* (application number 15615/07)).

This gives rise to the second major point that can be observed from the case law in this area – that most cases were pleaded under Article 10, that is, as freedom of expression cases. Such cases are concerned with a negative duty upon states to not necessarily limit the freedom of expression. In considering the validity of claims, the court has been primarily concerned with performing a balancing exercise between rights to freedom of expression under Article 10 and potential harm to others in terms of the right to a private and family life as a result of being exposed to hate speech (i.e. protected by Article 8).[39] Given this the ECtHR has tended not to look at such matters from an anti-discrimination perspective.

37 Stephanos Stavros, "A Duty to Prosecute Hate Speech under the European Convention on Human Rights?" (OxHRH Blog, 9 April 2015). Available at http://humanrights.dev3.oneltd.eu/a-duty-to-prosecute-hate-speech-under-the-european-convention-on-human-rights

38 For more on the ECHR and its approach to hate speech see J Cardozo, "Protecting Freedom of Expression: The Challenge of Hate Speech in the European Court of Human Rights Case Law", *Journal of International Law and Comparative Law* 17 (2009).

39 In *Jerslid*, for example, the court was concerned with the ability of a journalist to repeat the hate speech of others. *Vejdeland* concerned a case where individuals had been spreading negative propaganda about homosexual individuals on school sites. In *Feret*, the case concerned the freedom of a politician to make remarks that appeared to be hate speech under national law. For a broad discussion on arguments used from the perspective of religious freedom to justify the use of hate speech, see E Janssen, *Faith in Public Debate. On Freedom of Expression, Hate Speech and Religion in France & the Netherlands* (Cambridge: Interstentia, 2015).

A third important element that should be appreciated in this context is that there is very little case law where the court has discussed a positive duty to prevent hate speech. Its focus has rather been on a negative duty not to prevent the freedom of expression of others and how such a duty can be limited (*inter alia* in instances of hate speech). This again reflects the way most cases concerning hate speech are brought before the court. Given that most are the result of appeals against the imposition of national laws on hate speech, the court has quite logically focused on the limits of a potential negative duty not to infringe upon free speech. There is, with the exception of *AKSU*, very little in the way of case law available where the issue was the existence of a positive duty to prevent harmful expressive acts. Even though, therefore, the court has demonstrated in its reasoning (e.g. in *AKSU* at para 59) that there are strong grounds to think that a positive duty to prevent hate speech exists under Article 8, it has never ruled so definitively in a case where that was the main contention.

Given that there appears to be a positive duty to prohibit hate speech, one might ask does this not also mean that such a duty exists in terms of stigmatizing expressions in general? In answering this, it is important to consider the nuanced relationship that exists between expressions that are stigmatizing and expressions that constitute hate speech (see Chapter 4). The latter arguably represents a narrower range of expressions than the former and has a higher threshold. Expressions that are stigmatizing need not necessarily amount to hate speech. Imagine, for instance, expressions by a public official concerning the high unemployment among particular ethic groups or immigrants in general.[40] While such comments are undoubtedly stigmatizing, they are unlikely to be classified as hate speech. Most formulations of hate speech in law refer to expressions that incite hatred or discrimination against specifically defined groups.[41] Expressions that do not meet such a definition or are not targeted at those groups deemed vulnerable enough to find protection in the law will not constitute hate speech (at least legally speaking). The concept of hate speech concerns expressions of such gravity that they are likely to bring about a threat to public order, increase the chances of physical attack or directly encourage others to discriminate.[42] Remarks that are 'merely stigmatizing' may not meet such a threshold. Whilst they may induce a sense of embarrassment or shame (with

40 The Mayor of Antwerp in Belgium, for instance, has criticized the efforts that the Berber community in his city had made to integrate socially and economically into Belgian life. The Belgian prosecutor's office has since confirmed that such announcements do not amount to hate speech. See (in Dutch) http://www.knack.be/nieuws/belgie/racismeklacht-tegendewever- geseponeerd-parket-bevestigt-dat-feitelijke-uitleg-doen-geen-misdrijf-is/articlenormal-737565.html

41 M Van Noorloos, *Hate Speech Revisited – a Comparative and Historical Perspective on Hate Speech Law in the Netherlands and England and Wales* (Cambridge: Interstentia, 2011).

42 This appears to be the motivation behind offences such as incitement to hatred or discrimination as exist in France and the Netherlands, for example (Van Noorloos, 2011). In France, incitement to discrimination against certain groups was made illegal by 'La loi n_72–546 du 1er juillet 1972'. The same law also prohibits incitement to hatred for these groups.

potential attendant psychological effects on those concerned),[43] as in the example of the remarks made by a public official discussed above, they need not represent calls for acts of hatred or incitement to discrimination.[44] While all hate speech is stigmatizing, not all stigmatizing expressions need to be considered hate speech. The indications that the court has given to the existence of a positive duty to prevent hate speech cannot therefore be thought of as applying in a general sense to stigmatizing expressions, but rather to a special subset of expressions that represent a certain gravity and are against specific groups recognized to be vulnerable. Indeed, given the need to weigh limitations of expression against the right to liberty of expression enshrined in Article 10, it may be considered likely that only expressions of such gravity may be considered as demanding prohibition. In *Handyside v. the United Kingdom* (application number 5493/72), for example, the court stated (in para 49) of its reasoning (which it has often repeated since) that measures that aim to prevent expressions that merely "offend, shock or disturb" others are not permitted under Article 10. This will include many or even most of the types of SSEs discussed in Chapter 1.

Given the prominence of Article 10 in such cases, it would seem unlikely that speech that is merely stigmatizing would be viewed in a similar way to hate speech. Were a court to consider a discrimination case concerning a purely expressive act (i.e. not constituting treatment), Article 10 would likely be of application (as it has been in most hate speech cases heard before the court). This would bring with it the inherent limitations posed by Article 10 on limiting free speech, and therefore mean that expressions not deemed to be of sufficient gravity (i.e. perhaps those that are merely stigmatizing) could not be prohibited. Even if, therefore, a court was to decide that treatment was not a prerequisite to engage Article 14, the existence of Article 10 would likely mean that a large range of stigmatizing statements (i.e. those that fall below the threshold of hate speech) could not be prohibited.

4 The EU and its anti-discrimination initiatives

A The EU as an actor that is increasingly active in combating discrimination

Another important source of anti-discrimination law for many European countries comes from the EU and its initiatives in the area. Unlike the ECHR approach discussed above, there are no general EU anti-discrimination initiatives that are intended to apply in most contexts.[45] The EU has opted to legislate for certain

43 Crocker, "Social Stigma and Self-Esteem: Situational Construction of Self Worth", *Journal of Experimental Social Psychology* 35 (1999). B Major et al., "Coping with Negative Stereotypes About Intellectual Performance: The Role of Psychological Disengagement", *Personality and Social Psychology Bulletin* 24, no. 1 (1998).

44 As (Courtwright, 2009) points out, stigmatization is possible even in the absence of discrimination.

45 T Givens and R Evans Case, *Legislating Equality: The Politics of Antidiscrimination Policy in Europe* (Oxford: Oxford University Press, 2014).

specific anti-discrimination initiatives that apply in certain specific contexts. In spite of this, or perhaps even because of this, some of these (two of which are discussed below) approaches are seemingly able to impact upon stigmatizing expressions in a way that Article 14 ECHR is seemingly unable to. Given their formulation, however, they are only able to do so in very specific circumstances, limiting their potential application to stigmatizing expressions in general.

In the absence of a general instrument that is applicable to all matters of discrimination (not including the broad and ill-defined commitments to fighting discrimination contained within the treaties and the limited applicability of the Charter) the EU has created a number of piecemeal initiatives.[46] The first initiatives of the European Economic Community (EEC) in the area of anti-discrimination rights came in the 1970s with the creation of directives prohibiting gender discrimination in the workplace.[47] These provided rules concerning discrimination in terms of pay between men and women, and also concerning access to employment and employment training.[48] It was not until the late 1990s, however, that the EU started to become more active in the creation of anti-discrimination laws (i.e. beyond gender discrimination). This was because less of a consensus existed at the political level as to the need for such activity (in comparison with the consensus concerning the need for protection against discrimination in terms of gender). Given that this coincided with a period when the progress made by the ECtHR in anti-discrimination cases was considered to be limited,[49] political pressure began to grow on the EU to take its own measures in order to push a broad and progressive anti-discrimination agenda.[50] This pushed the EU into producing two new directives.[51] These were Council Directive 2000/43/EC

46 G De Burca, "The Trajectories of European and American Antidiscrimination Law", *American Journal of Comparative Law* (2011).

47 This included Council Directive 75/117/EEC of 10 February 1975 on the approximation of the laws of the Member States relating to the application of the principle of equal pay for women and men; and Council Directive 76/207/EEC of 9 February 1976 on the implementation of the principle of equal treatment for women and men with respect to access to employment, vocational training and promotion and working conditions (as amended by Council Directive 2002/73), and Council Directive 97/80/EC of 15 December 1997 on the burden of proof in cases of sex discrimination.

48 For further discussion see S Besson, "Gender Discrimination under EU and ECHR Law: Never Shall the Twain Meet?", *Human Rights Law Review* 8, no. 4 (2008); "Evolutions in Antidiscrimination Law within the European Convention on Human Rights and the European Social Charter System", *American Journal of Comparative Law* 60 (2012).

49 O'Connell, "Cinderella Comes to the Ball: Art 14 and the Right to Non-Discrimination in the ECHR".

50 T Simonovic Einwalter, "Far, but Not Far Enough: An Idealist Critique of the Racial Equality Directive", *Croatian Yearbook of European Policy & Law*, no. 4 (2008).This was set against the backdrop of a worrying rise in support for far right groups in a number of European countries in general. See: European Union Agency for Fundamental Rights, *Handbook on European Non-Discrimination Law* (2010).

51 The authority to create such legislation is described in Article 18 of the Treaty on the Functioning of the European Union (TFEU) which provides the EU with the competence to enact legislation with the aim of combatting forms of discrimination

of 29 June 2000 implementing the principle of equal treatment between persons irrespective of racial and ethnic origin (the RED) and Council Directive 2000/78/EC of 27 November 2000 establishing a general framework for equal treatment in employment and occupation (the EED). These are referred to collectively as the 'equality directives' and will be discussed below. They are interesting because both contain provisions that appear to be applicable to expressive activity. They thus make for an interesting comparison with regimes of more general application such as that envisaged under Article 14 ECHR. Such a comparison is interesting in illustrating the problems various anti-discrimination approaches are likely to have in engaging stigmatizing statements and expressions where treatment does not exist.

B A new approach to problems of discrimination (in certain areas)

(i) Areas of application

The RED applies only to discrimination on the basis of perceived membership of racial or ethnic groups,[52] whilst the EED applies to a broader range of categories (i.e. religion or belief, disability, age or sexual orientation).[53] The RED is, however, much broader in terms of the protection it offers applying to a wide range of contexts and not just employment (as is the case with the EED). These areas are described as:

> conditions for access to employment, to self-employment and to occupation, including selection criteria and recruitment conditions, whatever the branch of activity and at all levels of the professional hierarchy, including promotion; … access to all types and to all levels of vocational guidance, vocational training, advanced vocational training and retraining, including practical work experience; … employment and working conditions, including dismissals and pay; … membership of and involvement in an organisation of workers or employers, or any organisation whose members carry on a particular profession, including the benefits provided for by such organisations; … social protection, including social security and healthcare; … social advantages; … education; … access to and supply of goods and services which are available to the public, including housing.[54]

The RED can thus be thought of as having an extensive but not general application in terms of discrimination based upon the categories it applies to (i.e. race and ethnicity). Its limitations in this regard are apparent if one compares it to Article

described in Article 10 TFEU, i.e. based on "sex, racial or ethnic origin, religion or belief, disability, age or sexual orientation".

52 Directive 2000/43/EC Article 1 states, "The purpose of this Directive is to lay down a framework for combating discrimination on the grounds of racial or ethnic origin, with a view to putting into effect in the Member States the principle of equal treatment".

53 Directive 2000/78/EC Article1.

54 Directive 2000/43/EC Article 3.

14 ECHR which, in conjunction with the rights provided by other articles (and their expansive interpretation by the court),[55] can be applied to an almost undefined list of contexts (as section 3 discusses).[56] Whilst the Court of Justice of the European Union (CJEU) may, through creative jurisprudence, interpret the above domains widely, the presence of an exhaustive list of domains of application represents by its very nature a limitation in terms of the RED's potential applicability in comparison with that of Article 14 of the ECHR and. In terms of the EED, the area of application is even more limited, only concerning discrimination connected to matters of employment.[57] This poses obvious limitations in terms of the applicability of the EU approach to SSEs.

(ii) A hierarchy of protected categories

The RED and the EED create between them a complex web of anti-discrimination law that has the effect of creating a hierarchy of protected categories.[58] This is because the RED offers more extensive protection, in terms of applying to a far wider range of contexts (see above), but only applies to discrimination based on race or ethnicity. The EED, applying to the categories of religion or belief, disability, age or sexual orientation, on the other hand only offers protection in the employment context. Given that such matters are also covered by the RED, this means that a clear hierarchy exists with on the one hand the categories of racial or ethnic discrimination enjoying protection in a greater number of domains (and also in domains that can be interpreted widely, e.g. educational protection or social services) and on the other those categories protected in the EED which only enjoy protection in terms of discrimination related to employment. This hierarchy is important because it limits the potential reach of EU laws on discrimination to the area of employment for the categories described within the EED (i.e. religion or belief, disability, age or sexual orientation). This, therefore, represents an important limit in terms of the potential application to SSEs. Where such statements are made against groups that are not covered by any directive, e.g. nationality (for third country nationals),[59] these directives offer no protection (this can be contrasted with the non-exhaustive list described in Article 14 ECHR). It is important to bear this

55 See also the discussion of the 'within the ambit concept developed by the ECHR in section 3A. See also Baker, "The Enjoyment of Rights and Freedoms: A New Conception of the 'Ambit' under Article 14 ECHR".

56 See section 3B where the non-exhaustive nature of the term "other status" in Article 14 ECHR is discussed.

57 Directive 2000/78/EC Article 3.

58 Degener, "Intersections between Disability, Race and Gender in Discrimination Law", in *European Union Non-Discrimination Law and Intersectionality: Investigating the Triangle of Racial, Gender and Disability Discrimination*, ed. D Schiek and A Lawson (Farnham: Ashgate Publishing, 2011).

59 S Benedi Lahuerta, "Race Equality and TCNs, or How to Fight Discrimination with a Discriminatory Law", *European Law Journal* 15, no. 6 (2009). Third country nationals, i.e. not from the EU, are unable to find any protection in the EU if they are discriminated against on the grounds of nationality. They are still protected under the

hierarchy of protection in mind when considering the effect of the EU's equality directives and the CJEU's case law on stigmatizing expressions.

(iii) 'Direct' and 'indirect' discrimination are explicitly recognized

In terms of actions that may constitute discrimination, Article 2 of both directives refers to a *prima facie* "neutral provision, criterion or practice". This choice of words is interesting because it arguably appears to go beyond the focus on legal rights which is the focal point of many other anti-discrimination measures, including Article 14 of the ECHR.[60] The use of the term 'provision' appears to be included to cover the formation of law or guidelines. The inclusion of 'criterion' and 'practice', however, appears to signal the explicit intention on the part of the legislator to provide for a wide and expanded scope of what indirect discrimination is. The latter could include the use of expressions, statements and information by the state in a manner that could be stigmatizing. Unfortunately, given the lack of pronouncement by the CJEU on this issue thus far and the lack of clarification on this issue provided by the directive (e.g. in the recitals) one cannot give a definitive answer to this question. The potential recognition of expressive activities under the term 'practices' would be important in terms of the potential engagement of stigmatizing statements or expressions. It would in particular mean that the recognition of such activities would not need to be linked to alterations in individual legal rights (or treatment) associated with the ECHR's interpretation of what discrimination constitutes (*inter alia* in cases such as *Baczkowski* and *AKSU).* [61] This would not be inconsistent with attitudes in some EU Member States where an employer's failure to stop racist remarks or comments can be considered as direct discrimination.[62]

Another important factor is the definition of indirect discrimination opted for, with the reference to 'persons' in place of "a person" used in the definition of 'direct discrimination'.[63] In referring to 'persons' the equality directives make it

RED, however, if they are discriminated against on the basis of their race or their ethnicity.

60 See, for example, the discussion in section 5 on the *Baczkowski* case. See also Quinn and De Hert, "Self Respect—a 'Rawlsian Primary Good' Unprotected by the European Convention on Human Rights and Its Lack of a Coherent Approach to Stigmatization?" p41

61 See section 3 of this chapter and Quinn, "The Problem of Stigmatizing Expressions – the Limits of Anti-Discrimination Approaches".

62 See Dutch Equal Treatment Commission, opinion no. 2010–17, 15.01.2010. In this case, the Commissie Gelijke Behandeling (CGB) concluded subsequently that the employer had failed to properly investigate the worker's initial complaint and came to the opinion that led to a violation of the law. This case is discussed in a paper prepared for the European Acadamy of Law (ERA) seminar 'The Anti-Discrimination Directives 2000/43 & 2000/78 in Practice', 22–23 February 2011, Trier by Dick Houtzager. Available at http://www.era-comm.eu/oldoku/Adiskri/03_Burden_of_proof/2010_Houtzager_EN.pdf

63 See Directive 2000/43/EC Article 2(2).

clear that this concept is capable of offering protection to groups that suffer harmful effects because of a particular measure. This is in contrast to the concept of direct discrimination which, according to the definition proposed by the equality directives, is much more focused on the effects on particular, identifiable individuals. *Henrard* suggests that the choice of definitions opted for in the equality directives for direct and indirect discrimination show that the former is concerned with the treatment of identifiable individuals who have been treated unfairly whereas the latter is concerned with harm that "can be identified at group level".[64] In the case of the RED this involves anything that would put "persons of a racial or ethnic group at a particular disadvantage".[65] This overt sensitivity to 'indirect effects' caused at the group level is synonymous with many of the problems associated with instances of stigmatization. In particular, such an openness seems particularly fine tuned to indirect effects in terms of negative coping strategies and harm to the self-esteem of groups in society (see Chapter 2), key factors in many instances of stigmatization (including through stigmatizing statements or expressions). Given the apparent receptivity of the equality directives to expressive acts (discussed below),[66] one could argue that the legislator may have indicated a greater desire to limit stigmatizing expressions under the concept of indirect discrimination in a way that ECHR has hitherto failed to demonstrate, albeit it in a restricted set of contexts.

(iv) 'Harassment' as discrimination

Both the RED and the EED describe a version of discrimination in the form of 'harassment'.[67] In clarifying what such a form of discrimination is both the RED and the EED state:

> Harassment shall be deemed to be discrimination within the meaning of paragraph 1, when an unwanted conduct related to racial or ethnic origin takes place with the purpose or effect of violating the dignity of a person and of creating an intimidating, hostile, degrading, humiliating or offensive environment. In this context, the concept of harassment may be defined in accordance with the national laws and practice of the Member States.

64 This description, however, seems to be contradicted by the CJEU's reasoning in *Feryn* where the court found the general statement of an employer against employing individuals of North African descent to be direct discrimination under the RED. This is discussed in section 5.

65 K Henrard, "The First Substantive ECJ Judgment on the Racial Equality Directive: A Strong Message in a Conceptually Flawed, and Responsively Weak Bottle", *Jean Monnet Working Paper* No. 09/09.

66 See in particular the CJEU's interpretation of the equality directives in the *Feryn* case, discussed in section 5.

67 This type of discrimination is described in Article 2(3) of both the RED and the equality directive.

Such a potential form of discrimination seemingly goes further than is permitted under the requirement of treatment (discussed in section 3).[68] This is because it seemingly does not require any changes to the legal rights or privileges of the individual involved, i.e. the imposition of binding changes. The concept is, however, somewhat restricted by a requirement that harassment be directed to a defined and identifiable person. The use of the words "a person" would seem to indicate that any expressive activity of an individual, must have been directed towards an identifiable individual in order to be considered harassment. Similar expressive activities that were directed towards a group (numerous illustrations of which were provided in Chapter 1) would not appear to be sufficient to constitute harassment.[69] Using the notion of harassment to tackle stigmatising expressions may, therefore, be subject to the same potential problems discussed above regarding direct discrimination, i.e. that it will not apply to general stigmatizing statements made about entire groups but which do not refer to specific individuals. Once again, only CJEU case law will be able to firmly delineate the boundaries of this provision.

(v) 'Instruction to discriminate'

The RED and the EED also state that 'instruction to discriminate' should be considered as constituting discrimination. Neither of these directives, nor any of the others that employ this term provide guidance on what the term 'instruction to discriminate' means.[70] Such a formulation is, at the same time, remarkably similar yet different to criminal provisions concerning hate speech found in a number of European countries concerning 'incitement to discrimination'.[71] Such offences appear to be intended to apply in instances where individuals call for the discrimination of others.[72] In terms of calling for discrimination, this presumably mean acts of direct discrimination, given that indirect discrimination often involves

68 *Baczkowski & Others v. Poland* [2007] ECHR No. 1543/06.

69 Council Declaration of 19 December 1991 on the implementation of the Commission Recommendation on the protection of the dignity of women and men at work, including the Code of Practice to Combat Sexual Harassment, OJ C 27, 04.02.1992 p. 1; Commission Recommendation 92/131/EEC on the protection of the dignity of women and men at work, OJ L 49, 24.02.1992. Further interpretation of what this category of harassment means can be found in Council Resolution of 29 May 1990 on the protection of the dignity of women and men at work, including the Code of Practice to Combat Sexual Harassment. This framework provides that a finding of harassment should be made if a victim feels that given the circumstances in question the acts in question were directed at him or her, or if given the circumstances a complainant was the target of the harassment in question. See also European Union Agency for Fundamental Rights, *Handbook on European Non-Discrimination Law*.

70 Ibid. p33

71 Article 15 of Directive 2000/43/EC requires that Member States have sanctions that must be effective, proportionate and dissuasive. It does not, however, require that such sanctions exist in the form of a criminal offence.

72 See, for example, the French Criminal Code – Article 24 de la loi du 29 juillet 1881, or the Dutch Criminal Code – Wetboek van Strafrecht Article 137(d).

treatment that may appear neutral and where discriminatory effects are often unintentional.[73] The provisions of both the RED and the EED concerning 'instruction to discriminate' are notable in that they both refer to "persons" and not "a person" as was the case with the definition of 'harassment'.[74] This indicates a potentially wide reading of these provisions as it would seem to indicate that individuals making such statements need not refer to specific individuals but can be seen as instructing discrimination even where they refer to general groups.[75]

Criminal law approaches to hate speech (discussed in Chapter 4), including provisions targeting incitement to discrimination are capable of covering a range of stigmatizing statements.[76] Doubt may, however, be cast upon the breadth of any potential interpretation given the choice of the word 'instruction'. This term could be construed as meaning a 'command' or an 'order', i.e. a direction by someone to another (who must listen to such direction) to treat an individual or a group of individuals in a discriminatory manner. If this interpretation is correct, simple calls by individuals (such as political figures) to discriminate would not constitute an instruction to discriminate if they had no power to compel the addressee(s) of their message to act accordingly. Advocates of this view would argue that, had the drafters of the equality directives wanted to create a wider concept they could have opted for the term 'incitation to discrimination' which is well known in the criminal law of several European states (see Chapter 4). Such a provision would apparently include those who simply 'call' for the discriminatory treatment of others, even where they have no power to compel individuals to listen to their 'calls'. Whilst demands for differential treatment for individuals on the basis of categories described in the equality directives might be considered socially unacceptable in most societies (and are indeed stigmatizing), such actions will often not be illegal. Some of the categorizations described in the EED (i.e. belief, disability, age or sexual orientation) represent, for instance, aspects for which a higher degree of criticism is often permitted, especially on the part of private individuals who are not in a position to directly discriminate against people.[77] Given that the equality directives are intended (through transposition) to be applicable both to the state

73 This notion is not confirmed by Article 1(4) of both directives which confusingly states that instructions to discriminate shall constitute discrimination "within the meaning of paragraph 1" which includes both direct and indirect discrimination.

74 See Council Directive 2000/43/EC Article 2(4) and Council Directive 2000/78/EC Article 2(4).

75 The CJEU case of *Feryn* represented an instance where an employer gave statements that made it seem likely that he would discriminate against certain groups of potential candidates. In that case, however, the court decided to invoke the concept of direct discrimination. See section 5.

76 For a discussion of such laws in the Dutch context see E Janssen and A Nieuwnhuis, "De Verhouding Tussen Vrijheid Van Meninguting En Discriminatie in Het Wilders-Process," *Nederlands Tijdschrift voor de Mensenrechten-Bulletin*. Available at http://hdl.handle.net/11245/1.375450 (2012)

77 For a more in-depth discussion on the problems this hierarchy can produce see Schiek and Lawson, *European Union Non-Discrimination Law and Intersectionality: Investigating the Triangle of Racial, Gender and Disability Discrimination*.

and to private individuals this issue is extremely pertinent.[78] Preventing such individuals from being able to voice opinions, even if they are unsavoury, would entail a major curtailment of free speech, something that may be seen as harmful to the democratic character of a society.[79] Imagine, for instance, a political figure or private individual who believed because of his or her religion that a homosexual lifestyle was 'immoral' or that certain religions contained aspects that were 'backward'.[80] Whilst in most societies such comments may be viewed as being intolerant or even morally wrong, the right to hold such opinions and to be able to make such comments may be seen as a necessary freedom within a democratic society (see also discussion concerning Article 10 ECHR in section 3D). Given these factors, the author would argue that the selection of the term 'instruction' over the potential option of 'incitement' is indicative of a desire on the part of the legislator to narrow the potential scope for interpretation of this type of discrimination. In terms of SSEs this would limit applicability to a narrow range of instances (e.g. within an employment relationship) where the individual involved had the power to ensure that their instruction was implemented. This could occur, for instance, when a minister or civil servant is able to ensure that his discriminatory instructions are implemented (e.g. deny services or benefits to a particular individual).

5 A third anti-discrimination approach described by the CJEU in *Feryn*?

A 'Dissuasive force' in expressive statements can be classed as direct discrimination?

Although the number of cases that have come before the CJEU concerning the RED and the EED is growing, to date not many have concerned expressive acts.[81] One important case, however, is that of *Feryn*. [82] In this case, the CJEU

78 Citation 26 of Council Directive 2000/43/EC states Member States should provide for effective, proportionate and dissuasive sanctions in case of breaches of the obligations under this directive. This indicates the legislators desire that Member States create laws that are also applicable to private parties.

79 It is also important to remember that some EU Member States have no equivalent hate speech provision to 'incitation to discrimination' (e.g. the UK). The imposition of such a concept in such systems would, therefore, have been problematic.

80 In France UMP politician Christian Vanneste was prosecuted for comments he made about the danger homosexuals posed to the world. The French *Cour de Cassation* quashed his conviction, however, on the grounds that the law preventing incitation to discrimination on the basis of sexuality was too broad. See Chapter 4.

81 Many cases have concerned more traditional forms of treatment. These have included dismissal from employment, e.g. C-13/05 *Chacon Navas* CJEU 11 July 2006, Case C-411/05 *Félix Palacios de la Villa* CJEU, 11 July 2006, pension entitlements, e.g. Case C-267/06 *Maruko* 1 April 2008, Case C-427/06 *Bartsch* 1 April 2008, terms of employment, e.g. Case C-88/08 Hutter 18 June 2009, Case C-555/07 *Kücükdeveci* 9 January 2010, compulsory retirement, e.g., Case C-286/12 *Commission v. Hungary* 6 November 2012.

82 *Centrum voor gelijkheid van kansen en voor racismebestrijding v. Firma Feryn NV*. Reference for a preliminary ruling: Case C-54/07.

considered comments made by the owner of a business in Belgium who installed shutters and other security equipment in private homes. He stated that he had numerous vacancies that he could not fill.[83] The business owner complained that he only received applications from individuals of North African origin (e.g. people of Moroccan descent) but that it was useless for him to employ such individuals as it would not be what his clients desired. He stated that this was because his clients would not want such people entering their homes given the association they make between the community concerned and acts of criminality. The firm's owner was also on record as saying that such a situation was not his fault but that of Belgian society, and that as a businessman he had no choice but to operate his business in a way that would make a profit. Interestingly, there was no identifiable complainant in this case, it had been brought by a Belgian anti-racism agency that was created under the auspices of the RED.[84] Furthermore this agency had put forward no evidence that a specific individual had suffered discriminatory treatment at the hands of the employer.

This case provided a perfect context to test how widely the CJEU would be willing to interpret the types of potential discrimination that can be found in the RED, and in particular if they would be applicable to expressive acts.[85] Although the case itself did not involve an expression made by the state (or someone working for it), the facts in the case are somewhat analogous to certain forms of SSE. These could include instances where employees or representatives connected to the state make statements concerning the entitlement of certain groups to a range of rights including services such as healthcare and education, employment by the state and benefits.

Given the individual concerned had been talking about his own practices in hiring ethnic minority individuals, the concept of instructing to discriminate was not of application. In addition, the fact that no comments had been made against specific individuals precluded a finding of harassment by the court. It therefore opted to examine the case under the Article 2(a) of the RED, i.e. direct discrimination. In its decision the CJEU indicated that it was open to a potentially much wider vision of what even direct discrimination constituted. It ruled that the statements of the business owner had been discriminatory in that they may have deterred potential applicants from minority backgrounds from applying.[86] This was remarkable given that no individuals had themselves claimed that they had been treated in a discriminatory manner by the employer in question. The court, however, concluded that the statement made by the employer in question was likely to dissuade potential employees from applying for employment and so constituted discriminatory treatment.[87] This concept of 'dissuasive force' used by the

83 *Feryn* para 18.
84 The agency, called Centrum voor gelijkheid van kansen en voor racismebestrijding, was established under Article 13 Directive 2000/43/EC which demands Member States set up domestic anti-discrimination agencies.
85 U Belavusau, "Fighting Hate Speech through EU Law", *Amsterdam Law Forum* 4, no. 1 (2012).
86 *Feryn* para 25.
87 *Feryn* paras 22–28.

court is striking for being synonymous with many of the negative effects associated with stigmatization, including harm to self-esteem and the induction of negative coping strategies (discussed in Chapter 2). The ruling in *Feryn* may, therefore, demonstrate that the equality directives are capable of being applied to a wide range of stigmatizing expressions or statements, though doubts remain as to the exact significance of the case.

One potential reading of *Feryn* is that it appears to ignore the conceptual barrier of treatment. In doing so it appears to demonstrate that the CJEU's conception of discrimination also includes statements and expressions that would not seem to involve treatment.[88] Such a development could *inter alia* mean that anti-discrimination approaches may be capable of engaging stigmatizing expressions that are not accompanied by treatment in certain contexts (i.e. the restricted contexts outlined in the equality directives). Such a motivation appears to have been the implicit intention behind both the creation of the equality directives and the CJEU's decision in *Feryn*. In expanding the concept of discrimination to include aspects such as dissuasive speech the CJEU may have been responding to a perceived need to address issues that have been associated with inequality, especially in the labour and housing rental markets in some Member States. As the Dutch equality body has made known,[89] problems associated with the way vacancies and notices for other services have been advertised has long been an issue associated with unfair treatment of minorities in society.[90] In such instances traditional anti-discrimination approaches had only had a limited impact, especially given that in many cases there may be no identifiable complainant who can show that he or she has been treated in a discriminatory way.

B Feryn – a judgment too inconsistent in its reasoning to be relied upon?

There are reasons to be cautious about what exactly *Feryn* means. The decision itself has been criticized for problems in terms of conceptual consistency.[91] Perhaps most noticeable was the (perhaps unavoidable) decision of the court to classify the remarks in *Feryn* as direct discrimination. This may appear a little strange given that the definition of direct discrimination in the RED, where it is described as a situation where "one person is treated less favorably than another is, has been or would be treated in a comparable situation on grounds of racial or ethnic origin". Even if one accepts the court's willingness to expand the concept of treatment to include remarks and statements, etc., the lack of any identifiable victim in *Feryn* makes it difficult to reconcile with the requirement of showing

88 Henrard, "The First Substantive ECJ Judgment on the Racial Equality Directive: A Strong Message in a Conceptually Flawed, and Responsively Weak Bottle".

89 This report was cited in ibid. p14

90 See, for example, Opinions 2006–11 2007–100 by the Dutch Equal Treatment Commission (Commissie gelijke behandeling (CGB)). These are discussed in European Union Agency for Fundamental Rights, *Handbook on European Non-Discrimination Law*.

91 Henrard, "The First Substantive ECJ Judgment on the Racial Equality Directive: A Strong Message in a Conceptually Flawed, and Responsively Weak Bottle". pp24–27

that a person has been treated less favourably than another.[92] In *Feryn,* whilst the remarks made by the employer suggested the likelihood that individuals from an ethnic minority would face discrimination, they did not show that a specific person or individual had faced such treatment.

Feryn represents a strange ruling because it seems consistent with the spirit of the RED whilst being difficult to reconcile with its technical requirements. As the court pointed out, the drafters of the RED clearly intended that a lack of identifiable complainants need not be a bar to showing that practices are discriminatory.[93] This is something the court later confirmed in its ruling in the case of *Asociaţia Accept.* [94] However, when making its decision in *Feryn* the problem for the CJEU was that the concept of 'instruction to discriminate' was worded in such a way that it seemed to exclude circumstances such as *Feryn*, where the speaker in question was not actually instructing, commanding or even simply calling for anyone to discriminate but was in fact indicating that he was willing to discriminate himself. This left direct discrimination as the only real option. The statements of the employer provided evidence of a presumption of a discriminatory practice of employment, evidence which the employer did nothing to rebut.[95] Given this, the court could have probably ruled in a similar manner to the ECtHR's judgment in *Baczkowski* (see section 3) and ruled that the statements made by the employer were evidence of a discriminatory practice that constituted direct discrimination. Indeed, some parts of its judgement appeared to be leaning towards this by emphasizing the evidential value of the statements towards the existence of discriminatory practices by the employer. The reasoning produced by the court went much further however, and made it explicitly clear that the statements themselves were discriminatory because of their dissuasive force. In going further than it needed to, the court clearly wanted to set a precedent whereby such activities, which have long been a problem in discriminatory labour markets, could be engaged. Whilst such an aim may be commendable, doing so appears to have required the court to push a square peg into a round hole in terms of the conceptual approach it took. Given these problems of conceptual inconsistency, further case law will be needed to settle this issue. The wording of the equality directives makes it difficult to see how such a broad conception of direct discrimination can be maintained without continuing to bend the rules a little.

92 This relates to the traditional requirement of having a comparator with whom a comparison can be made in order to discern whether or not unjust treatment has occurred. See O'Connell, "Cinderella Comes to the Ball: Art 14 and the Right to Non-Discrimination in the ECHR".

93 *Feryn* para 25.

94 Case C-81/12 *Asociaţia ACCEPT* para 62.

95 As the court in *Feryn* pointed out at paragraph 30, Article 8 of Directive 2000/43 allows a presumption of discriminatory practices to exist where there is evidence. Once this occurs the burden of proof shifts to the alleged perpetrator of the discrimination to disprove that such discrimination is actually occurring.

For those who do not agree that the equality directives signal the emergence of a potential third generation of an anti-discrimination approach, this confusion may provide doubt that the decision in *Feryn* did indeed confirm such an expansion. This is because it is possible to argue that the court's ruling in *Feryn* does not fundamentally go further than the ECHR position stated in *Baczkowski,* where the focus was on the traditional concept of treatment and where statements and expressions were relevant because of their evidential value. This author would argue that the reference of the CJEU to the dissuasive force of the statements makes this doubtful. A better explanation would perhaps be that the court found two separate types of discrimination to have occurred (i.e. an expressive form of discrimination and a traditional form based upon the likelihood of treatment), but failed to delineate this clearly.[96] The more recent case of *Asociaţia ACCEPT* raises further doubts about whether *Feryn* can really be read as such a precedent. This case involved comments made about the potential recruitment of a homosexual football player by a Romanian football club. The comments were made by an individual who had close links with the organization of the club. The facts in question were therefore extremely similar to that of the *Feryn* case. In its preliminary ruling the court made no reference to the concept of dissuasive force, which appeared to play such a central role in the *Feryn* judgment. Its focus was rather entirely on the premise that the remarks created a presumption that the football club was operating discriminatory practices (i.e. treatment) and the need for the alleged discriminating party to rebut such a presumption. This could be interpreted as a clarification that the court views such remarks in a *Baczkowski*-like manner.

These rulings by the CJEU have thus created uncertainty as to whether dissuasive expressions alone can indeed constitute direct discrimination under the Equality Directives. From the perspective of this book it is important to remember that even if a potentially wider version of the *Feryn* judgment was accepted going forward it would still only apply within the well-defined contours of the EU Equality Directives.[97] Unlike Article 14 ECHR (which given the use of the phrasing "other status" can apply to an open ended group of categories) the EU equality directives are restricted to a limited group of categories in a well-defined set of contexts. As Chapter 1 described many forms of stigmatizing state expression are likely to fall outside such contexts and, therefore, will unlikely be affected by even an expansive reading of the *Feryn* judgment.

96 Henrard suggests that the court was describing two different acts of discrimination, one expressive and one more in line with the traditional concept of treatment discussed in this chapter. See Henrard, "The First Substantive ECJ Judgment on the Racial Equality Directive: A Strong Message in a Conceptually Flawed, and Responsively Weak Bottle". pp24–27

97 E Howard, "EU Anti-Discrimination Law: Has the CJEU Stopped Moving Forward?", *International Journal of Discrimination and the Law* 18 (2–3): 60–81.

Part II: Administrative law

6 The concept and need of administrative law

A The varying forms of administrative law

SSEs represent activities conducted by the state or individuals working for it. Given that in most jurisdictions administrative law plays a vital role in allowing those affected by the activities of the state to challenge decisions made that may affect them, it represents another area of law that one might naturally look to for protection from potentially harmful SSEs.

The sources of administrative law can be many and varied. In the US, the term 'applied constitutional law' is often used, reflecting the view that administrative law exists in order to make the state act within constitutional limits.[98] In France the *droit administratif* is provided primarily by a complex web of provisions produced by the *conseil d'etat* which in turn draws its authority from the constitution.[99] In the UK where there is no written constitution, the term administrative law has not historically been used but has gained traction in recent times.[100] However, for a long time there have been legal doctrines that seek to ensure that parliamentary approval for ministerial actions exists[101] and that such actions are made in accordance with certain principles, known as 'natural law', which are considered to be incumbent upon all decisions makers if they wish to operate in a just manner.[102] In recent years the ECHR has also provided an important source of administrative law in the UK and other European jurisdictions.[103] This has, to a certain extent, led to a convergence in administrative law across Europe.[104]

98 Those familiar with German administrative law similarly speak of administrative law as being 'concretized constitutional law'. See S Rose-Ackerman and P Lindseth, "Comparative Administrative Law: An Introduction", in *Comparative Administrative Law*, ed. S Rose-Ackerman and P Lindseth (Cheltenham: Elgar Publishing, 2011). p1 For a discussion on this see G Metzger, "Ordinary Administrative Law as Constitutional Common Law", *Journal of the National Association of Administrative Law Judiciary* 30, no. 2 (2010).

99 For a good overview of the historical development of French administrative law see G Bigot, *Introduction historique au droit administratif depuis 1789* (Paris: Presses Universitaires de France (PUF), 2002).

100 F Johnson Goodnow, *Comparative Administrative Law: An Analysis of the Administrative Systems, National and Local, of the United States, England, France and Germany* (London: Beard Books, 2000).

101 Craig, P, "Ultra Vires and the Foundations of Judicial Review", *The Cambridge Law Journal* 57, no. 1 (1998).

102 H Arthurs, *'Without the Law' - Administrative Justice and Legal Pluralism in Nineteenth Century England* (Toronto and Buffalo, NY: University of Toronto Press, 1985).

103 A Wilfred Bradley and K Ewing, *Constitutional and Administrative Law Volume 1* (Harlow: Pearson Education, 2007).

104 J Schwarze, "The Convergence of Administrative Laws of the EU Member States", *European Public Law* 4, no. 2 (1998).

The emergence of administrative law is a relatively modern phenomenon. It accompanied the expansion in the activities of the state in the nineteenth and twentieth centuries.[105] Before that period the activities of the state were relatively limited. If individuals obeyed the criminal law and respected the property rights of others they would probably have very little contact with the organs of the state itself. Over time both the organs of the state and the various functions they carried out expanded enormously.[106] States, in the West at least, developed new competences that involved, for example, the provision of healthcare and other social services, services which individuals would become entitled to by law.[107] In addition, the state would take a more active role in the regulation of commercial activities. The demand for such new competences went hand in hand with the increasing levels of democratization of the legislatures of most states.[108] In addition, the state became increasingly active in the regulation of our day-to-existence, bestowing upon itself the right to grant licences, permits and permissions for a wide range of activities.[109] In all of these areas the state's administration was granted ever more authority (or even required) to control and regulate the lives of its citizens.

The importance of some level of direct control by citizens over the state is essential given the unique powers that a state and its administration possess. Given the range and depth of such powers the potential for abuse by those who are responsible for carrying out such activities (i.e. civil servants) is vast.[110] Such abuse has the power to prevent individuals from pursuing their lives as they might wish. As a consequence, the availability of administrative laws that restrain public servant decision making and allows them to be challenged by private citizens in independent tribunals is essential.[111] Were

105 B Sordi, "Rěvolution, Rechsstaat and the Rule of Law: Historical Reflections on the Emergence of Administrative Law in Europe", in *Comparative Administrative Law*, ed. S Rose-Ackerman and P Lindseth (Cheltenham: Elgar Publishing, 2011).

106 For a discussion on the changes in the functioning of the state, and the services it offered (including social security) both during the war and immediately after, see R Brown, *The Administrative Process in Britain* (London: Methuen & Co, 1971).

107 For a good description of how administrative law development in the US mirrored these developments see W Funk and R Seamon, *Administrative Law* (Aspen, CO: Aspen Publishers, 2009). See in particular Chapter 1 for a historic analysis.

108 C Tilly, *Contention and Democracy in Europe, 1650–2000* (Cambridge: Cambridge University Press, 2003). See pages 213–217.

109 For a perspective on the need for more administrative law control given the economic and social development of 1930s America see E Metzler, "The Growth and Development of Administrative Law", *Marquette Law Review* 19, no. 4 (1935).

110 For a discussion on the potential negative effects that can arise as a result of government abuse and corruption in both developing and developed countries see S Rose-Ackerman, *Corruption and Government: Causes, Consequences, and Reform* (Cambridge: Cambridge University Press, 1999).

111 Metzler, "The Growth and Development of Administrative Law". p213 As Metzler stated in the US context, "With this increase in governmental undertakings it was only natural that there should have been an accompanying increase in the law which not only facilitated but controlled the functions. And it was natural that variations in the existing legal structure should develop to meet the new and changing situations, for while the application of our constitutional system had previously been concerned chiefly with individual needs it found an increasing necessity to be applied to public needs."

administrative law not able to provide the ability to challenge the administration in such areas, the risk that individual civil servants involved would be able act improperly without any recourse for the individuals would be greater. Sections B and C below discuss how systems of administrative law are able to provide such forms of control and what their relevance to SSEs would be (if they were applicable).

B The functions of administrative law

Given the broad range of potential application of administrative action and the potential for harm where abuse occurs, systems of administrative law have a key role in scrutinizing, and if needs be, restraining the actions of the state.[112] These potential roles are interesting in the context of SSEs because if they were applicable they could allow some of the negative effects that can be caused by them to be moderated or even avoided. Administrative laws can, in particular, allow individuals to challenge administrative acts on three common grounds.

(i) Checks on legality

Perhaps the most important ground for challenging an administrative law decision is its lack of legality. Such a ground relates to the fact that ministers, civil servants and others who represent the state should have a legal basis for their actions. Such a basis can often exist in statutes created by legislatures and various forms of secondary legislative instruments. Such judicial checks form the oldest and most established grounds for judicial review, especially in common law countries. In the US, such grounds for review are associated with the longstanding and fundamental principle of limiting the role of government.[113] In the UK the doctrine of *ultra vires* has long been established.[114] This doctrine allows courts to rule decisions or acts illegal if the minister or civil servant involved cannot refer to primary or secondary legislation that permits such decisions to be made.[115] Where secondary legislation is provided as a source of authority, such legislation must be within the bounds of what was laid down by the relevant primary legislation. In France a similar ground for review exists and is known as *excés de pouvoir.* [116] Such a basis for judicial review is important in allowing individuals to prevent ministers and civil servants from taking

112 P Cane, *Administrative Law* (Oxford: Oxford University Press, 2011). pp11–14

113 C Harlow, "Global Administrative Law: The Quest for Principles and Values", *The European Journal of International Law* 17, no. 1 (2006). p307

114 Craig, "Ultra Vires and the Foundations of Judicial Review". Chapter 1–004.

115 For more on *ultra vires* in the UK context see H Barnett, *Constitutional & Administrative Law* (Abingdon: Routledge, 2014). p594 See also M Elliot, J Beatson, and M Matthews, *Administrative Law – Texts and Materials* (Oxford: Oxford University Press, 2005). Chapter 1:4; P Craig, *Administrative Law (7th Edition)* (London: Sweet and Maxwell, 2012). Chapter 1–004.

116 J Ziller, "The Continental System of Administrative Legality", in *Handbook of Public Administration: Concise Paperback Edition*, ed. G Peters and J Pierre (Los Angeles: Sage Publications, 2007). For more on the concept of *légalité* in French administrative law see D Truchet, *Droit administratif (5e Édition)* (Paris: Themis, 2013).

actions for which they have no authority and which are capable of producing harmful effects for the individuals concerned.[117]

(ii) Checks of form

In addition to the concept of legality, administrative law also often requires that decisions are made in a certain manner, or in an appropriate form.[118] Such grounds do not seek to specify exactly what course of action an administrator should choose, but pertain more to how the decision is made.[119] At the heart of such grounds is the need to ensure that principles of good governance are observed. As Harlow states, good government in the administrative context involves ideals of "openness, fairness, participation, accountability consistency [and] rationality".[120]

In order to facilitate such 'good governance', many legal systems have special statutes or codes that contain special requirements relating to administrative decisions and actions.[121] In the US, for example, the Administrative Procedure Act[122] sets out a number of requirements that apply to administrative actions and which, if not followed, can give rise to grounds for judicial review. In the UK such requirements are derived under the broad umbrella of natural law and emanate from decades of judge made case law on issues surrounding administrative review.[123] Requirements of form are also prominent in the administrative law systems of civil law countries such as France[124] and Germany.[125]

117 For a comparison of the French concept of *excés de pouvoir* and the UK concept of *ultra vires* see B Stirn, D Fairgreave, and M Guyomar, *Droits et libertés en France et au Royaume-Uni* (Paris: Odile Jacob, 2006). p54
118 For a description of some of the approaches of form used around the world see D Esty, "Good Governance at the Supranational Scale: Globalizing Administrative Law", *Faculty Scholarship Series 428* (2006). p1524
119 Craig, *Administrative Law (7th Edition)*. discusses the rationale for procedural rights in Chapter 12. p341
120 M Aronson, B Dyer, and M Groves, *Judicial Review of Administrative Action (3rd Edition)* (Pymont, Australia: Law Book Co of Australasia, 2004). p1 Quote taken from Harlow, "Global Administrative Law: The Quest for Principles and Values". p193
121 For more on the importance of procedural correctness in ensuring good governance (and the consequent role for administrative law on a national and international level) see D Esty, "Good Governance at the Supranational Scale: Globalizing Administrative Law", *Faculty Scholarship Series 428* (2006).
122 Administrative Procedure Act (APA) (1946) Pub. L 79–404.
123 M Elliot, *The Constitutional Foundations of Judicial Review* (London: Hart Publishing, 2001). See page 101.
124 See R Chapus, *Droit administratif général* (Montchrestien, 2001). pp244–252
125 In the of case of Germany see the Administrative Procedure Act (Verwaltungsverfahrensgesetz, VwVfG) Part III, in France a good example can be found in the Loi n° 79–587 du 11 juillet 1979 relative à la motivation des actes administratifs et à l'amélioration des relations entre l'administration et le public (Version consolidée au 19 mai 2011), which requires public officials to make the motivations behind a number of actions clear to those who might be affected.

In the various existing systems of administrative a focus is given to several key requirements of form that are seemingly connected to the idea of good governance. Most important amongst these are a duty to consult individuals who may be affected by administrative decisions, a duty to give reasons for decisions (often demonstrating the varying factors that have been considered in reaching a decision) and a duty to periodically review decisions that have already been made. The existence of such aspects in administrative matters helps improve the overall experience of governance in several ways. Most notably it compels administrators to consider relevant criteria, to listen to the opinions of those who might be affected (including to those who may possess useful information unbeknown to the administrator) and to review matters for changes in circumstances.[126] A duty upon administrators to provide reasons is particularly important in allowing individuals to understand both the motivations behind a decision and the factors considered in making such a decision.[127] The availability of such reasons allows individuals to know whether the administrator in question acted properly in terms of other requirements, including those of legality and issues of form and, whether he or she considered all the relevant factual information that was objectively available to him or her. The need to implement such requirements can therefore be thought of as a need by administrators to incorporate recognized elements of good practice in their decision making.[128]

(iii) Checks on adherence to important substantive principles

In addition to matters of simple legality and form, an administrative or judicial review can allow decisions or actions to be assessed for their compatibility with important constitutional or other legal principles that pertain to the decision in a substantive sense. In other words administrative review can, in many circumstances, allow the actual decision to be reviewed in terms of its substantive content. Such issues therefore go beyond matters of legal authorization and form and assess a decision for its actual outcome (or sometimes its motivation).

The particular legal principles that might apply are many and varied and depend upon the jurisdiction. They may emanate from constitutional provisions. These may, for example, relate to non-discrimination or non-interference with speech or the requirement of neutrality with regards to religion.[129] On other occasions such principles may exist in specially created statutes that are designed to guide actions by the state

126 Esty, "Good Governance at the Supranational Scale: Globalizing Administrative Law". See Part III.

127 For a discussion on the evolution of this requirement in UK law see M Eliot, "Has the Common Law Duty to Give Reasons Come of Age Yet?", *University of Cambridge Faculty of Law Research Paper* (2012).

128 Esty, "Good Governance at the Supranational Scale: Globalizing Administrative Law".

129 A good example of such principles in the US context are the provisions in the US Constitution guaranteeing freedom of speech and equal protection (i.e. non-discrimination). These were introduced by the First and Fourteenth Amendments respectively.

and its officials. Such principles may even originate from international agreements such as the European Convention on Human Rights.[130] This latter instrument has been integrated into the legal systems of most European states to such an extent that it can be considered to have an almost constitutional level of importance.[131] This instrument has supplemented important legal principles that exist in its signatories' legal systems, a process that has been considerably enriched through the large case law that has been generated in the cases dealt with by the ECtHR in Strasbourg.[132] The principles generated within such case law will often be taken into account in administrative hearings throughout Europe when deciding if administrative acts are acceptable.[133]

What is significant from the point of view of this chapter, however, is not the many and varied principles that exist and can be applied to administrative decisions, including those to make stigmatizing expressions, but that the availability of administrative review by tribunals can act as a gateway by which decisions can be reviewed in the light of whatever principles may exist. In essence they allow routine and everyday practical decisions to be reviewed in the light of abstract but important legal principles.[134] In this sense administrative law, and the access it offers to administrative or judicial tribunals, represents an important gateway by which individuals may be able to apply important legal principles and doctrines that may offer them protection in terms of potentially harmful decisions by state officials. Whilst administrative review is by no means unique in offering such a gateway given that such principles and doctrines will be considered by courts in other contexts such as criminal law cases and disputes amongst individuals in private law matters (e.g. tort or contract), it is nonetheless an important one. Administrative law is perhaps unique in terms of its scope and the likelihood with which individuals are likely to have contact with it (see discussion above).

C What would the application of administrative law to SSEs mean?

Chapter 1 presented numerous examples of SSEs and the negative effects they can bring about. The potential application of administrative law to them is an

130 Quinn and De Hert, "Self Respect—a 'Rawlsian Primary Good' Unprotected by the European Convention on Human Rights and Its Lack of a Coherent Approach to Stigmatization?"

131 See, for example, from the UK perspective, D Vick, "The Human Rights Act and the British Constitution, *Texas International Law Journal* 37 (2002).

132 T Raine, "Judicial Review under the Human Rights Act: A Culture of Justification", *North East Law Review* 1 (2013). In the UK, for example, the need to take into account the jurisprudence of the ECtHR has transformed the nature of judicial review and UK administrative law.

133 H Keller and A Stone Sweet, *A Europe of Rights: The Impact of the ECHR on National Legal Systems* (Oxford: Oxford University Press, 2008). In the UK case of *R (Daly) v. Secretary of State for the Home Department* the House of Lords stated that administrators must justify themselves when they "limit" ECHR rights.

134 As Craig discusses on page 21 of *Administrative Law (7th Edition)*, , the ECHR has transformed the process of judicial review at the heart of administrative law in the UK. Courts must now analyse administrative decisions in the light of ECHR principles.

interesting prospect because it could in theory be used to avoid or moderate such negative effects. Each of the three roles identified above in sections (i)–(iii), could in certain circumstances feasibly be relevant in restraining SSEs. Requirements of 'legality', for example, could be important in ensuring that only appointed individuals are able to legally speak on behalf of the state. Such a requirement could be used to prevent unappointed or unqualified individuals from making harmful remarks on behalf of the state (including those that are capable of producing stigmatization).

Administrative law's demand for good practice could in theory be used to ensure that procedures were put in place to reduce the possibility of harmful outcomes from SSEs. This could include requirements to consult with target groups or other potentially affected groups. Such requirements are a staple of administrative law and are designed to ensure that administrators take measures to ensure that they are well informed about the potential harm they can bring about. Similarly requirements to provide reasons for decisions allow potentially affected groups and individuals to understand why a particular measure has been taken and to make representations where possible. Given that stigmatization often arises as a result of the perceived opinion of others (even where such perceptions are not accurate), the need to provide reasons could allow the reasonable intentions of the state to be discerned. This could help to avoid stigmatization where statements made or information released was capable of having an unintended stigmatizing effect, e.g. functional stigmatization (see Chapters 1 and 3).

With regard to the potential gateway function that administrative law offers it would mean that harmful expressions could be analysed for compliance with important principles of both international and domestic law. This could allow expressions to be tested against requirements of privacy, respect for human dignity, non-discrimination, neutrality and other potentially applicable legal principles. The context of an administrative act represents an important moment where individuals can seize a court or tribunal to examine the actions of public officials in order to affirm their legality not just in terms of procedural administrate law but also other potentially applicable legal approaches. As section 7 below discusses the application of administrative law may be something that in many cases is far from certain.

7 Most systems of administrative law are unlikely to recognize expressive acts as administrative acts

Perhaps the most important aspect in discerning whether such engagement is possible is how each system defines the concept of an 'administrative act'. This definition is pivotal as it defines what types of act by the state are in general capable of engaging administrative law and, therefore, being subject to administrative review. If a particular jurisdiction's definition of an administrative act is not capable of encompassing expressive acts, then it often means that the system of administrative law in general will find it difficult to engage such acts. The concept of an administrative act may be defined differently from jurisdiction to jurisdiction.

In some jurisdictions e.g. Germany and the US, the concept of an administrative act may be defined in legislation, whilst in others, e.g. in the UK and France, it may be largely defined in case law.[135]

Given the importance of administrative law in terms of the various types of legal scrutiny it can bring,[136] the definition of an administrative act can represent a critical traction point in determining whether expressive activities (including those that are stigmatizing) are capable of being scrutinized by administrative tribunals. The situation *vis-à-vis* a number of states from both common and civil law systems will be presented below in order to be as illustrative as possible. As the remainder of this section will show, a common factor is that expressive acts of the state are unlikely to be viewed as constituting administrative acts. This means that the various roles that administrative law plays in terms of the checks and balances described in sections (i)–(iii) above are unlikely to be applied to most forms of SSE.

A US federal administrative law

(i) The creation of the APA

The most prominent source of American administrative law is the Administrative Procedure Act (APA).[137] This act was introduced by Congress in 1946, following the enormous explosion in competences of the federal state after the events of the Depression, subsequent New Deal and then the Second World War.[138] These events required that the federal government expand rapidly and undertake numerous new roles and competences that were not previously foreseen.[139] The APA was intended to allow a greater level of judicial control over such activities and limit the impact of an ever expanding state on private individuals and business.[140] In particular, systems of administration and bureaucracy had seemingly become vested with powers that one might expect (under the doctrine of separation of powers) would only be vested separately in the judiciary and the legislature.[141] These powers broadly represent the ability to create rules and laws that

135 In the UK, for example, the explicit concept of an 'administrative act' does not exist. It can, however, in reality be discerned by looking at the case law concerning *locus standi*. See section B. See also ibid.

136 Rose-Ackerman and Lindseth, "Comparative Administrative Law: An Introduction".

137 Administrative Procedure Act 5 U.S.C §§ 551–599. For a comprehensive overview see W Fox, *Understanding Administrative Law* (New York: Matthew Bender & Co., 1992).

138 W Scheuerman, "The Economic State of Emergency", *Cardozo Law Review* 21 (1999–2000).

139 For more on the changing perception of the need for administrative control at the time see Metzler, "The Growth and Development of Administrative Law". For more on the APA is in general see Barnett, *Constitutional & Administrative Law*.

140 E Rubin, "It's Time to Make the Administrative Procedure Act Administrative", *Cornell Law Review* 89 (2002). M McCubbins, R Noll, and B Weingast, "The Political Origins of the Administrative Procedure Act", *Journal of Law, Economics and Organization* 15 (1999).

141 Rubin, "It's Time to Make the Administrative Procedure Act Administrative".

are binding upon individuals and to judge or adjudicate disputes involving the implementation of such rules. Such an investiture was seen by many as a source of concern given that it represented a blurring of the system of checks and balances that are at the heart of all modern democracies.

(ii) Differing concepts of an 'administrative act'

This tension described above is apparent in the APA which recognizes three types of legal act that *inter alia* require compliance with a number of procedural formalities. These are; (i) formal acts of rule making; (ii) informal acts of rule making[142] and (iii) formal acts of adjudication. In addition, the APA seemingly groups all other types of administrative action into a fourth category that can be thought of as (iv) informal acts of adjudication.[143] The APA aims to curb the use of such rule making and adjudicatory powers by introducing various procedural requirements for the first three of these types of acts. For rule making acts, agencies must, for example, publish a proposed version of the rule in question and allow time for private parties to produce their own comments. After receiving such comments agencies are required to produce the final version of the rule with a statement of basis and purpose.[144] Where the action in question concerns an 'adjudication', the agency concerned must provide notice to affected parties and the possibility of a hearing. Such a hearing must be recorded and any decision taken on the basis of the hearing.[145] A distinction is drawn between 'formal' and 'informal' acts of rule making, with the former requiring much more onerous procedures such as 'giving of evidence' and 'cross examination', aspects that are not required with informal acts of rule making. In reality, however, the formal procedure for acts of rule making is considered so onerous that it is rarely used, and only in situations where Congress has specifically demanded it in statute.[146] As a result, the two most important types of administrative act are those described in (ii) and (iii) above, i.e. informal rule making and formal adjudication. These acts may encompass a large range of familiar administrative acts, including, for example, rules relating to planning permission and advertisements on public property in

142 Rules are defined as "the whole or a part of an agency statement of general or particular applicability and future effect". See 5 U.S.C. § 551 (4) (2000).

143 For more on the wealth of informal activities that fall within informal adjudication see T Rakoff, "The Choice between Formal and Informal Modes of Administrative Regulation", *Administrative Law Review* 52, no. 1 (2000).

144 Section 533 (b) and (c). See also Rubin, "It's Time to Make the Administrative Procedure Act Administrative". p101

145 Section 544.

146 Rubin, "It's Time to Make the Administrative Procedure Act Administrative". On page 108 Rubin describes an interesting and absurd example of a "hearing, held pursuant to the Federal Food, Drug, and Cosmetic Act, to determine whether the peanut content of peanut butter should be 87.5% or 90%, which spanned a nine-year period and produced a 7,736 page transcript. Because the impracticalities of formal rulemaking are well known, Congress rarely requires this technique, and courts avoid interpreting statutes to require it, even in the rare cases where the statute seems to do so."

the first category, and individual decisions on applications for planning permission or licences concerning the sale of alcohol in the latter.

(iii) Many forms of expressive activity may be classed as 'informal agency action'

Many 'informal agency actions' fall outside of the first three categories described above. 'Informal agency processes' have been described as the "lifeblood of the administrative process".[147] They represent most of the types of acts that could be described as administrational in nature. Most of these acts can be conceptualized as falling under category (iv) as described above, i.e. informal adjudicatory acts.[148] Unlike the other categories above, acts of this type face very little restriction from the APA. When making such acts, agencies have almost no procedural requirements and there is little potential for judicial review of such decisions. Such acts cover a wide range of actions that are administrative but are not capable of falling under the description of informal/formal rules and formal adjudications (i.e. (i)–(iii) above). These include all agency actions that do not involve the creation of general rules or adjudications. Such actions could include decisions on the deployment of resources, decisions of general policy direction and numerous types of expressive activities of the state. As Rubin points out "every time an agency plans its future actions or evaluates its prior ones, allocates its resources, gives advice, makes a promise, issues a threat, negotiates, conducts an investigation … it is at least arguably engaged in informal adjudication".[149] The result is that a whole range (if not most) administrative acts fall outside of the legal definitions used in the APA. This seemingly includes most if not all expressive acts of the state (including thus SSEs). Such activities have been reasoned *inter alia* to include publicity related conferences and press releases.[150] An important consequence of this is that such acts do not have to comply with the procedural requirements envisaged within the APA for other types of administrative acts, nor can individuals petition a court for such formalities to be imposed.[151]

B UK administrative law

Like the US, the UK, being a common law system, has traditionally had a more restrictive understanding of what administrative law constitutes than that might be

147 A Aman and W Mayton, *Administrative Law (Second Edition)* (Westgroup, 2001). p2544

148 §551 (6), (7). The APA describes all acts that are not rule making as adjudications.

149 Rubin, "It's Time to Make the Administrative Procedure Act Administrative". p107

150 Aman and Mayton, *Administrative Law (Second Edition)*. Aman and Mayton provide a good overview of informal agency action in Chapter 9. On page 273 they describe agency press releases and similar activities as in general being exempt from review.

151 It should be remembered that whilst the APA is the most prominent piece of legislation contributing towards federal administrative law it is not the only one. Many set-piece possibilities for judicial review are also provided in legislation by Congress for specific contexts. An analysis of these is, however, beyond the scope of this work. For more see Fox, *Understanding Administrative Law*. Chapter 9

understood in many civil law countries.[152] The focus of such law is very much on the interaction of the state and its emanations with private individuals. Unlike the situation *vsz-à-vis* the APA in the US, there is no single definition of what constitutes an administrative act. Rather it is necessary to piece together what types of actions may give rise to a right to judicial review through an analysis of the relevant case law. In conducting a review of the laws in the UK that can be described under the umbrella of 'administrative law' one finds it difficult to detect provisions or cases that involve instances where the issues alone rest upon an expression.

One important area of law is related to the concept of *locus standi* or standing. Case law in this area has been carefully developed in order to allow harmful acts of public authorities to be scrutinized in court, but at the same time to prevent the activities of such authorities being hindered by spurious legal actions. A common theme in these cases is that an applicant should show a "direct interest" in a particular measure that has been taken.[153] The understanding of what constitutes a direct interest has evolved in recent decades from a position where individuals originally had to show that they themselves were directly affected,[154] to one where on very limited occasions public interest groups may bring cases where it would be in the public interest, i.e. to protect the rule of law.[155] This is only permitted on rare occasions, however, where to prevent a case bring brought would result in a manifest harm to the public interest. It is doubtful whether individuals might be able to avail themselves of such a limited opportunity in instances where stigmatizing statements have been made by public officials in society (that do not refer to specific individuals). There are no precedents (to the author's knowledge) as there are in the US of individuals challenging the expression of the state (see Chapter 7).[156]

152 For a comprehensive overview of the principles of UK administrative law consult Cane, *Administrative Law*; Barnett, *Constitutional & Administrative Law*; Craig, *Administrative Law (7th Edition)*.

153 Jurisprudence in this area is based on an interpretation of section 31(3) of the Senior Courts Act 1981, which states, "No application for judicial review shall be made unless the leave of the High Court has been obtained in accordance with rules of court; and the court shall not grant leave to make such an application unless it considers that the applicant has a sufficient interest in the matter to which the application relates". For an excellent discussion on the jurisprudence on this matter see blog by Mark Eliot (Cambridge University) available at http://ukhumanrightsblog.com/2013/07/30/standing-and-judicial-review-why-we-all-have-a-direct-interest-in-government-according-to-law-dr-mark-elliott See also *Administrative Law (7th Edition)*. Chapter 21

154 In *R v. Inland Revenue Commissioners, ex parte National Federation of Self-employed and Small Businesses Ltd* [1982] AC 617 Lord Diplock stated, "It would, in my view, be a grave lacuna in our system of public law if a pressure group ... or even a single public-spirited taxpayer ... were prevented by outdated technical rules of [standing] from bringing the matter to the attention of the court to vindicate the rule of law and get the unlawful conduct stopped."

155 See the reasoning of Lord Reed, for example, in *AXA General Insurance Ltd v. Lord Advocate* [2011] UKSC 46.

156 Nor is there any equivalent to the concept of 'government speech' as there is in the US. See Chapter 7 and N Murphy, "Context, Not Content: Medium-Based Press Clause Restrictions on Government Speech in the Internet Age," *University of Denver Sports & Entertainment Law Journal* 7 (2009).

A quote from a renowned UK scholar, Paul Craig in his reference text on administrative law sheds an interesting light on this situation. He states (in outlining the general domains of administrative law), "there are three principal ways in which individuals can be affected by government action: through primary legislation, rulemaking and adjudication".[157] Although his study does not itself constitute law, his work is given the status of a very useful piece of analysis. These three domains of government action are not able to capture a wide range of expressive activities of the state. These include many or most of the types of SSE described in Chapter 1. Take, for example, a health information campaign by the UK's National Health Service. The competence for the campaign and its specifications are unlikely to be described in the first category described by Craig, i.e. legislation or even the second category which in the UK context usually refers to secondary legislation.[158] Such actions are also not likely to be covered by the category of adjudication as described by Craig. They refer to decisions made by public authorities that have legal consequences for identifiable persons.[159] An example of such a category would include a decision by a municipal authority to refuse an individual planning permission to extend his or her property or to revoke his or her driving licence. SSEs, by contrast, usually do not alter the legal rights of individuals, indeed individuals are free to ignore such actions and act in any manner they wish. These same issues would be likely to apply to a number of other instances where expressions of the state are capable of causing stigmatization, including instances such as briefings, political announcements connected to potential policies and selective releases of information.[160] The common unifying factor once again is that such actions do not alter the legal rights or privileges of individuals.

157 Craig, *Administrative Law (7th Edition)*. pp339–340 Craig also states that in the UK the criteria for demanding the application of the principles of natural justice through judicial review are the existence of a right, interest or a legitimate expectation.

158 This is created in instances where Parliament in primary legislation invests the authority in another party to create further rules under the piece of legislation in question. In the context of administrative law, cases often relate to claims *ultra vires* where it is alleged that the public authority is acting outside the bounds permitted to it by primary legislation to make secondary legislation.

159 As Craig discusses 'natural justice', which has traditionally, with the doctrine of *ultra vires,* been the main component of administrative law in the UK, has-traditionally been applied in instances where administrative decisions have affected the rights of discernible individuals. See Craig, *Administrative Law (7th Edition)*. p339

160 Such activities occupy a grey area whereby a state will often mix political and information functions. See D Gelders and I Oyvind, "Government Communication About Potential Policies: Public Relations, Propaganda or Both?", *Public Relations Review* 36 (2010).

C Administrative law in France

(i) An expansive concept of administrative law

France has had both a much more overt and broad understanding of what administrative law is than its common law equivalents.[161] In comparison to US or British administrative law, the *droit adminstratif* is also more expansive; governing nearly all legal disputes that surround the state.[162] As a result the French conception of administrative law relates not to only the relationship of the state in the context of its activities that affect individual citizens, but also to internal matters such as how it treats its employees.[163] Furthermore, administrative law rules also cover interactions of the state that would, in common law countries, be subject to the same forms of private law that would govern relations between private individuals. Common examples include incidences where the state enters into a contract with a private party or where it causes tortious harm.

(ii) The importance of an acte juridique administratif

Despite such an overt recognition and broad definition of administrative law, the *droit administratif* also appears to have problems in recognizing purely expressive acts. In French law the concept of an *acte juridique administatif* exists which can be defined as:[164]

> L'acte juridique administratif est un acte juridique unilatéral, pris par une autorité administrative (française) dans l'exercice d'un pouvoir administratif et créant des droits ou des obligations pour les particuliers.
>
> [Translation] The legal administrative act is a unilateral legal act taken by an administrative authority in the exercise of an administrative power which creates rights or obligations for individuals.

French administrative law envisages two types of actions that a public authority can undertake and which are capable of giving rise to claims in administrative law. These are the *contrat administratif* and the *acte administratif unlilateral.* [165]

161 Bigot, *Introduction historique au droit administratif depuis 1789*; Johnson Goodnow, *Comparative Administrative Law: An Analysis of the Administrative Systems, National and Local, of the United States, England, France and Germany*; Stirn, Fairgreave, and Guyomar, *Droits et libertés en France et Au Royaume-Uni.*

162 For a detailed, though dated comparative analysis of British and French administrative law see C Harlow, "Administrative Liability: A Comparative Study of French and English Law", PhD thesis, The London School of Economics and Political Science (1979).

163 For more on the sources of French administrative law see Chapus, *Droit administratif général.* Chapter 1

164 R Odentand M Waline, *Encyclopédie juridique* (Paris: Dalloz, T.I., 1958, n° 6).

165 For more on the *acte administratif unlilateral* see Truchet, *Droit administratif (5e Édition)*, p237 and Chapus, *Droit administratif général.* pp540–555

Both involve legal acts, where the legal environment of private individuals (natural or legal) is altered. The former relates to relationships of a contractual type between public entities and private parties.[166] The second category is related to instances where acts by the state (or its associated organizations) are able to alter the legal order applying to individuals (i.e. an *ordonnancement juridique)* by itself and without negotiation with or consent of the parties affected. This would, for example, include instances where public authorities, according to their competences in legislation, set rules concerning a certain activity, e.g. the rules concerning planning permission in a certain area, or where a public authority is able to adjudicate on the course of action available to an individual or group of individuals, e.g. in approving or denying planning permission. This category therefore seemingly includes two of the types of government action that Craig described in the UK system of administrative law (i.e. rule making and adjudication)[167] and is similar to the US categories of 'formal and informal rule making' as described in the US APA. As was described above in discussing the position of the UK's administrative law, for administrative law to be applicable, the unilateral act in question must involve some alteration of an individual's legal environment. Such an alteration might, for example, involve the creation of new rights, or the removal of rights that pre-existed. This does not, however, usually occur with SSEs. Whilst such comments may result in a number of psychological consequences, which may in turn result in behavioural changes, they do not (in the legal sense at least) compel or prevent individuals from doing something. These factors arguably render the French concept of the administrative act of little use in engaging stigmatizing statements by public authorities.[168]

D Germany

The German legal system in general is renowned for its precise, logical and highly codified approach. Whilst the German system of administrative law fits this mould to a certain extent, it is less codified than other areas of German law with an important part of its content resulting from previous court decisions and even scholarly legal writings.[169] In terms of codified statute, an important source is the Administrative Procedure Act (*Verwaltungsverfahrensgesetz*, (VwVfG)), being the

166 Stirn, Fairgreave, and Guyomar, *Droits et libertés en France et au Royaume-Uni*. Unlike the situation in the UK where the normal laws that apply between private parties also regulate contracts involving the government, in France a different regime applies when one of the parties to a contract is the state or one of its associated organizations.

167 Craig, *Administrative Law (7th Edition)*. p339

168 This, of course, does not mean that such statements are not capable of engaging legal provisions at all. As discussed in Chapter 4 section 4 French criminal law, for example, and the criminal law in most Western democracies, contains provisions that could apply to some SSEs.

169 M Sing, *German Administrative Law in Common Law Perspective* (Berlin: Springer, 2001).

primary statute responsible for the control of administrative actions.[170] Like France and the US, the German legal system has opted for a very precise legal definition of what an administrative act is. Acts falling outside this definition are not recognized as administrative acts by the German legal system and are, therefore, not subject to the same legal checks and controls that would be applicable to administrative acts. Section 35 of the VwVfG defines the two main types of administrative action as administrative acts and general orders. They are defined as:

> Verwaltungsakt ist jede Verfügung, Entscheidung oder andere hoheitliche Maßnahme, die eine Behörde zur Regelung eines Einzelfalls auf dem Gebiet des öffentlichen Rechts trifft und die auf unmittelbare Rechtswirkung nach außen gerichtet ist. Allgemeinverfügung ist ein Verwaltungsakt, der sich an einen nach allgemeinen Merkmalen bestimmten oder bestimmbaren Personenkreis richtet oder die öffentlich-rechtliche Eigenschaft einer Sache oder ihre Benutzung durch die Allgemeinheit betrifft.
>
> [Translation] An administrative act shall be any order, decision or other sovereign measure taken by an authority to regulate an individual case in the sphere of public law and intended to have a direct, external legal effect. A general order shall be an administrative act directed at a group of people defined or definable on the basis of general characteristics or relating to the public law aspect of a matter or its use by the public at large.

The concept of the administrative act is of central importance to German administrative law. Whilst jurisprudence had long recognized the existence of the concept of an official administrative act, it was formally recognized in the constitution and in legislation after the Second World War.[171] German law therefore recognizes categories that are broadly similar to the French concepts of the *acte administratif unlilateral* and the *ordinance juridque*. Like French law, the key concept in German administrative law is the presence of "a direct, external legal effect" which is similar to the French requirement for the creation of "rights and obligations" ("*créant des droits ou des obligations pour les particuliers*").[172] Without such effects, even if acts are made by the public administration they cannot be recognized as administrative acts in terms of the VwVfG and so will not be covered by the procedural and substantive requirements that relate to such acts.[173]

170 For a comparative analysis with UK administrative law see G Nolte, "General Principles of German and European Administrative Law – a Comparison in Historical Perspective", *Modern Law Review* 57, no. 2 (1994).

171 It is, for instance, described in Article 129(1) of the Basic Law and later the Provisions of the Code of Administrative Court of 1960 before being found in Article 35 of the Administrative Procedure Act which was created in 1979. See Sing, *German Administrative Law in Common Law Perspective.*

172 Odent and Waline, *Encyclopédie juridique.*

173 This is also true of section 35 VwVfG which describes potential "stipulations" that may be attached to an administrative act. Such stipulations take the form of commands concerning the commencement or end of a privilege or burden or stipulations to cease certain actions.

As with the other jurisdictions described in this section, it is evident that such a framing of administrative acts in general is likely to result in difficulties in terms of the recognition of expressive acts. Most, if not all, of the SSEs described in Chapter 1 would probably not be engaged by such a formulation. None of these SSEs involved an "order, decision or other sovereign measure taken by an authority to regulate an individual case in the sphere of public law and intended to have a direct, external legal effect." None of the types of SSE discussed in Chapter 1, no matter how stigmatizing or lacking in respects in terms of official neutrality, creates any discernible "direct, external legal effect". In all cases individuals can be considered (at least legally speaking) as being free to simply ignore such expressions and conduct themselves as they wish without any direct legal or material cost. A legally binding order, decision or other sovereign measure would, however, render an individual obliged to conduct him or herself in a certain way (or possibly desist from doing so) or would impose a material cost or grant a material benefit on such an individual. A stigmatizing expression, however, does none of these, with the only burdens that it places on individuals being psychological in nature. Whilst such burdens may in some cases be considerable,[174] they do not represent 'legal effects' and are therefore unlikely to be viewed as administrative acts.

Conclusion

An important reason for the inability of many important legal approaches to be able to engage SSEs is because often they do not bring about binding consequences for individuals who are affected by them. This is despite the fact that as Chapter 2 discussed, such activities can bring about negative psychological consequences that can provoke harmful coping responses. With regard to many legal approaches, however, such factors do not represent the kind of binding consequence that are needed for them to be engaged. This chapter sought to illustrate this situation with two prominent examples.

The *first* approach considered (in Part I) was anti-discrimination law. The approach developed by the ECtHR under Article 14 ECHR was presented as an example of a general anti-discrimination approach that appears to be dependent upon the existence of discriminatory treatment. In short this relates to the presence of actions that can bring about binding physical consequences upon individuals or their legal order. This could include decisions to not restrict certain legal rights or to not allow certain individuals to access schools or services. There has been no case law before the ECtHR where the court has found an expression that was merely stigmatizing to constitute discrimination. Although it is possible that the ECtHR

174 C Miller and B Major, "Coping with Stigma and Prejudice", in *The Social Psychology of Stigmatisation*, ed. T Heatherton et al. (New York: Guilford Press, 2000); Major et al., "Coping with Negative Stereotypes About Intellectual Performance: The Role of Psychological Disengagement"; J Crocker, B Major, and C Steel, "Social Stigma", in *Handbook of Social Psychology*, ed. D Gilbert, S Fiske, and G Lindzey (Boston: McGraw-Hill, 1998). See also Chapter 1 section 5 for a description of such negative effects.

might find a case of stigmatization alone to amount to discrimination if the right case was to come before it this has not yet happened. The court has furthermore indicated (e.g. in *Baczcowski* and *Aksu*) that expressive activity alone that is not accompanied by such an act of treatment would not amount to discrimination as far as Article 14 is concerned.

This situation can be contrasted with approaches such as those foreseen by the EU's anti-discrimination directives. These directives require Member States to recognize certain forms of discrimination that seemingly do not require treatment (i.e. in the way that Article 14 ECHR does). This include acts of harassment and even potentially, according to the CJEU in *Feryn*, statements or expressions that are capable of having dissuasive force. Whilst there is doubt about how far the *Feryn* decision should be read, even an expansive reading would necessarily be limited by the contours of the directives themselves. These limit their application to discrimination against only an exhaustive list of categories and to only certain contexts. This is unlike the more generally applicable approach of Article 14, which through the use of the words "other status" can be applied to an non-exhaustive list of groups and also the broad interpretation of Article 8 (which Article 14 can be applied with) to a potentially enormous domain of contexts.

The author would argue that the differences in the potential breadth of the two frameworks are important in explaining why and where the concept of treatment is important and how it limits the potential application of anti-discrimination law to SSEs. In understanding why this is so one needs to imagine what could potentially occur where no requirement of treatment existed in a broad anti-discrimination approach (e.g. Article 14 ECHR). The result would be that a potentially extremely wide range of expressive activity would be engaged. This could include a wide range of derogatory remarks being made against a non-exhaustive list of groups in society. Whilst this would allow a potentially wide range of stigmatizing remarks to be engaged (including those made by the state), it would also represent an extremely serious infringement on liberty of expression. This would go far beyond what is conceived of as being acceptable in most liberal democracies where expression can only be inhibited in certain important, narrowly defined and objective circumstances (e.g. hate speech). Given the potential breadth and subjectivity of stigmatizing remarks (including those made by the state) that would be engaged by such an open anti-discrimination approach it would likely be considered unacceptable. This factor may also explain why anti-discrimination approaches that do not depend on the concept of treatment (e.g. the EU equality directives) have been crafted so as to apply to only an exhaustively defined list of categories and in restricted contexts. In doing so they can be used to potentially engage a range of expressive acts that are known to cause problems associated with discrimination for certain sensitive categories in certain situations but without representing a large scale infringement on liberty of expression in general.

The *second* approach considered (in Part II) concerned an entirely different legal approach that is also affected by the same issue. Administrative law has grown to become one of the most important legal mechanisms for citizens to check the decisions and actions of the state and civil servants. It can be used to impose requirements of legality, correct form and procedure. In addition the option of administrative review before a court or tribunal can also act as a gateway, allowing administrative acts to be checked against a range of legal requirements including constitutional and other norms.

In analysing the various existing systems of administrative law, it becomes apparent that various approaches are likely to have problems in engaging purely expressive activity such as SSEs. In defining what an administrative act is, many systems seem to be focused on actions that create changes in the legal rights or obligations of individuals. Such a focus is demonstrated, for example, by the notion of formal and informal rule making and adjudication in the American Administrative Procedure Act and the concepts of *acte administratif unlilateral* and *ordonnancement juridique* in the French *droit administratif*. Similar illustrative examples can be found in other civil law systems of administrative law such as the German *Verwaltungsverfahrensgesetz* and can be easily discerned in the practice of common law systems such as the UK. These concepts reflect notions of an administrative act as an act by the state that has a discernible effect on the legal rights of individuals. Such a situation appears consistent with the situation described by Hoods and Margretts (discussed in Chapter 1) where the use of information by the state (that does not refer to specific individuals) is largely constraint free given its minimum level of effects on those who are influenced by it.[175] Such systems accordingly see the use of information (including in statements and expressions) as actions that are not capable of having discernible legal effects on individuals. This seemingly includes situations where expressions or the provision of information are conducted in a manner that is stigmatizing for various individuals or groups in society. Most systems of administrative law can, therefore, be thought of as being blind to the negative psychological effects (described in Chapter 2) that are caused by SSEs. Without the presence of an accompanying act that alters an individual's legal rights in a discernible way (e.g. the refusal to grant legal privileges or the imposition of a financial burden) most systems of administrative law are, in general, simply unable to engage such expressions.[176] The result is that many SSEs can arguably often be said to represent *de facto* but not *de jure* administrative acts. The usual consequence is a likely non-engagement of administrative law with most SSEs. This means that the tools that administrative law offers to ensure good governance will be exercised will not be brought to bear on SSEs.

175 One important exception to this is the existence of data protection approaches which do not necessarily depend upon the existence of binding consequences for individuals. For more see Chapter 6

176 As this chapter made clear there may be 'set-piece' grounds for reviewing administrative action that takes the form of an expression. These set-piece grounds find themselves in statutes and refer only to certain specific activities in a specific contexts. Unfortunately it would be beyond the scope of this work to discuss these in any systematic manner. This is an area that the author proposes would be of interest for further research.

Both the non-engagement of general anti-discrimination and of administrative law with state expressions means states can when expressing themselves avoid the scrutiny that one would normally expect to apply to activities of the state. In Chapter 3 the author reasoned in his normative approach that one might expect such processes of scrutiny to be applied to SSES. In normative principles (ii)–(iv) the author reasoned that it is necessary to ensure that SSEs are only used where there is a good reason to do so. Anti-discrimination law is often available to vulnerable groups who are at risk not only from direct acts of discrimination but also stigmatization as a consequence. General anti-discrimination approaches *inter alia* require states to ensure that valid reasons exist for treating certain groups differently from others, including where there are stigmatizing consequences. With activity that is purely expressive in nature, however, state representatives will not have to worry (at least in terms of most anti-discrimination law) about having good reasons, even where they are referring to one group differently than they would towards another, e.g. through SSEs. Although this situation boosts freedom of expression, it creates a risk that those representing the state will be more likely to intentionally or unintentionally stigmatize particular groups.

Similarly, various systems of administrative law will not be able to provide their power as a verification tool designed to encourage good governance. SSEs as *de facto* administrative acts will in contrast to *de jure* administrative acts (that are regulated by administrative law systems) escape review in terms of legality, form and adherence to important legal principles. The result is a reduced imperative for good governance as far as such acts are concerned. In terms of legality, there will be no need for those involved in a state's administration to demonstrate that they have the authority to make the expression or statement in question. This means that in many states a state official may take it upon him or herself to make statements and expressions that purport to be on behalf of the state, without fear that individuals affected may be able to block them using administrative law.[177] In terms of form, administrators will not be pressed with the need to announce, consult or review their expressive acts. This is concerning because, as Chapter 1 demonstrated, careless statements by public authorities have a higher chance of producing stigmatizing effects. Requirements to consult and take into account the views of those affected could, in many circumstances, mean that such stigmatization could be avoided. Unfortunately, given that such expressive acts will rarely be classed as *de jure* administrative acts, the compulsion to implement such principles of good governance will be missing (though as Chapter 7 discusses, the state may choose to implement certain internal measures, e.g. codes of ethics to ensure this). As a consequence, it seems unlikely that many systems of administrative law will be able to play a meaningful role in ensuring that the normative principles described

177 There may of course be other mechanisms to restrain individuals falsely speaking on behalf of the state. A civil servant speaking without authority may for example be internally pursued under disciplinary laws and suspended or have their employment terminated as may be permitted under the prevailing employment law in question. Such individuals may also be the subject of criminal prosecution. For more on this see Chapter 7.

in Chapter 3 are met. This includes most notably principles (iii) and (v) which call respectively for stigmatizing acts to be verified for factual content and for stigmatizing statements made during the political process to be disassociated from the state itself. In terms of substantive principles, the absence of potential administrative review will mean that such individuals are able to make stigmatizing statements at will without fear of being engaged by the principles of law that would otherwise regulate their conduct if they were taking part in a *de jure* administrative act.

Bibliography

Aman, A, and W Mayton. *Administrative Law (2nd Edition)*. Westgroup, 2001.

Aronson, M, B Dyer, and M Groves. *Judicial Review of Administrative Action (3rd Edition)*. Pymont, Australia: Law Book Co of Australasia, 2004.

Arthurs, H. *'Without the Law' – Administrative Justice and Legal Pluralism in Nineteenth Century England.* Toronto and Buffalo, NY: University of Toronto Press, 1985.

Baker, A. "The Enjoyment of Rights and Freedoms: A New Conception of the 'Ambit' under Article 14 ECHR." *Modern Law Review* 69, no. 5 (2006): 714–737.

Barnett, H. *Constitutional & Administrative Law*. Abingdon: Routledge, 2014.

Belavusau, U. "Fighting Hate Speech through EU Law." *Amsterdam Law Forum* 4, no. 1 (2012): 20–35.

Belgian Linguistics (1968) 1 EHRR 252, 283.

Benedi Lahuerta, S. "Race Equality and TCNs, or How to Fight Discrimination with a Discriminatory Law." *European Law Journal* 15, no. 6 (2009): 738–756.

Besson, S. "Gender Discrimination under EU and ECHR Law: Never Shall the Twain Meet?" *Human Rights Law Review* 8, no. 4 (2008): 647–682.

Besson, S. "Evolutions in Antidiscrimination Law within the European Convention on Human Rights and the European Social Charter System." *American Journal of Comparative Law* 60 (2012).

Bigot, G. *Introduction historique au droit administratif depuis 1789.* Paris: Presses Universitaires de France (PUF), 2002.

Brown, R. *The Administrative Process in Britain.* London: Methuen & Co, 1971.

Burris, S. "Disease Stigma in U.S. Public Law." *Journal of Law, Medicine and Ethics* 30 (2002): 179–190.

Cane, P. *Administrative Law.* Oxford: Oxford University Press, 2011.

Cardozo, J. "Protecting Freedom of Expression: The Challenge of Hate Speech in the European Court of Human Rights Case Law." *Journal of International Law and Comparative Law* 17(2009): 427.

Chapus, R. *Droit administratif général.* Montchrestien, 2001.

Craig, P. "Ultra Vires and the Foundations of Judicial Review." *The Cambridge Law Journal* 57, no. 1 (1998): 63–90.

Craig, P. *Administrative Law (7th Edition).* London: Sweet and Maxwell, 2012.

Crocker. "Social Stigma and Self-Esteem: Situational Construction of Self Worth." *Journal of Experimental Social Psychology* 35 (1999): 89–107.

Crocker, J, B Major, and C Steel. "Social Stigma." In *Handbook of Social Psychology*, edited by D Gilbert, S Fiske and G Lindzey, 504–553. Boston: McGraw-Hill, 1998.

Cusack, M, J Gavin, and D Kavanagh. "Dancing with Discrimination: Managing Stigma and Identity." *Culture and Organization*, 9, no. 4 (2003): 295–310.

De Burca, G. "The Trajectories of European and American Antidiscrimination Law." *American Journal of Comparative Law* (2011): Research Paper No. 11–80.

Degener, T."Intersections between Disability, Race and Gender in Discrimination Law." In *European Union Non-Discrimination Law and Intersectionality: Investigating the Triangle of Racial, Gender and Disability Discrimination*, edited by D Schiek and A Lawson (Farnham: Ashgate Publishing, 2011).Eliot, M. "Has the Common Law Duty to Give Reasons Come of Age Yet? " *University of Cambridge Faculty of Law Research Paper* 7 (/2012).

Elliot, M. *The Constitutional Foundations of Judicial Review*. London: Hart Publishing, 2001.

Elliot, M, J Beatson, and M Matthews. *Administrative Law – Texts and Materials*. Oxford: Oxford University Press, 2005.

Esty, D. "Good Governance at the Supranational Scale: Globalizing Administrative Law." *Faculty Scholarship Series 428* (2006).

European Union Agency for Fundamental Rights. *Handbook on European Non-Discrimination Law*. (2010). Available at: https://www.google.com/search?ei=AVF-XPORDKqF1fAPlYOqiAo&q=European+Union+Agency+for+Fundamental+Rights%2C+Handbook+on+European+Non-Discrimination+Law+2010&oq=European+Union+Agency+for+Fundamental+Rights%2C+Handbook+on+European+Non-Discrimination+Law+2010&gs_l=psy-ab.3…9567.10263..10715…0.0..0.293.523.4j0j1……0….1..gws-wiz……0i71.3JFd7oi7eYY

Fox, W. *Understanding Administrative Law*. New York: Matthew Bender & Co., 1992.

Funk, W, and R Seamon. *Administrative Law*. Aspen, CO: Aspen Publishers, 2009.

Gelders, D, and I Oyvind. "Government Communication About Potential Policies: Public Relations, Propaganda or Both?" *Public Relations Review* 36 (2010): 59–62.

Givens, T, and R Evans Case. *Legislating Equality: The Politics of Antidiscrimination Policy in Europe*. Oxford: Oxford University Press, 2014.

Harlow, C. "Administrative Liability: A Comparative Study of French and English Law." *PhD thesis, The London School of Economics and Political Science* (1979).

Harlow, C. "Global Administrative Law: The Quest for Principles and Values." *The European Journal of International Law* 17, no. 1 (2006): 187–214.

Henrard, K. "The First Substantive ECJ Judgment on the Racial Equality Directive: A Strong Message in a Conceptually Flawed, and Responsively Weak Bottle." *Jean Monnet Working Paper* No. 09/09.

Howard, E. "EU Anti-Discrimination Law: Has the CJEU Stopped Moving Forward?" *International Journal of Discrimination and the Law* 18, nos 2–3: 60–81.

Janssen, E. *Faith in Public Debate. On Freedom of Expression, Hate Speech and Religion in France & the Netherlands*. Cambridge: Interstentia, 2015.

Janssen, E, and A Nieuwnhuis. "De Verhouding Tussen Vrijheid Van Meninguting En Discriminatie in Het Wilders-Process." *Nederlands Tijdschrift voor de Mensenrechten-Bulletin* (2012). Available at: http://hdl.handle.net/11245/1.375450

Johnson Goodnow, F. *Comparative Administrative Law: An Analysis of the Administrative Systems, National and Local, of the United States, England, France and Germany*. London: Beard Books, 2000.

Keller, H, and A Stone Sweet. *A Europe of Rights: The Impact of the ECHR on National Legal Systems*. Oxford: Oxford University Press, 2008.

Link, B, and J Phelan. "Conceptualizing Stigma." *Annual Review of Sociology* 27 (2001): 363–385.

Link, B, and J Phelan. "Stigma and Its Public Health Implications." *The Lancet* 367 (2006): 528–529.

Major, B, S Spencer, T Schmader, C Wolfe, and J Crocker. "Coping with Negative Stereotypes About Intellectual Performance: The Role of Psychological Disengagement." *Personality and Social Psychology Bulletin* 24, no. 1 (1998): 34–50.

McCubbins, M, R Noll, and B Weingast. "The Political Origins of the Administrative Procedure Act." *Journal of Law, Economics and Organization* 15 (1999): 180–217.

Metzger, G. "Ordinary Administrative Law as Constitutional Common Law." *Journal of the National Association of Administrative Law Judiciary* 30, no. 2 (2010): 421–494.

Metzler, E. "The Growth and Development of Administrative Law." *Marquette Law Review* 19, no. 4 (1935): 209.

Miller, C, and B Major. "Coping with Stigma and Prejudice." In *The Social Psychology of Stigmatisation*, edited by T Heatherton, R Kleck, M Hebl and J Hull, 243–272. New York: Guilford Press, 2000.

Murphy, N. "Context, Not Content: Medium-Based Press Clause Restrictions on Government Speech in the Internet Age." *University of Denver Sports & Entertainment Law Journal* 7 (2009): 26–61.

Nolte, G. "General Principles of German and European Administrative Law – a Comparison in Historical Perspective." *Modern Law Review* 57, no. 2 (1994): 191.

O'Connell, R. "Cinderella Comes to the Ball: Art 14 and the Right to Non-Discrimination in the ECHR." *Legal Studies* 29, no. 2 (2009): 211–229.

Quinn, P. "The Problem of Stigmatizing Expressions -the Limits of Anti-Discrimination Approaches." *International Journal of Discrimination and the Law* 17, no. 1 (2017): 23–50.

Quinn, P, and P De Hert. "Self Respect—a 'Rawlsian Primary Good' Unprotected by the European Convention on Human Rights and Its Lack of a Coherent Approach to Stigmatization?" *The International Journal of Discrimination and the Law* 14 (2014): 19–53.

Raine, T. "Judicial Review under the Human Rights Act: A Culture of Justification." *North East Law Review* 1 (2013): 81–108.

Rakoff, T. "The Choice between Formal and Informal Modes of Administrative Regulation." *Administrative Law Review* 52, no. 1 (2000): 159–174.

Rose-Ackerman, S. *Corruption and Government: Causes, Consequences, and Reform.* Cambridge: Cambridge University Press, 1999.

Rose-Ackerman, S, and P Lindseth. "Comparative Administrative Law: An Introduction." In *Comparative Administrative Law*, edited by S Rose-Ackerman and P Lindseth, 1–20. Cheltenham: Elgar Publishing, 2011.

Rubin, E. "It's Time to Make the Administrative Procedure Act Administrative." *Cornell Law Review* 89 (2002): 95–190.

Scheuerman, W. "The Economic State of Emergency." *Cardozo Law Review* 21 (1999–2000): 1869–1870.

Schiek, D, and A Lawson. *European Union Non-Discrimination Law and Intersectionality: Investigating the Triangle of Racial, Gender and Disability Discrimination.* Farnham: Ashgate Publishing, 2013.

Schwarze, J. "The Convergence of Administrative Laws of the EU Member States." *European Public Law* 4, no. 2 (1998): 191–210.

Simonovic Einwalter, T. "Far, but Not Far Enough: An Idealist Critique of the Racial Equality Directive." *Croatian Yearbook of European Policy & Law*, no. 4 (2008): 196–223.

Sing, M. *German Administrative Law in Common Law Perspective.* Berlin: Springer, 2001.

Solanke, I. *Discrimination as Stigma.* Oxford: Hart, 2017.

Sordi, B. "Révolution, Rechsstaat and the Rule of Law: Historical Reflections on the Emergence of Administrative Law in Europe." In *Comparative Administrative Law*, edited by S Rose-Ackerman and P Lindseth, 23–36. Cheltenham: Elgar Publishing, 2011.

Stirn, B, D Fairgreave, and M Guyomar. *Droits et libertés en France et au Royaume-Uni.* Paris: Odile Jacob, 2006.

Stone Sweet, A, and T Burnell. "Trustee Courts and the Judicialization of International Regimes: The Politics of Majoritarian Activism in the European Convention on Human Rights, the European Union, and the World Trade Organization. " *Journal of Law and Courts* 1, no. 1 (2012): 61–88.

Tilly, C. *Contention and Democracy in Europe, 1650–2000.* Cambridge: Cambridge University Press, 2003.

Timmer, A. "Toward an Anti-Stereotyping Approach for the European Court of Human Rights." *Human Rights Law Review* 11, no. 4 (2011): 707–738.

Truchet, D. *Droit administratif (5e Édition).* Paris:Themis, 2013.

Van Noorloos, M. *Hate Speech Revisted – a Comparative and Historical Perspective on Hate Speech Law in the Netherlands and England and Wales.* Cambridge: Interstentia, 2011.

Vick, D. "The Human Rights Act and the British Constitution." *Texas International Law Journal* 37 (2002): 329–372.

White, R, and C Ovey. *The European Convention on Human Rights.* Oxford: Oxford University Press, 2009.

Wilfred Bradley, A, and K Ewing. *Constitutional and Administrative Law Volume 1.* Harlow: Pearson Education, 2007.

Ziller, J. "The Continental System of Administrative Legality." In *Handbook of Public Administration: Concise Paperback Edition*, edited by G Peters and J Pierre. Los Angeles: Sage Publications, 2007.

6 Stigmatizing state expressions – a threat to privacy?

1 Introduction

> Civilization is the progress toward a society of privacy. The savage's whole existence is public, ruled by the laws of his tribe. Civilization is the process of setting man free from men.
>
> Ayn Rand[1]

Privacy is a concept that has evident links to the phenomenon of stigmatization. As Chapter 2 discussed, individuals who possess a trait that they feel is stigmatized may often wish to keep it concealed from their peers and society at large. This desire to keep aspects of oneself hidden is synonymous with a number of concepts of privacy that relate to the ability of individuals to live in isolation to the extent they might wish. This can include concepts of informational privacy that value the ability of individuals to control what information concerning them is available to others. As section 2 will discuss, however, privacy is a concept which finds no universally accepted definition. Indeed, many definitions of privacy have been put forward, with some relating to concepts that are far wider than the ability to live in isolation where desired (including control of one's information). These definitions include notions of privacy that relate to the ability of individuals to determine their own course in life, part of which entails being free from unnecessary impediments in doing so.

This chapter will look at illustrative examples of laws that have been inspired by both narrow visions of privacy (focused primarily on informational autonomy) and wide concepts (concerned with the ability to be free from undue impediments or steering forces). In terms of the former, section 3 will look at perhaps the most well developed and widely applicable legal framework to ensure informational self-determination – the European Union's General Data Protection Regulation (GDPR). The framework of rights and duties for data controllers/processors and data subjects set out in this regulation may be of relevance to both the preparation of certain expressive acts as well as to the acts themselves (where the processing of personal data is involved). The GDPR may thus have relevance not only for SSEs that contain personal data but also those SSEs that required the processing of

1 A Rand, "*The Fountainhead*" (Indianapolis, IN: Bobbs Merrill, 1979).

personal data in their preparation. Section 4 looks at related case law derived from Article 8 of the European Convention on Human Rights (ECHR) which will still apply in certain situations in which the GDPR will not (e.g. in the context of a criminal investigation).

Concerning a wider notion of privacy, section 5 looks at further case law of the European Court of Human Rights (ECtHR) that seemingly relates to an ability of individuals to develop their own personality and relationships. This case law of the court has shown that it views privacy both as a concept that relates to controls on the use of personal information (i.e. related to a specific individual) and also as a wider notion that is potentially related to the concept of stigmatization. This includes the right to form one's own personality and freedom to choose and form relationships in life. This case law raises the question of whether the creation and use of harmful stereotypes in stigmatizing state expressions (SSEs) could represent an infringement of an individual's Article 8 rights. This chapter will demonstrate that privacy approaches are more likely to be applicable to SSEs when they refer to specific individuals but are less likely to be relevant when SSEs target groups of individuals. An important reason for this is the need to protect the liberty of expression that exists at the heart of democratic societies and which is often recognized as a fundamental right (e.g. in Article 10 ECHR). Given this imperative it seems likely that negative effects such as stigmatization (which often are applied to groups) may not be seen as sufficient to warrant the infringement of free speech. As the author discuses in section 5, whilst his normative position (established in Chapter 3) foresees the necessity of some forms of stigmatizing expression (e.g. 'functional stigmatization' or 'fair criticism') the court's case law in relation to both Articles 8 and 10 suggests that a much broader range of SSEs will be permitted.

2 Varying concepts of privacy and their relationship with SSEs

A Privacy is a multifaceted concept

Privacy is a term that is omnipresent in our informational society. Individuals seek it, business and governments claim to respect it. It would be difficult to find an individual that did not value his or her privacy in one way or another. Despite this, it is a concept that is notoriously difficult to define in a concise manner. The former French justice Minister Robert Badinter went so far as to say that "respect for the secret of privacy was such that it went beyond definition".[2] Others described privacy as merely a term to describe a number of problems "not related by a common denominator or core element. Instead, each problem has elements in common with others, yet not necessarily the same element—they share family resemblances with each other".[3]

2 S Gutwirth, *Privacy and the Information Age* (New York: Rowman & Littlefield, 2002). p34

3 C Bennet, "In Defence of Privacy: The Concept and the Regime ‚*Surveillance and Society* 8, no. 4 (2011). Quote originally taken from D Solove, *Understanding Privacy* (Cambridge, MA: Harvard University Press, 2008).

The contextual variations in which privacy is invoked and its intrinsic illusiveness as a concept have greatly complicated definition. A plethora of pseudonyms that are used interchangeably with privacy including 'private life, 'private sphere', intimacy' and 'secrecy' have only complicated this further. This has led some scholars to give up on a global definition and to rely on a more contextual approach.[4] For both legal and sociological purposes a global, catch all definition of privacy is therefore not available. A complete analysis of all potential definitions of privacy is beyond the scope of this book, though some useful illustrations can be summarized to demonstrate the breadth that exists.

In 1967, Westin, for instance, conceptualized four states of privacy: solitude, anonymity, reserve and intimacy.[5] Solove, on the other hand, argued that the conceptions of privacy could be grouped in six categories:[6]

> (i) the right to be let alone;[7] (ii) limited access to the self – the ability to shield oneself from unwanted access by others; (iii) secrecy – the concealment of certain matters from others; (iv) control over personal information – the ability to exercise control over information about oneself; (v) personhood – the protection of one's personality, individuality, and dignity; and (vi) intimacy – control over, or limited access to, one's intimate relationships or aspects of life.

By contrast, Roessler introduced three dimensions of privacy:[8] 'decisional privacy', which is necessary for individual autonomy; 'informational privacy', i.e. control over information relating to a person; and 'local privacy', i.e. privacy of the household, of one's flat or room and thus privacy of private objects. The last category relates thus to a realm of private space. Banisar and Davies came up with another similar, yet different categorization as follows:[9] a) informational privacy, concerning the collection and handling of personal data; b) bodily privacy, with regards to the protection of a person's physical integrity against invasive procedures, such as clinical trials; c) privacy of communications, covering the security and confidentiality of every form of communication; and d) territorial privacy, concerning protection of the domestic and other environments, such as the workplace.

4 Examples of such contextual contexts are 'home privacy', 'informational privacy' and 'relational privacy'. See Gutwirth, *Privacy and the Information Age*. p34
5 Westin, A F. *Privacy and Freedom* (New York: Atheneum, 1967).
6 D J Solove, *Understanding Privacy* (Cambridge, MA: Harvard University Press, 2008). p13
7 S D Warren, SD and L D Brandeis, "The Right to Privacy", *Harvard Law Review*, 4, no. 5.
8 B Roessler. "New Ways of Thinking about Privacy". In *Oxford Handbook of Political Theory*, ed. Anne Philips, Bonnie Honig, and John Dryzek, 694–713 (Oxford; Oxford University Press, 2006).
9 D Banisar and S Davies, "Global Trends in Privacy Protection: An International Survey of Privacy, Data Protection, and Surveillance Laws and Developments", *John Marshall Journal of Information and Technology and Privacy Law*, 18, no. 1 (1999).

B Privacy can be understood in both a narrow and a broad sense

Although a full analysis of all proposed concepts of privacy is beyond the scope of this chapter, some useful generalizations can be made. Arguably two classifications can be made that are most relevant to SSEs. These are the concepts of 'informational privacy' and 'privacy as liberty'. Both can be considered as motivational forces behind a number of important legal approaches that are worth consideration in terms of their potential applicability to SSEs.

(i) Informational privacy

Informational privacy relates to the notion that an individual should have autonomy over who has access to information concerning him or her and what can be done with such information. The need for such autonomy can be found in many traditional conceptions of privacy which broadly relate to the right to be left alone or in isolation.[10] The importance of such autonomy has taken on a new dimension in the information age where personal data is processed on an industrial scale for many purposes. Even before the digital age, however, the threats posed by gathering personal information were apparent. These included persecution (and even murder) and the discrimination of minorities. On the individual level numerous risks have also long existed including blackmail, social isolation (where information that is not considered socially acceptable is made public) and a ride range of criminal activity. Given these risks, the ability to control the use of one's personal information is often seen as an essential element of a free democratic society.

Laws inspired by this concept of privacy are many and varied. They may relate to the creation of new information concerning individuals (e.g. relating to medical dossiers, its utilization or its dissemination)[11] or may demand that individuals have a right not to be monitored in certain domains.[12] Such concepts may call for the creation of private spaces, either in the physical or digital sense where individuals have a right not be monitored by others (including the state).[13] The existence of such spaces is required in order to allow individuals to act as they wish without fear of being monitored and having such information made available to other individuals.[14] Rules inspired by such principles may prevent journalists from taking photographs of people in their private homes, or employers from reading the personal email correspondence of their employees, for example. In addition to rules relating to activity pursued in certain domains, information pertaining to certain sensitive relationships may also be the subject of restrictions. This may

10 R Post, "Three Concepts of Privacy", *Faculty Scholarship Series*, 185 (2001).

11 E Mantovani and P Quinn, "Mhealth and Data Protection – the Letter and the Spirit of Consent Legal Requirements", *International Review of Law, Computers & Technology*, (2013). doi:10.1080/13600869.2013.801581

12 See, for example, *Von Hannover v. Germany* (No. 59320/00). Such spaces could be inside one's home, or even in spaces that although not public may not be secluded.

13 In terms of online space see the ECHR Article 8 case of *Copland v. UK* (No. 62617/00). This case involved the monitoring of an employee's email messages.

14 Gutwirth, *Privacy and the Information Age*.

include, for example, information created under the auspices of patient-doctor relationships, relationships with legal advisers, financial advisers or other sensitive contexts.[15]

Other legal approaches in this category may seek to prevent individuals or organizations from creating information that relates to specific individuals and using it without certain legal conditions being met (including, for example, consent of the data subject).[16] Data protection legislation is a prominent example of such a perceived form of privacy (discussed further in section 3). The aim of such initiatives is to place limits on the ability of individuals or organizations to create, use or transfer personal data relating to others and, where it is allowed, to lay out transparent conditions for the use of data.[17] In some domains, for example that of medical information, the rules on the creation, use and transfer of such data may be particularly strict.[18] The European Union's (EU's) new GDPR, for example, creates a number of rights (for data subjects) and obligations (for data controllers and processors) connected to the processing of personal data. As section 4 discusses, further these rights and obligations may, in some contexts be relevant to SSEs.

(ii) Privacy as liberty

The concept of informational privacy represents a narrow concept linked to traditional ideas of a right to be able to exist in isolation.[19] Other more expansive notions value broader factors including, for example, the need for individuals to be able to live their life in the manner in which they see fit. This can relate to a need to prevent direct barriers to such self-determination or even forces that might be capable of having a steering effect.[20] In terms of the former one can imagine a wide range of traditional legal protections such as freedom from (wrongful) imprisonment, protection of private property and measures against discrimination. Such impediments can directly prevent individuals from exercising self-determination and must therefore be prevented where they cannot be justified. In addition to such clear obstacles to self-determination however there exist a range of other forces that are capable of exerting a steering effect upon individuals. Whilst not

15 For a discussion on laws related to patient confidentiality see: J Mason, *Mason & McCall Smith's Law and Medical Ethics* (Oxford: Oxford University Press, 2005).

16 In the UK, for instance, the taking and publishing of photos at an individual's wedding without the permission of the participants was described as a breach of an obligation of confidentiality under Article 8 ECHR. *Douglas v. Hello! Ltd* [2005] EWCA Civ 595.

17 S Gutwirth and P De Hert, "Privacy, Data Protection and Law Enforcement. Opacity of the Individual and Transparency of Power", in *Privacy and Criminal Law*, ed. E Claes, A Duff, and S Gutwirth (Antwerp: Intersentia, 2006).

18 Mantovani and Quinn, "Mhealth and Data Protection – the Letter and the Spirit of Consent Legal Requirements". See also the guidance document produced by the Article 29 Working Party (00323/07/EN WP 131).

19 H Nissenbaum, "Protecting Privacy in the Information Age: The Problem of Privacy in Public", *Law and Philosophy* 17 (1998).

20 Gutwirth, *Privacy and the Information Age.*

being able to block individual freedom to self-determine *tout court*, they are able to exert influence and therefore weaken an individual's ability to choose freely how he or she should live his or her life (see Chapter 2 on the properties of stigmatization). Importantly these include forces that are able to exert a psychological force on individuals. A broader concept of 'privacy as liberty' would arguably require that limitations be placed upon forces that seek to pressure individuals (*inter alia* through stigmatization) to choose to live in one way or another.

This can arguably include forms of propaganda and various forms of symbolic gestures found in many SSEs. Given the harm that they are capable of producing, a broad notion of privacy as liberty could in certain contexts foresee a need to restrict SSEs. As the discussion of Rawls' ideas in Chapter 3 demonstrated, many positions and viewpoints on the just organization of society would argue that it is important that the state, where possible, show its self to be neutrally disposed *vis-à-vis* the choice of way of life made by the various groups of people that make up a pluralist society.[21] Many examples of SSEs show the problems that can be produced where such an ambition is neglected.

Examples of legal approaches motivated by this broad concept of privacy are many and varied. These range from international human rights agreements such as the European Convention of Human Rights (ECHR) to constitutional and legal provisions within the legal order of particular states. In terms of the latter, provisions demanding the protection of privacy are notable in many constitutions, including, for example, the German and Spanish constitutions.[22] In terms of the former Article 8 (which is further discussed in section 5) is renowned for the extremely broad, non-exhaustively defined and even ever changing scope of protection it offers to 'private and family life'.[23]

C The relevance of privacy to SSEs

There are clear links between the protection of privacy and the phenomenon of stigmatization. The types of links may be subtly but importantly different depending on the concept of privacy involved. The potential links between privacy, stigmatization and SSEs in particular are discussed below from the perspective of both 'informational privacy' and a wider sense of 'privacy as liberty'.

21 J Rawls, "The Priority of Right and Ideas of the Good", *Philosophy & Public Affairs* 17, no. 4 (1988).

22 In certain constitutions, such a broad version of privacy may be supported by several articles in combination. This is the case with the German Constitution with Articles 4, 5 and 11 relating to freedom of conscience, religion, expression, correspondence and communication respectively. In the Spanish Constitution Section 18 of the Spanish Constitution contains a broad provision applying to personal and family privacy (i.e. similar to Article 8 ECHR).

23 Stefan Theil, "Is the 'Living Instrument' Approach of the European Court of Human Rights Compatible with the ECHR and International Law?", *European Public Law* 23, no. 3 (2017).

(i) Informational privacy

Where informational privacy exists, it allows individuals to be able to control what aspects others learn about them.[24] In doing so they are able to reveal (or not) only the aspects concerning them which they desire. This means they may be able to hide certain facets of their personality that are perceived to put them at a disadvantage. This can range from the seemingly innocuous, e.g. idiosyncratic sexual desires, to the serious, e.g. past convictions for serious crimes.[25] In certain instances this may be because revealing such information could bring about concrete negative results (e.g. criminal prosecution, violent attack or the likelihood of suffering from acts of discrimination). Even where this is not the case, however, individuals will often desire to keep aspects of their personhood to themselves where it is perceived that their peers (or society at large) might not approve. In such cases one is essentially speaking of keeping a stigmatized trait hidden (or as Goffman described preventing oneself from becoming discredited).[26] Imagine, for instance, an individual who chooses to hide his or her sexual orientation, political preference or religious feelings (or lack thereof) for fear of offending others.[27] Humans in all societies possess a strong sensitivity towards the perceptions and opinions of their peers and as a consequence a desire to have control over what other people know about them.[28]

Where individuals have full control over information relating to them they are in effect able to prevent themselves from being connected to stigmatizing stereotypes that exist within their peer group or within society at large. Informational self-determination in such a context essentially allows individuals to prevent information relating to them being used in a way that would allow them to be associated with a trait that is stigmatized. This process involves linking a particular group with a negative stereotype.[29] From the perspective of SSEs this could occur with statements, expressions or information releases that show individuals to have properties that could be linked to a stigmatized trait (see Chapter 1 for numerous illustrations). Some of these may be more obvious than others. Imagine, for instance, a statement from a police department that "Mr John Smith of Clapham, London has been arrested on suspicion of acts of terrorism". For the individual

24 K Einiar Himma and H Tavani, *The Handbook of Information and Computer Ethics* (Englewood Cliffs, NJ: Wiley, 2008). See pp 131–165 for more on informational privacy.

25 G Herek, "Sexual Stigma and Sexual Prejudice in the United States: A Conceptual Framework", *Nebraska Symposium on Motivation* 54 (2009).

26 I Goffman, *Stigma: Notes on a Spoilt Identity* (Englewood Cliffs, NJ: Prentice Hall, 1963). See Chapter 2 of this book.

27 A Simon, "The Relationship between Stereotypes of and Attitudes toward Lesbians and Gays", in *Stigma and Sexual Orientation: Understanding Prejudice against Lesbians, Gay Men, and Bisexuals. Psychological Perspectives on Lesbian and Gay Issues*, ed. G Herek (Thousand Oaks, CA: Sage Publications, 1998).

28 S Neuberg, D Smith, and T Asher, "Why Do People Stigmatise?: Toward a Biocultural Framework", in *The Social Psychology of Stigma*, ed. T Heatherton et al. (New York: Guilford Press, 2000).

29 B Link and J Phelan, "Conceptualizing Stigma," *Annual Review of Sociology* 27 (2001).

involved, who will be no doubt easily be identifiable by a large number of people, such a statement would be stigmatizing whether he is innocent or not. Similarly imagine a promotional flyer for a local sexual health clinic that incidentally included a picture of a local resident who happened to be walking past. Such information could be misconstrued by some as indicating that the resident concerned was visiting the clinic and therefore had a sexual health issue. Given the sensitivity of such matters and the stigmatizing nature of many sexual health conditions this could be a source of concern for the individual involved.[30] On a more public level the same is true where a minster accuses an opponent of having links to organized crime or of having an extramarital affair. Whether or not the allegations are true they are capable of having a stigmatizing effect on the individuals concerned. Given the potential for harm to be caused by the use of personal data, it is worth inquiring (see sections 3 and 4) what role legal processes linked to the theme of informational privacy can play in restraining SSEs that use personal data.

(ii) Privacy as liberty

Whilst laws relating to informational privacy may be of use in challenging SSEs where they concern specific individuals, they may be limited in instances where they do not. Unfortunately, as Chapter 1 illustrated, there is an enormous range of possible SSEs that whilst not referring to specific individuals are highly stigmatizing. This is because SSEs usually link groups of people to negative stereotypes. As a result, most SSEs need not refer to specific individuals in order to be stigmatizing. Imagine, for instance, an example where a minister states that unemployed people are lazy. Where this occurs information contained within SSEs may intentionally or unintentionally give the perception that groups within society possess stigmatized traits. This may occur, for example, where public authorities release figures showing that it is individuals from within a certain minority that are most likely to be found committing a certain type of crime (e.g. related to domestic or sexual abuse) or that certain groups are most likely to suffer from a health issue (e.g. related to drug or alcohol abuse).[31] Such information can be highly stigmatizing for the group concerned because it means that they will be associated with a particular stigmatized trait, e.g. a certain criminal activity or a certain health problem. Even though the SSE in question might not refer to specific individuals, individuals belonging to the group in question will nonetheless feel stigmatized because they will be connected to the stigmatized trait by association.

30 E Lawson et al., "HIV/Aids Stigma, Denial, Fear and Discrimination", (Toronto: The African and Caribbean Council on HIV/AIDS in Ontario (ACCHO), Behavioural and Epidemiological Studies Unit, University of Toronto, 2006).

31 W Tufail, "Rotherham, Rochdale, and the Racialised Threat of the 'Muslim Grooming Gang'", *International Journal for Crime, Justice and Social Democracy* 4, no. 3 (2015). There has been considerable criticism of the Muslim minority in the UK in recent years as a result of a very small number who have taken part in paedophilic criminal activity or terrorism related offences.

Given the power the state has in terms of its perceived moral authority and its ability to disseminate its message, it (and those connected with it) is also able to create new stereotypes that can be connected to pre-existing groups. This might occur, for example, when a political figure states that 'foreigners come to our country to claim benefits' or that 'foreigners are increasing the crime rate'. Such expressions do not need to refer to individuals to be stigmatizing. They are stigmatizing simply because they create a stereotype that is easily applicable to various groups in society. Indeed, in certain circumstances a public official/minster, etc. need not even name a particular group or minority given that the stereotype they are invoking is of evident application to one.

Given that the ECtHR has indicated that there is a duty to prevent hate speech one might ask to what extent privacy as liberty approaches can be used to limit the stigmatizing activities of the state.[32] As Chapter 2 discussed stigmatization is capable of exerting important psychological forces on individuals that are capable of altering individual behaviour. The adoption of various coping mechanisms, for example, is a common response to a stigmatizing environment (see Chapter 2). Where stigmatization is particularly severe, an individual's self-esteem may be eroded.[33] This may cause individuals to lose confidence that their desires and beliefs are acceptable. In such circumstances elements of self-loathing and of internalization (in terms of the negative appraisals of others) can occur.[34] The result of such occurrences can be that individuals loose not only the desire to live according to their version of the good, but also the belief that such a version is an acceptable choice. The ability to resist stigmatizing forces is thus an important element of such liberty to define oneself.[35] As Chapter 3 discussed, the possession of self-respect has been proposed as being of importance in allowing individuals to resist stigmatizing forces and potential harm to self-esteem. Rawls reasoned that one of the key ways such self-respect could be facilitated was by ensuring that the state showed respect towards the opinions and beliefs individuals had concerning their version of the 'good life'.[36] Given that SSEs are able to do the opposite those sharing Rawls ideas on the need to protect self-respect might look towards laws inspired by privacy as liberty in order to restrict them. Some of the ECtHR's case law under Article 8 is seemingly motivated by a need for individuals be able to follow their own preferred version of life or form their own personalities. Its relevance in terms of SSEs is discussed further in section 4.

32 *AKSU v. Turkey* (Applications nos 4149/04 and 41029/04).

33 M Leary, "The Social and Psychological Importance of Self-Esteem", in *The Social Psychology of Emotional and Behavioral Problems*, ed. R Kowalski and M Leary (Washington, DC: APA, 1999). Link and Phelan, "Conceptualizing Stigma", See also Chapter 2 for a further discussion.

34 A Courtwright, "Justice, Stigma, and the New Epidemiology of Health Disparities", *Bioethics* 23, no. 2 (2009). p92

35 P Quinn and P De Hert, "Self Respect—a 'Rawlsian Primary Good' Unprotected by the European Convention on Human Rights and Its Lack of a Coherent Approach to Stigmatization?", *The International Law of Discrimination and the Law* 14 (2014).

36 J Rawls, *A Theory of Justice* (Cambridge, MA: Harvard University Press, 1999). p155

3 Information privacy approaches and SSE

A The GDPR as the world's most sophisticated informational privacy approach

Data protection began to arise as an issue with the creation of automated forms of data processing in the 1960s. From the 1970s onwards various European states began to enact data protection laws, often to regulate who could access databases used for public administration that were being built up by public bodies.[37] Later, data protection began to receive international attention exemplified first by the Council of Europe's Convention 108[38] and later the EU in its Data Protection Directive 95/46/EC.[39]

The latest iteration of the EU's data protection approach is the General Data Protection Regulation (GDPR).[40] This regulation has to a large extent harmonized data protection law across Europe. In general, it offers three important guarantees (which can be further broken down into more specific rights and obligations) that offer protection to potential data subjects (i.e. those whose personal data may be processed). These are: (i) that there is a valid legal base for the processing of data; (ii) that it is processed in line with data protection principles outlined within the GDPR; and (iii) that data subjects are provided with a number of data protection rights.

In terms of having a correct legal base, the most well known is that of consent, i.e. where an individual gives his or her permission for their personal data to be used in some manner.[41] Even where a controller/processor does not require consent (because some other legal base is available) it can still only process data according to certain principles.[42] Requirements such as 'purpose limitation', 'data minimization' and 'storage limitation' limit the manoeuvring space of data controllers and do not allow them to process data in ways that were not originally foreseen at the time of collection or for an indefinite period of time. This might be important, for example, where a public official tries to publish details of an individual who had given permission for his or her data to be used for some other purpose by the state (or when some other legal grounds existed for that processing – see section D). Imagine where a minister used the example of certain

37 Banisar and Davies, "Global Trends in Privacy Protection: An International Survey of Privacy, Data Protection and Surveillance Laws and Developments"..

38 Council of Europe, Convention for the Protection of Individuals with Regard to Automatic Processing of Personal Data (ETS No. 108, 28.01.1981).

39 Directive 95/46/EC of the European Parliament and of the Council of 24 October 1995 on the protection of individuals with regard to the processing of personal data and on the free movement of such data, *OJ L* 281, 23.11.1995, pp. 31–50.

40 Regulation (EU) 2016/679 of the European Parliament and of the Council of 27 April 2016 on the protection of natural persons with regard to the processing of personal data and on the free movement of such data, and repealing Directive 95/46/EC (General Data Protection Regulation) *OJ L* 119, 4.5.16 , pp. 1–88.

41 The conditions for consent for personal data can be found in Article 7. For sensitive personal data the conditions are found in Article 9(2).

42 Many of these are described within Article 5 (and Article 9 for sensitive data) of the GDPR.

families that claimed a high amount of social security for a prolonged period of time after he had accessed databases on social security recipients. Given the requirement of 'purpose limitation' (i.e. only using personal data for certain specified purposes), the processing of personal data for other purposes (including to prepare an SSE) would likely contravene the GDPR, even where the state had a correct legal basis for processing the data to begin with (i.e. the administration of social security). Similarly, the principle of storage limitation may require public authorities to delete certain personal data after a certain period of time, meaning they would not be available for use to prepare or execute SSEs.

The existence of data subject rights means that data subjects can *inter alia* request that their personal data is deleted or amended where incorrect.[43] This could be relevant to SSEs in two ways. First it allows potentially concerned individuals to have their data deleted or amended before it can ever be used in expressive activity by the state. If their personal data is not available, there is no chance it can be used either in the preparation of SSEs or in the acts of expression themselves. Second, data subject rights can be used to have personal data amended or removed. This could be useful where personal details have been published by public bodies, e.g. online. It addition to these rights, data controllers can be subject to extensive fines when they process personal data incorrectly. Such fines (which can be substantial) could also, in theory at least, be applicable to the processing of personal data in the form of an SSE (or any form of state expression for that matter).[44]

B The GDPR and SSEs

Whilst data protection undoubtedly has a role to play in limiting the processing of personal data in general the question arises as to what role it can play in limiting SSEs. When most people think of the application of data protection, they imagine the regulation of the use of data in the computerized processing of personal information. This might, for example, include databases or various forms of digitized organized storage systems. However, many state expressions do not possess such a character. Purely expressive activity need not be of a digital character, it can consist, for example, of verbal expressions. It also need not be of a structured nature, i.e. as databases and other forms of organized storage are. These factors therefore call into question (at least in an intuitive sense) the applicability of the EU's data protection framework. The remainder of this section will look at these questions by looking at the potential applicability of the GDPR to SSEs in two ways. The first will involve the expressive act itself, asking whether such acts can

43 Data subject rights are described within Articles 12–23 of the GDPR. The right of erasure is contained within Article 17.

44 See Article 83 of the GDPR. Some states have opted to exempt public bodies from fines under the GDPR. In Ireland, for example, the government had originally proposed to exempt public bodies from fines but later amended the Data Protection Bill 2018 to allow fines of up to 1 million euros. See https://www.irishtimes.com/news/politics/government-departments-may-face-1m-fines-for-data-breaches-1.3440007

constitute the processing of personal data as defined in the GDPR. The second (discussed in section C below) will involve looking at linking such acts to more traditional forms of processing data, acts that may, for instance, be necessary to prepare and facilitate SSEs.

The applicability of the GDPR in general depends on the applicability of the concept of 'processing of personal data' found within the GDPR which determines the applicability of the regulation. Given the varying form SSEs can take one might ask whether, even if they refer to specific individuals, they involve the processing of personal data. In order to answer this question, it is necessary to break this requirement into two separate subcomponents, each of which is relevant to the questions of applicability of the GDPR to SSEs.

(i) Do SSEs involve the processing of data as understood in the GDPR?

Of key importance to the application of the GDPR is that personal data must actually be 'processed'. This implies that something must actually happen with personal data beyond its transient existence. However, the definition of processing is very broad, with storage of data seemingly being sufficient to constitute processing. The question remains whether such a definition would apply to many forms of SSEs, especially those that may be of a verbal nature. Whilst certain forms of expressive activity could involve the publication of data in structured form (including, for example, extracts from databases) most expressions will not. Many will be verbal in nature, and may relate data in a manner that is unstructured. Even where personal data is presented in a way that is not verbal it may, for example, involve the replication of verbal comments that have been made (e.g. where text or video are shown on a website). Even where this is the case personal data may be presented in an completely unstructured way, for example, where somebody is named on a website in connection with a series of events. Despite the seeming incongruity with the traditional image of what 'data processing' constitutes, it seems likely that many forms of SSE could be considered as capable of constituting 'processing'. Indeed, the GDPR opts for an extremely wide definition, stating in Article 4(2) that processing includes:

> any operation or set of operations which is performed on personal data or on sets of personal data, whether or not by automated means, such as collection, recording, organization, structuring, storage, adaptation or alteration, retrieval, consultation, use, disclosure by transmission, dissemination or otherwise making available, alignment or combination, restriction, erasure or destruction.

In doing so the GDPR makes clear that question of automation or computerization is not determinative, seemingly opening the way for manual activities such as many of the forms of non-automated expression described in Chapter 1. Furthermore, the dissemination of material is explicitly described and includes the notable wide description of "otherwise making available". The sheer breadth of this description would seemingly include most forms of state expressive activity that use personal data.

(ii) Do SSEs use personal data?

Perhaps the most important limitation of data protection approaches such as the GDPR is that they only apply to the processing of data that is of a 'personal nature'. The GDPR, for instance, makes clear that it does not apply to data that is anonymous or not personal in nature.[45] Data is only personal in nature if it can 'reasonably likely' be linked to a particular individual. In the case of anonymous data, such data will not be personal in nature and the GDPR will simply not apply.[46] Where this is the case data can be processed without the need for a legal basis, to respect data processing principles or facilitate data subject rights. In effect data protection law does not apply and any party, including the state, is free from associated restrictions, including using such data to prepare an SSE or within the expression itself.

This limitation is important because many individuals can feel personally affected by SSEs that do not refer to them specifically. Imagine disparaging comments made by a minster that refer to a particular minority or to immigrants in general. A member of a particular minority might feel personally highlighted, especially where they interact with others who are not part of their community. Imagine an immigrant who lives in a small village (where there are not many other immigrants) or works in an organization where there are not many others from his or her community present. As Chapter 2 discusses in depth, stigmatization of such a sort is able to have considerable effects, even where stigmatizing remarks or ideas are not addressed to specific individuals. The obvious limitation of data protection approaches to instances that involve the processing of personal data will limit its ability to contribute to the regulation of such potentially harmful expressions. One important exception to this is where personal data is used in the preparation of such expressions (discussed below).

C The use of data in preparative acts

In addition to acts of expression themselves it is important to consider the application of the GDPR to acts of data processing that may make them possible. This includes acts of preparation or other forms of processing necessary to arrive at a conclusion that might be presented in an SSE. Personal data used in an SSE may have been sourced from databases or other information that the state is in possession of. In order to be able to make the expression in question and provide such data, the individual or organization speaking on behalf of the state may have had to access it in databases or in some other filing systems. This provides an important secondary role for data protection frameworks such as the GDPR, even instances where an expression itself may not include personal data. The need to prepare many acts of expression (including, for example, the complex analysis of data) means that the GDPR not only has relevance with regard to SSES that use personal data but also to some which do not. This is because in order to make generalizations or remarks concerning groups it

45 GDPR Recital 26.

46 P Quinn, "The Anonymisation of Research Data — a Pyric Victory for Privacy That Should Not Be Pushed Too Hard by the EU Data Protection Framework?", *European Journal of Health Law* 24 (2017).

may often be necessary to analyse personal data on (sometimes numerous) individuals to arrive at a conclusion.

The use of such data may provide a point at which individuals could intervene in order to prevent processing that would be required in order to create expressions that were stigmatizing (even sometimes where the expression itself did not contain any personal data). This is because some expressions that do not possess personal data may nonetheless still have required the processing of personal data when they were being prepared. Depending on the context in question, the state may need consent to gather and process data in ways that could facilitate expressive activity. In certain instances, specially crafted legislation may grant the ability for the state to process personal data, though under certain conditions. Where neither of these factors exist, the processing of personal data will not be permissible. Data protection therefore acts to restrict the types of personal data the state can collect and process. Where the state is prevented from knowing certain things about individuals in society it will, in a number of instances, be prevented from forming stigmatizing conclusions or stereotypes regarding either individuals or the groups to which they belong. The application of the GDPR may therefore in certain instances prevent the analyses that lead to SSEs occurring. In this way frameworks such as the GDPR may well have a role in preventing the creation of harmful stereotypes (which can be used in expressions) that require the analysis of personal data

D Exceptions limiting the impact of the GDPR

Consent is described above as one of the most important legal bases for the processing of personal data but it is not the only one. There are a number of other potential legal bases that can be used to justify the processing of personal data without the consent of data subjects that may be linked to an SSE. In such cases, the possibility for individuals to prevent the processing of their data, e.g. through withholding consent, may be limited. The exceptions provided for in the GDPR are important because in theory they could be linked to a number of the illustrative examples of SSEs provided in Chapter 1. Article 6(1)(e) of the GDPR, for example, allows Member States (where the possibility exists in law) to process personal data without consent for reasons of general interest.[47] This effectively provides the option for the state to create legislation in appropriate contexts to process personal data for suitable goals without consent. Other more specific exemptions are provided in order to process perusal data in order to manage its social security systems or for reasons of public health.[48] Exceptions such as these allow the state to process personal data for certain specific and important purposes without having to gain the consent of those involved. As Chapter 1 illustrated, expressions in these areas (e.g. related to public health or the fight against crime) can often be stigmatizing.[49]

47 Article 9(2)(G) of the ECHR allows a similar exemption for sensitive (or 'special') data.

48 Article (9(2)(h).

49 Theil, "Is the 'Living Instrument' Approach of the European Court of Human Rights Compatible with the ECHR and International Law?"; P. Quinn, "Crisis Communication in Public Health Emergencies: The Limits of 'Legal Control' and the Risks for Harmful Outcomes in a Digital Age", *Life Sciences, Society and Policy* 14, no. 1 (2018).

Yet another potentially important exemption exists for sensitive personal data that has already been manifestly made public by the data subject.[50] This exemption effectively means that potential controllers do not need another legal base to process the data in question. This could, for example, include information published in various forms of news media or even information that has been posted on certain forms of online social media (depending on whether the type of social media involved can be considered as indeed making data manifestly public, i.e. open to all). This exemption is potentially significant with regard to SSEs given that if such data can be used it will allow those expressing themselves on behalf of the state to both link specific individuals to traits that are already stigmatized and also to use the information from a number of individuals to create new forms of stigmatizing stereotypes. Imagine, for instance, a politician that, in seeking political gain, chooses to highlight embarrassing tweets of members of another political party that were made many years ago. Alternatively, in some instances a state could try to harvest a large amount of data that had been manifestly made public in order to make models or predict behaviours in certain areas. This could, for example, be in areas related to public health or public order. Even where this is done with the best intentions, it is possible to give rise to new forms of negative stereotypes that could be communicated to the public through SSEs.[51]

Perhaps one of the most important exceptions can be found in Article 2(2)(d) which states that the GDPR does not apply to processing "for the purposes of the prevention, investigation, detection or prosecution of criminal offences or the execution of criminal penalties, including the safeguarding against and the prevention of threats to public security". Unlike the exceptions described above, which simply provide a legal base to process this data in question, this exemption effectively excludes the type of processing from the application of the GDPR. This means that not only is there no need to worry about having a legal base outlined in the GDPR but that there is also no need to comply with the rest of regulation (e.g. in relating to the data processing principles or data subject rights). Whilst other laws may still apply (i.e. outside the realm of data protection),[52] this effectively creates a broad domain where the state can process personal data without having to comply with the requirements of the GDPR.[53] As Chapter 1

50 Article 9(2)(e).

51 Quinn, "Crisis Communication in Public Health Emergencies: The Limits of 'Legal Control' and the Risks for Harmful Outcomes in a Digital Age".

52 *Marper v. UK* ECHR 1581 (Application nos 30562/04 and 30566/04).

53 Whilst the GDPR may not apply, other legal provisions may do so. These include various laws at the local level, and at the European level the Directive (EU) 2016/680 of the European Parliament and of the Council of 27 April 2016 on the protection of natural persons with regard to the processing of personal data by competent authorities for the purposes of the prevention, investigation, detection or prosecution of criminal offences or the execution of criminal penalties, and on the free movement of such data, and repealing Council Framework Decision 2008/977/JHA. The protection this latter instrument offers is considerably less than the GDPR. Unfortunately, a full analysis is beyond the scope of this book. For more see C Jasserand, "Law Enforcement Access to Personal Data Originally Collected by Private Parties: Missing Data Subjects' Safeguards in Directive 2016/680?", *Computer Law & Security Review* 34 (2018).

illustrated with numerous examples related to terrorism and security matters, this is concerning given that this area is a rich source of SSEs.

4 The ECHR and informational privacy attacks against individuals

Data protection approaches such as the GDPR may be applicable in the case of some SSEs but not others. One reason for this is that there are a number of exceptions to the full or partial application of data protection law (described above in section 3D). For individuals in such situations (e.g. relating 'the fight against crime') the lack of application of data protection law does not mean that they are without total protection of the law. This is because other approaches related to privacy may apply even where data protection does not. These could include, for example, laws related to wrongful attacks on the character of individuals or even simply the publication, storage or processing of information that is considered sensitive in nature. The ECtHR has rules that states must put in place measures to prevent the harmful use of information in such contexts (where it cannot be justified). In *Marper* the ECtHR confirmed that Article 8 of the ECHR can be of application where personal data is processed by the state. In that case (which related to the detection of crime) the court affirmed that the state could only make use of such information where it has a valid goal, where it is both necessary and proportional and where it is described in law.[54] Two important areas of protection that may be relevant to SSEs may likely apply as a result of Article 8. The first is the use or release of sensitive information that is of a private nature. The second relates to wrongful attacks on the integrity or reputation of individuals. The potential relevance of these two areas of case law for SSEs is discussed below.

A The use of private information

The ECHR has confirmed that the ability to control what happens to one's private information falls within Article 8 ECHR. It stated in *Marper* [55] that; "The mere storing of data relating to the private life of an individual amounts to an interference within the meaning of Article 8". This is important because it will also apply in areas where the GDPR does not, e.g. in matters related to the prevention of crime or the maintenance of public security. This means that where certain expressions (or their preparation) use personal data and are not covered by data protection law such as the GDPR, Article 8 may still offer protection to data subjects. This protection essentially requires that the use of personal data be for a valid purpose, that it be described in law and

54 D Kim, "Case: *S. and Marper v. United Kingdom*", *Chicago-Kent Journal of International and Comparative Law* 9, no. 1 (2009).

55 *Marper v. the United Kingdom*, judgment (Grand Chamber) of 4 December 2008, § 67.

that it be both necessary and proportional.[56] *Marper* confirmed this in a case involving the storage of data by the state (fingerprints and DNA), the court has also confirmed that it will apply to other forms of operation. In *Peck v. the United Kingdom*[57] the ECtHR confirmed that releasing information such as images of individuals captured on CCTV to the public could amount to a violation of Article 8.[58] Indeed the protection offered by Article 8 goes far beyond incriminating camera images and can be applied to many forms of private information. The case law of the court has also required that states put in place adequate legal tools to provide individuals with mechanisms of redress where they have been harmed by the release of such information.[59] These factors mean that states should be wary of releasing private information into the public domain, including ***inter alia in*** the context of an SSE.

Although most of the case law of the court relates to accidental release of data, there are also cases that clearly relate to various forms of expressive activity, including publishing information in official publications such as a state gazette.[60] The court's case law under Article 8 does not mean, however, that states cannot release any private information (even where it is stigmatizing). What it does mean is that it can only do so where it has valid grounds for so doing as outlined in Article 8(2) of the ECHR (i.e. where there is a valid aim, the measure is described in law and it is necessary and proportional). This means that states may be able to engage individual privacy rights in a number of areas where these conditions are met. This means that in areas related to public health, the fight against crime or national security the state will be able to collect and use personal data where it is described in law and is necessary and proportional. SSEs will thus be permissible in these areas where these conditions are met. Article 8 could arguably be considered as a source of law that could provide some of the elements the author argued for in his normative position in Chapter 3 (i.e. the ability of the state to use stigmatizing expression in certain contexts, e.g. functional stigmatization, fair criticism, etc.). This role is, however, limited by the need to respect individual rights under Article 10 to freedom of expression, meaning that the court has limited room to intervene in matters of expression, even where they may be stigmatizing.

56 The permissible aims of a measure must fall within those described in Article 8(2), i.e. "[the measure] is necessary in a democratic society in the interests of national security, public safety or the economic well-being of the country, for the prevention of disorder or crime, for the protection of health or morals, or for the protection of the rights and freedoms of others".

57 *Peck v. United Kingdom* (2003) 36 EHRR 41.

58 The court found that the disclosure of the footage by a municipal council had not been accompanied by sufficient safeguards and constituted disproportionate and unjustified interference with the applicant's private life, in breach of Article 8 of the Convention.

59 *Armonas v. Lithuania* ECHR (2009) 48 EHRR 53, [2009] EMLR 7, 36919/02.

60 *Sõro v. Estonia* (Application no. 22588/08).

B Unjustified attacks upon reputation

Not all SSEs are harmful because they release real facts or data concerning specific individuals. Some may relate to unwarranted attacks upon an individual's character and reputation. Imagine, for example, a situation where somebody is accused of having 'terrorist sympathies', of being promiscuous, or an alcoholic. SSEs that make such assertions need not invoke specific facts or evidence but can cause harm by accusation or inference alone. In such instances the SSE may result intentionally or unintentionally in individuals being linked to stigmatizing stereotypes (see section 2 above). The court confirmed in the *Axel Springer* case that "[T]he right to protection of reputation is a right which is protected by Article 8 of the Convention as part of the right to respect for private life".[61] In the case of *Axel* the ECtHR effectively confirmed that states must have laws in place that prevent serious and unfounded attacks on an individual's reputation. This includes serious and unfounded attacks on individual character (e.g. related to libel or defamation). Article 8 will not, however, be engaged by every form of attack upon reputation no matter how slight. As the court stated:

> "In order for Article 8 to come into play, however, an attack on a person's reputation must attain a certain level of seriousness and in a manner causing prejudice to personal enjoyment of the right to respect for private life … The Court has held, moreover, that Article 8 cannot be relied on in order to complain of a loss of reputation which is the foreseeable consequence of one's own actions such as, for example, the commission of a criminal offence.

With these comments the court effectively established a threshold below which Article 8 would not be of application. This means that not all SSEs that are capable of constituting an attack on an individual's reputation are likely to be capable of infringing Article 8. Moderate attacks on character which are common in the political process, for example, are likely to fall under this category. This could include instances where political figures, for example ministers, raise such issues in order to politically harm those perceived as opponents (Chapter 3). In cases involving disputes over freedom of expression the ECtHR will also consider individual rights under Article 10 ECHR, which protects freedom of expression. The requirements of this article (which is further discussed in section 5D) means that the court will only prohibit expressions (including SSEs) where they cause harm that is serious enough to warrant infringement of an individual's Article 10 ECHR rights. This will not always be the case with SSEs, particularly where the stigmatization that occurs can be relatively minor in nature.[62] In addition the ECtHR has drawn a distinction between harm to reputation that occurs through the use of facts and value judgements. The former represents a statement of factual

61 *Axel Springer AG v. Germany*, judgment (Grand Chamber) of 7 February 2012, §§ 83–84.

62 See Chapter 2 section 3 for a discussion on how the stigmatizing forces can range from being mild to severe in nature.

information and can accordingly be proved or disproved. The latter represent an individual appraisal of the value of certain facts. Value judgements, unlike allegations of fact are not provable or disprovable. It is for this reason that the court has stated that value judgements are a protected form of free speech under Article 10. As a result of this, appraisals of the value of certain individuals should not, according to the court, be prohibited.[63] Accordingly calling individuals opportunistic, immoral or undignified would represent a value judgement and thus find protection under Article 8. Again, this means that a significant number of SSEs that expressly link individuals to stigmatized traits will enjoy protection under Article 10 ECHR. This arguably limits the role of the ECHR to meet some of the requirements of the author's normative vision given that some expressions can be very stigmatizing even where they are based on fact (i.e. not value judgements).

5 Legal approaches related to wide concepts of privacy – attacks on groups

Sections 3–4 considered laws linked to themes of informational privacy. Whilst these may have some relevance to SSEs, they are limited to those SSEs that relate to specific individuals (or where their data has been used in preparation of the SSE). However, as Chapter 1 illustrated, many SSEs need not refer to specific individuals at all. SSEs are noteworthy because they can bring about harm without referring to specific individuals at all. This means that informational privacy approaches may not be capable of having much effect on most SSEs. The rest of this chapter will consider ECtHR case law that seemingly relates to a broader conception of privacy that goes beyond the use of personal information. Laws related to broader concepts of privacy are common. They find their home within international treaties, constitutional provisions and national legislation. Such provisions may often be of potentially extremely broad application but are unlikely to have the precision and complexity of approaches designed to ensure informational privacy such as the GDPR. Article 8 of the ECHR provides the perfect example of this. As section 4 above discussed the ECtHR has produced important case law concerning informational privacy. This, however, represents only one facet of the ECtHR's Article 8 jurisprudence. It has interpreted the broad protection Article 8 offers to private and family life as offering protection to individuals in a wide array of circumstances and contexts. This can range from access to schools and other public services, rights related to housing or guarantees against unjustified surveillance.[64] Indeed the court itself has described the ECHR and Article 8 as being a 'living instrument', with a breadth that knows no fixed limit, allowing its protection to be adapted with changing times. Given this, it is perhaps not a surprise that some of the court's case law can be linked to themes of privacy as liberty as described above in section 2.

63 *Lingens v. Austria* (1986) 8 EHRR 407.

64 Theil, "Is the 'Living Instrument' Approach of the European Court of Human Rights Compatible with the ECHR and International Law?"

Article 8 ECHR in particular offers a broad protection to individuals to define their own beliefs, opinions and personalities, and (unless there are good reasons) to live life according to their own vision of the good.[65] In addition as section B below describes the court has in its jurisprudence also seemingly recognized the relevance of the phenomenon of stigmatization. The ECtHR has stated that Article 8 protects *inter alia* the ability of individuals to form their own personality free from unnecessary obstruction. It is its case law related to this article which is most relevant to the ability of individuals to be able to determine their own course in life.[66] Despite this potential relevance to SSEs there are a number of issues which may serve to limit its application in reality. These issues are discussed further below.

A The ECtHR recognizes psychological aspects of privacy

The ECHR has shown itself on a number of occasions to be concerned by activities that are capable of having a psychological impact on individuals that would make it difficult for them to form their own personalities and social relationships without hindrance.[67] This has most notably occurred in the context of cases concerning Article 8, which perhaps more than any other article covers the broadest range of potential rights. It has a potentially enormous and ever expanding coverage.[68] The ECtHR has stated this coverage extends to the notion of personal autonomy, a notion that according to the court is "an important principle underlying the interpretation [of Article 8]".[69] In *AKSU v. Turkey* the court furthermore stated that personal autonomy can embrace "multiple aspects of [a] person's physical and social identity".[70] In addition, the court has recognized "[the] negative stereotyping of a group when it reaches a certain level is capable of impacting on [a] group's sense of self identity and the feeling of self-worth and self-confidence of members of the group."[71] These aspects can, according to the court, entail an

65 For an interesting discussion on how the ECHR has acted to protect sexual minorities under the concept of privacy see P Johnson, "'An Essentially Private Manifestation of Human Personality': Constructions of Homosexuality in the European Court of Human Rights", *Human Rights Law Review* 10, no. 1 (2010).

66 Other ECHR articles also have the potential to contribute to the general protection of an individual's ability to define themselves as he or she would wish. These include Article 3 (freedom from inhuman and degrading treatment) and Article 9 (religious freedom and freedom of conscience). Unfortunately, a full description is beyond the scope of this chapter.

67 For a discussion on how these approaches can vary between Articles 8 and 9 see J Marshall, "Women's Right to Autonomy and Identity in European Human Rights Law: Manifesting One's Religion", *Res Publica* 14, no. 3 (2008).

68 S & Marper v. United Kingdom [2008] ECHR 1581 p66.

69 Pretty v the United Kingdom, Application no. 2346/02 (ECHR, 29 April 2002) para 61.

70 *AKSU v. Turkey* [2011] ECHR 499 para 58.

71 For more on the anti-stereotyping approach of the ECtHR (with a particular perspective on gender issues) see A Timmer, "Toward an Anti-Stereotyping Approach for the European Court of Human Rights", *Human Rights Law Review* 11, no. 4 (2011).

engagement of Article 8 ECHR. In *Marper v. UK* [72] the court stated that a right to a "physical and social identity" includes the right to "establish and develop relationships with other human beings and the outside world". In addition, the court stated that "the concept of private life moreover includes elements relating to a person's right to their image". The statements indicate that the ECtHR views privacy (in terms of personal liberty) as being able to go beyond a mere freedom from physical impediments to also include psychological forces that may act as barriers to liberty. In particular it has recognized Article 8 also covers a person's ability to "view themselves as they wish' and that person's ability to live his or her own life in the manner that they wish as falling within the concept of 'a right to a private life".[73] This is striking for its similarity to the notion of self-respect described by Rawls, a notion that lay at the heart of the author's normative reasoning in Chapter 3.

B The court has also directly linked Article 8 and the protection of privacy to stigmatization

The ECtHR has, on several occasions, explicitly made the connection with stigmatization and personal liberty in a number of Article 8 cases. Whilst these cases may not revolve around the concept of stigmatization, the court's references to it are nonetheless significant, confirming that the court is receptive to recognizing issues linked to stigmatization when considering Article 8. In *Marper* [74] the court was concerned with the system of retention of genetic samples from individuals that have been arrested for crimes in the UK.[75] The court found the application of this system to minors in a blanket manner to be a breach of their Article 8 rights. After finding that the retention of genetic data constituted an engagement of the claimant's Article 8 rights, the court proceeded to decide whether such engagement was justified. The court was particularly concerned with the retention of DNA samples taken from individuals who were never convicted, including in this case children. It stated that:

> of particular concern in the present case is the risk of stigmatization stemming from the fact that persons in the position of the applicants, who have not been

72 *S & Marper v. United Kingdom* ([2008] ECHR 1581).

73 For many examples of how this right is viewed as manifesting itself in differing contexts see N Koffeman, "(The Right to) Personal Autonomy in the Case Law of the European Court of Human Rights (Nota Opgesteld Ten Behoeve Van De Staatscommissie Grondwet)", *External Research Report - Leiden University* (2010). Available at https://openaccess.leidenuniv.nl/handle/1887/15890

74 *S & Marper v. United Kingdom* ([2008] ECHR 1581).

75 The UK system was (and is) one the most stringent in the world, one that allows the retention of cellular samples and DNA profiles after the arrest of individuals for many crimes even if the detention did not lead to a trial, let alone a conviction. These powers were provided by the Police and Criminal Evidence Act 1984.

> convicted of any offence and are entitled to the presumption of innocence, are treated in the same way as convicted persons.[76]

The case of *A, B and C v. Ireland* ([2010] ECHR 2032) involved Irish applicants that were forced to travel to the UK to obtain an abortion as a result of the ban on obtaining such procedures in the Irish Republic. Two of the applicants alleged that their rights under Article 8 were breached as they could not obtain an abortion where they were resident.[77] The courts accepted that their rights under Article 8 were clearly engaged as the ban on abortion in Ireland affected the claimants' right to form a family as they wished. The court also recognized that there was an element of stigmatization for the women involved (in being forced to travel to a neighbouring country for an act that was considered illegal and immoral at home),[78] but did not consider that it was sufficient to render the illegality of abortion in Ireland disproportional.[79] The case demonstrates that whilst the court is willing to recognize stigmatization as a factor to be considered when deciding upon the proportionality of a measure, its presence may be acceptable under certain circumstances and may not necessarily render a measure a breach of Article 8.

In the case of *S.A.S. v. France* [80] (a case which considered both Article 8 and Article 9) which concerned the permissibility of the French law banning the wearing of the full face veil in public, the court referred to the opinion of the National Advisory Commission on Human Rights that a blanket ban on the public wearing of the full face veil would "run the risk of stigmatizing Muslims".[81] Additionally, the court quoted a 2006 report from the United Nations Special Rapporteur on Freedom of Religion which stated that when looking at restrictions on religious dress, the administration or judiciary should ask itself:

> [I]is the restriction in question appropriate having regard to the legitimate interest that it seeks to protect, is it the least restrictive, has it involved a balancing of the competing interests, is it likely to promote religious intolerance and does it avoid stigmatizing any particular religious community?[82]

In addition to cases that focus on Article 8 in isolation the court has invoked the concept of stigma in a number of cases that involved the application of Article 8 in

76 *S and Marper v United Kingdom* [2008] ECHR 1581 para 66. One aspect that convinced the court of this was the fact that genetic profiles could be used to discern familial relationships with other individuals.

77 *A, B and C* paras 212–214.

78 For more on the stigma surrounding abortion see: A Kumar, L Hessini, and E Mitchell, "Conceptualising Abortion Stigma", *Culture Health and Sexuality* (2009).

79 *A, B and C* para 241.

80 *S.A.S. v. France* (Application no. 43835/11).

81 *S.A.S v. France* para 18. Most of the court's discussion in *S.A.S* concerned Article 9. The court did, however, state that the issues at hand meant that the court could also have heard the case under Article 8.

82 *S.A.S v. France* para 92.

conjunction with Article 14, i.e. discrimination cases.[83] In the case of *Kiyutin v. Russia*, [84] for example. the court found that the discriminatory deportation of foreigners with HIV would *inter alia* bring about an increased level of stigmatization. The ECtHR stated:

> that people living with HIV are a vulnerable group with a history of prejudice and stigmatisation and that the State should be afforded only a narrow margin of appreciation in choosing measures that single out this group for differential treatment on the basis of their HIV status.[85]

In the case of *Bayev v. Russia* [86] the court also concluded that a discriminatory law outlawing presenting gay propaganda to children would have harmful stigmatizing effects on both gay adults and pubescent children. The court notably stated that "by adopting such laws the authorities reinforce stigma and prejudice and encourage homophobia, which is incompatible with the notions of equality, pluralism and tolerance inherent in a democratic society".

On other occasions, however, the court has failed to explicitly mention issues of stigmatization despite its obvious relevance in the case before it. A prominent example was the case of *AKSU* (discussed further in section C). This case involved the publication of passages in both an academic textbook and dictionary that were insulting to the country's Roma community. Whilst the court acknowledged the negative effect this could have on the Roma community, it failed to overtly raise stigma as an issue to be considered despite the obvious existence of stigmatizing factors in the case. Whilst this may, to a certain extent, represent an issue concerning the terminology that the court chooses to employ, it also shows that the concept of stigmatization is by no means one that exists at the forefront of its thinking.[87]

C The ECtHR has never found a stigmatizing expression alone to engage Article 8

Most ECHR cases concerning harmful expressions (such as hate speech) fall into one category – appeals under Article 10 ECHR against a conviction under hate speech legislation. Despite the fact that the court has invoked both a negative and

83 Chapter 5 discusses the application of anti-discrimination law to SSEs in further depth. This will not be duplicated here. See also P Quinn, "The Problem of Stigmatizing Expressions – the Limits of Anti-Discrimination Approaches", *International Journal of Discrimination and the Law* 17, no. 1 (2017).

84 *Kiyutin v. Russia* (Application no. 2700/10) [2011] ECHR 439.

85 *Kiyutin v. Russia* para 64.

86 *Bayev and Others v. Russia* (Application nos 67667/09, 44092/12 and 56717/12).

87 The obvious applicability of issues of stigmatization to the case was only highlighted by Judge Gyuluman in his dissenting opinion. He evoked the Council of Europe High Level Meeting on Roma in October 2010. This adopted the "Strasbourg Declaration on Roma" CM (2010) 133.. Available at http://unipd-entrodirittiumani.it/public/docs/the_strasbourg_declaration_on_roma.pdf

a positive duty under Article 8, and that the court has seemingly accepted that certain harmful expressions are capable of engaging Article 8, the ECtHR has never actually found the state itself to have violated the Article 8 rights of individuals with its own expressions.[88] As one research paper points out "all the hate speech-related applications brought before the ECtHR concerned either a claim that the state sanctioned an expression which was not hate speech or the state did not sanction expressions of hate speech".[89] As Chapter 4 described, however, many types of stigmatizing state expression would not fall into such a category (given the subtle nature of many forms of stigmatization which would be unlikely to meet the threshold of hate speech).

At present little in the case law of the court indicates that Article 8 can be engaged by stigmatizing statements or expressions alone (i.e. in the absence of other more corporeal factors).[90] This raises doubts about whether the ECtHR would actually apply Article 8 to the types of statements and expressions this book is concerned with. In most of the above examples, the ECHR considered stigmatization as a factor only in deciding whether a breach of Article 8 had occurred. As with Article 14 cases (discussed in Chapter 5) this has been where Article 8 had already been obviously engaged by some other, more corporeal engaging factors (e.g. in *Marper* the retention of sensitive personal information or in *A.B.C.* controls on access to abortions).[91] In these cases it did not find 'stigmatization alone' (i.e. as would be the case with a stigmatizing expression) to be capable of engaging Article 8. Thus, whilst the ECtHR has been willing to consider stigmatization when deciding if some other engaging factor was a breach of Article 8, it has thus far not seen fit to find stigmatization alone (i.e. stigmatizing statements) as something that is capable of engaging Article 8.

AKSU represents an important exception whereby the alleged infringement was brought about by expressive activities. In that case the court implied that the publication of certain materials in an academic text and in a dictionary (that contained offensive terms and assertions concerning the Roma community) represented an "interference" with the Article 8 rights of the respondents. The individuals concerned sought to argue that the state had a positive duty to prevent harmful expressive activity against the group. In that case the court considered that the state had a duty to balance the conflicting Article 8 rights of the Roma community with the right to freedom of expression of those who had published the remarks in question.[92] The

88 See *Hate Speech and Beyond: Targeting the Gulen Movement in Turkey*, Paper 16, June 2014 (Rethink Institute, Washington DC).

89 Ibid. Quote taken from page 31.

90 Chapter 1 section 1 discussed the concept of 'nodality' raised by Hoods and Margretts. This concept described activities of the state that are purely informational and involve few if any physical impositions. See C Hood and H Margretts, *The Tools of Government in the Digital Age* (New York: Palgrave Macmillan, 2006).

91 There is an important similarity here with the concept of 'treatment' discussed in Chapter 5 concerning the ECtHR's anti-discrimination approach. It reflects a consistent problem legal approaches have in engaging acts that are solely expressive in nature and do not have binding consequences.

92 The case of *AKSU* can, therefore, be thought of as a general exception to the rule of thumb described above where expression cases that come before the court are usually analysed mainly in the context of Article 10 and without a consideration of Article 8.

ECtHR stated that the essential object of Article 8 was to "protect the individual against arbitrary interference by the public authorities". The court stated furthermore that this does "not merely compel the State to abstain from such interference: in addition to this negative undertaking there may be positive obligations inherent in the effective respect for private life".[93] Such a duty may, therefore, require the adoption of measures designed to secure respect for private and family life. These obligations may involve the "adoption of measures designed to secure respect for private life even in the sphere of the relations of individuals between themselves".[94]

Unfortunately, however (in the opinion of the author), the analysis in this case was somewhat lacking in coherence. This is because the court made no effort to elaborate what exactly had engaged Article 8 rights, opting effectively to take such engagement for granted and not in need of further elaboration. The ECtHR did not specifically invoke the concept of stigmatization, though it did invoke a related concept of 'negative stereotypes'. The court accordingly did not confirm that there was an engagement of Article 8 rights arising from the stigmatizing content of the remarks (or from any other factor for that matter).[95] Thus, whilst the *AKSU* judgment may show that expressive activities such as entries in dictionaries and academic reports can be capable of engaging Article 8, it does not confirm why. Although the remarks in question were undoubtedly stigmatizing for members of the Roma community, it is not possible to know if this is the reason why the court felt that an engagement had so obviously occurred.

An important factor that should be considered is that in *AKSU* the court seems to have viewed the remarks in question as constituting hate speech. The ECtHR highlighted the fact that the Turkish court had considered the case under parts of the criminal code concerned with hate speech and its judgment can be read as implicitly accepting this.[96] This factor means that thinking of ASKU as a case that concerned remarks that were 'merely stigmatizing' would be dubious. As Chapter 4 discussed, hate speech arguably goes beyond stigmatization in its generation of an atmosphere of hate and fear and the problems that it can pose for public order. Individuals who respond to hate speech by altering their behaviour may often be acting rationally to avoid threats, intimidation or even the possibility of violence. This is often not the case with stigmatization where individual responses may appear irrational and

93 *AKSU v. Turkey* [2011] ECHR 449.
para 59.

94 *Tavlı v. Turkey* (Application no. 11449/02), § 28, 9 November 2006, and *Ciubotaru*, cited above, p5000.

95 *AKSU.* See dissenting opinion of Judge Gyulumyan at para 8. Whilst the *AKSU* judgment did mention the concept of stigmatization (once) it was not in the pronouncement of the majority, but in the minority opinion of Judge Gyulumyan, who was quoting the Council of Europe's "Strasbourg Declaration on Roma" and the problems of stigmatization that are associated with hate speech.

96 *AKSU* paras 36 and 37. The court invoked Article 312 of the old Turkish Criminal Code and Article 216 of the new code.

be highly subjective.[97] In addition to a possible grounding in hate speech (and not stigmatization), the court also looked into the authenticity of the remarks made, i.e. in terms of their factual legitimacy.[98] Such questions indicate a focus more centred on issues associated with concepts such as slander, libel and others that are focused on the factual truth of an assertion. As Chapter 1 discussed the stigmatizing nature of acts and expressions is not necessarily linked to their factual basis (or lack thereof). Pointing out an embarrassing truth for a group can be stigmatizing but will not be slanderous or libellous. Imagine the public proclamation that 'Germans were responsible for the Holocaust'.[99] This statement may have some factual accuracy but will nonetheless be stigmatizing. The ambiguities in the court's reasoning and the presence of other potential engaging factors makes relying on the *AKSU* decision as an authority to suggest that statements or expressions that are merely stigmatizing may, in general, be capable of engaging Article 8 dubious.

D The role of Article 10 should not be forgotten

The limited role the ECtHR has played so far in hindering stigmatizing expression must be seen in the context of the requirements it has also outlined arising out of Article 10 ECHR.[100] This article guarantees that individuals cannot have their freedom of expression infringed unless there is a valid (and also necessary and proportional reason for doing so). As Chapter 5 discussed, Article 10 guarantees the right of individuals to express themselves even when it can "offend, shock or disturb others".[101] Whilst such a requirement may seem startling it is in reality a core element of all democratic societies. Without this, the ability to freely discuss and debate within democratic societies would be severely limited. Given this the court has a limited room for manoeuvre to infringe upon the liberty of expression of private individuals. Whilst the court has been willing to find valid exceptions to this right in order to prevent hate speech[102] it has not yet done so for lesser forms of harmful speech including expression that was merely stigmatizing (including SSEs). In such cases the question thus arises not only of whether the ECtHR

97 See C Miller and C Kaiser, "A Theoretical Perspective on Coping with Stigma", *Journal of Social Issues* 57, no. 1 (2001); M Deal, "Aversive Disablism: Subtle Prejudice toward Disabled People", *Disability & Society* 22 (2007) and Chapter 1 section 5 of this book.

98 *AKSU* para 70 the court stated, "In the Court's opinion, these conclusions cannot be considered to be unreasonable or based on a misrepresentation of the relevant facts".

99 Example taken from Quinn and De Hert, "Self Respect—a ""Rawlsian Primary Good' Unprotected by the European Convention on Human Rights and Its Lack of a Coherent Approach to Stigmatization?" p42

100 See "Freedom of Expression in Europe Case-law Concerning Article 10 of the European Convention on Human Rights" produced on behalf of the ECHR. Available at https://www.echr.coe.int/LibraryDocs/DG2/HRFILES/DG2-EN-HRFILES-18 (2007).pdf

101 *Handyside v. the United Kingdom*, 7 December 1976, Series A No. 24, § 49.

102 See, for example, *Belkacem v. Belgium* (2017) ECHR 253.

would be willing to see stigmatization as being capable of engaging Article 8 but also whether it would be sufficiently severe to warrant prohibition given the requirements of Article 10.

One matter that further complicates this discussion is that applicability of Article 10 to state speech is not certain. The rights enshrined within the ECHR are in general intended to offer protection to private individuals and not the state. Indeed, the reality is the ECHR represents a list of rights which individuals can impose against the state. The possibility for the state to invoke Article 10 in order to guarantee its freedom of speech is indeed questionable at best.[103] This raises the question of whether the court would even consider the effect of Article 10 if it were to hear a case concerning an SSE (as it would do in a case that involved private speech). As Chapter 4 discusses state expression is a complex affair and may also involve elements of private speech. This is true for individuals with a political character such as ministers and mayors. Furthermore, where public servants (or the 'human component' as Chapter 4 discusses) use harmful expression such as hate speech the criminal law may, in many jurisdictions, see them as acting outside the course of their duty and thus speaking as private individuals. Laws forbidding highly stigmatizing expression (were they to exist) would, therefore, in a number of circumstances be likely to attract the potential application of Article 10 of the ECtHR.[104]

E The ECHR and SSEs – a story not yet finished?

It is thus not possible at present to state that the ECHR is willing, using Article 8, to limit some or any stigmatizing state expressions made against groups (and not specific individuals). Whilst the court has recognized a need to limit hate speech, such acts of expression exist at the extreme end of harmful expression and can in some respects even be considered as being conceptually different (see Chapter 4). The vast majority of SSEs are likely to fall below the bar of hate speech.[105] Despite the harm that SSEs can cause there is thus at present little indication the ECtHR would ever be willing to see them as constituting a violation of Article 8.

This does not mean, however, that one can state with confidence that the court would never be willing to do so. It is important to bear in mind that the court has considered relatively few expression cases under Article 8. Most such cases are actually heard under Article 10 which safeguards freedom of expression. This reflects the dynamics of most expression cases and how they are brought before

103 This is unlike the application of the First[t] Amendment to state speech under the US Constitution. For more see Chapter 7.

104 Article 10 also offers protection to state employees in many instances where the state may attempt to prohibit their expression. See, for example, *Vogt v. Germany*, judgment of 26 September 1995, Series A No. 323.

105 Mantovani and Quinn, "Mhealth and Data Protection – the Letter and the Spirit of Consent Legal Requirements"; Quinn, "The Problem of Stigmatizing Expressions – the Limits of Anti-Discrimination Approaches".

the court. Most relate to appeals against the imposition of national hate speech laws. By contrast few cases come before the court where the complainant is seeking to have speech or expression (including SSEs) prohibited. The sample of cases available that can provide guidance on this matter is thus somewhat limited. Given this, one could surmise that the reason the court has not ruled an SSE is capable of constituting an engagement of Article 8 is because the right case has not come before it. Were this to happen (e.g. with an SSE that was extremely stigmatizing for a sensitive or vulnerable group) there is at present no reason to think that it would not be able to consider an SSE as capable of engaging Article 8, though it would, of course, have to contend with the requirements of Article 10 ECHR as discussed above in section 5D.

Conclusion

Stigmatization as a phenomenon undoubtedly has links with the concept of privacy. This includes privacy viewed in a narrow sense as informational self-determination and in a wider sense as allowing individuals to be free from steering forces. The first relates primarily to the need for individuals to be able to prevent themselves from being linked to traits that are stigmatized. Such a possibility is important given the very real consequences stigmatization can have (discussed in Chapter 2). Two examples of legal approaches that could be connected to these themes were discussed within this chapter. These included the EU's GDPR and case law of the ECtHR under Article 8 ECHR. Both require controls on the use of personal data and limit how it can be used. The GDPR in particular outlines a number of rights and obligations that could potentially have relevance for both the preparation of SSEs and state expressions themselves. Requirements such as consent or a right of access and erasure could allow individuals to have their data deleted before it can be used in an expression. They could also be of relevance in certain cases where an expression has already occurred, for instance potentially allowing details of individuals to be removed from a website or from social media. Whilst the case law of Article 8 ECHR may be less precise in nature than the GDPR, its applicability is seemingly broader, potentially applying in certain instances where the GDPR does not (including in areas related to the detection of crime and public security). In addition to the use of data that can be considered of a private nature (i.e. linked to a specific individual), Article 8 can be understood as prohibiting certain expressions that may represent an attack on an individual's personality or which may be defamatory. These provisions mean that whilst the state may well be able to use personal data in SSEs (or in their preparation) it may have to take into account the effect it can have on particular individuals, including where it can bring about potentially stigmatizing effects. It will also only be able to do so where this is necessary to meet one of a number of goals envisaged within Article 8(2) ECHR.

This legal framework will, however, probably not apply to SSEs that do not contain personal information. This is important given that the vast majority of SSEs (as highlighted in Chapter 1) will not contain personal data. The GDPR, for example, specifically excludes its application to data which is not personal in nature (i.e. data which cannot be linked to a specific individual). Similarly, the ECtHR's case law in cases like *Marper* involved instances where personal information was being used in ways that raised serious concern. Given this, this chapter then asked whether legal approaches inspired by a broader conception of privacy exist and whether it would be applicable to SSEs. Whilst the ECtHR has recognized a broader concept, allowing individuals to lead their life in a manner they would wish, it has thus far not ruled that a purely expressive act (by the state or anyone else) is capable of engaging Article 8. The only exception to this is perhaps with regard to hate speech, where the court has indicated that there is a positive duty on states to take measures to prevent it. As Chapter 4 discussed, however, hate speech is in many ways conceptually different from remarks that are merely stigmatizing. In addition, many forms of SSE are likely to be considered of an intensity that would be far below that normally considered as hate speech.

The importance of such a threshold is underlined by the fact that the ECtHR must take into consideration Article 10 ECHR and the protection it offers for liberty of expression. This article allows infringement of expression only in certain circumstances and where it is necessary and proportional. Whether the court would be willing to do so in many instances of expression is doubtful, especially given that many forms of SSE can be considered mild in comparison to phenomena such as hate speech. Given the need to respect the threshold which Article 10 sets, including the right to "shock, offend and disturb", it seems unlikely that the ECtHR would see many of the examples of SSE discussed in Chapter 1 as being sufficiently harmful to require prohibition under Article 8. A tolerance of many moderately harmfully stigmatizing expressions is not necessarily a bad thing however, given as the author argued in Chapter 3 in his normative prospectus that it is often necessary for the state to stigmatize certain groups to achieve a valid aim (e.g. through functional stigmatization or fair criticism). In addition, the democratic character of the modern state means that expecting it to totally refrain from all forms of stigmatization is not realistic (see discussion on political forms of stigmatization in Chapter 3).

Privacy approaches arguably, therefore, have some, albeit limited, role to play in meeting the normative position demanded by the author. In the limited instances that they are applicable they may allow SSEs to be scrutinized in the manner that was envisaged in the author's normative approach (most notably those principles that demand that SSEs only occur for good reasons). The extent of applicability, however, remains to be seen. If courts such as the ECtHR were willing to find expressive acts that refer only to groups as capable of infringing privacy rights then the requirements of Article 8(2) (relating to where engagement may be permitted) would seemingly allow for an analysis of the necessity and proportionality of the measures in question (i.e. SSEs). This would seemingly allow unnecessarily harmful SSEs to be checked whilst those SSEs that are necessary to be permitted. Similarly, the existence of Article 10 will ensure that a high level of freedom of expression, especially concerning political expression (though the question of precisely which forms of SSE it could apply to is still open). Whilst this was also something the author argued for in his normative position, the threshold which the ECtHR has set for allowing engagement under Article 10(2) means that only the most extreme forms of harmful expression are capable of being sanctioned. This threshold seemingly does not permit the form of fine-tuned analysis that the author called for in his normative position given that the overwhelming majority of SSEs will fall below it (see Chapter 3).

Bibliography

Banisar, D, and S Davies. "Global Trends in Privacy Protection: An International Survey of Privacy, Data Protection and Surveillance Laws and Developments." *John Marshall Journal of Information and Technology and Privacy Law*, 18, no. 1 (1999): Fall 1999.

Bennet, C. "In Defence of Privacy: The Concept and the Regime." *Surveillance and Society* 8, no. 4 (2011): 485–496.

Courtwright, A. "Justice, Stigma, and the New Epidemiology of Health Disparities." *Bioethics* 23, no. 2 (2009): 90–96.

Deal, M. "Aversive Disablism: Subtle Prejudice toward Disabled People." *Disability & Society* 22 (2007): 93–107.

Einiar Himma, K, and H Tavani. *The Handbook of Information and Computer Ethics.* Englewood Cliffs, Hoboken, NJ: Wiley, 2008.

Goffman, I. *Stigma: Notes on a Spoilt Identity.* Englewood Cliffs, NJ: Prentice Hall, 1963.

Gutwirth, S. *Privacy and the Information Age.* New York: Rowman & Littlefield, 2002.

Gutwirth, S, and P De Hert. "Privacy, Data Protection and Law Enforcement. Opacity of the Individual and Transparency of Power." In *Privacy and Criminal Law*, edited by E Claes, A Duff and S Gutwirth, 61–104. Antwerp: Intersentia, 2006.

Hate Speech and Beyond: Targeting the Gulen Movement in Turkey, Paper 16, June 2014. Washington, DC: Rethink Institute.

Herek, G. "Sexual Stigma and Sexual Prejudice in the United States: A Conceptual Framework." *Nebraska Symposium on Motivation* 54 (2009): 65–111.

Hood, C, and H Margretts. *The Tools of Government in the Digital Age.* New York: Palgrave Macmillan, 2006.

Jasserand, C. "Law Enforcement Access to Personal Data Originally Collected by Private Parties: Missing Data Subjects' Safeguards in Directive 2016/680?" *Computer Law & Security Review* 34 (2018): 154–165.

Johnson, P. "'An Essentially Private Manifestation of Human Personality': Constructions of Homosexuality in the European Court of Human Rights." *Human Rights Law Review* 10, no. 1 (2010): 67–97.

Kim, D. "Case: *S. and Marper v. United Kingdom.*" *Chicago-Kent Journal of International and Comparative Law* 9, no. 1 (2009): Available at: http://scholarship.kentlaw.iit.edu/ckjicl/vol9/iss1/6

Koffeman, N. "(The Right to) Personal Autonomy in the Case Law of the European Court of Human Rights (Nota Opgesteld Ten Behoeve Van De Staatscommissie Grondwet)." *External Research Report – Leiden University* (2010). Available at: https://openaccess.leidenuniv.nl/handle/1887/15890

Kumar, A, L Hessini, and E Mitchell. "Conceptualising Abortion Stigma." *Culture Health and Sexuality* (2009): 1–15.

Lawson, E, F Gardezi, L Calzavara, W Husbands, T Myers, and W Tharao. "HIV/Aids Stigma, Denial, Fear and Discrimination." Toronto: The African and Caribbean Council on HIV/AIDS in Ontario (ACCHO), Behavioural and Epidemiological Studies Unit, University of Toronto, 2006.

Leary, M. "The Social and Psychological Importance of Self-Esteem." In *The Social Psychology of Emotional and Behavioral Problems*, edited by R Kowalski and M Leary. 6, 1, 85–96. Washington, DC: APA, 1999.

Link, B, and J Phelan. "Conceptualizing Stigma." *Annual Review of Sociology* 27 (2001): 363–385.

Mantovani, E, and P Quinn. "Mhealth and Data Protection – the Letter and the Spirit of Consent Legal Requirements." *International Review of Law, Computers & Technology* (2013). doi:10.1080/13600869.2013.801581

Marshall, J. "Women's Right to Autonomy and Identity in European Human Rights Law: Manifesting One's Religion." *Res Publica* 14, no. 3 (2008): 177–192.

Mason, J. *Mason & McCall Smith's Law and Medical Ethics.* Oxford: Oxford University Press, 2005.

Miller, C, and C Kaiser. "A Theoretical Perspective on Coping with Stigma." *Journal of Social Issues* 57, no. 1 (2001): 73–92.

Neuberg, S, D Smith, and T Asher. "Why Do People Stigmatise?: Toward á Biocultural Framework." In *The Social Psychology of Stigma*, edited by T Heatherton, R Kleck, M Hebl and J Hull, 31–61. New York: Guilford Press, 2000.

Nissenbaum, H. "Protecting Privacy in the Information Age: The Problem of Privacy in Public." *Law and Philosophy* 17 (1998): 559–596.

Post, R. "Three Concepts of Privacy." *Faculty Scholarship Series* 185 (2001).

Quinn, P. "The Anonymisation of Research Data — a Pyric Victory for Privacy That Should Not Be Pushed Too Hard by the EU Data Protection Framework?" *European Journal of Health Law* 24 (2017). doi:10.1163/15718093-2341416

Quinn, P. "The Problem of Stigmatizing Expressions -the Limits of Anti-Discrimination Approaches." *International Journal of Discrimination and the Law* 17, no. 1 (2017): 23–50.

Quinn, P. "Crisis Communication in Public Health Emergencies: The Limits of 'Legal Control' and the Risks for Harmful Outcomes in a Digital Age." *Life Sciences, Society and Policy* 14, no. 1 (6 Feb. 2018): 4.

Quinn, P, and P De Hert. "Self Respect—a "Rawlsian Primary Good" Unprotected by the European Convention on Human Rights and Its Lack of a Coherent Approach to Stigmatization?" *The International Law of Discrimination and the Law* 14(2014): 19–53.

Rand, A. *The Fountainhead.* Indianapolis, IN: Bobbs Merrill, 1979.

Rawls, J. "The Priority of Right and Ideas of the Good." *Philosophy & Public Affairs* 17, no. 4 (1988): 251–276.

Rawls, J. *A Theory of Justice.* Cambridge MA: Harvard University Press, 1999.

Roessler, B. "New Ways of Thinking about Privacy." In *Oxford Handbook of Political Theory*, ed. Anne Philips, Bonnie Honig, and John Dryzek, 694–713 (Oxford: Oxford University Press, 2006).

Simon, A. "The Relationship between Stereotypes of and Attitudes toward Lesbians and Gays.". In *Stigma and Sexual Orientation: Understanding Prejudice against Lesbians, Gay Men, and Bisexuals. Psychological Perspectives on Lesbian and Gay Issues*, edited by G Herek, 62–81. Thousand Oaks, CA: Sage Publications, 1998.

Solove, D. *Understanding Privacy.* Cambridge, MA: Harvard University Press, 2008.

Theil, Stefan. "Is the 'Living Instrument' Approach of the European Court of Human Rights Compatible with the ECHR and International Law?" *European Public Law* 23, no. 3 (2017): 587–614.

Timmer, A. "Toward an Anti-Stereotyping Approach for the European Court of Human Rights." *Human Rights Law Review* 11, no. 4 (2011): 707–738.

Tufail, W. "Rotherham, Rochdale, and the Racialised Threat of the 'Muslim Grooming Gang'." *International Journal for Crime, Justice and Social Democracy* 4, no. 3 (2015): 30–43.

7 Carte blanche to stigmatize or a pragmatic reality in a liberal democracy?

1 Introduction

> [T]he theory rests upon a fundamental distinction between belief, opinion and communication of ideas on the one hand, and different forms of conduct on the other. For shorthand purposes we refer to this distinction ... as one between "expression" and "action." ... [I]n order to achieve its desired goals, a society or the state is entitled to exercise control over action—whether by prohibiting or compelling it—on an entirely different and vastly more extensive basis. But expression occupies a specially protected position. In this sector of human conduct, the social right of suppression or compulsion is at its lowest point, in most respects non-existent.
>
> Professor Thomas Emmerson[1]

Using illustrative examples, previous chapters of this book have demonstrated how a range of important legal approaches are likely to have difficulty in engaging the expressive activity of the state. These approaches were selected because they can often be used by individuals to restrain the state from acting in a way that harms them or because they are used in situations that are linked to the concept of stigmatization. They are, therefore, important because they provide private individuals and organizations with binding law that can be enforced in a court of law. Were these mechanisms to be available for use against purely expressive acts they would create the possibility for private individuals to use the courts to halt stigmatizing state expressions (SSEs) or seek remedial measures where harm has been caused. As Chapters 4–6 illustrated, however, this is often not the case. This essentially means that states (and often individuals connected to them) can express themselves without fear of being challenged in court. This provides an expansive freedom of expression and therefore permits many forms of SSEs. The restraint-free nature of this freedom is especially noteworthy when compared to other domains of action where the state can be challenged in a court of law.[2]

1 T Emerson, "Toward a General Theory of the First Amendment," *Yale Law Journal* 72 (1963). Quote taken directly from S Goldberg, "The Government-Speech Doctrine: 'Recently Minted,' but Counterfeit," *University of Louisville Law Review* 49. p55

2 For a discussion on a comparison of these domain see the concept of 'nodality' in Chapter 1.

The question then arises, is this state of affairs intentional or simply the unintended product of the way legal systems are constituted? As section 2 of this chapter discusses, this is a question that often does not have a clear answer in most legal systems. In Europe, for example, there are few legal provisions found in constitutions, statues or human rights instruments that appear to grant the state a high degree of freedom in terms of liberty of expression. Rather it appears that such a situation seems to exist as a result of the cumulative non-engagement of a range of important legal approaches (as has been illustrated thus far in this book). One prominent exception to this can, however, be found in the American concept of 'state speech'. This is a doctrine developed by the US Supreme Court that grants the executive (of which the president is the ultimate head) the right to express itself almost without restriction on any matter of its choosing. Unlike most European legal systems, the US Supreme Court has thus effectively ruled that the state enjoys a right to freedom of expression under the US Constitution. The far ranging effects of such a doctrine are illustrated on a daily basis for all to see with the incendiary tweets of President Trump and the lack of any possibility of taking legal action in response to them.

The fact that there are few hard law approaches available that are capable of impacting upon the expressive activity of the state does not mean that no other mechanisms of control exist. As sections 4–5 discuss alternative mechanisms of control and restraint (to hard forms of law) also exist. These include control over day-to-day state activities by the executive, intervention by legislatures and the creation and implementation of various forms of soft law pertaining to the conduct of public bodies and public servants. Each of these can provide some form of restraint on the expressive activities of the state. These forms of constraint may have several advantageous properties that hard forms of law do not. These include the fact that they are relatively inexpensive, fast and flexible, often not requiring the existence or creation of legislation. Soft law can, for example, be both more flexible and more precise (applying to very specific contexts) and adaptable to changing situations. Not requiring the same lengthy legislative processes as hard law it can be redrafted quickly in response to new problems that are perceived, including with regard to discrimination and stigmatization.

Despite these advantages such methods of control also suffer from important disadvantages in comparison to hard forms of law. Perhaps the most important is that they can often not be activated externally and independently by private individuals, e.g. through an independent court. Individuals (without the help of binding law) can do little to compel executives or legislatures to take action. Where soft forms of law are available, they may not provide any mechanisms that can be activated externally by private individuals but may rather depend on individuals who work within the executive for activation. Even where a mechanism (such as a complaints body) can be activated, complaints will usually not be heard in a truly independent court. As section 3 discusses, this leaves such tribunals (together with the executives or legislatures) open to very majoritarian forms of control. Given that the prejudices and misconception that lie behind many stigmas are often found in majoritarian attitudes to minorities and vulnerable groups, such forms of control may also be influenced by them. The result is that the individuals involved in creating and operating them (and who are ultimately answerable to masters who derive their power and authority from majoritarian political approval) are arguably less likely to be able or willing to recognize or respond to stigmatizing expressions where they occur. Consequently, although alternative mechanisms of control do exist, their effectiveness is questionable and their ability to bring about the normative position described by the author is limited.

2 The expressive freedom of the state can exist in a *de jure* or *de facto* sense

A A de facto *state of freedom of expression is most common*

This book has demonstrated that it is often not easy to challenge the expressive activity of the state in a court or legal tribunal. This situation is common to most Western states. One might expect, given that such a situation is both fundamental to the relationship of the state with its citizens and so seemingly common, that this situation would be well outlined or codified in law. However, this is usually not the case. The freedom enjoyed by the state to express itself is often not explicitly described in constitutions, legislation or other legal codes. Often there is no one judgment or decision that exempts SSEs and other expressive activities from legal challenge. It is rather the cumulative non-applicability of a range of legal approaches that brings about a *de facto* situation of non-restraint. As the chapters of this book have discussed this includes diverse areas such as the criminal law, anti-discrimination law, administrative law and various forms of law that can be grouped under the need to protect individual privacy. What unites this diverse range of legal approaches is that they often provide mechanisms for individuals to hold the state to account for its actions before a court of law. It is not the non-application of one of these approaches that is responsible for this existence of a zone of non-constraint but rather the lack of engagement of all or many of them. This is the situation in most European countries where it is often difficult to find any overt declaration in law concerning SSEs (or the lack of potential restraint that can be exerted upon them). Given this situation of non-restraint (from most forms of binding law) the question arises of the nature of this wide freedom of expression that states seemingly enjoy. Are there no limits upon what a state can say (beyond the limited legal approaches such as hate speech law that may be applicable in some jurisdictions – see Chapter 4)? Is it possible to go further and say that states have a legal right to say (almost) whatever they wish, even where it may be stigmatizing (or worse)? The importance of freedom of expression for private actors is often invoked from various perspectives as being central to the democratic nature of our societies.[3] Often though such freedom is emphasized against the state (often in the form of a negative right not to be interfered with) and is rarely

3 R Post, "Racist Speech, Democracy, and the First Amendment", *Faculty Scholarship Series* 208 (1991).

invoked as giving the state itself rights. This raises the question as to whether a right corresponding to a 'freedom of state expression' actually exists and what legal status it would enjoy if it did. Whilst important rights relating to freedom of speech do exist (including, for example, Article 10 of the European Convention on Human Rights (ECHR) and various constitutional guarantees) these rights normally relate to private citizens to use against the state (i.e. where it is attempting to inhibit free speech and not the other way round. There are few examples of constitutional or legislative provisions that overtly guarantee the state a right to express itself in a manner that it wishes. Rather there is often what appears to be an unspoken and *de facto* situation of non-restraint *vis-à-vis* state expressions (as opposed to a *de jure* situation where such a right is explicitly described in law). In this *de facto* context there is an almost subconscious and unwritten acceptance that a state has the right to express itself freely, even if it does so in way that is stigmatizing and thus capable of producing harmful effects. The subconscious nature of this acceptance is demonstrated by the relative lack of legal cases or academic writing concerning the constraints that may be placed upon state speech.[4]

This *de facto* and silent acceptance of a lack of constraint upon state expression (as is seen in most European countries) can be contrasted the situation in the US where the subject of constraint of state expression has received much attention both in legal judgments and in academic writing.

B The US Supreme Court's overt acknowledgement of 'government speech'

The US Supreme Court has fostered the development of an overt doctrine which, rather than ignoring the expressions of the state, acknowledges and places them on an almost untouchable pedestal. It has focused on an area of activity known as 'government speech'.[5] The concept of 'government speech' is intricately tied to the First Amendment to the US Constitution, which is usually invoked to protect private speech in the US.[6] Unlike most constitutional rights which are concerned with providing rights to citizens, the First Amendment also appears to provide *de*

4 For a legal perspective concerning primarily the ECHR see P Quinn and P De Hert, "Self Respect—a 'Rawlsian Primary Good' Unprotected by the European Convention on Human Rights and Its Lack of a Coherent Approach to Stigmatization?", *The International Journal of Discrimination and the Law* 14 (2014). For a more political science based perspective see Dave Gelders, Geert Bouckaert, and Betteke van Ruler, "Communication Management in the Public Sector: Consequences for Public Communication About Policy Intentions", *Government Information Quarterly* 24, no. 2 (2007); D Gelders and I Oyvind, "Government Communication About Potential Policies: Public Relations, Propaganda or Both?", *Public Relations Review* 36 (2010).

5 C Taylor, "Hate Speech and Government Speech", *Journal of Constitutional Law* 12, no. 4 (2010).

6 The effects of the First Amendment on criminal law are discussed in Chapter 4. It provides the US with an extremely libertarian character in terms of hate speech law. See also Post, "Racist Speech, Democracy, and the First Amendment"; R O'Neil, "Hate Speech, Fighting Words, and Beyond – Why American Law Is Unique", *Albany Law Review* 76, no. 1 (2013); Taylor, "Hate Speech and Government Speech".

facto rights to states in terms of liberty of expression.[7] The application of the First Amendment to government speech is, however, very different from its application to private speech. In the latter context the First Amendment is used to justify a near total lack of restriction on the speech of private individuals (i.e. restricting the state from doing anything to infringe upon private speech). When the First Amendment is applied to the state itself, however, far from having a restrictive effect on the state, it has the opposite effect, seemingly allowing the state to say almost anything that it wishes.[8] It is this basic freedom that forms the core of the government speech doctrine. This doctrine is very interesting from a comparative perspective given that no equivalent doctrine appears to exist in most European countries. In the era of President Donald Trump, a president who seems to relish causing offence daily through *inter alia* the use of Twitter, the effects of this far reaching concept are clearer than ever.

The Supreme Court has outlined the notion of government speech in a number of cases.[9] In *Rust v. Sullivan* [10] the Supreme Court examined the legality of the federal government's ban on federally funded family planning including providing abortion counselling or information on obtaining an abortion. When asked about abortion, doctors working at federally funded institutions were advised to state that their centre does not advocate abortion. In that case the court relied on the argument that if the state were only able to express itself in ways that did not offend any group of individuals the results would be impractical and absurd. The court accordingly stated:

> To hold that the Government unconstitutionally discriminates on the basis of viewpoint when it chooses to fund a program dedicated to advance certain permissible goals, because the program in advancing those goals necessarily discourages alternative goals, would render numerous Government programs constitutionally suspect. When Congress established a National Endowment for Democracy to encourage other countries to adopt democratic principles ... it was not constitutionally required to fund a program to encourage competing lines of political philosophy such as communism and fascism.[11]

The court's remarks in *Rust* demonstrate aptly how it perceives the state is under no obligation to avoid offence to certain groups, or to appear neutral when

7 Such rights are *de facto* in the sense that they only protect the state where it is not in violation of individual constitutional rights.

8 N Murphy, "Context, Not Content: Medium-Based Press Clause Restrictions on Government Speech in the Internet Age", *University of Denver Sports & Entertainment Law Journal* 7 (2009).

9 For an excellent review of the recent Supreme Court jurisprudence on government speech and its implications for novel modes of communication see H Norton and D Keats Citron, "Government Speech 2.0", *Denver University Law Review* 87 (2010).

10 *Rust v. Sullivan* 500 U.S. 173 (1991).

11 *Rust v. Sullivan* 594. Also quoted in Norton and Keats Citron, "Government Speech 2.0". p904

expressing its opinion on a matter.[12] The practical attraction of such a stance is readily apparent, for it would be difficult for the state to express itself on any matter if, in doing so, it would have to avoid offence.[13] As Chapter 3 discussed, the ability of the state to express itself using various information is important in allowing it to achieve its aims.[14] It would otherwise be impossible for the state to declare itself in favour of any particular course of action, policy or even moral standpoint if it had to avoid all possible offence. In *Johanns* [15] the court recognized that in adopting such a principle it was effectively recognizing that tax payers would have to frequently fund various forms of government expression and speech that they might not agree with.[16] Such a situation, according to the court, rather than representing an oppressive act by the state, represents a necessity for a complex and well run state that has to take into account the interests of the whole of society. Such a line of argument reasons that in a pluralistic society all state expressions are likely to cause offence to some group or other who happen to disagree with the state's position on a particular issue.[17]

Whilst the doctrine of government speech is very appealing from a practical perspective, it raises concerns for those concerned with the appearance of a basic level of neutrality from the state towards all groups in society. As was discussed in Chapter 3, [18] this is important in showing that all citizens are valued equally and in doing so fostering a sense of self-respect.[19] Where a state is able to criticize certain groups freely in society without any threat of judicial restriction, there clearly exists the possibility to harm the self-respect of individuals through stigmatizing expressions and other types of statements. It also makes it difficult to envisage how law can be used to ensure the normative position argued for by the

12 It has been reasoned that if a state were to attack certain groups or religions it might run afoul of constitutional provisions against discrimination (i.e. the equal protection clause) or requirements of secularism (i.e. the establishment clause). These arguments have, however, thus far not been tested before the Supreme Court and remain highly speculative. See Taylor, "Hate Speech and Government Speech".

13 The Supreme Court seems to have been motivated by a similar fear or 'plurality angst' in restraining the development of the anti-discrimination approach under the equal protection clause. See also K Yoshino, "The New Equal Protection", *Harvard Law Review* 124 (2011).

14 These include public health information campaigns, tackling criminality, announcements related to national security, the criticism of anti-social behaviour and the facilitation of democratic discussion.

15 *Johanns v. Livestock Marketing Association*, 544 U.S. 550 (2005).

16 Norton and Keats Citron, "Government Speech 2.0". p908

17 It is important to stress that there may be soft forms of law (such as guidelines codes of conduct) that may be applicable, even if hard forms of law are not. This may even be the case in the US where the government enjoys protection under the First Amendment. For more see section 4.

18 See Chapter 3 for a discussion of how state can harm the self-respect of individuals and why this is problematic.

19 J Rawls, *Political Liberalism* (New York: Columbia University Press, 1993). See also C Stark, "Rawlsian Self-Respect", in *Oxford Studies in Normative Ethics*, ed. M Timmons (Oxford: Oxford University Press, 2012).

author in Chapter 3 is met. The doctrine of government speech clearly ignores such issues, focusing itself entirely on facilitating the practical day-to-day operation of the state and upon issues of accountability. In doing so it ignores the psychological effects that it can have on its citizens through its expressions, including those brought about by SSEs. This approach is fitting with the almost libertarian commitment to free speech found elsewhere in the US legal system (see, for example, the discussion of hate speech in Chapter 4).[20] The concept of 'government speech' is furthermore interesting because it represents an overt denial of the importance of such issues, in comparison to the situation in many other states where an apparent blindness to such issues appears to be the incidental result of the way many such laws are fashioned. Whether the approach of most other states is truly incidental or represents the denial of an inconvenient truth is debatable. In many regards, however, the practical outcome is similar, with it being difficult to challenge state expression through mechanisms such as administrative law (see Chapter 5). This arguably permits the state to use expressive activity to achieve the important goals and aims that were discussed in the normative position in Chapter 3 (see discussion concerning 'functional stigmatization' and 'fair criticism') whilst making it difficult to ensure that unnecessarily harmful SSEs are prevented.

C Pure state speech – no danger to private speech?

In the US, opponents of unlimited governmental speech would argue that when the state chooses to support a particular viewpoint in its expression, it inadvertently (or sometimes intentionally) reflects only a part of the many viewpoints in society. In doing so it strengthens such viewpoints at the expense of others. Such viewpoints tend to rely on a 'crowding out' argument that sees government as having unrivalled powers of communication and expression due to its organizational abilities and its perceived moral credibility.[21] Given such advantages, it is argued that when the state chooses to speak on such matters, it can often have the ability to crowd out other messages that may be opposed to its own. The US Supreme Court recognizes the possibility that the state might harm freedom of speech by supporting one group's message in society and crowding out another. It accordingly does not permit the state to censor voices in fora that the state has established as a venue for open debate and exchange of ideas.[22] However, it makes a distinction between instances where the state promotes the voices of one group of citizens over others and where the state itself decides to speak its own viewpoint. The former is not permitted and constitutes a violation of the First Amendment. The latter, however, is permitted, with the court having adopted an approach that seemingly allows the state to speak as loudly as it wishes, even where it is has, as a result of its facilities, the possibility of drowning out opposing views. The only requirement is that in such instances the expression actually be the state's own, and not

20 See also O'Neil, "Hate Speech, Fighting Words, and Beyond – Why American Law Is Unique"; Taylor, "Hate Speech and Government Speech".

21 Norton and Keats Citron, "Government Speech 2.0".

22 Murphy, "Context, Not Content: Medium-Based Press Clause Restrictions on Government Speech in the Internet Age".

that of a private party which it has decided to boost. In reality this theoretical distinction is extremely difficult to apply to real life practical situations.

These requirements were underlined in the seminal *Pleasant Grove City v. Summum* case.[23] This case involved a local municipality that ran a local park in which it had in the past allowed various organizations to add statues and other types of monuments. Some of these had been of a political or religious nature, including a statue related to the Ten Commandments which had been donated by a Christian group.[24] Despite the wide range of previously accepted contributions the municipal authority rejected (in what was a no doubt stigmatizing move) an object by the Summum group (a religious minority) to erect a monument to their faith in the park. The Summum alleged that this was a violation of their right to freedom of expression under the First Amendment as the state had facilitated the expression of other groups but had denied the chance for them to express themselves in a similar manner. The Supreme Court did not, however, agree with this assessment and classified the statues in the park not as private expression, but as government speech which is protected under the First Amendment. Supporting this the court stated that:

> the City has 'effectively controlled' the messages sent by the monuments in the Park by exercising 'final approval authority' over their selection. The City has selected those monuments that it wants to display for the purpose of presenting the image of the City that it wishes to project to all who frequent the Park; it has taken ownership of most of the monuments in the Park, including the Ten Commandments monument that is the focus of respondent's concern.[25]

In reaching such a conclusion the court demonstrated once again that its inspiration was largely practical, as it tried to invoke the absurd possibilities that would occur were it to find otherwise. In order to exemplify this fear the court invoked the idea that if the state had to allow all parties to express themselves equally, the state of New York would have had to reject the Statue of Liberty or, having accepted it, would have had to accept all other offers of statues of a similar size, no matter what the statues represented.[26] Courts in the US have applied this logic not only to high level pronouncements connected to the executive function of the state but also to smaller more basic units that are not usually associated with carrying out a political function. It has thus been applied to state structures as diverse as schools[27] and universities.[28]

23 *Pleasant Grove City v. Summum* 129 S. Ct. 1125 (2009).
24 The park included, for example, a statue dedicated to the September 11 attacks. The park even contained a monument donated by the Fraternal Order of the Eagles.
25 *Summum* 11344.
26 For a discussion on how the Supreme Court has expressed similar sentiments in limiting the extent of its anti-discrimination approach under the First Amendment see Yoshino, "The New Equal Protection".
27 *Page v. Lexington County School District One* 531 F.3d 275 (4th Cir. 2008) (not a Supreme Court decision but from the US Federal Circuit).
28 *Rosenburg v. Rector and Visitors of the University of Virginia* 515 U.S. 819 (1995), *Board of Regents of the University of Wisconsin System v. Southworth* 529 U.S. 217 (2000).

D Government speech – a blank cheque?

The doctrine of government speech is striking in the *carte blanche* freedom it appears to give the state. Although, as sections 4 and 5 discuss, some restraints exist they do so in forms of soft law by virtue of the political process.[29] The result of this is that the medium of expression represents one of the most constraint free ways in which a state can act. One difficulty that often exists is separating government speech from those instances where the government is imposing itself unevenly upon private speech. In attempting to do this the US Supreme Court has relied upon the existence of potential political mechanisms that demonstrate executive control over the speech in question. This was, for example, the case with the *Johanns v. Livestock Marketing Case.*[30] This case involved an advertising campaign by the government that supported certain meat products over others. In that case the court stated that the advertisements amounted to government speech, stating:

> the beef advertisements are subject to political safeguards more than adequate to set them apart from private messages. The program is authorized and the basic message prescribed by federal statute, and specific requirements for the promotions' content are imposed by federal regulations promulgated after notice and comment. The Secretary of Agriculture, a politically accountable official, oversees the program, appoints and dismisses the key personnel, and retains absolute veto power over the advertisements' content, right down to the wording. And Congress, of course, retains oversight authority, not to mention the ability to reform the program at any time. No more is required.[31]

The link between expression and the democratic character of government is an important theme for the Supreme Court in its reasoning (and also one at the centre of the author's normative position discussed in Chapter 3). This is because, in addition to liberty of state expression being indispensable for the effective functioning of the state, it has also been deemed indispensable if citizens are to be able to hold the government to account for its actions and if necessary change it through the ballot box.[32] Without liberty of expression, such reasoning suggests that it would not be possible for a government to communicate its thinking on an issue, including its motivations for past actions and its intentions for future ones.

29 The US Office of Government Ethics is, for example, responsible for producing guidelines and codes on a variety of matters concerning the activities of Members of the Executive, including on matters of communication. See, for example, the communication on "LA-15-03: The Standards of Conduct as Applied to Personal Social Media Use", dated 9 April 2015. Available at https://www.oge.gov/web/oge.nsf/Resources/LA-15-03:+The+Standards+of+Conduct+as+Applied+to+Personal+Social+Media+Use

30 *Johanns v. Livestock Marketing Case* 544 U.S. 550 (2005).

31 *Johanns v. Livestock Marketing Case* also quoted by Norton and Keats Citron, "Government Speech 2.0". p908

32 Ibid.

Without the availability of such information, the Supreme Court was of the opinion that it would be difficult for citizens to hold the executive branch to account.[33] This would render making a democratic assessment at election time difficult. The Supreme Court has accordingly adopted an approach which sees government speech not as a bad thing to be discouraged for fear that it will overwhelm private speech, but as a good thing that allows accountability and which is accordingly something to be encouraged as much as possible. This connection to accountability is likely the reason the Supreme Court uses 'executive control' as a mechanism to assess whether the speech in question is indeed government speech. Where Congress or an executive minister has the means to control the expression in question, e.g. by removing funding for the programme in question or disciplining the staff involved, the speech in question will likely be deemed government speech. Where such control does not exist, the Supreme Court reasons that such expression does not enjoy the protected status that government speech provides. Given that some systems of legislative and executive control of spending have been described as representing constitutional myths (discussed in section 5D), the US Supreme Court's assertion that control of such expression can be performed through the ballot box is arguably questionable.[34] The fact that such systems of control are based on majoritarian control means they may also be receptive to stigmatizing ideas and prejudice. As section 4 discusses this may reduce the likelihood that they are able to either recognize stigmatizing expressions when they occur or be willing to do anything to prevent them.

3 An impossible balance – the benefits and harms of constraining state expression

A Expression exists within legal black and grey holes

The book has shown how the expressive activity of the state often exists in a 'black' or 'grey' area in terms of their ability to be challenged in a court of law.[35] It often is possible to draw a distinction between those acts that are capable of engaging important legal approaches such as administrative law and those that are not, in terms of their ability to have direct effects that are binding on private individuals.[36] Where such effects do not occur the possibility of restraining the acts

33 As the court stated in *Board of Regents of the University of Wisconsin System v. Southworth* para 235: "When the government speaks, for instance to promote its own policies or to advance a particular idea, it is, in the end, accountable to the electorate and the political process for its advocacy. If the citizenry objects, newly elected officials later could espouse some different or contrary position."

34 J Wehner, "Assessing the Power of the Purse: An Index of Legislative Budget Institutions", *Political Studies* 54 (2006). See also section 5 of this chapter for a discussion of the types of control mechanism used in France and the UK.

35 These expressions, which are used throughout this chapter, have been taken from A Vermeule, "Our Schmittian Administrative Law", *Harvard Law Review* 122 (2009).

36 See Chapter 1 and C Hood and H Margretts, *The Tools of Government in the Digital Age* (New York: Palgrave Macmillan, 2006). Chapter 2

of the state using binding law may be limited. Key legal approaches will often not apply, leaving control solely in the hands of the administration, and ultimately its political masters.

As Chapters 1 and 2 discussed the idea that expressive activity is incapable of producing any harmful effects upon individuals is simplistic. Many in reality can be considered as existing in an in-between zone in terms of their ability to impose effects upon individuals. In the case of SSEs, they can bring about important psychological effects, but do not have binding effects in terms of an individual's rights or obligations.[37] They are, as a consequence, generally constraint free (at least in terms of binding law). Such a lack of engagement is in large part because many key legal approaches law do not recognize the imposition of psychological burdens on individuals (without any further tangible consequence) as an alteration of an individual's legal rights. The effect is to create a 'grey area' in terms of the legal protection that is available to individuals from expressive acts of the administration, including those that are stigmatizing.[38] A wide range of expressive activities fall within this grey area, where the potential psychological burden can vary immensely. Imagine, for instance, the difference between an information campaign that attempts to dissuade individuals from allowing their dogs to litter on street pavements, to another which states that the wearing of certain religious symbols (such as the full face veil for Muslims) is not acceptable in a certain society.[39] The psychological burdens in the former are arguably trivial whilst in instances such as the latter they can be grave.

Such legal black or grey holes may not be limited solely to the area of statements (including stigmatizing ones) by the state. The existence and the potential justification for areas of 'non-justiciability' in a democratic society have been discussed by scholars for many years. One noticeable example was Carl Schmitt, a controversial legal jurist in the Weimar Republic.[40] He was *inter alia* particularly interested in the extent of control that could be written in to the legal systems of democracies.[41] A key focus for Schmitt was how democratic states acted in the

37 As this author stated, in Quinn and De Hert, "Self Respect—a 'Rawlsian Primary Good' Unprotected by the European Convention on Human Rights and Its Lack of a Coherent Approach to Stigmatization?" stigmatization is rather defined by its potential to induce negative psychological effects in individuals.

38 Some forms of protection may exist in other forms of law such as criminal law (discussed in Chapter 4) and important substantive principles in human rights, e.g. ECHR, and constitutional law (see Chapter 6). In general, however, stigmatization is not a concept that is embraced directly by the law. See: Burris, "Disease Stigma in U. S. Public Law", *Journal of Law, Medicine and Ethics* 30 (2002).

39 In the case of *S.A.S. v. France* (Aplication no. 43835/11) the ECtHR has upheld the right of the French state to make the wearing of full face veils in public illegal.

40 For a good description of the legal paradoxes Carl Schmitt described in terms of the imposition of the rule of law on the democratic state see E Kennedy, *Constitutional Failure: Carl Schmidt in Wiemar* (Durham, NC: Duke University Press, 2004).

41 For a good review of his ideas concerning the problems associated with liberal democracies see J McCormick, *Carl Schmitt's Critique of Liberalism: Against Politics as Technology* (Cambridge: Cambridge University Press, 1999).

context of an emergency, where the state may have to deal with unforeseen events. Such events according to Schmitt posed big problems for democratic states that aspire to operate in accordance with the *rule of law*. For him it was impossible for the law to describe in advance what would happen in all circumstances, especially emergency situations which are very unpredictable.[42] Traditionally, in times of emergency, the functions and actions of the state would be controlled by a sovereign who would, by virtue of his or her position, have the ability to decide how to act. This provided non-democratic states with the flexibility needed to respond to unpredictable or emergency situations. A democratic state that was strictly operated under the principle of the *rule of law*, would not by contrast, Schmitt argued, possess such a level of flexibility.[43] This is because its underlying requirement is that public officials should only act when and how the law specifies. In order to meet such a requirement in the strict sense, a state would need to specify when and how public officials would act in all circumstances. Schmitt believed that it is simply not feasible for states to attempt to regulate all administrative actions (including in particular emergency situations) with comprehensive *ex ante* type legal rules.[44] This view sees such a level of precision as being impossible, especially in emergency circumstances where unforeseen problems occur. Laws could not, by their very nature, hope to specify all actions that might be required by state officials in all situations, especially given that many of them might be unknown at the time the law was created.

B The need for a 'black hole' – explaining the lack of constraining law on state expressions

Although Schmitt was primarily concerned with emergency situations in formulating the ideas discussed above, the author of this book would argue that such reasoning also has utility in being able to explain other gaps that appear in the ability of law to engage expressions by the state. Vermeule has argued that these Schmittian limitations can be seen, for instance, in the form of 'black and grey legal holes' throughout administrative law.[45] He describes the existence of such holes in numerous areas of US administrative law, many of which do not represent the existence of emergency situations. The holes are used to allow the executive, through direct action or through the many public agencies that exist, to act in a

42 For an English language version of Schmitt's most important work (translated by George Swabb) see C Schmitt, *Political Theology: Four Chapters on the Concept of Sovereignty* (Cambridge, MA: MIT Press, 1985 (1922)).

43 It should be acknowledged that Carl Schmit is not a figure without controversy. This includes, for example, concerns over alleged sympathies with elements of Nazi ideology. For a more extensive critique see R Gross, *Carl Schmitt and the Jews, the "Jewish Question", the Holocaust and German Legal Theory* (Wisconsin: University of Wisconsin, 2007). See also J Bendersky, *Carl Schmitt: Theorist for the Reich* (Guildford, UK: Princeton University Press, 1983). pp195–243

44 Vermeule, "Our Schmittian Administrative Law".

45 Ibid. Vermule is primarily concerned with US law, but theorizes correctly that such aspects are likely to exist in other versions of administrative law also.

flexible manner, unconstrained by the rules of administrative law and its usual requirements. 'Black holes' describe areas where administrative law simply acknowledges that it has no control of administrative activities, thus allowing free rein to officials to act as they wish in a certain area. 'Grey holes' describes areas where judicial review of administrative acts exists, but it is limited in terms of its scope and intensity. The result, according to Vermeule, is often to have a pretence of judicial control over legal actions that in reality amounts to little more than a sham.[46] In terms of black holes, numerous techniques exist in order to exempt certain types of administrative action from judicial review.[47] These include exceptions for certain state organizations (e.g. diplomatic or intelligence services),[48] limits as to the potential reviewability of certain types of activities and often exemptions for the actions of senior individuals in the executive (e.g. the president of the United States).[49] The author of this book would also argue that expressive acts of the state can often be considered to exist within such administrative law black and grey holes. Whilst most or many of the examples discussed in this book do not represent emergencies or existential threats to the state, the use of such expressions or statements can be useful in allowing a quick reaction to unforeseen circumstances (e.g. in public health or security situations). In addition, it may be difficult to foresee what form such expressions should take given that everyday situations may require an enormous variety of different responses. Indeed, as Chapter 1 discussed, speed and flexibility of use are two important aspects that make nodality instruments (including SSEs) both effective and attractive as a policy tool of the state. This need arguably explains why the fact that there are very few legal approaches that are able to get to grips with expressive activities of the state has in general not been seen as problematic.

C Do the expressive activities of the state merit a home within one of administrative law's black holes?

Whilst many expressive activities may fall within some form of emergency context, a much larger number cannot be thought of as related to an emergency situation. Indeed, a look at many of the instances of expressive activity described in Chapter 1, including the release of stigmatizing statements, shows that many expressive acts of the state occur in what can be considered day-to-day contexts. Whilst these

46 Ibid. p1103

47 In US administrative law such acts are referred to as 'agency acts'. Like the other European systems of administrative law, the American APA divides all administrative acts into one of two bins, "rules" and "orders". Rules are defined, whereas orders are a catch-all category that includes anything "other than rule making". Ibid. p1109

48 The American APA, which represents the core of the US administrative law approach, for example, only regulates actions that are defined as having being carried out by a government agency. Some acts, although undeniably emanating from the state, are not classed as emanating from a recognized government agency and so are exempt. ibid. p1109

49 Examples excluded by the American APA include acts of the military abroad and acts of the diplomatic services. See bid. p1112

may not be considered as truly emergency situations, they often require a fast and flexible response to a situation in flux (i.e. situations that are in some ways analogous to emergency situations).[50] Take, for instance, the example of public health information campaigns or communications relating to crime. Whilst some of these may well have constituted emergency situations (e.g. where there is an outbreak of an infectious disease or a terrorist attack), it would be difficult to categorize others as being an emergency context, e.g. campaigns aimed at reducing smoking or announcements by municipalities concerning more mundane criminal matters. Often such situations may not represent an 'extraordinary emergency' for the life of the state as a whole (such as may be the situation in a war, for example), but may still represent a situation that requires a flexible and immediate response that can only be met with nodality type instruments,[51] i.e. statements, expressions and the use of information as discussed in Chapter 1. [52] Imagine, for example, a police operation to find a missing child or a fugitive, in such instances the only suitable and effective responses may be immediate statements or information releases by the state. Given the variation in the type of incidents that could be involved and the type of communication that may be required in response, it is difficult if not impossible to foresee how the law could accurately detail such activities in advance.

Whilst Schmitt, and those who usually invoke him are primarily concerned with emergency situations, his arguments could also be applied to certain areas of state actions that are in a state of constant evolution. As described above, expressive acts of the state are often used in contexts where events demand rapid action of the state. Given that expressive activities require relatively few resources and are subject to few legal restraints, their use often represents both the fastest and most flexible means of action available. Such means are unhindered by the need to deploy organizational resources, the need to create new laws and usually are relatively light in terms of their impact on individuals. As a result of these factors, it is often such measures that public officials turn to when circumstances warrant immediate action. The reality of the modern world is that even day-to-day situations that would usually not be thought of as constituting emergencies on a national scale require rapid and potentially unforeseen responses, including the provision of information from public authorities in a manner that had not been predicted beforehand. Failure to provide such information can result in harmful consequences, including unnecessary panic and a failure by the state to avoid situations that could produce negative circumstances.[53] Imagine, for instance, a

50 P. Quinn, "Crisis Communication in Public Health Emergencies: The Limits of 'Legal Control' and the Risks for Harmful Outcomes in a Digital Age", *Life Sciences, Society and Policy*14, no. 1 (2018).

51 See: Hood and Margretts, *The Tools of Government in the Digital Age*. Chapter 2

52 For an in-depth description of nodailty instruments see ibid.

53 Quinn, "Crisis Communication in Public Health Emergencies: The Limits of 'Legal Control' and the Risks for Harmful Outcomes in a Digital Age". A failure to disseminate accurate information on public health issues such as emerging epidemics can, for example, lead to situations where stigmatizing rumours and myths arise.

situation in which a number of violent attacks have occurred against women in a certain area of a city at night. In such cases a public alert to be aware and report any suspicious activity can be amongst the most simple and effective responses. Whilst responses other than simple expressive acts may be conceivable, e.g. increasing the number of police in the area or creating harsher punishments for the perpetrators of such crimes, these responses require greater effort in terms of time and resources (and perhaps even the creation of new law). The first of these requires the deployment of state resources which may be stretched and required elsewhere whilst the second requires legislative action, which, in most modern democracies, is notoriously slow. In addition, the judicial constraints on such non-nodal activities are considerable in comparison with the relatively constraint free use that is possible for nodal instruments. An alternative state of affairs where expressive activity was open to real time judicial review would likely create problems in terms of being able to use an expedient and flexible response to a dynamic situation. Some of the reasons for this are discussed below.

(i) The need for expedient information

As Chapter 1 demonstrated, expressive activities and the emission of information are frequently used in fluid and fast changing situations, including those of an emergency nature. One such example may, for instance, be in a disaster situation provoked by a public health crisis or a natural disaster. In such instances public officials often have to react quickly and convey messages to citizens that may require them to act in a way that protects their interests.[54] In the case of a public health emergency, for example (see Chapter 1), public officials may advise individuals to take precautions, e.g. to avoid kissing when greeting or to wash hands frequently or where they can obtain treatment or vaccination.[55] When a storm is approaching, public officials will warn individuals in the affected region to take shelter and avoid unnecessary travel. The examples are numerous and probably beyond exhaustive definition. In such instances public officials will need to act quickly and decisively. If expressive acts were to be classified as acts that were subject to judicial review (e.g. because they were stigmatizing) this might reduce the expediency and effectiveness of such acts for two reasons. First, no matter how streamlined a court process was it would entail a delay. Judicial review would slow down such procedures given the inevitable delays involved. Second, even where courts did not intervene in such instances, public authorities would feel constrained by the potential applicability of legal proceedings to such acts. This would be because public servants would have to consider such requirements in planning

54 Hood and Margretts, *The Tools of Government in the Digital Age*. See also C Hood, "Intellectual Obsolescence and Intellectual Makeovers: Reflections on the Tools of Government after Two Decades", *Governance* 20 (2007).

55 For a good repository of information concerning the use of public communication in vaccination campaigns visit the website of the TELL ME project. It contains a range of deliverables that describe such uses of information. The website can be found at www.tellmeproject.eu

and executing such announcements and would have to tailor such announcements so as to allow them to be compatible with the requirements of the law. Doing so would require more time and further resources. This would probably be impracticable not only in emergency situations, but also in a wide range of day-to-day situations that might nonetheless demand highly adaptive responses that are difficult to predict beforehand (see below).

(ii) The need for flexibility of form

Flexibility is required by the state, not only in the context of infrequent emergencies that threaten the lives or property of citizens, but also in the day-to-day operation of the modern state. Modern states are involved in such a range of differing activities that it is almost impossible to categorize them all. If one also includes expressive activity within this, the complexity becomes all the more evident. Within the accepted roles of many public servants and elected officials there are requirements to make announcements and provide information on issues of importance that may vary from moment to moment. This may include, for instance, announcements by the local police requesting information on crimes committed in a certain area or the provision of information concerning roads or streets that are dangerous for pedestrians. In addition, public officials may be active in the provision of information related to any one of a number of issues that may arise in civic life. Public officials may, for example, provide messages encouraging individuals not to litter or allow their dogs to foul public streets in response to uncivil behaviour that has increased in a certain area. Other public officials may see it as part of their role to advise their citizenry on healthy eating or lifestyle habits where they find problems to exist.[56] Such roles may not be specifically described in legislation but may have developed organically over time.

It is not possible to exhaustively categorize the various contexts in which public officials may act. This is not only because of the potential breadth of possible interventions that public officials might be able to make, but also because the nature of such interventions is constantly changing as a result of changing socio-economic and technological circumstances. Public officials may, for instance, at the time of writing send messages or information through social media platforms such as Twitter or Facebook, activities that could not have been envisaged ten years ago.[57] Given that our societies and the technologies that they use are constantly evolving, it is likely that public officials in the future will make pronouncements, send messages and provide information to the public in ways that are equally difficult to envisage today.[58]

56 See Chapter 1 section 2 for a description of stigmatizing examples of such activities.

57 For an example of how public agencies have used social media to communicate in disaster situations see S Muralidharan et al., "Hope for Haiti: An Analysis of Facebook and Twitter Usage During the Earthquake Relief Efforts ,*Public Relations Review* 37, no. 2 (2011).

58 See: R Thackeray et al., "Adoption and Use of Social Media among Public Health Departments", *BMC Public Health* 12 (2012).

The ability of public officials to express themselves freely in matters of current importance represents one of the few possibilities for public officials to react to changing circumstances without the need to wait for changes in the legal landscape. A restriction on the ability of public officials to act in such a manner would therefore render the state unable to intervene in a diverse range of areas whilst awaiting the required changes in the legal landscape needed in order to allow officials to respond to a particular context.

D An expressive legal black hole allows a democratic element to be contained within administrations

Many of the expressive actions above represent activities of the state that are relatively uncontroversial. Most individuals, academics and commentators would accept that a state should be active in such areas, i.e. that a state should use nodality type instruments where possible to combat threats to public health, security threats, threats to public order and other similar problems that governments and states of all ideologies are likely to face.[59] Indeed, were a state not to do so, it might even be seen as a dereliction of duty.[60]

As many of the other examples of stigmatizing state expression in Chapter 1 demonstrated, in numerous other instances state expression may not be dedicated towards serving such important and practical ends, but may in reality be the result of the partially political character of most public bodies (see discussion on 'Statements made for political purposes' in Chapter 3). Such a character stems from the democratic nature of the modern Western state, where individuals with elected office are tasked with exerting a certain level of control over civil service administrations. Such a situation can exist on the national (e.g. ministers) or the local level (e.g. mayors). Individuals of this type are to a large extent free to make their opinions known on a wide variety of subjects, including even those that have little to do with their competences as state officials.[61] The most prominent contemporary

59 S Burris, "Stigma, Ethics and Policy: A Commentary on Bayer's 'Stigma and the Ethics of Public Health: Not Can We but Should We'", *Social Science & Medicine* 67 (2008); R Bayer, "Stigma and the Ethics of Public Health: Not Can We but Should We; N Guttman and C Salmon, "Guilt, Fear, Stigma and Knowledge Gaps", *Ethical Issues in Public Health Communication* 18 (2004); B Link and J Phelan, "Stigma and Its Public Health Implications", *The Lancet* 367 (2006).

60 Legal duties often exist for states to act in some way to protect the interests of individuals who may face threats to health or security. In recent decades the ECtHR has been moving towards protecting rights that were previously considered social and economic rights and, therefore, beyond the protection of the ECHR. See E Palmer, "Protecting Socio-Economic Rights through the European Convention on Human Rights: Trends and Development in the European Court of Human Rights", *Erasmus Law Review* 2, no. 4 (2009).

61 Public officials often condemn individuals in society when they have not broken any law and cannot be the subject of legal measures. Recently in the UK, for example, the Mayor of London condemned a housing association that erected small spikes to prevent homeless people sleeping in an unwanted place on private property. Even though such action was not illegal it resulted in public revulsion. See http://www.independent.co.uk/

example is President Trump who seems to relish social media tirades on an eclectic range of issues. At a lower level a local mayor, for example, may pronounce that he or she feels that there are too many immigrants coming into the country, or a minister may state that the cultural activities of a certain minority are unacceptable, even though in reality he or she has no legal powers to control such behaviour. Unlike the other types of roles of the state described above the political pronouncements of state individuals may vary from individual to individual according to his or her particular political orientation. One mayor may, for example, pronounce him or herself in favour of increasing LGBT rights whilst his or her successor may make pronouncements to the contrary.[62] As Chapter 3 discussed, such expressions can present problems in terms of the expectation that a state should demonstrate neutrality in terms of its perception of the choices of various individuals in terms of their vision of what represents 'the good'.[63] This results from the perceived link between such individuals and the state and the resultant perception that their messages emanate from the state also.

The existence of stigmatizing messages in society that emanate from such individuals may represent an unavoidable price that must be paid in order to allow a sufficient level of freedom of speech in political life to foster the requisite level of democratic debate needed in order to allow a democratic society to function adequately. As Chapter 3 discussed, restrictions on the expressions of such individuals would make it difficult for them to explain their views on matters of importance to society, to explain why they have opted for a particular course of action and to explain how they intend to act in the future. Voters expect to know the views of their elected representatives on a variety of matters (often even when it relates to matters that are outside their competence). All of these types of information are arguably indispensable in allowing individuals not only to act in order to protect their interests as they would wish, but also in allowing individuals to make an informed choice at the ballot box when the time comes.[64] The existence of administrative black holes in these areas may, therefore, represent the creation of a zone of 'non-legal restraint' that is required in order to allow a state to function in a democratic manner. Whilst this presents the state with the flexibility it arguably needs to communicate to address an important range of issues it makes it difficult to see how the law and legal approaches can play a role in bringing about the normative perspective the author discussed in Chapter 3 given that this perspective

news/uk/home-news/homeless-spikes-row-boris-johnson-calls-for-stupid-spikes-to-be-removed-but-faces-criticism-over-own-record-on-rough-sleepers-9514421.html

62 In the ECtHR case of *Baczkowski & Others v, Poland* [2007] ECHR No.1543/06 the Mayor of Warsaw made remarks that were highly critical of the gay community in Poland. He later banned a gay pride parade for 'traffic reasons'.

63 Rawls, *Political Liberalism*. Rawls did, however, qualify this to allow the state to condemn behaviour or beliefs that were intolerant of others and contrary to the idea of a tolerant society.

64 Norton and Keats Citron, "Government Speech 2.0".

required the state to be prohibited from making certain forms of (highly) stigmatizing expression.

4 Alternative forms of control to binding law

A Alternative potential forms of control to hard law

The emphasis in this chapter (and in this book as a whole) thus far has been on the potential of binding forms of law to engage with and hold the (stigmatizing) expressive activities of the state to account. Given that the author is a legal scholar this naturally forms a clear focus for him. However, as the author has been describing a situation of non-restraint *vis-à-vis* expressive activities, this book would be incomplete without a discussion of the other forms of regulation/control that can be exerted (i.e. in the absence of hard forms of law). Such control can take a number of forms. This can include control over spending on programmes that involve public communication, political pressure in general and codes of conduct or ethical codes that are applicable to public employees (discussed further in section 6).

As this section discusses briefly (before sections 5–6 take a more illustrative look), each of these is able to exert some form of control on public agencies and public servants (including on expressive activity).[65] It is, therefore, of course not correct to say that expressions of the state are restraint free simply because they may not be engaged by binding legal frameworks. Indeed, alterative control mechanisms may offer certain advantages which hard law does not. The most important of these is flexibility, given that such forms of regulation need not depend upon the existence of legislation or other forms of hard law. New soft law relating to government communication can be drawn up quickly. Similarly, soft law also need not be dependent upon the existence of independent courts for enforcement. Forms of control such as executive control and even codes of conduct can be implemented with simplified (and thus more rapid) procedures. Such forms of control are, however, likely to have a number of disadvantages concerning their ability to limit SSEs. Whilst these factors may vary from mechanism to mechanism (e.g. executive, legislative control or codes of conduct, they all also have one important disadvantage when compared to hard forms of law) – they are more likely to be subject to majoritarian control or influence (discussed further below).

B Hard law v. majoritarian control

There are arguably two central elements to a modern democratic society. The first is the possibility for free and fair elections allowing the majority in society to influence and arguably direct its governance. The second is the presence of legal rules and the rule of law. This latter element *inter alia* ensures that executives

65 Gelders and Oyvind, "Government Communication About Potential Policies: Public Relations, Propaganda or Both?"

(ostensibly supported by the majority) are not able to abuse their authority and act unfairly towards minority groups and individuals. The need for such protection is evident not only in our darkest past, but in contemporary times where populist politicians attempt to appeal to the majority with promises of being tough on various minority groups, most notably immigrants (as President Trump has sought to do on a number of occasions).[66] Without such protection there is little to stop the state and its various bodies either causing minorities and individuals harm or encouraging others to do so, arguing that they are only implementing the 'will of the people'. Hard law often plays a crucial role in this regard, providing rules that private individuals can (through an independent judiciary) enforce against the state and thus limit the potential for majoritarian imposition.

The concept of majoritarian imposition resonates strongly with the theme of stigma. As Chapter 2 discussed, a central theme of the phenomena is that it relates to the perception of an individual or group of individuals concerning how they are thought of by their peers. A common element of stigmatization is that stigmatized individuals (rightly or wrongly) feel that they are held in low esteem by their peers or society at large. Protecting individuals from stigmatization thus, to a certain extent, entails preventing individuals from being exposed to the harmful opinions and attitudes of the rest of society. There are interesting parallels between efforts at minimizing stigmatization and the rule of law. In terms of the rule of law a key element is the existence of binding (or hard) laws that cannot simply be ignored by the executive or anyone else.[67] They can be invoked by individuals before an independent court or tribunal to ensure that the state acts in a manner that is consistent with legal requirements. Requirements found in hard law thus play an important role in in protecting minorities and individuals.[68] Whether they be in constitutions, legislation or case law they provide individuals with a shield that can be wielded with the aid of independent courts and tribunals to protect themselves from unjustified majoritarian imposition.

Many non-hard law methods of constraint arguably have properties that make them more susceptible to majoritarian control. One common problem is that they often cannot be enforced by private natural or legal persons in independent courts or tribunals.[69] The availability of independent courts, a hallmark of the separation of powers, plays a crucial role in democratic societies in protecting the rights of minority groups and private individuals against the will of the majority. They allow private individuals to enforce their rights *inter alia* against an executive that draws its legitimacy in large part from democratic majoritarian approval. Crucial factors in the presence of such guarantees are the ability of affected individuals to invoke

66 https://www.nytimes.com/interactive/2018/03/30/upshot/crime-immigration-myth.html

67 G O'Donnell, "Why the Rule of Law Matters", *Journal of Democracy* 15, no. 4 (2004).

68 S Croley, "The Majoritarian Difficulty: Elective Judiciaries and the Rule of Law," *Crime and Justice* 283 (1995).

69 H Gribnau, "Soft Law and Taxation: The Case of Soft Law in the Netherlands", *Legisprudence* 1, no. 3 (2015).

such laws before a court and to have their case heard by a tribunal that has total independence from the executive. Protections in the form of hard law thus arguably offer the best protection for minority individuals against the threat of majoritarian imposition. This explains the focus of this book on such matters given that stigmatization (and also SSEs) is a phenomenon that is in many ways defined by the perception of majority opinion and often prejudice. Whilst other methods exist to prevent harmful inhibitions (including stigmatizing expressions) they are weaker in the protection they may be able to offer. In particular, other forms of control are more open to majoritarian input in both their inception and management. Some of these are discussed below.

(i) Political control (of the executive)

In terms of its day-to-day running the modern state is controlled by an executive. It is able, through complex forms of delegation, to manage the day-to-day business of the state. Control of the executive ultimately rests with elected officials or those that have been appointed by them. One would hope that most executives in most democratic states have no desire to unnecessarily stigmatize vulnerable minority groups in society. Even in the most well intentioned societies, however, biases and prejudices are likely to exist against certain groups. Such prejudices may both inform the results of elections and also influence the actions of members of the executive who may hope to gain favour amongst the electorate in future elections. This may often explain the willingness of ministers to organize harmful communication initiatives concerning groups that through being vulnerable are often the subject of biases or prejudices on the part of the society as a whole (e.g. immigrants).[70] In such a context, where elected members of the executive are likely to be both informed by prejudices and stereotypes or even be incentivized to appeal to them, it is possible or even likely that majoritarian stereotypes and prejudices could influence decision makers concerning the authorization of potentially stigmatizing communication or impair their ability to recognize where stigmatization occurs. This lessens the ability (and potentially even the desire) of executives to recognize and stop SSEs.

(ii) Legislative control

In many countries legislatures have the power to hold the executive to account or even topple a government. Such bodies have a key role in holding executives to account for their actions. Legislatures are thus in theory able to operate as a democratic brake on the activities of the executive. It may, therefore, be possible for groups that are able to influence parties that are able to command a majority in

70 In 2013 the UK government, in a controversial decision, approved the driving of mobile vans around London carrying billboards telling illegal immigrants they should go home. See https://www.theguardian.com/politics/2013/oct/22/go-home-billboards-pulled

legislatures to exert (limited) control on the executive.[71] As section 5 discusses, such control is in reality rather crude, being limited to approving general departmental spending allocations and, in extreme cases, to bringing down an executive. Whilst vulnerable or minority groups may hope to have representation in such legislatures, this does not equate to control of them. Majority control of such bodies is needed to enact laws or sanction (or bring down governments). Again, it is likely that majority groups in legislatures are likely to possess many of the same prejudicial and stigmatizing attitudes as society in general. Where they do not, they may be incentivized to adopt them for the sake of electoral expediency. This can mean that many of the prejudices and stereotypes that are present in society (and which bring about stigmatization) can infiltrate the large groups that are likely to control parliament. As with members of the executive this is likely to effect both the desire of a legislature to prevent stigmatizing expressive activities and, in reality, even to recognize them when they are occurring.

(iii) Soft law codes, etc.

Anybody who has experience in matters such as discrimination, the plight of minorities and holding public bodies to account will testify that there are other regulatory approaches beyond hard law that are capable of providing an important contribution.[72] Other forms of control, including (as described below in section 6) ethical codes and codes of conduct, also no doubt have a role to play. Such codes are flexible, require less burdensome procedural requirements (compared, for example, with court proceedings) and can be quickly adapted to changing circumstances and concerns. Whilst such approaches certainly have something to bring to the table, without the existence of some forms of protection in hard law, this protection may be limited and, in a number of ways, compromised, including by its exposure to majoritarian control and the problems associated with it.[73] In particular they can be contrasted with binding law in two important ways.

First individuals may have less power to enforce codes of conduct or ethical codes than they do with harder forms of law. Depending on the type of code they may or may not be able to commence proceedings against a public body or employee for having contravened it. Even where they can they are unlikely to be able to do so in an independent court. A tribunal, if available, may be made up of members of the executive or other public servants under its control. Ultimately it is the executive and its political masters (associated with majoritarian control) that

71 See section 5 for a discussion on the limitation of such control in the context of spending on expressive activities.

72 L Carlson, "Constructing Human Rights from Soft Law: The Swedish Journey Towards Protection against Unlawful Discrimination", *Scandinavian Studies in Law* 58 (2013); F Zerilli, "The Rule of Soft Law: An Introduction", *Focaal—Journal of Global and Historical Anthropology* 56 (2010).

73 J Gersen, "Soft Law: Lessons from Congressional Practice", *Stanford Law Review* 61 (2008).

is responsible for the establishment of such a tribunal, opening it up to the same majoritarian influences as discussed above.

Second, the rules or codes that outline procedures for how tribunals deal with disputes will usually have been drafted by the executive or parts of the state under its control.[74] Whilst this allows such codes to be drafted quickly and flexibly, it means that they do not face the same scrutiny as hard law does in its creation.[75] There may be little or no oversight on the part of legislatures (including cross party committees), review by second chambers or review for constitutionality. It is rather the executive that is master in such situations and it can accordingly choose what form the code in question will take.

These factors mean that checks and balances that might otherwise be expected to limit majoritarian biases and prejudices may not be deployed in the case of soft law tools. As discussed above, this may arguably make executives and the public bodies they control less willing, or even able, to recognize the harms that SSES can bring about and even, where they do, to take action to prevent them.

5 Control over spending on expressive activities

A Legislators and executives as the main overseers of financial control

The expressive activities of the state may in a number of contexts require the allocation of specific funding in order to be executed. This is more likely in large communication programmes (e.g. on public health themes) than it may be for the expression of single individuals, e.g. minsters or mayors. Large scale communications programmes may require the committal of important resources of the state. Public information campaigns may, for example, require advertising space to be purchased in the printed media or online.[76] Individuals may have to be employed to co-ordinate informational activities. Such activities may require the committal of expertise in a way that may represent a significant cost in time and resources to the state. Where this occurs states can effectively prevent such forms of communication by revoking the funding necessary for them.

In the UK (as in many other countries) the courts have an extremely limited, almost non-existent level of control over the expenditure of various government departments. This has been an accepted principle of the UK constitutional arrangement since the sixteenth century.[77] Control is effectively limited to

74 R De Ruiter, "EU Soft Law and the Functioning of Representative Democracy: The Use of Methods of Open Co-Ordination by Dutch and British Parliamentarians", *Journal of European Social Policy* 17, no. 6 (2010).

75 R Creyke and J McMillan, "Soft Law v Hard Law", in *Administrative Law in a Changing State: Essays in Honour of Mark Aronson*, ed. L Pearson, C Harlow, and M Taggart (London: Bloomsbury Publishing, 2008).

76 Guttman and Salmon, "Guilt, Fear, Stigma and Knowledge Gaps".

77 J Jowell and M Oliver, *The Changing Constitution* (Oxford: Oxford University Press, 2004). p384 Whilst UK courts have been willing to intervene in the supply side of government expense, i.e. taxation, they have been extremely reluctant to get involved

ensuring that the UK Treasury has received the consent of Parliament for the total allocation of funds to the department in question. Such a level of control is very mild, however, given that the department (i.e. the relevant part of the executive) in question does not need to spell out exactly how the money it receives will be spent.[78] This leaves the department in question with relative freedom to decide how and where its budget may be spent. Such spending may include activities ranging from the procurement of items needed for departmental activities to expenditure on informational programmes or other informational activities (i.e. activities that are ostensibly nodal in nature). Under the UK constitutional system courts have very limited powers to regulate specific allocations of departmental expenditure.[79] This means that to a large extent, once a department has been legally allocated funds by Parliament for a certain purpose, e.g. public health, it is free to spend such money in any way it sees fit in pursuing aims connected to that purpose (including discretionary communication programmes).

Courts may only interfere with such choices when they interfere with the rights or privileges of individuals.[80] Such actions fall into the latter of the two categories described by Craig (discussed in Chapter 5 Part 2), i.e. rule making and adjudication. One can imagine an instance of the former where a government department decides that people who fall within a certain category are entitled to a grant of government funds for one reason or another. The second may occur where a court decides whether an individual falls into a category it has already outlined and is therefore eligible to receive such a benefit. Both of these types of cases involve government expenditure and both may be subject to judicial review. What makes such instances open to the scrutiny of the court is not the fact the state funds have been allocated to them, but rather the fact that the spending of such funding impacts upon individual rights or privileges. Where this happens, individual cases that involve the allocation of funds may indeed be the subject of judicial scrutiny under the guise of various administrative law requirements, but in such cases the issue at hand is in reality the rights of individuals to the funds or the material benefit in question and not the right of the state to spend taxpayers' money *per se*. Where no such interface with individual rights and privileges exists (e.g. where the

in matters of how money is spent. Even in the second half of the twentieth century where judicial intervention increased in areas such as welfare payments, intervention has often been limited to procedural questions querying the application, for example, of principles of natural justice to individual cases of dispute. For more on natural justice see P Craig, *Administrative Law (7th Edition)* (London: Sweet and Maxwell, 2012). Chapter 12

78 See also B Morgan and K Yeung, *An Introduction to Regulation* (Cambridge: Cambridge University Press, 2007).

79 In the well-known case of *R. v. Secretary of State for Foreign Affairs*, ex parte World Development Movement [1995] 1 All ER 617, the court intervened in the case of a UK government grant to build a dam in Peru. Even on that occasion, however, where the court questioned the spending as inappropriate the UK government was able to go ahead with funding the grant by deploying funds from another source.

80 See the comments by Craig, *Administrative Law (7th Edition)* discussed in the previous section.

state engages in purely expressive activity), there is little possibility for courts to intervene on behalf of individuals. This situation is *inter alia* facilitated by the restrictive attitudes of the courts concerning the issue of standing (discussed in Chapter 5).

In France a similar logic exists to the UK, although with more clearly demarcated institutions that are tasked with scrutinizing government expenditure. The *Cour des Comptes* (Court of Auditors) exists to examine all public accounts including those of publicly owned enterprises.[81] Like the Public Accounts Committee (PAC) in the UK (see below) its function is primarily that of auditor which allows it to advise both the executive and parliament as to whether departments have been spending the money allocated to them correctly. As is the case with PAC for the UK Parliament, the reports of the *Cour des Comptes* are not themselves binding, but are meant to arm the French legislature with sufficient evidence to make binding votes on public finances.[82] It is ultimately the legislature that has final say on the legality of allocation of state funds.[83] To do this the *Cour des Comptes* produces reports and studies that are requested by both the *Assemblée Nationale* and the *Sénat*. In its scrutiny of public expenditure it has a role before the budget is approved and afterwards in an audit function. When undertaking such studies a primary aim is to ensure that money is spent in a legal way and that the spending in question achieved value for money.[84] Where cases of illegal action are discovered the *Cour des Comptes* can invite a prosecution.[85]

B *Weakness of non-judicial methods of control spending on expressive activities*

Given that little control exists over departmental expenditure in terms of judicial action, control of such activities rests with executives and ultimately parliaments. The UK provides a good example of this situation. Under its constitutional arrangements, for example, Parliament has ultimate control over government expenditure. This function is exercised by the PAC, which is composed of Members of Parliament. In reality Parliament has only control in the *de jure* sense, with *de facto* control resting with the executive and more specifically the Treasury. It is this part of the executive that has the most oversight of departmental spending, in addition to the bureaucratic capabilities needed to analyse departmental expenditure in greater detail. The reality of politics in the UK means that the government

81 For a comparison of the makeup and role of the *Cour des Comptes* with similar institutions in other European countries see S Jacob, *Institutionnaliser l'évaluation des politiques publiques: Étude comparée des dispositifs institutionnels en Belgique, en France, en Suisse et aux Pays-Bas* (Brussels: Peter Lang, 2005).

82 This competence is outlined in Article 47–2 of the French Constitution. The role of the *Cour des Comptes* was recently updated by the loi constitutionelle du 23 juillet 2008.

83 Article 47 de la Constitution de la Cinquième République française.

84 Loi organique n°2001–692 du 1er août 2001 relative aux lois de finances. This law provides that public servants must show effectiveness (*efficacité*) in the spending of credits that have been attributed to them.

85 Code des jurisdictions financiérers, Article R 143–3.

of the day has to have a parliamentary majority in the main chamber of Parliament, the House of Commons. Given this, it is almost inconceivable, at least in political terms that a Parliament would vote down the budget of the government of the day, as that budget would have been formed according to the desires of the political party that controls most of Parliament. This political reality significantly weakens the ability of Parliament to exact control upon the expenditure of government departments.

In addition, Parliament does not vote on the minute details of parliamentary expenditure, but approves expenditure in terms of annual budgets at the departmental level.[86] Parliament does not have the time, expertise or resources to analyse all aspects of departmental budgets in detail. Considering that some departments are very large with an enormous range of competences this is understandable. The UK's National Health Service (NHS) has an annual budget of 140 billion which can be broken down into numerous complex smaller sub-departmental budgets including ***inter alia*** for public health information campaigns. With such large and complex budgets, Parliament is unlikely to be able to analyse the spending that will be committed to individual projects.[87] Given that information campaigns and other expressive activities by the state are often opted for because they are perceived as a cheap solution,[88] it is extremely unlikely that parliamentary scrutiny will extend to such relatively modest expenditure projects.

Yet another issue with regard to relying on legislative or executive control of departmental spending programmes is that such scrutiny is often exercised on an *ex post facto* basis. This can be seen in the UK with the work of the PAC. This committee normally conducts reviews of departmental expenditure of the various departments for the previous year. The purpose of this is to highlight wasteful spending patterns, allowing savings to be made in future budgets. Such reviews are intended to provide information that can be used by the executive and Parliament to curb waste in future budgets. While this may be logical and may encourage efficiency in terms of resource utilization, it means that expenditure is examined after it has occurred. The result is that, for example, any significant expenditure on public (or other) health information campaigns will only be analysed after they have occurred. Whilst spotting wasteful excess in terms of spending might allow future savings to be made, the termination of a public information programme long after it has already propagated stigmatizing ideas and statements will probably not be able to reverse the damage that has been caused. The genie will in a sense already be out of the bottle.[89]

86 J Von Hagen, "Fiscal Rules, Fiscal Institutions, and Fiscal Performance", *The Economic and Social Review* 33, no. 3 (2002).

87 The NHS as an organization is necessarily categorized as having a high degree of decentralized budgetary control. See N Flynn, *Public Sector Management* (SAGE, 2007).

88 See Hood, "Intellectual Obsolescence and Intellectual Makeovers: Reflections on the Tools of Government after Two Decades". See also Chapter 1 of this book.

89 It has been recognized that stigmatizing rumours and opinions can take on a life of their own once established in a community. Thus, whilst a state may be able to create stigmatizing rumours or ideas it may be very difficult for them to remove them or stop them from gaining ground in the community once established. See Burris, "Stigma, Ethics and Policy: A Commentary on Bayer's 'Stigma and the Ethics of Public Health: Not Can We but Should We'".

A further weakness of relying on this type of scrutiny mechanism, to the exclusion of the potential judicial mechanisms, is that it is primarily resource focused.[90] The UK's PAC, for example, will focus on items such as efficacy and value for money in its analysis. It is not specialized in matters of human rights or ethical practice and its activities will reflect this, with its members often being selected for their mastery of financial or accounting matters. Whilst this may seem logical for a body that is tasked with holding the executive financially accountable, it means that bodies like the PAC cannot be considered fit for purpose in terms of holding all executive functions to account. This means that in matters of state expression, one may not find much utility in looking to mechanisms designed to control public expenditure to challenge potentially harmful expressions, including stigmatizing ones.[91] Even in terms of financial control, the weaknesses of such measures led the Procedure Committee of the UK House of Commons to conclude that the level of budgetary control was in fact a constitutional myth. A similar situation of a constitutional myth can be applied to the system of budgetary control in many other states.[92]

6 Ethical codes, codes of professional conduct and the democratic process

As section 4 discussed soft law mechanisms can play a role in restraining the actions of the state. Whilst they may be more open to majoritarian (and thus potentially stigmatizing) influences they are nonetheless capable of having some restraining effect upon the activities of public bodies. This can include areas related to expression. Whilst it may be difficult to challenge such matters in an independent court (as a number of chapters in this book have illustrated), public employees involved in matters of communication are not simply able to say what they wish without fear of repercussion. Other forms of soft law control exist, though they may not be accessible to those individuals that are directly affected by the communicational activities in question (i.e. they may not, for example, provide access to a tribunal for affected individuals).[93] Where hearings or tribunals are available, they are unlikely to meet the standards of a fully independent court. Such forms of soft law may exist in the form of guidance that is intended to assist public servants in working out how they should carry out their functions in a legal manner. Clarification may often be necessary because legislation may either not be explicitly clear on some matters, leaving public servants unsure as to how they should act in a number of situations. Public bodies may even be required by law to create soft law guidelines in order to guide public

90 Jowell and Oliver, *The Changing Constitution*. See Chapter 15.

91 Quinn, "Crisis Communication in Public Health Emergencies: The Limits of 'Legal Control' and the Risks for Harmful Outcomes in a Digital Age".

92 Wehner, "Assessing the Power of the Purse: An Index of Legislative Budget Institutions". p778

93 G Weeks, *Soft Law and Public Authorities: Remedies and Reform* (Portland, OR: Bloomsbury Publishing, 2016).

officials.[94] Some form of restraint on expressive activities may be provided by codes of conduct or ethical codes. Such codes may be directly or indirectly related to matters of communication. The subsections below provide some illustrative examples.

A Codes of conduct

Many public employees and agencies are likely to be subject to codes of conduct. The purpose of such codes is to identify the main principles by which public employees should operate. Such codes have been becoming more common in recent years, including gaining prominence in continental Europe (where the term 'deontological code' is commonly used),[95] where they have been inspired to a certain extent by the example of the UK (and other English speaking contexts).[96] In the US the Office of Government Ethics periodically releases an updated "Standards of Ethical Conduct for Employees of the Executive Branch" on a range of matters which directly and indirectly include communication (including the use of social media). Other similar codes exist for different branches of the government such as the Judiciary.[97] In the UK the *Civil Service Code of Conduct* requires public employees to refrain from acting "in a way that unjustifiably favours or discriminates against particular individuals or interests". They should also carry out responsibilities in a way that is "fair, just and equitable" and reflects a commitment to "equality and diversity".[98] Similar principles exist in civil service codes in many states including (but not limited to) Belgium[99] and France.[100] In some instances codes of conduct may exist that deal particularly with efforts at communication and may demand that civil servants communicate in ways that are not likely to worsen discrimination and create unnecessary harms.[101] In some instances codes of conduct may

94 This is the case, for example, with the director of public prosecutions in the UK who is required to produce guidelines to aid the decisions of prosecutors. See Prosecution of Offences Act (1985) Section 10.

95 Intervention by Jean-Marc Sauvé (vice président du Conseil d'état) "Quelle déontologie pour les hauts fonctionnaires?" Presentation made at the École Nationale d'Administration on 27 March 2013. Available at http://www.conseil-etat.fr/Actualites/Discours-Interventions/Quelle-deontologie-pour-les-hauts-fonctionnaires (In French)

96 A De Becker, "Juridische Status Van Een Ethische Code: Waar Plaats Je Zo'nCode in De Hiërarchie Van De Continentale Normen?", *Bestuurskunde* 23, no. 4 (2014). (In Dutch)

97 D Bratton and V Candy, "Federal Government Ethics: Social Media", *International Journal of Management & Information Systems* 17, no. 3 (2013).

98 The current UK Civil Service Code of Conduct (dating from March 2015) is available at https://www.gov.uk/government/publications/civil-service-code/the-civil-service-code

99 See, for example, the "Deontogishe Code Vlaamse Overhied (applicable in the Flemish Region of Belgium) which demands civil servants to act objectively and to avoid discrimination". Available at https://overheid.vlaanderen.be/deontologische-code (In Dutch)

100 The French law of conduct for civil servants demands *inter alia* that public servants show neutrality when communicating in public with a view to maintaining the impartiality of the state. See: J Auby, *La Fonction Publique* (Paris: Dalloz, 2002). p300 (In French)

101 See, for example, the Code of Conduct for Federal Communicators (Code de déontologie des communicateurs fédéraux). Available at http://www.fedweb.belgium.be/

exist in legislation, whilst in other instances such requirements may take the form of soft law. Depending upon the type of legal system in question the legal value of such codes may vary. In the UK, where the legal system is more open to using such forms of soft law in hard legal cases, such codes are likely to carry more legal weight. They may, for example, be understood to form part of the employment conditions of public employees.[102] This raises the possibility of particular individuals being sanctioned or suffering consequences when they fail to act as expected. This could feasibly occur when they are responsible for communication practices that are contrary to whatever code a particular employee may be bound by. In continental Europe, the legal status of such codes (where they are not contained in legislation) is more dubious. Many continental systems do not recognizes codes or circulars as binding sources of law. As a consequence, the contents of such codes may not bind public employees in the same manner (i.e. forming a condition of their employment). In such instances the ability of such codes to weigh on the decision making of a public employee will accordingly be reduced. Even where this is the case, they may still be used in order to judge or appraise the behaviour of public servants.[103]

Whilst soft law codes may be weaker in terms of their enforceability, they do have a number of advantages. Most importantly they are low cost to implement, both in terms of resources and the time required.[104] Unlike formal laws they do not require multiple sittings of a legislature or perhaps the analysis of a constitutional court. With the former comes the need for public consultation and a vote in which majoritarian approval may be required. With the latter comes the need to adhere to constitutional norms and requirements. All of these pose serious requirements that must be complied with. Another important factor is that soft forms of law can often be more precise. Given that it is non-binding, it can advise public servants to carry out activities in response to certain situations that might not be possible for legislation which has to remain more general in nature. The low cost nature of such rule making also means that soft law rules can be made more quickly and more frequently.[105] This allows a faster response to changing situations and (at least in theory) to the plight of vulnerable groups or minorities (including in terms of risk of stigmatization where there is a willingness to do so (see section 4)). Where evidence is available of changing situations, including in the potential for harms or better outcomes, soft law can be used to bring about a more expedient response.

sites/default/ files/downloads/broch_commcollection10_deontologischecode_fr.pdf (In French)

102 De Becker, "Juridische Status Van Een Ethische Code: Waar Plaats Je Zo'n Code in De Hiërarchie Van De Continentale Normen?"

103 J Maesschalck and F Schram, "Meer Dan Een Brochure of Affiche: De Deontologische Code Als Kernelement Van Een Effectief Ambtelijk Integriteitsbeleid," *Burger, Bestuur & Beleid* 3, no. 1 (2006). (In Dutch)

104 L Senden, *Soft Law in European Community Law* (London: Hart, 2004).

105 G Schaffer and M Pollack, "Hard vs. Soft Law: Alternatives, Complements and Antagonists in International Governance", *Minnesota Law Review* 94 (2010).

B Ethical codes linked to professional status

Many individuals who act on behalf of the state, including to communicate to the public, may also be subject to other forms of professional codes of conduct or ethics. Unlike codes of conduct that may apply to public employees in general, such codes may apply to specific individuals by virtue of the profession they belong to. One of the most important examples of such codes is the professional codes of conduct that bind doctors, nurses and other medical professionals. In most countries such medical professionals must, in order to be active professionally, be registered with a national body, and agree to act professionally in manner that is considered compatible with their profession. Such codes aim to ensure that individuals belonging to certain professions act in a way that is ethically and professionally consistent with that which might reasonably be expected. In the UK, for example, doctors must be a member of the British Medical Council, which has issued guidelines on "Good Medical Practice" (including requirements related to communication and non-discrimination).[106] Where there are concerns that such standards have not been met, special panels of inquiry, described as 'fitness to practice panels' are able to issue warnings, impose conditions on a doctor's practice, suspend a doctor or even remove them from the medical register. Examples of similar bodies can be found in most other European countries, including Belgium,[107] France,[108] Germany,[109] Ireland[110] and the Netherlands. Although such codes may not relate directly to communicational practices, they are likely to be relevant indirectly, posing requirements that can be applied contextually to matters of pure communication. This may include, for example, the application of medical ethics including the principle of non-maleficence (or 'do no harm') in contexts that involve public communication

Conclusion

A A high level of restraint on the freedom of state expression is not synonymous with the functioning of a democratic state

As Chapter 1 discussed the use of nodal methods of action have traditionally represented a constraint free means of action through which the state may act in a

106 http://www.gmc-uk.org/Good_medical_practice___English_1215.pdf_51527435.pdf

107 In Belgium the Ordre des médecins is the relevant body. Its ethical code (Code de déontologie médicale) can be found at https://ordomedic.be/fr/code/contenu (In French)

108 In France the Le Conseil national de l'Ordre des médecins is the primary professional body. Its main ethical code (Code de déontologie médicale) can be found at https://www.conseil-national.medecin.fr/sites/default/files/codedeont.pdf (In French)

109 The German Medical Association (Bundesärztekammer (BAK)) is unlike the other examples presented here in that it is not a unitary organization but is rather a composite organizations from each German Lander. For a model code see http://www.bundesaerztekammer. de/fileadmin/user_upload/downloads/pdf-Ordner/MBO/MBO_EN_Novellierung_2015.pdf

110 The ethical code produced by the Irish Medical Council can be found at http://www.medicalcouncil.ie/News-and-Publications/Reports/Guide-to-Professional-Conduct-Ethics- 8th-Edition.html

flexible manner in order to attain its goals, often free from legal challenge by private individuals or entities. Various chapters in this book have illustrated how various forms of hard and binding law are likely to have difficulty engaging expressive acts of the state and individuals connected to it. Given that individuals are not legally bound by the provision of information, including through statements and expressions, the use of expressions and the provision of information arguably represents the least intrusive types of government action in terms of the effects it has on individual liberties. Tools including the use of information are used to respond expediently, flexibly and at low cost to dynamic and potentially fast changing situations. Whilst soft forms of law such as codes and circulars may suggest suitable courses of action for public servants and organizations, they may not be binding and may be difficult for private individuals or organizations to invoke.

Whilst this situation raises concerns one should not forget the problems that could arise if this was not the case. If civil servants and ministers were faced with potential restraint from a range of potentially binding legal approaches (and the possibility for legal challenge) in such instances, it would reduce their ability to respond to such situations in a fast and effective manner (as would be the case for most normal administrative acts). Imagine, for instance, a situation where a minister of health had to consult and consider the views of potentially thousands of citizens before he or she launched an information campaign that was intended to tackle a pandemic of infectious disease that had exploded with almost no warning. Public bodies must act flexibly, especially in terms of communication when dealing with such issues. Equally, it is difficult to imagine security alerts and notices designed to respond to fast moving threats posed by crime and terrorism having to undergo such formal rigour, or be the subject of frequent legal challenges. In such cases the potentially collateral psychological damage that may be caused by occasional stigmatization may be considered insufficient to warrant tying the hands of the state in such a way that it would lose its flexibility to act. This partly explains why (as Chapters 4–6 illustrated) many binding legal approaches have difficulty engaging SSEs. A converse situation would arguably represent the dreaded iron cage of law invoked by Max Webber which would prevent the state from acting purposely and quickly when needed.[111]

In addition to such operational requirements, it is important to remember that a state's administration is not solely a technocratic machine designed to implement the law in a manner that is blind to all ideology and partisanship. It also has an unavoidable political flavour given that those who are in ultimate charge of it, and who are tasked with exerting some influence on it, are usually elected. The democratic nature of a state's administration is perhaps most evident through the

111 T Kelly, "Unlocking the Iron Cage – Public Administration in the Deliberative Democratic Theory of Jürgen Habermas", *Administration and Society* 36, no. 1 (2004).For more on how Schmitt was inspired by Max Webber see A Mitzman, *The Iron Cage: A Historical Interpretation of Max Webber* (New York: Transaction Publishers, 1970).

statements and expressions that it makes. This is exemplified by the never ending stream of tweets produced by US President Trump. Indeed, unlike with other types of activities, it is in such areas that those running the state's administration are the least constrained and, therefore, most able to act according to their personal ideological or political orientation. As Chapter 1 illustrated, this may manifest itself in partisan statements by the administration that may be hard to reconcile with the requirement of neutrality that is usually expected from the state itself. Furthermore, the ability of those involved in government to express themselves freely in such areas does have some important advantages that are central to the functioning of a democratic state. It allows individuals, especially those in charge of the administration, to explain their beliefs and opinions on a wide range of issues and to explain how they have acted in the past and how they will act in the future. Such information is useful for individuals to predict the future actions of the state and act in a manner that will protect their interests. Without it, individuals might find it difficult to predict the various policy directions the state might take in the future. In addition to this, the availability of such statements and expressions allows a high level of democratic accountability. Without the ability of those in prominent positions to express themselves freely it would arguably be difficult for citizens to discern their opinions on a range of beliefs and their motivations for past and future actions. Without knowing such information, it would arguably be difficult for citizens to exercise democratic control effectively through the ballot box. Such reasoning lies behind the US legal concept of government speech which sees expression of the state as largely sacrosanct.

B Hard law is not the whole story

Whilst expressive acts may be free from interference with most forms of binding law, it would not be correct to say they are likely to be free from all forms of restraint. As this chapter has discussed there are a range of non-hard law mechanisms that are able to have limiting impacts on such activities. These range from political control exercised by the executive or legislature to the imposition of various forms of soft law regulation such as guidelines, codes and circulars. Whilst each of these forms of control is able to have a varying level of impact on the control of expressive activity of public bodies and public servants, each is deficient in various ways if compared to the type of control that one could expect from binding legal approaches.

Most important is that it may be difficult or impossible for affected individuals to force the state to implement such mechanisms of control. It is not possible, for instance, to force executives or legislatures to intervene to prevent certain expressive acts. Both branches of the state enjoy a certain freedom of initiative. Legislatures have near total freedom of initiative and as various chapters of this book have discussed, executives are generally considered to be free to express themselves as they wish on whatever matters they see fit. This is something which the US Supreme Court has recognized overtly and which seems to exist in a *de facto* manner in most European states.

As section 4 discussed, the majoritarian nature of executive and legislative control is important with regard to the potential for SSEs. This is because stigmatization as a phenomenon often manifests itself in majoritarian attitudes, biases and prejudices against minority or vulnerable groups. As Chapter 2 discussed the phenomena are often based on misconceptions and prejudices towards groups which are not likely to be majoritarian in nature. This is relevant to the control that may be exerted through political means (such as that exerted by executives and legislatures). Given that such entities draw their legitimacy from the democratic process (which by its very nature is majoritarian based) they are likely to be fertile breeding grounds for the prejudices and misconceptions that give rise to stigmatization in society as a whole. The ability of executives and entities to be able, or even willing, to recognize stigmatizing expressions (against what may be marginalized groups that may be small in nature) is thus questionable. On the contrary it may often be deemed politically expedient to adopt attitudes that are stigmatizing towards certain groups given that these may be views that the electorate itself is considered to possess. This factor furthers the ability of the executive or legislature to exercise control on the use of stigmatizing expressions in many cases.

Control through the use of soft law instruments arguably exists somewhere in between control that is purely political in nature and the legal certainty offered by hard forms of law. Such instruments, like hard law, may exist in written form and may on certain occasions offer the possibility for decisions to be reviewed in terms of correctness. Unlike forms of hard law, such as administrative law, this may even extend to the expressive activities of the state where specific and applicable ethical codes or conduct may exist. Such codes can also be created more quickly and in a more flexible manner than hard forms of law. They may also be able to offer more flexible and specific forms of guidance than harder forms of law that may be more general in nature. These potential advantages *vis-à-vis* the expressive activity of the state is to a large extent limited by the limited access private individuals may have to processes of appeal and review. On many occasions such processes may only be initiated internally by public bodies or structures or the individuals that work for them (for example, against individual civil servants in the form of disciplinary proceedings). Even where it is possible for such forms of review to be activated externally, the type of proceedings available is unlikely to meet the standard that exists for legal proceedings concerning issues of hard law. The tribunals available are unlikely to meet the high standards of independent courts. Such courts exist in a different branch of the state administration than the executive. This is in contrast to the kind of tribunals that may decide upon soft law matters which may often be composed of individuals who are not only part of the executive, but even close to the decision that has been made. Although efforts may be made to increase impartiality these are unlikely to meet the level of impartiality found within independent courts.

Another factor to be taken into consideration is that the creation and implementation of soft law is more majoritarian than that of hard law. Proposed legislation in many states is often analysed (for example, by constitutional courts) for compatibility with such requirements, which *inter alia* are designed in order to protect minority groups from majoritarian impositions. The same goes for independent courts. They are vested with an almost total level of independence in order to ensure that they can where necessary ignore majoritarian interests, prejudices and misconceptions. Tribunals designed to hear soft law related disputes are unlikely to have such a level of independence, making them also more prone to the sort of majoritarian prejudices and misconception that feed stigma. These factors may mean that where soft law does exist it may be contaminated by majoritarian prejudices in both its formulation and implantation. This may reduce the ability to be able to recognize SSEs or restrict them when they occur.

Bibliography

Auby, J. *La Fonction Publique* (Paris: Dalloz, 2002).

Bayer, R. "Stigma and the Ethics of Public Health: Not Can We but Should We." *Social Science & Medicine* 67 (2008): 463–472.

Bendersky, J. *Carl Schmitt: Theorist for the Reich*. Guildford, UK: Princeton University Press, 1983.

Bratton, D, and V Candy. "Federal Government Ethics: Social Media." *International Journal of Management & Information Systems* 17, no. 3 (2013): 175–184.

Burris, S. "Disease Stigma in U.S. Public Law." *Journal of Law, Medicine and Ethics* 30 (2002): 179–190.

Burris, S. "Stigma, Ethics and Policy: A Commentary on Bayer's 'Stigma and the Ethics of Public Health: Not Can We but Should We'." *Social Science & Medicine* 67 (2008): 473–475.

Carlson, L. "Constructing Human Rights from Soft Law: The Swedish Journey Towards Protection against Unlawful Discrimination." *Scandinavian Studies in Law* 58 (2013): 75–100.

Craig, P. *Administrative Law (7th Edition)*. London: Sweet and Maxwell, 2012.

Creyke, R, and J McMillan. "Soft Law v Hard Law." In *Administrative Law in a Changing State: Essays in Honour of Mark Aronson*, edited by L Pearson, C Harlow and M Taggart. London: Bloomsbury Publishing, 2008.

Croley, S. "The Majoritarian Difficulty: Elective Judiciaries and the Rule of Law." *Crime and Justice* 283 (1995): 690–794.

De Becker, A. "Juridische Status Van Een Ethische Code: Waar Plaats Je Zo'nCode in De Hiërarchie Van De Continentale Normen?" *Bestuurskunde* 23, no. 4 (2014). (In Dutch)

De Ruiter, R. "EU Soft Law and the Functioning of Representative Democracy: The Use of Methods of Open Co-Ordination by Dutch and British Parliamentarians." *Journal of European Social Policy* 17, no. 6 (2010): 874–890.

Emerson, T. "Toward a General Theory of the First Amendment." *Yale Law Journal* 72 (1963): 878–879.

Flynn, N. *Public Sector Management*. SAGE, 2007.

Gelders, D, and I Oyvind. "Government Communication About Potential Policies: Public Relations, Propaganda or Both?" *Public Relations Review* 36 (2010): 59–62.

Gelders, Dave, Geert Bouckaert, and Betteke van Ruler. "Communication Management in the Public Sector: Consequences for Public Communication About Policy Intentions." *Government Information Quarterly* 24, no. 2 (2007): 326–337.

Gersen, J. "Soft Law: Lessons from Congressional Practice." *Stanford Law Review* 61 (2008): 573–628.

Goldberg, S. "The Government-Speech Doctrine: 'Recently Minted,' but Counterfeit." *University of Louisville Law Review* 49: 21–57.

Gribnau, H. "Soft Law and Taxation: The Case of Soft Law in the Netherlands." *Legisprudence* 1, no. 3 (2015): 291–326.

Gross, R. *Carl Schmitt and the Jews, the "Jewish Question", the Holocaust and German Legal Theory*. Wisconsin: University of Wisconsin, 2007.

Guttman, N, and C Salmon. "Guilt, Fear, Stigma and Knowledge Gaps." *Ethical Issues in Public Health Communication* 18 (2004): 531–552.

Hood, C. "Intellectual Obsolescence and Intellectual Makeovers: Reflections on the Tools of Government after Two Decades." *Governance* 20 (2007): 127–144.

Hood, C, and H Margretts. *The Tools of Government in the Digital Age*. New York: Palgrave Macmillan, 2006.

Jacob, S. *Institutionnaliser l'évaluation des politiques publiques: Étude comparée des dispositifs institutionnels en Belgique, en France, en Suisse et aux Pays-Bas*. Brussels: Peter Lang, 2005.

Jowell, J, and M Oliver. *The Changing Constitution*. Oxford: Oxford University Press, 2004.

Kelly, T. "Unlocking the Iron Cage – Public Administration in the Deliberative Democratic Theory of Jürgen Habermas." *Administration and Society* 36, no. 1 (2004): 38–61.

Kennedy, E. *Constitutional Failure: Carl Schmidt in Weimar*. Durham, NC: Duke University Press, 2004.

Link, B, and J Phelan. "Stigma and Its Public Health Implications." *The Lancet* 367 (2006): 528–529.

Maesschalck, J, and F Schram, "Meer Dan Een Brochure of Affiche: De Deontologische Code Als Kernelement Van Een Effectief Ambtelijk Integriteitsbeleid", *Burger, Bestuur & Beleid*3, no. 1 (2006). (In Dutch)

McCormick, J. *Carl Schmitt's Critique of Liberalism: Against Politics as Technology*. Cambridge: Cambridge University Press, 1999.

Mitzman, A. *The Iron Cage: A Historical Interpretation of Max Webber*. New York: Transaction Publishers, 1970.

Morgan, B, and K Yeung. *An Introduction to Regulation*. Cambridge: Cambridge University Press, 2007.

Muralidharan, S, L Rasmussen, D Patterson, and J Shin. "Hope for Haiti: An Analysis of Facebook and Twitter Usage During the Earthquake Relief Efforts." *Public Relations Review* 37, no. 2 (2011): 175–177.

Murphy, N. "Context, Not Content: Medium-Based Press Clause Restrictions on Government Speech in the Internet Age." *University of Denver Sports & Entertainment Law Journal* 7 (2009): 26–61.

Norton, H, and D Keats Citron. "f Government Speech 2.0." *Denver University Law Review* 87 (2010): 899–943.

O'Donnell, G. "Why the Rule of Law Matters." *Journal of Democracy* 15, no. 4 (2004): 32–46.

O'Neil, R. "Hate Speech, Fighting Words, and Beyond – Why American Law Is Unique." *Albany Law Review* 76, no. 1 (2013): 467–498.

Palmer, E. "Protecting Socio-Economic Rights through the European Convention on Human Rights: Trends and Development in the European Court of Human Rights." *Erasmus Law Review* 2, no. 4 (2009): 397–425.

Post, R. "Racist Speech, Democracy, and the First Amendment." *Faculty Scholarship Series* 208 (1991).

Quinn, P. "Crisis Communication in Public Health Emergencies: The Limits of 'Legal Control' and the Risks for Harmful Outcomes in a Digital Age." Life Sciences, Society and Policy14, no. 1 (6 Feb 2018): 4.

Quinn, P, and P De Hert. "Self Respect—a 'Rawlsian Primary Good' Unprotected by the European Convention on Human Rights and Its Lack of a Coherent Approach to Stigmatization?" *The International Journal of Discrimination and the Law* 14 (2014): 19–53.

Rawls, J. *Political Liberalism*. New York: Columbia University Press, 1993.

Schaffer, G, and M Pollack. "Hard vs. Soft Law: Alternatives, Complements and Antagonists in International Governance." *Minnesota Law Review* 94 (2010): 706–799.

Schmidt, C. *Political Theology: Four Chapters on the Concept of Sovereignty*. Cambridge, MA: MIT Press, 1985(1922).

Senden, L. *Soft Law in European Community Law*. London: Hart, 2004.

Stark, C. "Rawlsian Self-Respect." In *Oxford Studies in Normative Ethics*, edited by M Timmons, 238–261. Oxford: Oxford University Press, 2012.

Taylor, C. "Hate Speech and Government Speech." *Journal of Constitutional Law* 12, no. 4 (2010): 1115–1189.

Thackeray, R, B Neiger, A Smith, and S Wagenen. "Adoption and Use of Social Media among Public Health Departments." *BMC Public Health* 12 (2012): 242–248.

Vermeule, A. "Our Schmittian Administrative Law." *Harvard Law Review* 122 (2009): 1096–1149.

Von Hagen, J. "Fiscal Rules, Fiscal Institutions, and Fiscal Performance." *The Economic and Social Review* 33, no. 3 (2002): 263–284.

Weeks, G. *Soft Law and Public Authorities: Remedies and Reform*. Portland, OR: Bloomsbury Publishing, 2016.

Wehner, J. "Assessing the Power of the Purse: An Index of Legislative Budget Institutions." *Political Studies* 54 (2006): 767–785.

Yoshino, K. "The New Equal Protection." *Harvard Law Review* 124 (2011): 747–803.

Zerilli, F. "The Rule of Soft Law: An Introduction." *Focaal—Journal of Global and Historical Anthropology* 56 (2010): 3–18.

Author's note

The aim of this book was not to undertake a comprehensive analysis of every type of legal approach and its possible interaction with stigmatizing state expressions (SSEs). Its aim was rather to raise the profile of a problem that had come to the attention of the author in his own scholarship. This was a problem that has thus far received limited attention by legal scholars in general.[1] Despite the illustrative nature of this book it has nonetheless covered a vast range of concepts and ideas. The purpose of this note is to distil this mass into a simple message that the reader will (hopefully) retain long after completing the book. It is the author's hope that this message will provide food for thought not only for legal scholars and those involved in the legal process but also, where possible, for those individuals involved in the expressive activity of the state. The following pages are split into two parts. The first will summarize the central message the author would like to convey to the reader in four (relatively) succinct points. These points represent the core message this work was intended to transmit. The second will present some simple recommendations that could be considered in order to reduce the potential problems with SSEs that have been identified.

Four core concepts developed in this book

1 The expressive activities of the state are relatively restraint free

The use of information by the state can be harmful even where it does not contain information that relates to specific individuals. As Chapter 1 discusses most types of informational or expressive instrument of the state (or 'nodality tools') are associated with a high level of flexibility, a low level of cost and a lack of legal restraint. This makes them attractive in terms of being a tool that can be used to address a wide range of situations where a fast and flexible response may be needed. In addition, such tools come with an expectation that they produce little binding consequences on individuals, i.e. effects that cannot simply be ignored. As

1 S Burris, "Disease Stigma in U.S. Public Law", *Journal of Law, Medicine and Ethics* 30 (2002).

a result there is often an implicit assumption that a lack of control on the use of such tools poses little problem.

2 Expressive activities by the state can be used in a stigmatizing manner

Despite the assumption of there being few or no binding consequences to the use of 'nodality instruments', as Chapter 1 discusses they can in the form of SSEs be used to stigmatize various groups in society. This can occur even where they do not refer to specific individuals. Such stigmatization can usually be placed into one of three categories:

- i Incidental (or 'functional') stigmatization that occurs whilst attempting to achieve an important goal (e.g. statements related to public health/crime/national security, etc.).
- ii Intentional stigmatization (or 'fair criticism') through statements or information that is designed to get individuals to change behaviour that is not perceived as desirable.
- iii Stigmatization through statements or expressions by individuals that can be connected to the state but which also have a political character, e.g. ministers, mayors, etc. (or 'stigmatization through the political process').

3 Stigmatization through SSEs produces serious consequences that cannot be ignored

Stigmatization is an omnipresent phenomenon that informs our thoughts, decisions and actions in life. It is tied intimately to human nature yet also influences and feeds off our complex culture.[2] The phenomenon will likely always be with us in some form or other. It can even be thought of as having some positive aspects related to social control of harmful or immoral behaviours or activities.[3] It is necessary however to realize that processes of stigmatization can bring about harmful situations at both the individual and the group level.[4] On the individual level the result can be lowered individual aspirations and expectations. This can

2 For a good general overview of stigmatization and the various ways in which it can be conceived see: J Dovidio, B Major, and J Crocker, "Stigma: Introduction and Overview", in *The Social Psychology of Stigma*, ed. T Heatherton et al. (New York: Guilford Press, 2000).

3 Some, for example, argue for the use of stigmatization in certain contexts in healthcare communication, e.g. in anti-smoking campaigns. See, for example: R Bayer, "Stigma and the Ethics of Public Health: Not Can We but Should We", *Social Science & Medicine* 67 (2008). Such a position is by no means universally accepted, however see: S Burris, "Stigma, Ethics and Policy: A Commentary on Bayer's 'Stigma and the Ethics of Public Health: Not Can We but Should We'".

4 B Link and J Phelan, "Conceptualizing Stigma", *Annual Review of Sociology* 27 (2001); I Goffman, *Stigma: Notes on a Spoilt Identity* (Englewood Cliffs, NJ: Prentice Hall, 1963); D Reidpath et al., "'He Hath the French Pox': Stigma, Social Value and Social Exclusion", *Sociology of Health & Illness* 27, no. 4 (2005).

manifest itself *inter alia* in healthcare avoidance and a reduced desire to seek necessary goods in life (e.g. education and employment).[5] On the societal level such effects can worsen problems of marginalization experienced by already vulnerable minorities.[6] There is thus arguably a need to restrict SSEs in certain contexts.

Stigmatization by the state may be particularly corrosive. It can create or strengthen negative feelings individuals have concerning themselves or others. Given the symbolic value of the relationship we have with the state and its position as a guarantor of our rights in society, its attitudes towards its citizens are of great importance. Where the state displays negative attitudes towards members of a particular group, the 'self-respect' of the affected individuals can be threatened.[7] This can result in a loss of belief that an individual's view of the good (i.e. their project in life) is valuable and worth striving for. In addition to causing direct stigmatization SSEs can increase incidences of secondary stigmatization, i.e. incidences where as a result of having the information in question individuals act in a way that is stigmatizing (or even discriminatory).

4 Legal approaches may (sometimes for good reasons) have trouble engaging state expressions

Despite the potentially harmful consequences of state stigmatizing expressions individuals who are negatively affected may often have difficulty in finding any form of legal redress. This is mainly because stigmatization is occurring in the context of an activity that is purely expressive in nature. As a result, legal approaches that are normally expected to control the activities of the state or protect individuals from its effects may have difficulty in 'gaining traction'. Many approaches look for the creation of binding consequences in order to engage state activity. Several illustrative examples of this problem are discussed in this book. Systems of administrative law, for example, foresee 'administrative acts' as those that 'create rights or obligations',[8] whilst the focus of the European Court of Human Rights (ECHR) in terms of an anti-discrimination approach appears to be on the presence of a similar concept, i.e. 'treatment'.[9] Other approaches in the criminal law (i.e. concerned with hate speech) may often be limited in their

5 For more on such issues see: Link and Phelan, "Conceptualizing Stigma"; A Courtwright, "Justice, Stigma, and the New Epidemiology of Health Disparities", *Bioethics* 23, no. 2 (2009).

6 C Miller and B Major, "Coping with Stigma and Prejudice", in *The Social Psychology of Stigmatisation*, ed. T Heatherton et al. (New York: Guilford Press, 2000).

7 This book focuses in particular on Rawls' conception of self-respect. For a succinct description see: J Rawls, *A Theory of Justice* (Cambridge, MA: Harvard Press, 1971). p386

8 See Chapter 5 for a discussion of various illustrations. In French law the concept of an *acte juridique administatif* exists which can be defined as "une acte juridique unilatéral, pris par une autorité administrative (française) dans l'exercise d'un pouvoir administratif et créant des droits ou des obligations pour les particuliers".

9 See, for example, the cases of *Baczkowki and Others v Poland* (Application No. 1543/06) and *AKSU v. Turkey* (Application No. 4149/041). These are discussed in Chapter 6 section 5.

application to particular types of extreme expression directed towards certain categories. Even where such laws do apply, they may be hampered by the existence of immunity laws that prevent prosecution of the state itself or senior political figures.[10] The cumulative result of these issues is a general lack of engagement of prominent legal approaches with the expressive activity of the state, including where such activity is stigmatizing. In some instances other forms of control may be available (including soft law or legislative/executive control), though they may be associated with a number of important disadvantages, including, most notably, often not being invocable before a truly independent tribunal.

Recommendations

As the brief overview above discusses, a propensity to stigmatize, and be stigmatized, is an integral part of the human condition.[11] This propensity is related to our social nature and the value we place on the opinions of our peers and those we interact with. The use of stigmatization is furthermore arguably central to important mechanisms of social control including *inter alia* the criminal justice system. As a consequence it is important to emphasize that it is neither desirable nor possible to attempt to rid society of stigmatization altogether.

The focus of this book is rather on the stigmatization produced by the state in its expressive activity. This represents a specific type of stigmatization that, as Chapter 3 demonstrates (using the ideas of Rawls) is in many circumstances questionable. This is because of the importance of the attitude of the state to individual self-worth. Whilst the stigmatizing responses of one's peers may be painful, the stigmatizing attitudes of the state are likely to be even more so and have an increased likelihood of bringing about harmful effects that may be associated with stigmatization in general. There is therefore a need to determine when it is acceptable for the state to stigmatize and when it is not. Chapter 3 suggests five principles that could be used to guide state action in terms of stigmatizing expressions. They are:

- i There are no instances where states need to intentionally damage an individual's self-respect.
- ii The state should only take action that may harm self-esteem (i.e. stigmatize) where doing so would be needed to secure the fundamental liberties or equality of opportunity of others.
- iii There is a duty upon states not to harm individual or group self-esteem through the release of incorrect information.
- iv The state should not criticize individuals for their ideas or lifestyle choices unless they threaten the fundamental rights or the equality of opportunity of others.

10 The importance of immunity provisions is discussed further in Chapter 9 sections 9–12.

11 R Kurzban and M Leary, "Evolutionary Origins of Stigmatization: The Functions of Social Exclusion" *Psychological Bulletin* 127, no. 2 (2001).

v Stigmatizing statements made during the political process should be clearly identified as neither emanating from, nor representing the opinion of the state itself but of an individual or group with political motives.

Based on the discussion that was involved in forming these principles and the research that was conducted to produce the subsequent chapters concerning potential legal approaches the author makes six simple recommendations. They relate to diverse areas of law and in so doing recognize that there is no one simple solution to the problems described above. These recommendations are general in nature. As a consequence, further research and development would be needed to adapt them to a particular jurisdiction. Some represent alterations to binding legal approaches whilst others recommend the development of soft law approaches such as codes of conduct. Whilst the author does not realistically expect any jurisdiction to adopt all of these approaches directly, he hopes to raise the profile and dangers associated with SSEs amongst scholars (both legal and otherwise) and policy makers involved in these areas who may be able to make more tailored recommendations based on a specific jurisdiction.

Recommendation 1 – Further measures to prevent intentional attacks on self-respect by state officials

Of the principles described above, principle (i) can undoubtedly be described as the most important. As Chapter 3 discusses there is little or no conceivable need for the state or those connected with it to intentionally harm the self-respect of individuals through extreme stigmatization of the group they belong to.[12] However, as is discussed in Chapter 4 , whilst in many states legislation exists that is able to engage the most serious forms of 'hate speech' (likely to threaten the self-respect of individuals) the formulation of such laws is usually highly selective. This means that wide groups of individuals can be attacked (even severely) without fear of the application of the criminal law. This is because legislation relating to harmful acts in most states relates only to expressive acts made against particular categories. Imagine, for instance, groups such as 'individuals with red hair', 'the obese', 'the unattractive', 'the unintelligent' or the 'left handed' (and many others); categories such as these are unlikely to find protection in hate speech laws that have been pragmatically defined in reaction to historical patterns of abuse concerning prominent minorities or other vulnerable groups. Whilst there may often be a political price to pay for attacks on groups that are not protected, the criminal law in many jurisdictions would be silent on such issues. This is concerning given that (as such laws will also be applicable to the 'human component' of

12 For more on the importance of self-respect see: Courtwright, "Justice, Stigma, and the New Epidemiology of Health Disparities"; C Roland and R Foxx, "Self-Respect: A Neglected Concept", *Philosophical Psychology* 16 (2003); D Sachs, "How to Distinguish Self-Respect from Self-Esteem", *Philosophy and Public Affairs* 10 (1981); C Stark, "Rawlsian Self-Respect", in *Oxford Studies in Normative Ethics*, ed. M Timmons (Oxford: Oxford University Press, 2012); D Statman, "Humiliation, Dignity and Self-Respect", *Philosophical Psychology* 13, no. 4 (2000).

the state) it means that individuals connected to the state will be able to launch intensely stigmatizing attacks without fear of prosecution.

Whilst accepting that it is unacceptable for the state to launch such stigmatizing attacks, the author of this book recognizes that there is no simple solution to this problem. One possible solution could be the use of broad hate speech provisions applicable to all that criminalize insults and defamation against undefined groups in society (as exists in Germany where such laws are based on the protection of human dignity – see Chapter 4). Whilst these could be invoked to criminalize severely stigmatizing attacks against all groups that were capable of harming self-respect (and not just a few pre-defined ones), they are also capable of impacting severely on liberty of expression. In addition, the potential breadth of application of such provisions is enormous, meaning that it may be difficult for those subject to such laws to foresee their engagement in advance (something that is incongruous with most visions of what constitutes good criminal law). Given these reasons the author is doubtful as to whether such laws would be considered acceptable in most other Western states that have both different conceptions of the requirements of dignity as a concept and have also not undergone a similar historical experience to Germany.[13] Consequently the author would suggest that it is possible to seek a middle ground. This would involve more specialized criminal law provisions that only apply to agents of the state such as civil servants (and not political figures, e.g. Members of Parliament or the executive) and individuals when they were purporting to represent the government. Whilst such laws would need to be generally applicable (i.e. to undefined groups) they would have a high threshold so as demarcate as much as possible the type of expressions that would be engaged. Such a threshold would arguably serve to meet the concerns linked to liberty of expression (something the European Court of Human Rights (ECtHR) has raised in its Article 10 jurisprudence concerning restriction of the speech of government employees).[14] The author suggests that such a threshold would engage expressions such as incitation to hatred or speech that clearly intends to dehumanize particular groups. This type of formulation would allow for 'functional stigmatization' or 'fair criticism' where necessary (see Chapter 1).[15] Such a threshold (applying to hateful or dehumanizing speech) would only apply to speech that arguably has little role to play in the open debate and discussion that are needed in a democracy. It

13 For more on how various legal cultures differ in the conception of dignity see: C McCrudden, "Human Dignity and Judicial Interpretation of Human Rights", *The European Journal of International Law* 19, no. 4 (2008). As the author points out in Chapter 4 the German Constitutional Court adopts a more communitarian approach, whilst the predominant approach to dignity in the US Supreme Court, the Canadian Supreme Court and the Hungarian Constitutional Court is more individualistic.The South African Constitutional Court appears to be significantly split on the issue.

14 See, for example, *Vogt v. Germany* (Application No. 17851/91). This issue is discussed in further depth in Chapter 6 section D.

15 Such a formulation would also protect the right to 'shock, offend and disturb that the ECtHR has identified in its jurisprudence *inter alia* in *Vogt*.

would thus allow civil servants and other agents of the state to engage in political activities under certain circumstances (as the ECtHR has demanded in its Article 10 jurisprudence). As is briefly discussed in Chapter 4 models for such selective application of the criminal law exist in some civil law countries (e.g. France) that have special offences for civil servants that engage in discriminatory acts (albeit against certain predefined categories).[16] The author suggests that such offences can be considered a useful template. In addition to any practical impact the existence of such laws would raise awareness amongst civil servants in terms of their responsibilities in this area.

Recommendation 2 – The need to demonstrate necessity where some types of stigmatizing expression are used

An important theme that arises in several of the chapters of this book is the seeming lack of engagement of legal approaches that could be useful in determining the necessity of a measure. This was, for example, the case with the anti-discrimination approach of the ECtHR and its jurisprudence under Article 8 (unless personal information is involved), described as 'privacy as liberty'. The lack of any finding of a clear engagement with convention rights thus far means that there may be a lack of incentives in individual states to develop legal tools that would be capable of engaging such acts and determining (in certain contexts) whether they are necessary.[17] This is relevant to principles (ii) and (iii) described above. These principles accept that the state can stigmatize certain groups of individuals where it is necessary in order to complete an important aim, i.e. 'functional stigmatisation' or 'fair criticism'.[18] This accepts the need of the state to commit both incidental and even intentional stigmatization where there is a valid purpose. Given that non-engagement has thus far been found where expressions are merely stigmatizing there is no obligation upon states to develop processes that would be capable of determining if such conditions existed.

In order to ensure that the state acts in accordance with the normative principles outlined here it is necessary to have some kind of legal mechanism that is capable of recognizing expressive acts and determining whether they are needed

16 See Articles 432–437 of the French criminal code, for example. The *Code pénale* foresees a special criminal offence for those who discriminate against the protected categories whilst carrying out a public function. Where public officials are guilty of such an offence they are punished more severely than those individuals who may have committed the offence but who are not in a public position.

17 This may, for example, explain why many systems of administrative law (discussed in Chapter 5) have difficulty in engaging administrative acts. Jurisprudence from the ECtHR could incentivize states to create approaches that would be more willing to engage with certain expressive acts.

18 These aspects relate to the lexical ordering of Rawls' principles of justice. They are discussed in Chapter 3. This lexical ordering allows one to prioritize the protection of (i) rights and liberties or (ii) opportunities over (iii) social goods such as the provision of ''self-respect'.

or permitted. This may well be problematic, but otherwise the result of a lack of engagement is a lack of control and a lack of need to adhere to principles (ii) and (iii) above. There are admittedly practical problems with such engagement (e.g. with Article 8) that may require creative solutions (e.g. the need to demonstrate a legitimate aim, legality and necessity). This may, for example, require the need to develop a new line of case law that deals specifically with the expressive activities of the state in place of applying approaches that were envisaged to deal with more corporeal or concrete actions that are not of an expressive nature.

Once again, the question of a realistic threshold will be key. The engagement and analysis of all expressive activities of the state is of course not practically feasible (see Chapter 7). In modern pluralist societies there will always be one group of people that for one reason or another find a particular measure to be offensive to their background culture or beliefs. A more practical threshold might, for example, involve expressive activities that are likely to stigmatize already vulnerable minority groups or activities that were intended to stigmatize others, e.g. through criticism of beliefs, behaviours or lifestyles, etc. Whilst expressions that reach such a threshold could still occur, they would come with the need to demonstrate a need to make such an expression. Such an arrangement would represent a pragmatic balance between the ideals set out in principles (ii) and (iii) above and the practical needs of the state to express itself with flexibility. The ECtHR can for example encourage such a process by recognizing that expressions that are 'merely stigmatizing' are capable of engaging Article 8.[19] This would *inter alia* create a requirement for systems of administrative law in signatory states to be better able to engage such expressive activities and, where needed, to provide some form of remediation.[20]

Recommendation 3 – The use of restatement or retractions of stigmatizing expressions should be encouraged

In addition to considering the potential engagement of a legal approach with stigmatizing expressive acts, there is also a need to consider how such engagement could bring about benefits for those who have suffered harm. Courts are likely to have difficulty in granting a remedy of any practical significance (though in certain

19 As Chapter 6 discusses, the ECtHR has not as yet made such a recognition. It has, however, not ruled it out. Such a recognition may not yet have occurred because the right type of cases have not come before the court. See also: P Quinn and P De Hert, "Self Respect—a 'Rawlsian Primary Good' Unprotected by the European Convention on Human Rights and Its Lack of a Coherent Approach to Stigmatization?", *The International Journal of Discrimination and the Law* 14 (2014).

20 As P Craig, *Administrative Law (7th Edition)* (London: Sweet and Maxwell, 2012) discusses on page 21, the ECHR has transformed the process of judicial review at the heart of administrative law in the UK. Courts must now analyse administrative decisions in the light of ECHR principles and where national legislation is incompatible they must, under the Human Rights Act (1998), issue a declaration of non-conformity.

circumstances remedies such as injunctions may be of use in instances where expression is continuous, e.g. on a website). This may appear problematic as in many cases the whole point of undertaking legal action is often assumed to be a desire or need to obtain practical relief (often from actions that might otherwise be binding). With stigmatizing expressions however their potential harm is in reality related to their symbolic value, in particular as indications of the attitude the state holds towards certain groups of citizens. In the context of the search for a suitable remedy such symbolic value may be able to moderate both primary (i.e. produced by the original expression) and secondary stigmatization (produced by repeated expression or negative attitudes by third parties). The fact that symbolic forms of relief may in reality be the only feasible type does not therefore mean that undertaking legal action is a pointless exercise.

Of particular interest may be remedies in the forms of requirements to restate or clarify a particular expression. Such remedies may allow individuals to understand the intention behind a particular expression (where it is not clear). This can on certain occasions allow messages to be diffused of their stigmatizing content. This may occur where individuals, for example, are able to understand why certain stigmatizing information (for a certain group) has been released to the public. Imagine, for instance, an announcement that a health problem is prominent in a particular community. Where individuals are able to see that such information has been released in order to protect the important interests of individuals (e.g. in order to protect public health or security) they are less likely to see such expressions as stigmatizing and also therefore less likely to suffer harm to self-respect. Remedies of this type may also have a role in relation to principle (iii) discussed above. This is because they can be used to compel state officials to clarify certain expressions, including explaining the reasons and context in which they were made. Where this is able to better demonstrate that a particular expression was made in order to achieve valid aims it may act to reduce its stigmatizing content. Such types of remedy will also have a role to play in terms of principle (iii) as they will allow the retraction of information that is incorrect.

However, remedies of this type are found and used more in certain jurisdictions than others. In particular, they are more commonly found as private law remedies in the civil law world (e.g. Germany).[21] There may be a merit in their expansion including to the common law world. These types of remedy have the advantage that they do not prevent the state from expressing itself but may require it to modify its expression or add to it on certain occasions. This could occur at a later data and thus not form a problem in the contexts of a crisis. In addition to private law however the requirement to provide reasons is often found in systems of administrative law. The author would suggest that subject to a potential finding of engagement either at the level of the ECtHR or national levels such a requirement could also be extended to similar categories of expressive acts (as well as more conventional types of administrative act).

21 A Bruns, "Access to Media Sources in Defamation Litigation in the United States and Germany", *Duke Journal of Comparative & International Law* 10 (2000). p285 E Wenzel, *Das Recht Der Wort – Und Bildberichterstattung (4th Edition)* (1994). Sections 13.57 and 13.68.

Recommendation 4 – An appreciation of the 'dissuasive force' of stigmatization

Stigmatization is a phenomenon that is closely related to discrimination.[22] As Chapter 5 describes some traditional anti-discrimination approaches may find it difficult to engage expressions that are not accompanied by acts of 'treatment' (i.e. acts that bring about binding effects that individuals cannot simply ignore).[23] As many of those familiar with issues of discrimination will be aware, individuals can suffer harmful consequences through stigmatization even in the absence of any discriminatory treatment (at least in the traditional sense). This is because the psychological forces that are unleashed in processes of stigmatization can have very real practical consequences that are in many ways synonymous with those produced through discrimination. Amongst these is the concept of 'dissuasive force'. Imagine, for instance, a prominent local official or mayor who makes negative comments concerning a particular minority or gender and their suitability as employees. Such comments are likely to discourage individuals from the community in question from applying for employment with the state. This means that even if there are non-discriminatory employment procedures in place, stigmatizing remarks may have a harmful effect and deter individuals from undertaking activities that they might otherwise have done.[24]

Whilst treating all stigmatizing remarks by the state as discrimination may neither be practical nor desirable, there is a need to recognize the harmful effects that such remarks can have in particular situations.[25] This is particularly true when public officials openly question the entitlement of certain individuals to obtain important goods (e.g. employment, healthcare, social security from the state) that they are legally entitled to. Whilst such remarks may not be acts of discrimination in the traditional sense (i.e. involving treatment), they are through the induction of psychological processes (such as coping responses associated with stigmatization) able to bring about analogous effects. The author welcomes the steps that have been taken in some areas in recent years to this effect, including, for example, the recognition of particular expressive acts within the anti-discrimination framework in the European Union's

22 Link and Phelan, "Conceptualizing Stigma".

23 See, for example, the cases of *Baczkowki and Others v. Poland* (Application No. 1543/06). and *AKSU v. Turkey* (Application No. 4149/041). These are discussed in Chapter 6 section 5 in these cases the ECtHR discusses the requirement for 'treatment' in order to find acts of discrimination under Article 14.

24 Such an effect has also been observed with benefit claimants in the UK who have felt ashamed by the comments of others and as a consequence have not claimed benefits they are legally entitled to. See Baumberg Geiger et al., "Benefits Stigma in Britain" (2012) Project report. Elizabeth Finn Care https://kar.kent.ac.uk/id/eprint/36377

25 Harmful expressions are particularly able to cause problems in the employment market and worsen problems of structural discrimination that exist for vulnerable minorities. See, for example, Opinions 2006–11 2007–100 by the Dutch Equal Treatment Commission (Commissie gelijke behandeling (CGB)). These are discussed in European Union Agency for Fundamental Rights, *Handbook on European Non-Discrimination Law* (European Union Agency for Fundamental Rights/Council of Europe, 2010).

Equality Directives.[26] In the *Feryn* [27] judgment the Court of Justice of the European Union (CJEU) showed its apparent willingness to embrace the concept of 'dissuasive force' in the contexts of the employment market. The author believes this potentially represents a key moment where the power of stigmatizing expressions (and their relationship to discrimination are clearly being recognized in judicial terms). It is hoped that this will set a judicial and legislative precedent where the concept of dissuasive force is further recognized in expressions made in certain contexts (including *inter alia* by the state).[28] As a consequence the author would call for this development to be pursued, removing the potential doubts over this interpretation that remain.[29]

Recommendation 5 – Codes of conduct concerning political speech by ministers and the use of state resources for such purposes

The recommendations above relate to the control of stigmatizing statements made by the state or its employees (e.g. civil servants). Another category of stigmatizing expression (as described above) relates to statements made by political figures that can be linked to the state. It is not desirable to hold such individuals to the same requirements in terms of their attitudes to the various groups in society as state agents or employees. This is because in a democratic society it is expected that such individuals will voice the views of the electorate. Whilst this may result in offence being caused to other groups in society it is difficult to envisage the operation of a democratic society without a high level of freedom of expression for such individuals. As principle (v) above recognizes, whilst there is a need to accept that a certain level of stigmatization will always occur through such processes, efforts should be made where possible to dissociate stigmatizing messages from the state itself. In such instances it is desirable for political actors (and in particular those with a close association with the state such as ministers, etc.) to emphasize that such views are their own and not those of the state.

26 The two directives discussed are Council Directive 2000/43/EC of 29 June 2000 implementing the principle of equal treatment between persons irrespective of racial and ethnic origin and Council Directive 2000/78/EC of 27 November 2000 establishing a general framework for equal treatment in employment and occupation. These directives recognize, for example, the concepts of 'harassment' and 'instruction to discriminate'.

27 *Centrum voor gelijkheid van kansen en voor racismebestrijding v. Firma Feryn NV.* Reference for a preliminary ruling: Case C-54/07.

28 This concept is already accepted in some jurisdictions including the Netherlands. See: K Henrard, "A First Substantive CJEU Judgement on the Racial Equality Directive: A Strong Message in a Conceptually Flawed and Responsively Weak Bottle", *Jean Monnet Working Paper* (2009).

29 Further jurisprudence will be necessary to confirm this apparent precedent in *Feryn,* however, in particular given that the court chose not to invoke the concept of 'dissuasive force' in the *Asociaţia Accept* Case C-81/12 25 April 2013 ruling, a case with similar facts.

None of the legal approaches looked at in this book offer anything substantial in this regard. The author would suggest that binding legal approaches are unlikely to provide an answer in this area. Voluntary codes of conduct and standards of behaviour are more realistic. These already exist in many countries.[30] They are often concerned with rules outlining when and where state funds can be spent (e.g. in the context of election campaigns).[31] Such rules and codes should (where they do not already) also encourage political figures to dissociate their remarks from the state when they are stigmatizing purely for political purposes and not utilize the machinery of the state for their dissemination.[32] There may also be a role for standards bodies and parliamentary committees in making such clarifications and for condemning instances where such rules have not been respected. Whilst measures of this type will not be able to prevent stigmatization of groups arising through the political process, they should encourage the development of a political culture that at least has an awareness of these issues. Such a culture should seek to assert shared values concerning the need for the state to show a respectful attitude to all groups as a form of civic culture that can be respected by individuals from all political persuasions.

Recommendation 6 – Limitation of immunity for extreme speech

As Chapter 4 discusses, a further issue relating to political figures concerns their potential immunity from the application of criminal law. Such immunity may apply

30 K Sanders, M Canel Crespo, and Holtz-Bach C, "Communicating Governments: A Three- Country Comparison of How Governments Communicate with Citizens", *The International Journal of Press/Politics* 16, no. 4 (2011).

31 In the UK one important code of conduct produced by the Cabinet Office is the *Proprietary Guidance on Government.* On page 5 it states, "Publicly funded government communications cannot be used primarily or solely to meet party political objectives. However, it is recognized that the governing party may derive incidental benefit from activities carried out by the Government. ... The Ministerial Code requires ministers to uphold the impartiality of the Civil Service. They must not ask civil servants to act in any way that conflicts with the Civil Service Code. Ministers must ensure that public resources are not used to support publicity for party political purposes". Available at: https://gcn.civilservice.gov.uk/wp-content/uploads/2011/02/propriety-guidance.pdf Another potential example in the UK is Article 10 of the *Ministerial Code on Special Advisers* (who work for ministers) which recognizes the more political role they may take. It states "Special advisers are able to represent Ministers' views on Government policy to the media with a degree of political commitment that would not be possible for the permanent Civil Service. Briefing on purely party political matters must be handled by the Party machine." Article 12 states "Special advisers must not take public part in political controversy whether in speeches or letters to the Press, or in books, articles or leaflets; must observe discretion and express comment with moderation, avoiding personal attacks; and would not normally speak in public for their Minister or the Department". Available at: https://www.gov.uk/government/uploads/system/uploads/attachment_data/file/62451/special-advisers-code-of-conduct.pdf

32 This of course represents an ideal position that would be confronted by problems related to the practical reality of ministerial communication in a democracy. See: D Gelders and I Oyvind, "Government Communication About Potential Policies: Public Relations, Propaganda or Both?", *Public Relations Review* 36 (2010).

to individuals by virtue of them being part of the executive and/or parliament. This can *inter alia* result in exemption from the application of hate speech laws. Given that normative principle (i) above requires that individuals connected with the state are prevented from intentionally harming the self-respect of individuals through severely stigmatizing remarks (e.g. including the incitement of hate or severe dehumanization) such immunity is concerning. Immunity provisions may mean that individuals will be able to engage in hate speech and face a delayed prosecution or no prosecution at all. Hate speech laws usually only engage the most extreme forms of stigmatizing expressions (see Chapter 4). Such forms of expression contribute little to democratic debate and arguably are able to bring about severe stigmatization and threaten the self-respect of those involved.

Given this, immunity laws should be qualified to allow application of laws for hate speech. This would arguably bring about little or no infringement of democratic debate. In addition, such a situation would not mean that such figures were subject to additional criminal laws, but only to those that apply to the population in general. This would reverse a 'perverse paradox' that currently exists in some states, where although the general population are restricted by wide-ranging hate speech laws, senior political figures can use harmful expressions freely in the context of parliamentary duties. As Chapter 4 discusses, such a situation exists in several civil law European countries where powerful hate speech laws may be blocked by powerful immunity provisions. It is difficult to understand why, if certain types of expressions are not permitted amongst the general populace (who also have a right to engage in political debate), they should be permitted by senior political figures. In order to minimize the potential disruptive effects of such a measure the author would recommend any qualification of immunity only be applicable to those types of hate speech law that have both a high threshold and are narrowly defined and are therefore reasonably foreseeable in terms of application. This could, for example, relate to types of expression that are targeted at particular minorities, groups or communities that have a history of vulnerability and are at risk of marginalization. This would be less likely to run afoul of rights covering liberty of expression such as Article 10 ECHR. The author would, for example, point to Germany (where defamatory statements are not covered by immunity provisions) as a possible inspiration to show that such a nuanced system of immunity is possible.

Bibliography

Baumberg Geiger, B, K Bell, D Gaffney. "Benefits Stigma in Britain." (2012). Project report. Elizabeth Finn Care. Available at: https://kar.kent.ac.uk/id/eprint/36377

Bayer, R. "Stigma and the Ethics of Public Health: Not Can We but Should We." *Social Science & Medicine* 67 (2008): 463–472.

Bruns, A. "Access to Media Sources in Defamation Litigation in the United States and Germany." *Duke Journal of Comparative & International Law* 10 (2000): 283–305.

Burris, S. "Disease Stigma in U.S. Public Law." *Journal of Law, Medicine and Ethics* 30 (2002): 179–190.

Burris, S. "Stigma, Ethics and Policy: A Commentary on Bayer's 'Stigma and the Ethics of Public Health: Not Can We but Should We'." *Social Science & Medicine* 67(2008): 473–475.

Courtwright, A. "Justice, Stigma, and the New Epidemiology of Health Disparities." *Bioethics* 23, no. 2 (2009): 90–96.

Craig, P. *Administrative Law (7th Edition)*. London: Sweet and Maxwell, 2012.

Dovidio, J, B Major, and J Crocker. "*Stigma: Introduction and Overview*." In *The Social Psychology of Stigma*, edited by T Heatherton, R Kleck, M Hebl and J Hull, 1–30. New York: Guilford Press, 2000.

European Union Agency for Fundamental Rights. *Handbook on European Non-Discrimination Law*." (European Union Agency for Fundamental Rights/Council of Europe, 2010).

Gelders, D, and I Oyvind. "Government Communication About Potential Policies: Public Relations, Propaganda or Both?" *Public Relations Review* 36 (2010): 59–62.

Goffman, I. *Stigma: Notes on a Spoilt Identity*. Englewood Cliffs, NJ: Prentice Hall, 1963.

Henrard, K. "A First Substantive ECJ Judgement on the Racial Equality Directive: A Strong Message in a Conceptually Flawed and Responsively Weak Bottle." *Jean Monnet Working Paper* (2009).

Kurzban, R, and M Leary. "Evolutionary Origins of Stigmatization: The Functions of Social Exclusion." *Psychological Bulletin* 127, no. 2 (2001): 187–208.

Link, B, and J Phelan. "Conceptualizing Stigma." *Annual Review of Sociology* 27 (2001): 363–385.

McCrudden, C. "Human Dignity and Judicial Interpretation of Human Rights." *The European Journal of International Law* 19, no. 4 (2008): 655–724.

Miller, C, and B Major. "Coping with Stigma and Prejudice." In *The Social Psychology of Stigmatisation*, edited by T Heatherton, R Kleck, M Hebl and J Hull, 243–272. New York: Guilford Press, 2000.

Quinn, P, and P De Hert. "Self Respect—a 'Rawlsian Primary Good' Unprotected by the European Convention on Human Rights and Its Lack of a Coherent Approach to Stigmatization?" *The International Journal of Discrimination and the Law* 14 (2014): 19–53.

Rawls, J. *A Theory of Justice*. Cambridge, MA: Harvard Press, 1971.

Reidpath, D, K Chan, S Gifford and P Allotey. "'He Hath the French Pox': Stigma, Social Value and Social Exclusion. " *Sociology of Health & Illness* 27, no. 4 (2005): 468–489.

Roland, C, and R Foxx. "Self-Respect: A Neglected Concept." *Philosophical Psychology* 16 (2003): 247–287.

Sachs, D "How to Distinguish Self-Respect from Self-Esteem." *Philosophy and Public Affairs* 10 (1981): 346–360.

Sanders, K, M Canel Crespo and C Holtz-Bach. "Communicating Governments: A Three-Country Comparison of How Governments Communicate with Citizens." *The International Journal of Press/Politics* 16, no. 4 (2011): 523–547.

Stark, C. "Rawlsian Self-Respect." In *Oxford Studies in Normative Ethics*, edited by M Timmons, 238–261. Oxford: Oxford University Press, 2012.

Statman, D. "Humiliation, Dignity and Self-Respect." *Philosophical Psychology* 13, no. 4 (2000): 523–540.

Wenzel, E. *Das Recht Der Wort – Und Bildberichterstattung (4th Edition)*. Köln: O. Schmidt, 1994.

Index

For Product Safety Concerns and Information please contact our EU representative GPSR@taylorandfrancis.com
Taylor & Francis Verlag GmbH, Kaufingerstraße 24, 80331 München, Germany

www.ingramcontent.com/pod-product-compliance
Ingram Content Group UK Ltd.
Pitfield, Milton Keynes, MK11 3LW, UK
UKHW022012180926
475701UK00003B/319

* 9 7 8 1 0 3 2 2 4 1 1 2 8 *